RAW

RAW
My Autobiography

Antony Worrall Thompson

BANTAM PRESS

LONDON · NEW YORK · TORONTO · SYDNEY · AUCKLAND

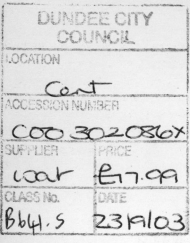
TRANSWORLD PUBLISHERS
61–63 Uxbridge Road, London W5 5SA
a division of The Random House Group Ltd

RANDOM HOUSE AUSTRALIA (PTY) LTD
20 Alfred Street, Milsons Point, Sydney,
New South Wales 2061, Australia

RANDOM HOUSE NEW ZEALAND LTD
18 Poland Road, Glenfield, Auckland 10, New Zealand

RANDOM HOUSE SOUTH AFRICA (PTY) LTD
Endulini, 5a Jubilee Road, Parktown 2193, South Africa

Published 2003 by Bantam Press
a division of Transworld Publishers

A catalogue record for this book is available from the British Library.
ISBN 0593 049276

Typeset in 11/13pt Sabon by
Falcon Oast Graphic Art Ltd.

Printed in Great Britain
by Mackays of Chatham, Chatham, Kent

1 3 5 7 9 10 8 6 4 2

Paper used by Transworld Publishers are natural, recyclable products made from wood grown
in sustainable forests. The manufacturing processes conform to the environmental regulations
of the country of origin.

To my late mother. I know I've been rough
on her in this book but I owe my life to her,
and of course my dad.

ACKNOWLEDGEMENTS

First things first. I need to do the brown-nose thing and thank my publishers, Transworld, for commissioning the book. I'm flattered that they thought I had a story to tell. Doug Young was my main man, who encouraged me and cajoled the words out of me (finally), about a year late. But to Doug I say it was meant to be late; it's fate. I wouldn't have been able to write about my jungle exploits if I had been the perfect author, handing my copy in on time. And I shall never forget the editor who turned my ramblings into chapters and coherence, so a big thank-you to Caroline North – you're pretty good at this writing lark – and to all the team I've encountered at Transworld.

And then there are my agents, Fiona Lindsay, Linda Shanks and more recently Lesley Turnbull of Limelight Management, without whom I would probably still be a broke chef. But they give me more than just management – they're my mates.

To my TV mentor, Peter Bazalgette, formerly of Bazal Productions, now Endemol UK Plc, and his team, especially Linda Clifford – both gave me the opportunities that changed my career. They, with Tim Hinks, guided me from nervous amateur to competent performer on programmes such as *Ready, Steady, Cook* and *Food & Drink*. I would love to have mentioned more about Jeni Barnet of *Good Food Live*, who I've worked with several times over the last couple of years. I think she deserves so much more credit. She is a brilliant performer and a wonderful person. She should be on terrestrial television rather than satellite.

I'm lucky that so many of my friends from my London years had the patience to stay with me: Rex, Melissa, my gorgeous god-daughter Chelsea and her sister Tamsin, Michael Proudlock and my other gorgeous god-daughter Laura, Steve Thomas, Brian

Turner, Annie Bonnet from the Leatherne Bottel, Michel and Robyn Roux from the Waterside Inn, Patrick Gwyn-Jones from Pomegranates, Richard and Kate Smith from the Beetel and Wedge, Jimmy and Kay Nissaire and Peter and Christine Goring from my east London days – to name but a few. They'll tell Jaybe how I've changed, and I'm very glad to have done so. The names above won't mean much to you, readers, but they mean one hell of a lot to me.

I also feel privileged to have gone from industry colleague to friend of Fay Maschler, restaurant critic of the *Evening Standard*, and her fab husband Reg. Don't get the wrong message – this is an above-board friendship. From her first review of Dan's restaurant in 1979, she has been happy to give me a good kicking whenever she felt I deserved it, and more often than not she has been right. She has given me some excellent advice over the years. Fay's sister, Beth Coventry, herself an excellent and, may I say, underrated restaurateur and chef, has also been a friend and inspiration. Her no-nonsense approach to cooking helped me simplify my approach and ultimately led to the sort of food I am producing at Notting Grill.

Family is a difficult one. My upbringing was quite Dickensian. We weren't that close, but I still loved them. I put my mother through hell as a child; she didn't need that. I didn't understand what being a single mother entailed. Sorry. To my grandfather and grandmother, great people without whom I wouldn't have had an education of such quality and a childhood of such excitement.

Ex-wives don't often feature in an acknowledgement list, but to mine, Jill and Militza, I just wanted to say the 'ex' bit wasn't your fault. You were both unlucky to meet me before I had grown up. To Militza, thanks for my two great Aussie boys, Blake and Sam, to whom I haven't been the best of dads – but you've done a great job, and I'll make it up to them in time.

My life would be impossible without a great team around me. A special thank-you to Jo Hynes, who ploughed through my hand-written manuscript and transformed it into type, a great PA who remarkably managed to stick with me for five years. To Louise, ex-Delia, my current PA, who took over my working life at its busiest point – a job that must be above and beyond the call of duty; certainly no time for polishing the nails.

To my great team of chefs and front-of-house, who over the years have produced miracles in my various absences. A special thank-you to my current team at Notting Grill: especially George, my manager; Antonio, a mate and longest-serving member of staff;

Fernando, George's assistant; Candido, top man and a rock in the kitchen. And not forgetting my partners at our function venue Luxters, Nick, Lisa and Ian.

To Jonathan Townsend at The Partnership, who searches for and discovers licensees to make and develop my ever-increasing range of equipment and food products. He has turned me into the largest chef brand in Europe, something I haven't quite got my head round. To all the licensees who have developed the 'dream', thanks for all your support and technical know-how.

To Lizzie Wilson, who came to us as a seventeen-year-old seven years ago to help with Toby-Jack and later Billie-Lara. She has been unbelievably supportive, a wonderful surrogate daughter and mate who has been invaluable in helping me and Jaybe develop and nurture two smashing 'normal' kids, forever a star, forever a friend.

A big thank-you to our little team at Shiplake who keep me sane, keep the flower and vegetable garden looking fab and who are happy to help out at the drop of a hat: Jim, Mike, Charlie and Paul.

To Simon 'the Bulldog' Bowen, who has seen me though many ups and downs, both as friend and lawyer, and to his gorgeous French wife Chantal, who very occasionally manages to turn the bulldog into a loveable poodle. To Simon's partners and associate, Richard and Isabel Cruickshank, who in recent years have dealt with my legals.

I believe it is important to have friends outside your industry – you can only talk so much food, even if it is your main passion. It's so refreshing having new friends Rory and Tessa Bremner; the ageless Penny Smith; great friends Tim Etchells and his delicious armlock Nicky, both in the exhibition world; neighbours and mates Anne and John Sawbridge; Nicki and Mike Ryan and Julian Glasspole, co-drinkers, co-boating enthusiasts and joint swamp-owners – all of whom live in different worlds, creating fascinating new areas of conversation. As you get older you don't need so many friends, but the ones you have must keep you happy, keep you stimulated and occasionally have strong shoulders on which you can cry.

To the 'new' mates that Jaybe brought into my life. Nicky Nardelli, no shrinking violet, a perennial who has become part of Shiplake's furniture; whenever she's not around you feel there's something missing. To Dominic, Nicky's son, who has become another 'son' to me and Jaybe. To Katie 'I love you really' Fingret, Jay's old flatmate, who winds me up something rotten and I love her for it. To Sarah and Sue, the tottering totty, glamour to the last, great mates, great fun. Sue's lovely husband Terry, who managed to tame the untamable. Kate's equally lovely husband James, another ex-Kings boy, another tamer of wild women. And to the biggest girlie of the lot, Dave Cannon, and partner Casper, who are responsible for many of my laughter lines. (I'm a lucky guy to know this terrific bunch.)

To Andrea Riva, who owns and is ever-present at my favourite restaurant, Riva in Barnes, the perfect restaurateur, great friend, and godfather to Billie-Lara.

To Michael Feeney Callan, another workaholic, a brilliant biographer with such luminaries as Richard Harris, Sean Connery, Antony Hopkins and soon Robert Redford in his portfolio. He dealt with my numerous one a.m. calls to him, when everything got too much or I had writer's block, in a sensitive way, with honest advice and reassuring words. As a virgin author of anything other than cookbooks, I needed all his years of experience to see me to the finishing line. There were also times when Jaybe couldn't see any light at the end of the tunnel either, so a big thank-you goes to Mike's wife Ree and their children Corey and Paris, who provided shoulders to cry on in her time of need.

Some of my greatest thanks must go to David Wilby and his perennial petal Margot. Employing him in 1983 at Ménage à Trois was one of the best things I ever did. How he survived that rocky first year, when I was at one of my lowest points, I'll never know. But he did, and as head chef he steadied the ship, which like the *Titanic* was a major success on the surface but had a weak keel and could have easily hit an iceberg. Now twenty years later he steadies Notting Grill, but more than that he has cemented our relationship and introduced us to new friends John and Helen, Mark and Shel. He deserves huge credit for my success; without him I couldn't do half of what I manage to achieve.

To my father, long gone but not forgotten, a kind gentle guy who undoubtedly gave me the thespian roots that surface from time to time.

And finally to the Sheils, my new family: Frank, Maeve, Rufina, John and Ciara, without whom I would never have met the lady who changed my life, Jaybe. No superlatives in the world could ever describe how much Jaybe means to me. Quite honestly, I could have finished this book at the point where we met, as ever since then I've been living the dream.

There are so many people who have meant so much to me over my life; so many I need to thank, but as with all books, space is the key. So to those I omit, big apologies.

PREFACE

ON THE RECENT TV PROGRAMME *I'M A CELEBRITY – GET ME OUT OF
Here!*, some of the stories I told about my life were condensed into
1½ minute clips and I was subsequently likened to Pinocchio.
Admittedly, when my experiences are edited in this way my life
does look extraordinary, but I can assure you that in real time
things make sense.

My life has been quite a journey, an amazing series of downs and
ups. You could say it's been character-building. I've never let it get
me down, and of course there is plenty to regret, plenty I would
have done differently given a second chance, but life isn't like that.
I now live for the day, I rarely look back and it's probably only
because of my fantastic 'new' family that I look forward. I think it
was Samuel Johnson who said something like 'I would rather have
a rich life than die rich'. That sums me up completely.

It may seem that I've been tough on my mother in these pages,
but I've tried to reflect the way I felt then. Looking back, of course
I loved her, but I also despaired of her. It can't have been easy for a
single divorced mum in the fifties and sixties, but at the time I
didn't see it that way: it was very much about me, me, me. And to
give her her due, she knew nothing of my abuse at school, as those
were the days when schools hid their shame under the carpet.

But if you're going through hell, there's no point in stopping to
be consumed by life's fire. You just have to keep going, and hope
you'll come out the other side. I didn't really emerge from that hell
until I met Jacinta, or Jaybe as I refer to her in the text. Jaybe
proved to me that a leopard could change his spots. And,

importantly, she instigated closure between me and my mother. I wish I had had time to understand where Mum had been coming from during my earlier years, but at least she died happy in the knowledge that I had completed my journey from hell to tranquillity, and I did this by finding a woman who could handle me, who could understand me and who could love me un-conditionally. It's amazing how love can change your whole outlook on life, close a few doors and yet open a lot more.

In my later life I have perhaps been fortunate, but success doesn't grow on trees – it has to be worked at. Luckily I'm a workaholic. I haven't written about this period in great detail as, being public property, it is already fairly well known – and also because it's far less interesting than the first thirty years of my life. I've also deliberately sheltered my children – my two older boys in Oz and my youngsters – because I feel they need a 'normal' life free from the pressures of being in the public eye. As far as I'm aware, they're all quite normal and, thank goodness, apart from *I'm a Celebrity*, they've hardly ever seen me perform on telly.

I've tried to recreate my very early memories accurately, building up the story from conversations with my mother and others who were around during this part of my life. Even so, there are bound to be errors. If there are, I apologize, but I've written in the belief that the facts are as true as my memory allows. Where I deem it necessary to protect the guilty or the innocent, and to avoid hurt-ing feelings, I have changed some names.

This is my first substantial piece of prose, and I have to admit to getting a bit carried away. Perhaps I should have accepted the offer of a ghostwriter, but I didn't, and one year turned into two and one hundred thousand words into 220,000. Every word was written by me in longhand using my lucky pen. I have no idea which buttons to push to turn on the computer; one day I'll have to come into the twenty-first century. Understandably, from the publisher's point of view, one third of the book hit the cutting-room floor, so I'm very sorry if some of my nearest and dearest went out in this tumble of words. Shit happens.

All of my life I have constantly been in trouble for telling it how it is. Nothing changes, and my autobiography reflects this rough edge – hence its title, *Raw*. I apologize in advance for some of my graphic language. Maybe the leopard hasn't changed all his spots.

CHAPTER ONE

'O ROMEO, ROMEO! WHEREFORE ART THOU ROMEO? OH NO, I'M OUT of here!'

And so, on 1 May 1951, my life began. In true romantic style, my mother was playing Juliet and my father Romeo with the Royal Shakespeare Company at Stratford-upon-Avon when she was caught short on stage by her waters breaking as Henry Antony Cardew Worrall Thompson gave notice of his arrival, unusually for him, three weeks early. The story goes that I was born in the Green Room of the theatre but, knowing how prone my mother was to exaggeration, I suspect I actually made it to the nursing home before bouncing on to the world's stage.

I was Henry after Henry IV, the Shakespearean role my father loved the best. Antony, my mother's choice, and the name she later decided to call me by, was inspired by her favourite Shakespeare play, *Antony and Cleopatra*. My third given name, Cardew, was taken from my maternal grandfather's family tree, which could be traced back to Cornelius Cardew, the mayor of Truro in 1797. My ancestor had owned two schools near the Cornish city and, on the evidence of historical records, he was a right bastard. He governed his schools with the stick rather than the carrot, using the Church as an excuse for his fire-and-brimstone approach to education. It was a type I was to encounter later in my childhood.

The nursing home was on the banks of the Avon. I was told that my father's understudy, rowing up the river one day, found me in a cot in the garden and deposited a Welsh threepenny bit in my hand with a note reading: 'Richard was here.' I promptly swallowed the coin. How this was discovered I never really found out, but when it was there was uproar, with Matron apparently threatening to call the police unless the perpetrator of this hideous crime owned up and apologized. To keep the peace, he did. I would love to have seen Richard Burton, that famous Welshman, being reprimanded and scolded like a naughty child.

Richard became one of my 'luvvie' godfathers. But don't get too excited, folks – I saw him on no more than half a dozen occasions during my lifetime. Still, I guess it's quite nice having his name on my curriculum vitae, especially as he was my father's understudy rather than the other way round. My father's name was Michael Worrall Thompson, though he went by the stage name of Ingham, and he came from an acting family. While I never knew him that well, I was always very proud of him and of his reputation as a good, if not great actor.

It is obvious from the stories of my early life that I was a bit of an inconvenience. Soon after my birth, my mother, Joanna Duncan, was asked to play the lead role in *Brigadoon*, which involved an eighteen-month tour of the UK. Not surprisingly, my father was appalled that she was considering doing any such thing and pleaded with her not to go. Fat chance. Till the day she died my mother was strong-willed to the point of being pig-headed. So she went, and so did I. Touring with a baby was not much fun for either mother or child, especially in the days of terry-towelling nappies, buckets of bleach and clothes lines strung between water pipes in the dressing room. When we were featured in two or three of what would now be described as red-top rags – the *Daily Sketch* dubbed me the '18,000-mile baby' – fortune smiled on my mother in the form of an American company which picked up on the story. They were in the advanced stages of testing the first disposable nappies and offered her a free supply of them for the rest of my babyhood. I wonder if she ever entered them on her tax return. Anyway, I duly became Britain's first 'disposable' baby. It's funny, but now that I've gone 'green' and try to do my bit to save the planet, I'm dead against disposables because of the time they take to decompose. Apologies to any new mothers, because it's probably not what you want to hear, but it's true.

During my eighteen months with *Brigadoon* I was dragged from pillar to post, with hundreds of landladies at digs all around the country acting as surrogate aunts. As for my poor old dad, it must have been tough on him, rarely seeing my mother apart from on the odd Sunday, and it is not surprising that he fell by the wayside. In the 1950s affairs weren't the public issue that they are today, and the press wasn't nearly as cut-throat, but theatre luvvies, then as now, loved to gossip and it wasn't long before my mother was acquainted with my father's infidelity. He was immediately given his marching orders and no amount of pleading, tears or remorse would change her mind. He loved my mum but she, being pig-headed, was unforgiving. Personally, I think it was a decision she would come to regret.

Yet even before my father's affair things hadn't been going well between them. The particular pressures and lifestyle of the theatre made it easy to fall into the habit of drinking too much, and they both did that. Money was scarce, and rows and bickering were the order of the day. Dad was partial to the odd flutter on the horses, and, inevitably, what began as the odd flutter gradually turned into an obsession. In the end he was betting every day. It fell to my mother to place his bets and she soon worked out that, given his less-than-glittering success rate, it made sense to keep the money instead and simply pay out if and when the occasional nag came up trumps. What he didn't know couldn't hurt him, after all. Things went swimmingly at first, and Mum was able to supplement her meagre theatrical income quite nicely. I guess it was just robbing Peter to pay Paul, really, and if my father had had the money he would only have drunk it.

But disaster was just around the corner. One day, just as he did on many other days, Dad placed a combination bet, a yankee. He always picked horses with long odds, so he had more chance of being struck by lightning than of winning. But, you've guessed it, on this particular day the yankee came up. The sum of £14,000 had been lost by my mother's own gamble. My dad had been standing at the gates of heaven only to be snatched away at the last moment and thrown into hell. It was the beginning of the end, and their relationship would never be the same again. My father's affair, it seems, was just the straw that broke the camel's back.

Getting divorced was not the common occurrence in the 1950s that it is today. It brought shame upon the whole family, or so my maternal grandparents thought, anyway. The marital home in Chelsea had to be sold and it was arranged for my mother to be dispatched to a flat in Hove. It might as well have been purgatory as far as she was concerned. She was a wild one, and she loved

London. That was where her friends were, and where she wanted to be, but she had me to consider.

As for me, I was blissfully unaware of all this. The only recollection I have of my father at this time is of being wrapped up in a camel coat with a velvet collar, velvet beret and brown, buckled shoes at the age of three to be towed by a male visitor around the Lanes in Brighton on a pub crawl. This was Dad's first and last attempt after the divorce to spend time with his son. I was not to see him again until I was twenty-five.

My mother was dominated by an even more powerful woman: my grandmother. Gran was an upper-crust type of the old school, and a fearsome woman, or so I thought. I dreaded the visits she demanded. For one, I had to behave, I had to pretend to be nice. Mother insisted on this because, while I was a total inconvenience to her, I was at the same time her lifeline.

My mother had had a brother called Andrew, the apple of my grandparents' eyes. He could do no wrong. At Eton he had been captain of cricket and house captain; afterwards, he followed his father into the Grenadier Guards and became an excellent soldier. Even when he was sent home wounded from the Second World War he fell on his feet. For his convalescence he was barracked at Windsor Castle. The King's two daughters, Princess Elizabeth and Princess Margaret, used to wander through the tented city where the wounded were recovering, giving their royal waves and exchanging niceties with 'our boys'. Andrew struck up a friendship with Princess Elizabeth, later to become our Queen.

According to my grandfather's fireside stories, this friendship blossomed in all the right directions. He used to recount stories of dinners for eight at Windsor Castle, where Andrew would be seated next to Elizabeth and opposite the King. My grandfather must have been bursting with pride. But I never knew the man who would have become my uncle. So I never knew whether or not he was a nice person, or what his feelings were towards my mother, who clearly had been jealous of him. And none of us will ever know if or how his friendship with Princess Elizabeth might have developed, though it is fascinating for me to speculate about what the consequences might have been. Instead Andrew chose to play the hero and return to the battlefield. He was killed rescuing one of his platoon in the last week of the war. What followed was unspeakable and would have a lasting effect on my mother.

At the time of Andrew's death my mother was working overseas with ENSA, the Entertainments National Services Association, entertaining the troops. She had been evacuated to Canada at the start of hostilities and before joining ENSA had decided to pursue an acting career in the USA, much to the displeasure of my gran, whose view of Americans was not flattering. She considered them to be uncouth and unnecessary. But it would seem that my mother deliberately enjoyed upsetting the applecart, and she turned a deaf ear to family pleas to return home and find a nice young Englishman.

My grandfather, meanwhile, was serving with the Indian Army, training troops for General Slim's Burmese campaign. His wife, ever faithful, divided her time between the North-West Frontier in India and Washington, where she worked on breaking German coded messages. She was in India when she received the news of her son's death. She and my mother immediately returned to England, arranging to meet at Southampton Docks. Shocking, bitter words were said by my distraught grandmother: 'Why, why, why, couldn't it have been you?' Those words haunted my mum until the day she died. She was never, ever going to be anything other than second best.

This was why I was her lifeline. The moment I was born I became Andrew; I was grandma's substitute son. My mother resented this but she milked it for all it was worth. To ensure that I was looked after, my gran became my mother's financial drip feed, while I became her hostage. 'If you want to see your grandson, then cough up the dough,' was the gist of it, though I'm sure the threat was made in a far more subtle way.

My mother had no choice other than to accept the flat in Hove, but she was just biding her time until she was able to contrive some more satisfactory arrangement. I hampered her lifestyle and her freedom of movement, and something was going to have to be done about that. There were going to have to be some changes. And in the middle of 1954, there were.

CHAPTER TWO

IN 1954 MY MUM AND I MOVED TO OUR UNFURNISHED, RENTED FLAT IN Farm Road in Hove. One of my earliest memories is how excited I was about the large, communal garden and about being so close to the sea. What more could a toddler ask for, after all? My mother was absolutely gutted, but I couldn't have been happier. Just me and Mum: quality time for ever. The idyll lasted about a month.

It was explained to me over a glass or six of Dry Sack sherry (for her) and a Kia-Ora orange squash (for me) at a pub called the Tree Trunk run by Valentina Hoolihan, a friend of my mother's. Looking back, it was probably quite a sleazy place: loads of red lamps, barrels for tables and perpetually full of smoke. Everyone seemed to smoke in those days, and I would be given cigarette cards from the packets to keep me quiet, which wasn't difficult as I was a self-sufficient child. I would hide behind the barrels, examining the strange, red faces, hideous with raucous laughter. I saw the regulars as families of rather large, fat pigs and the Tree Trunk as their sty. For Mum I was a talking point, an ice-breaker in her constant quest to be loved by everyone in Brighton. It wasn't London, but still. When I got a bit older I realized that Mother never stopped acting. She was like a pot of honey, a magnet for the worker bees.

But I digress. I was in the middle of my Kia-Ora, Mum was sipping a sherry and we were having a 'chat'.

'Darling, you like going to the pier, don't you?'

'Yes.'

'You like me buying toys for you?'

'Yes.'

'You like having Geoffrey to tea?'

Geoffrey was my only friend in Brighton. Needless to say, he was the son of a publican.

'Yes.'

'Well, to do all these things, Mummy has to earn some money.'

I was wondering what she was getting at.

'Well,' she went on, 'I've found this lovely place for you to stay at while I'm working.'

'But I want to stay with you.'

'You can't, darling.'

'Why not?'

'Because Mummy has to work in London.'

I was struck dumb for a moment, then: 'I hate you!' I yelled, and with that I was out of the door and off, running as fast as my tiny legs would go. My destination was the comforting familiarity of the West Pier. I sheltered underneath it, in among the wrought-iron supports, throwing pebbles into the sea. But at three years old your options are limited, and by the time the sun began to set I was bored, my temper had cooled and it was time to try to get home to Farm Road. It's hard to believe that a three-year-old would be able to find his way from Brighton to Hove, but in those days, having no car, we walked everywhere, and the route from Hove to the Tree Trunk was a well-travelled one. We rehearsed it at least three times during the week and again every Sunday.

When I eventually toddled into the flat I was surprised to find several of the 'pigs' comforting my mother. I was dispatched straight to bed without my usual cup of steaming Ovaltine or Horlicks. Left alone with Fred, my teddy bear, I found it hard to sleep. It wasn't made any easier by the bursts of hearty laughter coming from Mum and the 'pigs' in the sitting room next door. My tantrum, it seemed, had been forgotten. Perhaps my mother's plans had been, too.

But the next morning, a Monday morning, I was awoken at 7.30 and, dazed, put into clothes I had never seen before: a grey fluffy flannelette shirt, grey shorts, long grey socks, black shoes, grey tie, navy blazer with some sort of crest on the pocket. On top of all that, when it was time to go – where? – I was kitted out in navy duffel coat and navy cap and frogmarched the three quarters of a mile from Farm Road to St Ann's Road and up a few steps to what was to me a huge, forbidding front door.

Mother whacked the heavy doorknocker a couple of times. The door was opened by a girl of about sixteen whose name, I was to learn, was Rosemary. Mother told her who we were. 'You are expected. Please follow me,' she said curtly. Holding on to my mother's dress I shuffled into a big, book-laden study with floor-to-ceiling windows. Behind a desk sat Little Red Riding Hood's wolf in her grandmother's clothing, a tall, lean, lady wearing a full-length blue skirt, a white, lacy shirt with a ruffled collar and the obligatory string of pearls and brooch. The hair was elegantly swept up in a bun on top of a finely proportioned head. She must have been in her late fifties, and she was a formidable-looking woman. When she stood to shake my mother's hand she seemed to tower over her. Unlike my mother's fat piglet friends, this wolf was definitely a female. She invited my mother to sit down and they talked for a short time, then my mother got up to leave. I started to sob. 'Don't worry, little one, you're going to have fun here,' the wolf growled. Desperate to spend a final few seconds in my mum's skirt folds, I didn't respond. I had to be dragged off her. If my mother was upset, she didn't show it. She kissed me and, with the words 'See you on Sunday' she was gone.

Rosemary whisked me away down the back stairs to the basement, where about twenty other boys were sitting on long benches, finishing their breakfast. They were all older than me except for one, whose face was already familiar: it was Geoffrey, the publican's son, who was my only friend in Brighton. He was to remain my only friend for the next four years. Geoffrey was round and smiley whereas I was skinny and sulky, but he needed me and I needed him.

St Ann's was a kindergarten for boys up to the age of seven. As the official school starting age was five, I was being given a valuable head start on the educational front, though I didn't of course appreciate that at the time. However, in terms of emotional damage, no one will ever know how deeply I may have been affected by being sent away to board at the age of three. My over-riding memory is of feeling incredibly unwanted. I don't recall anything specific from those first weeks other than that I looked forward to Sundays, when I could see my mum. She was usually fairly late picking me up, having been to bed in the small hours the same morning – drinking perhaps; performing, definitely. About the only plus point I can think of about boarding at such a tender age is that it makes you very independent very quickly, and I suppose my mother realized this. At any rate, it didn't come as a huge surprise to her when I told her that I would like to walk home each Sunday rather than have her collect me. Even though in those days people didn't worry so much about small children wandering the streets on their own, it is still astonishing that she agreed. I had only just turned four.

I would be longing to see my mum, but otherwise Sundays were not all that exciting. After walking to Farm Road, I'd play with my Dinky toys while mother slapped her face on, as she put it, and then it was off to the Tree Trunk to meet up with other actors and actresses on their day off. I think I was the only child there, and whether I was pitied I don't know. But I was allowed to have anything I wanted if it kept me quiet. I would usually be found under a table, in my own little world, playing cops and robbers with my Dinky toys in among the legs around me, human or wooden. I suppose we must have had a lunch of some sort, though I don't remember what. At that time food wasn't high on the AWT agenda. I can't recall my mother cooking, although she must have done or I wouldn't be here to tell the tale.

I was four when I first attempted to cook myself, on one of those walk-home Sundays. I had been given a key to the flat with strict instructions not to wake Mother. Some days it was noon before she emerged, make-up smeared, hair tangled. It was not a pretty sight, but she was my mum and I loved her. This particular Sunday a thought struck me. Perhaps if I were to cook her breakfast, it might encourage her to get up a bit earlier.

My first foray into a world that would later become my own involved a valiant if ultimately disappointing attempt at scrambled eggs on toast. I knew that involved eggs – two, I thought – a splash of milk, a knob of Echo margarine and our tatty blue frying pan. But how did you break the eggs? I had seen Mum crack the top of a boiled egg with the back of a teaspoon. Thwack! went the spoon on the egg. It sort of dented, but didn't actually break. I picked the fragments of shell from the top of the egg only to find that there was an opaque film preventing me from getting at the inside. After fiddling with it for an age I managed to push my finger through the film. Success. Putting the egg into a bowl, though, was easier said than done. It eventually occurred to me that if I squeezed the egg in the same way as I squeezed my tube of toothpaste, the egg would pop out. It did, too, but with such force that it completely overshot the bowl and redecorated the kitchen wall instead. Five eggs later,

I'd finally got two into the bowl. I reached for the Cerebos salt. The container had a picture on it of a small boy chasing a chicken and trying to cover it in salt. I pulled open the spout and poured. It does come out quickly, doesn't it? So, my recipe so far: two abused eggs, one tablespoon of salt. What was next? Milk. We won't even go down that route, except to say that a small thumb pushing down on a gold-foil top is asking for trouble. Another minor makeover for the kitchen, and I had a little milk in the eggs.

The next feat was the cooking part. The facilities had hardly been designed with me in mind. I was a small and scrawny four, a shade less than three foot tall. The hob on the cast-iron electric cooker was at hat level, the toaster grill at eye level, the controls eighteen inches above the hob at the rear. After assessing the options, I pulled up a chair from the kitchen table. Somehow I manoeuvred the heavy pan, the eggs and myself up on to the chair. Everything was going very well indeed. The eggs went in the pan, the pan on the stove, the heat went on, and step one had been accomplished. I even added the knob of margarine. Now, what was step two? Ah yes, toast. Slap two slices of bread under the grill. Meanwhile the eggs, for some extraordinary reason, seemed to have stuck to the bottom of the pan. I scraped and they came away, along with what appeared to be some of the pan but was probably just bits of black egg. I was absorbed in stirring in the lumps when I caught a whiff of the unmistakable carbon smell of burned toast. Calmly, I pulled out the blackened bread, turned it over and offered it back up to the mercies of the grill. Off came the pan, out came the toast. I arranged the carbon-coated slices on a plate, tipped out the circular eggy lump on top of them, found a knife and fork, pulled out a tray and off I went, down the corridor, ready to impress mother with my culinary triumph. Surely that breakfast must have ended up in the bin, but if so it was done without my seeing it, and I still remember my feeling of utter triumph from that day.

It was at about this time that my mother decided to get married again. It was a fait accompli. The first time I met her husband-to-be, a writer, was at the register office on the day of the wedding. From my vantage point he seemed tall. He had glossy, shiny cheeks and a shock of red hair. He didn't appear to like me, and I didn't like him. He was a gatecrasher in my life, someone who had wheedled his way into my mum's affections while I was away at school and unable to protect her. He wasn't to last, though, and when the short-lived marriage hit the buffers I heaved a huge sigh of relief.

I found out much later that when the sparks flew on their wedding night, it was not in the way my mother had intended. My potential new dad turned out not to be interested in women and, instead of treating my mum to a night of unbridled passion, he knocked her out with one punch and then locked himself in the bedroom, ignoring her cries of pain. Whether this man was simply gay, as my mother believed then, or whether he was something rather more sinister, as subsequent events were to suggest, it is impossible to say. Whatever the case, he had married my mum to cover up his true sexuality and protect his family name. It was not a wise decision. Little did he know that she was a five-foot-four-inch bundle of trouble. She was not the kind of woman to put up with a sham relationship for the sake of appearances and she didn't want her second marriage to fail. She tried every trick in the book to convert him but it wasn't to be.

The final straw for her was when he began to abuse me. My bogus stepfather babysat me if mother needed to be at the theatre when I was home from school, and used to take a bath with me. I saw nothing odd in this – at that age, bathtime is just fun time. And as for what he did in the bath, to me it was just vigorous splashing. I don't suppose anybody would ever have known anything about it if my mother hadn't come home early one evening feeling unwell and caught him red-handed. I'm sure the earth must have moved for him in a big way when she smashed him silly with the blue frying pan.

His response was to scoop me up in his arms and make a dash through the flat for the balcony. Out there – we were both still stark naked – he screamed at my mother that he would throw me over the balustrade if she didn't back off. As we lived on the fourth floor this was a serious matter. My mother was shaking. Even I could see she was dumbstruck. Then she sprang into action. Without a word, she picked up the phone and started dialling. My captor was puzzled: she didn't appear to be ringing the police. She wasn't. She was ringing his mother.

'Good evening, Mrs Carter,' she said, 'I think there is something you should know about your son.'

As quick as a flash, my mum's husband had deposited me back in her arms and in the same movement swiftly disconnected the call. You should have seen my mum. Her eyes were blazing, and she seemed to puff out her chest and grow several inches taller. She had him in the palm of her hand now, and she squeezed metaphorically, gently at first, but with each expletive, volcanically delivered in a way only an actor knew how, her grip grew tighter. 'Fuck' wasn't a word often heard in the 1950s, but my mother was clearly no stranger to it. During her tirade I heard more fucks than I had so far had hot dinners.

'You dirty fucking bastard! If you ever touch my son again, if you ever set foot in this fucking flat again, if I ever fucking see you again, not only will I tell your beloved mother what a worm you are, what a despicable piece of human excrement, but I'll tell all the newspapers, and the police . . .' and so it went on, for what seemed like hours.

As for me, I hadn't got a clue what any of this was about. I can remember the row, remember my mother's husband threatening to throw me off the balcony, but of course I didn't understand the significance of him thrashing about in the bath until long afterwards.

My mother's threats must have worked, because I don't recall ever again seeing my would-be stepfather. He was a mummy's boy, and the last thing he wanted was to bring shame on his family by being outed for the pervert he was, which was why he had married my mother in the first place.

Although I was too young to grasp that I had been abused, I wonder whether it did have some subconscious effect on me, because it was around this time that I started behaving a bit strangely at school. It started with horrendous nightmares. They were always the same. I was being chased by a terrifying monster, a monster with fishy breath, a monster that seemed to develop more and more arms and legs, a monster whose body seemed to contain a lot of mini monsters, all growing out of its flesh. Just as it was about to catch me I would go into an uncontrollable spin, as if I'd been placed on a spinning top and then thrown off, at a ferocious speed, spiralling away from my pursuer. It didn't matter what I read before bed, what sweet thoughts were in my head as I dozed off – as soon as I was deeply asleep, the monster would be back.

Worse was to follow. Apparently I fell into the habit of peeing under my pillow. The monster had burning breath, you see, and I guess I imagined I was quelling the flames. Whenever I had one of these nightmares, I would always wake up in the morning topsy-turvy, with my head at the bottom of the bed. There was no sympathy from the staff, just a scolding. I would then be marched to the basement where I was shown a washboard and given a big cake of carbolic soap. 'You filthy little boy! I want those sheets whiter than white!' And with those words ringing in my ears, I would have to scrub and rinse my sheets, scrub them and rinse them. Then I would be marched into the garden and made to hang them on the line in front of all the other children. Still my humiliation was not complete. In that morning's lessons I would then have to wear a dunce's hat or sit in a corner of the classroom until lunchtime.

In my waking hours I seemed like a normal, bright child, top of my little class, great at spelling. I could tell the time at four, tie my own little grey tie, do up my shoelaces – you know the sort of thing, the basic, functional skills we all take for granted, appreciating only a generation later, when we come to teach them to our own children, what a mountain they are to climb. But the nights got worse before they got better. At five I started sleepwalking. And it wasn't any old sleepwalking, getting into bed with another pupil, say, or raiding the kitchen, this was going down two flights of stairs, across the hall, out of the front door, down another set of stairs and walking in my pyjamas the mile and a half to my favourite penny-in-the-slot ride – an animal that you sat on – which was on the Brighton seafront near the Palace Pier. I did this four times. The police would find me there – they had police on the streets in those days – wait for me to wake up, and then take me down to the local nick. They were nice to me, gave me Ovaltine and custard-cream biscuits. It was comforting being looked after by these kindly men. I missed the presence of men. I suppose I missed my dad.

The first time they found me they obviously established where I came from – I must have given them the school address rather than my mother's, because apparently she knew nothing about the sleep-walking until years later – and after that returning me to St Ann's became a bit of a routine. They would drive me back in their shiny, black police Wolseley with its grown-up smell of old leather, and let me turn on the bell (no sirens in those days), just like on *Dixon of Dock Green*, before delivering me into the not-so-safe hands of our fearsome governess, Mrs Townsend – the wolf – who would smile sweetly at the officers, thanking them profusely for their efforts and apologizing on my behalf.

But once that front door was closed I was subjected to a one-handed blitzkrieg. The first time it happened it caught me unawares. Wham, a stinging slap nearly knocked me off my feet as it connected with my left cheek. I could feel my bottom lip going, but I was determined not to cry. The tears were welling in my eyes but they never reached my cheeks. When she failed to elicit the desired reaction, the wolf hauled me by my ear to the basement, where I was given a chipped white enamel cup of water and a plate of dripping-coated bread.

'This is all you will get all day,' she told me, before handing me over to the young assistant: Rosemary, the girl who had opened the door to Mum and me on my first day at St Ann's. I liked her, and she had a soft spot for me, too. She probably felt sorry for me, but however it came about, we were friends, even though she was seventeen and I was only five. Rosemary was as terrified of the wolf as I was, so she did what she was told. Which, in this instance, was to escort me, along with my meagre food rations, to the coalhole under the road. It was dark, and made darker still by the piles of black coal and coke it contained.

Rosemary was choking with emotion as she led me into this dungeon. 'I'm sorry,' she said miserably. 'It's not me, it's Mrs Townsend's decision. I'll look after you when she lets you out after tea.' And then the door closed, the bolts were drawn and I was all alone: just me, my food, the coal, and my now black pyjamas. Only then did the floodgates open, and out they poured, tears as big as peardrops. I could hardly draw breath, so violent were my sobs. But still I didn't scream. I just sat there, not understanding what heinous crime I had committed. And in truth, apart from endangering myself, my only transgression was to have embarrassed the wolf, which hardly constituted a crime. In any case, I had not done either of these things voluntarily. But Mrs Townsend was one of the old school, the school of Victorian values such as 'children should be seen and not heard', and 'spare the rod and spoil the child'. She was the first malign force in my life. Not even my mother's second husband made such an impression on my formative years.

In all I was sentenced to the coalhole four times – each time my sleepwalking took me to my seafront animal. On all these occasions the police picked me up and returned me to the school. Every time I got the whack, then the torrent of verbal abuse from the wolf, the rations of water and bread and dripping and a six-hour sojourn in the hole. Not only was my mother never told about the sleepwalking, but she never knew about my incarceration, either, and when I did tell her, years later, I'm sure she didn't believe me. Back then, when she inquired on Sundays how my week had been, I replied merely: 'Fine.' I may have been a boy of few words, but if I was fine, it was only insofar as the word could be taken as an acronym of Fucking Insecure, Neurotic and Emotional.

My fourth spell in the coalhole brought results. I had found a small metal bar in the darkness among the coal – I've no idea what it could have been or how it got there, but there it was – and, scrambling to the top of my hill of coal, managed to use it to force off the heavy, cast-iron coalhole cover. It was through this hole that the coalman delivered the coal straight from the pavement into the basement, and it was through this hole that I escaped, wriggling up on to the pavement, blinking in the sunlight. I was free!

I knew exactly where I wanted to go. My favourite place, asleep or awake, was the section of the Brighton seafront where my penny-in-the-slot ride was waiting for me. And this time it was different, because not only was I awake, but I had cast off my shackles. I had bucked the system, and there was no going back. The shine was rather taken off my triumph by the man in charge of the amusements, who refused to let me on my animal unless I had money to put in the slot, which of course I didn't. God knows what he or the rest of the outside world must have made of this street urchin. There were plenty of small kids out playing in the streets or on the seafront in those days, but they weren't usually covered in coal dust. So I went down to the beach, where I kicked things around and threw the occasional pebble in the sea before deciding to walk into town, through the Lanes, and up to the main drag running from the station towards Hove.

As I strode down the road, I saw something that stopped me in my tracks. There, right in front of me, was a shop window full of naked women! They weren't, of course – women, I mean – they were mannequins. But they were still naked. Both my mother and my grandmother were uptight about nudity, so I'd never seen my mum in the altogether. I was completely transfixed. How passers-by must have interpreted my antics doesn't bear thinking about. There I was, looking at the mannequins from every imaginable angle, lying down on the pavement to get a different perspective.

After a while I was diverted when a small dog entered my field of vision. I loved dogs. My gran had a Lhasa apso, Tomu, which she had brought back with her from Nepal, and my one regret about living in the Hove flat was that there I couldn't have a pet of my own. The terrier rolled on the ground alongside me to have its tummy rubbed. As we played I had the feeling I was being watched. I was. Out of the corner of my eye I glimpsed a pair of brown eyes with yellowy whites above a yellowy-white beard. I looked up and took in long, unkempt grey hair, ruddy cheeks and a big face, smiling at me from behind what had once been a good-quality pram, cream with a navy hood. The man whistled to his dog and it ran obediently over to him. I got up and followed it. I had no fear of strangers, having met hundreds of them at theatres where my mother worked or in the Tree Trunk.

'What's his name, mister?'

'That's Ronnie,' replied the man. I remember thinking that was funny because Ronnie was my granddad's name. We exchanged names, too. The man was called Harry. He carried lots of things with him in that pram, and he was nice. He talked to me normally, not as an adult to a small child. We chatted away as we walked towards the beach, where he shared with me the remnants of what must have been his lunch.

Then we just walked around, talking as we went. I don't remember what about, and even then I didn't much care. Just having somebody to talk to was all that mattered. What I do remember is that Harry, who might easily have been dismissive and grumpy, and was certainly a tramp, was kind and caring. And best of all he was a man. The only man in my life was my granddad, and I didn't see him that often. Otherwise my world was all women: Mother, Gran, Mrs Townsend, Rosemary. That afternoon Harry was happy, Ronnie was happy and I was happy. And it's important to be happy.

At teatime we stopped at a café on the seafront. Harry seemed to know everybody there. We were given tea and cake, and Ronnie got a biscuit and a bowl of water. My eyes were on stalks when I was presented with the biggest chunk of lardy cake I had ever seen. The tea was delicious: warm, sweet and milky. It was bliss. Back at St Ann's it must have been another story, but I hadn't a care in the world. As evening fell we left Brighton and were heading east along the beach, Harry picking up anything he could find to add to his estate in the pram, me playing with Ronnie, throwing stones, chasing the dog through the surf. It was a new and exciting life, and it was to last for another three days. We slept in beach huts and arches. Harry would cover me with his coat, unnecessarily, as it was summer, but it was comforting all the same. For me all this was a wonderful adventure.

On the evening of the fourth day we camped on the clifftops at Rottingdean. As I settled to sleep with Ronnie snuggled up beside me, I was disturbed by the familiar jangling of a bell. The bell of a police car. I heard stern voices. Then Harry was shouting, the police were shouting and I was taken away. So were Harry and Ronnie, but not Harry's pram. I often wondered whether Harry was ever reunited with his worldly goods. I never knew what happened to Harry and Ronnie, and I never saw them again.

As for me, I was returned to St Ann's. This time there was no violence, merely a lot of questions from a woman in a navy suit, an official-looking lady, presumably from the council. When the interrogation was over I was taken out of the room to be welcomed by Rosemary, who gave me one of the biggest hugs of my life. She squeezed me so hard that I was yelping with pain. Rosemary was no heavyweight – I've seen more meat on a butcher's pencil – and her protruding bones dug into me sharply. Mrs T. was, amazingly, calm, almost pleasant, as she explained in gentle tones that in future I would be sleeping in Rosemary's bed. I don't know whether Rosemary had been consulted about this. I doubt it, but she didn't utter a word except for the regulation courtesy reply, 'Yes, Mrs Townsend.'

Whatever Rosemary felt about it, I was delighted. I loved Rosemary, and now she was to be my personal night chaperone. Everything seemed to go swimmingly after that. The nightmares came less and less often and sleepwalking was intercepted by Rosemary. I even had the chance to see a real naked woman. If I woke up when Rosemary came to bed I was instructed to avert my eyes while she got undressed. I would obediently turn my head away from her, but I could see her reflection in the window. I've no idea what the other children must have thought about this special treatment. I was a loner, and I don't remember my fellow pupils at all, except for Geoffrey, the publican's son. There were about twenty of us, I think, but my only memory of the other boys is that none of them had blond hair like I did.

By the time I was six, my mother was mapping out the next stages of my education. Discussions were held with my maternal grandparents. My grandfather, being of military stock, wanted me to be prepared for Wellington College, his old school. My gran, of course, wanted me to follow in her son Andrew's footsteps and therefore to be prepped for Eton. Neither of these options met with the approval of my mother. She decided that I was to be prepared for King's School, Canterbury, probably on the suggestion of one of her friends.

However, it was my grandparents who were going to be paying for my schooling for the next twelve years. So I can only surmise that, combined with her stubbornness, it was my mother's emotional blackmail over grandparental access to me that won the day. There were rows, of course. My grandparents couldn't argue that King's was a common school, but it certainly wasn't Eton or Harrow or Wellington. In truth, their reservations were rooted in the fact that they didn't know any of the governors at King's, so no strings could be pulled there. They were furious, but in the end they went along with my mother's choice. She was very pleased with her-self. Me? I just went with the flow.

CHAPTER THREE

DURING MY TIME AT ST ANN'S MY MOTHER HAD GONE IN FOR A change of career. Soon after the launch of independent television in 1955, she went to work for a new television company, ATV. She wanted to train as a director, but she started as a floor manager. It was not a good career move for somebody who was, by all accounts, an excellent actress. I remember traipsing around studios in my school holidays while my mother laid great big lines of green and red tape on the set, marking the positions for furniture and scenery. God, was it boring. But I idolized my mum, so I did what I was told: held tape measures, stuck down bits of tape.

On the plus side, along with Mum's new job came two fantastic additions to the family: a television and a car. The television was a Bush portable, with a round screen, black and white, of course. We watched it all the time, and because of my mother's work, it was always ITV. The car was a grey Austin A35 with red mock-leather upholstery. It was the bee's knees. At last there were trips to the country, to the coast, and whole new vistas opened up to me.

Mum's connections in independent television and her theatrical roots also opened up opportunities for me in advertising. I am told that my first performance had actually been given before this, at the tender age of about two, when my bare botty appeared on the telly displaying those new disposable nappies. There followed commercials for the Gas Board, sliced bread and several others requiring a cute little blond boy. All they meant to me were long, tedious days hanging around endlessly and then being pushed from pillar to post, but you'd have thought that at least they would have

built up a healthy savings account for me. My mother's needs, however, were greater than mine. Besides, in those days the payments
for children were small and there were no repeat fees, just good old
exploitation. I can't imagine I was any good at it, either. I was shy
and not too receptive to being told what to do.

I lived in my own world. My mum's luvvie friends tolerated me,
but didn't show a great deal of interest. I played with some of their
kids sometimes, but that was about the extent of my relationship
with them. Among them were Googie Withers, who lived in
Brighton before she decamped to Australia, Jack Hawkins, whose
wife Doreen got on well with my mum, John Le Mesurier, Diana
Dors, Ralph Richardson and John Gielgud. There was always a
'face' around, though many of Mum's circle didn't become famous
until later, but that's all they were to me – faces, theatrical types
who would come and go. My mother loved it, of course. She was
desperate to hold on to her roots, which were gradually being
eroded by her new career in television. Although it was a move she
regretted, she was good at what she did and she did finally make it
up the ladder to become a director.

I passed my entrance exams for Milner Court, the prep school for
King's, Canterbury and settled down to see out my last months at
St Ann's in relative tranquillity. It was not only the kindergarten
that would soon be consigned to memory but Brighton and Hove,
too. My grandmother, who felt she wasn't seeing enough of me,
took the decision to let one of two properties she owned in
Markham Street in Chelsea – a tiny maisonette that connected to
her own house – to my mother, and we moved there when I left St
Ann's.

Living next door to my grandparents was very different from our
bohemian existence in Hove. I didn't really know them that well –
they had spent a good deal of time out of the country visiting far-
away lands such as South Africa, the Falklands or India, fulfilling
my grandfather's military duties – and I had always been a bit
frightened of them. They were very posh, very correct. My gran
took it upon herself to train and groom me. In the school holidays,
when my mother was at work, she looked after me, and I slept in
her house, even though my mother was only next door. My gran
had a thing about mattresses. Each bed had to have at least three.
It made for snuggly sleep in a bed so soft that I would sink into the
middle, almost engulfed by the mountains of mattress on each side.
Every night my grandfather would kiss me goodnight, and every

night I would tell him the same thing: 'You smell, and you need a shave.' He would chuckle and the twinkle in his eye shone a little brighter. As he tucked me up, he would always say, 'Snug as a bug in a rug. Sleep tight, and don't let the bedbugs bite.' In fact, it was such a ritual that he wasn't allowed to leave until he had said it. He was a warm, kind man, I discovered, once I got over my fear of him. We used to have long talks, during which he regaled me with stories of his adventures in India, or of wars, of shooting tigers (there were several skins and heads around the house) and of glamorous parties. He had lived through exciting and decidedly non-PC times.

Born in 1888, twenty-seven years after his eldest sibling, my grandfather was the youngest of twelve children. His roots were a mixture of Scottish and Cornish with the Scottish surname, Duncan, being passed down the male side of the family. I wish I had taken the opportunity to find out more about his family history while he was alive; all I know is that we have some very colourful cousins. One of Grandfather's sisters married a Philby and became the mother of Kim Philby, the notorious spy of the 1950s. I never knew him, but it's a great talking point to have a spy in the family, although of course in those days we were never allowed to mention his name. Two or three siblings went off to run diamond mines in South Africa. Another sister married a Montgomery – who, as Bishop Montgomery, officiated at my grandparents' marriage – and their son grew up to become the famous first Viscount Montgomery of Alamein. A third sister was a lady-in-waiting to Queen Victoria and married a prince of Saxe-Coburg. A brother, Jack, did brilliantly in the army and was knighted; another, embarrassingly, was Sheriff of Dublin during British rule and played a major role in quelling the Easter Rising of 1916.

My grandmother's family was equally posh. She was a Davies, one of four children, two sons and two daughters. They lived in a large house in Camberley in Surrey and had a pad on the Isle of Wight as well. The household was all very Upstairs, Downstairs, with a cook, a butler, chauffeurs and gardeners. She would tell me about the carriages they drove in, with Dalmatians running along behind. Her family used to breed Dalmatians. I have painful memories of one, called Sally, my grandmother had when I was a toddler, which gave me, with one crunch, my first broken nose at the age of one and a half. I still have the scar.

Unlike many Victorian families, the Davieses decided to educate their daughters, so it was off to a Swiss finishing school for Gran to learn how to write cheques and control the servants. I have kept her schoolbooks, filled with instructions on managing a household, all recorded in stilted, formal language. I also have some amazing photographs of her as a young woman – petite and beautiful, a real catch.

After being presented at court she decided to train as an actress at the Weber-Douglas school, but before she had time to embark on her new career she fell for my grandfather and was whisked off to India to become an army wife. In the hottest months she refused to go up to the hill stations with the other wives, preferring to return to England. She told me magical stories of great balls and dinners on the cruise ships going to and from India, and tales of hair-raising trips in the early days of commercial air travel after the war. Although passengers travelled in great luxury – meals served on board were freshly cooked and served on fine china, wine was sipped from crystal glasses and even the miniature salt and pepper pots were made of solid silver – the flight could be very uncomfortable. There were no pressurized cabins then, no heating, and journeys were longer with frequent refuelling stops. Gran didn't exactly travel light: she would be accompanied by a whole set of alligator suitcases containing her evening gowns and make-up, several hatboxes and racks and racks of shoes. Standards had to be maintained, even though when they first went to Kathmandu there were no roads around or over the surrounding mountains. My grandmother told me that they used to dismantle their Rolls-Royces and Morris Ambassadors, transport them to Kathmandu by elephant, and reassemble them there.

In India and Nepal she devoted her time to general good deeds, winning medals for her skills and acts of courage. She helped to run Girl Guide groups and, having great regard for many alternative forms of religion, turned her hand to faith healing. She also continued the family hobby of dog-breeding with Tibetan mastiffs, and even persuaded the monks to allow her to breed her beloved Lhasa apsos, the temple dogs. She was one of the first people to bring them to this country.

In Britain, because of his Indian connections my grandfather was called upon to look after any visiting maharajas. He told me that one of them once upped and died on him while staying at Windsor Castle. This was a ticklish problem and could have led to an embarrassing international incident if he hadn't dealt with it in the right way. The maharaja's body couldn't be shipped back to India because his religion required it to be burned on water within twenty-four hours of his death. So my grandfather had to arrange for a pyre to be built on a barge which was towed down the Thames away from the castle before being set alight. The barge continued on out to sea to dispose of the remains. This very un-British funeral was conducted in the utmost secrecy. Grandfather was also asked to help organize the rather more high-profile funeral of George VI and shortly afterwards was on duty as a gold staff officer at the coronation of Queen Elizabeth II.

Grandfather always said that those who retired early, died early, and he wasn't ready for that. When his army days were over he took up a new and unexpected career, much to the amusement of his club and his old regiment, as a male model. I don't mean the type who bares all, obviously – he did advertisements for insurance companies and the like. Then out of the blue he added acting to his CV, following in the footsteps of his wife – when they returned to the UK my grandmother had taken up her long-deferred acting career, doing a great deal of theatre work – and daughter. He usually had small roles, playing judges, army generals or cads, but he appeared in some big productions too, including movies starring Lauren Bacall and Peter Ustinov. He also featured in *North-West Frontier* with Kenneth More.

My grandfather taught me that if you really want to do something, you should let nothing stand in your way. He would never allow me to say, 'I can't do that,' insisting that in our family there was no such word as 'can't'. I didn't follow the career path he hoped I would – can you imagine me in the army? – and he did not live to see my chosen career develop, so I'll never know what he would have thought of it.

My grandmother was much stricter with me than my grandfather was. She had very set, old-fashioned ideas on the matter of bringing up children. A cool, Bette Davis-type character, she was still very glamorous in her twilight years. She was a doer, a highly organized lady. She wrote everything down and kept her house-keeping accounts to the last penny, a habit that was to catch me out in later years. She employed a woman who 'did', a housekeeper, who worked for her for forty-one years. From the day Mrs Woodward went to work for my grandmother until the day she died, on the job, she was known to my gran only as Mrs Woodward and she called my grandmother Mrs Duncan. I never even knew what Mrs W.'s Christian name was. My grandmother herself was incapable of boiling an egg without cracking it. I suppose her years being waited on hand and foot by servants in India did not stand her in good stead for real life in 1950s Britain.

I, meanwhile, had an embarrassing and excruciatingly painful problem, and eventually I had no choice but to mention it to my grandmother. My 'willy', as I called it, was giving me terrible gyp, and it hurt to pee. After I was seen by a private consultant in Harley Street, it was decided that I should be circumcised. When this was explained to me all I could say was, 'How much are they going to cut off? It's so little already, there won't be much left!' I panicked. It didn't bear thinking about. Nobody had made it clear that it was just the skin they would be cutting. So, not surprisingly, I was petrified. Even at the age of six I recognized that this was a very important part of my anatomy. As I was put under the anaesthetic, the surgeon promised me that I wouldn't feel a thing and that he would make a neat job of it. He was right on one count but completely wrong on the other. He performed the operation beautifully, paying great attention to detail, but when I woke up afterwards the pain was agonizing. I immediately tried to check my new dimensions only to discover that my equipment was wrapped in a wet, orange gauze. The wound took about seven days to heal and what was left underneath took weeks to return from its alarming shade of maroon to a more normal pink. My mother and grandmother kept reassuring me that the surgeon's handiwork was exemplary, and I must admit that when I spot a circumcision of the 'butcher at birth' variety attached to a colleague in the shower, I do feel relieved that my operation was carried out by an expert.

Life with Gran got better. As a bond grew between us she started to soften, and we shared some stifled laughs, which pleased her. My mother rarely saw me except on Sundays. She worked very hard and, I suspect, socialized pretty hard after work as well. Her friend Valentina Hoolihan, who had owned the Tree Trunk in Brighton, had herself moved to London, to St James's in the West End, where she had opened a club called Wilde's. I was dragged up there a few times. Once again my mother seemed to be the centre of attention. She was back in her beloved West End, and clearly she was loving every minute of it.

She was a bit of a looker, my mum: good legs, lovely blonde hair, breasts accentuated by the 1950s equivalent of the Wonderbra. All the women then seemed to wear tight-fitting, Jayne Mansfield-style cashmere jumpers. Although she was prudish about nudity, I often walked into her bedroom while she was getting ready to go out and I was struck by the complicated procedures involved in simply getting dressed and putting her face on. It all looked so uncomfortable, especially the stomach-flattening girdle with suspenders for attaching the silk stockings.

I can see now what her exertions were in aid of, though they went unrewarded. I never got a new daddy, just loads of 'uncles', one or two of whom I tolerated. As for the others, I either totally ignored them or was just plain rude. 'I don't like you,' was one of my favourite opening gambits. This must have been very frustrating for my mother. I went with the territory – it was a case of love me, love my son – and life for a single mum was hard. Many of these 'uncles' vanished as quickly as they had appeared, a pattern that was to continue for the next twelve years. During that time, I was often reminded that I was the reason my mother was lonely, unhappy and unloved.

There were two who stuck around, Tony Pelly and Frank the Car. Tony, who was in theatre management, was a tall, grey-haired man, gentle and a gentleman. I adored him. He would have done anything for my mum or for me. He took me on trips to the coast. I particularly loved going to Rye and to the sand dunes near Poole in Dorset. I badly wanted him to be my new dad but my mum wouldn't marry him. She didn't tell me why until I was in my teens: for a start, she didn't find him sexy. He had no money, either, and his ex-wife was a friend of hers. And yet he must have been a regular caller for the best part of fifteen years. Frank the Car was a car-dealer: a pig from the Brighton days whom I learned to like. He was a lovable rogue, a black sheep of good stock who lived on a beautiful part of the River Thames near Richmond. Charming and elegant in a fat sort of way by night, he turned into a Cockney all-right-my-son? type by day. But Mr Ten Per Cent was more of a Mr Pickwick where my mother was concerned – he did her some cracking deals on her booze and cigarettes. The only problem was that he and Tony Pelly didn't get on at all, so they had to be scripted into my mother's life in such a way that they never met each other, which could get complicated.

Tony and Frank the Car were the nearest I was going to get to a father figure and I loved them for that, but of course they were both only part-timers in this respect. So I got the treats but not the paternal discipline I undoubtedly needed. It is perhaps not surprising that, having been brought up around pubs and clubs, I took a great interest in what adults drank and wanted to try everything. Wine wasn't very popular in the fifties. My mother was a South African dry sherry girl, and occasionally she'd take a Bell's whisky or a gin and tonic, none of which appealed to my sweet tooth. My gran, on the other hand, had good supplies of Harvey's Bristol Cream, cherry brandy and crème de menthe, which were much more to my taste. My gran's remedy, or punishment, for my overindulgence was a tablespoon of caster sugar soaked in poor-quality olive oil, a treatment that made me immediately throw up again. 'You'll feel better for it,' she said firmly. All of the bottles were eventually locked away and I was confined to a tipple more appropriate to my age: a glass of Ribena or Robinson's Lemon Barley Water.

In the summer months my grandmother would decamp to her beloved house in Shiplake-on-Thames, near Henley. Every May she packed her necessities into her Morris Traveller and moved there with Tomu, the Lhasa apso, until mid-October. Shiplake has been a constant in our family since my grandmother's parents, the Davieses, fell in love with four ex-workers' cottages they found there. They bought the first for the princely sum of 89 guineas, I think it was, and waited patiently for the others to come on to the market, snapping them up one by one for their four children. Two of the siblings eventually sold their houses to Gran and the other brother, who ended up owning two cottages each. I spent a lot of time at Shiplake in my school holidays. Sometimes I went just for a weekend, sometimes for several weeks, depending on my mother's plans. It was my spooky paradise. I thought of it as spooky because it was tucked down a country lane and in my early years had no electricity, just gaslights that flickered and cast demonic shadows on the walls. The monstrous images of moths or mayflies that had strayed too close to the light I believed were ghosts.

The Shiplake house may have been primitive – the loo was in an outhouse that was also home to a copper for the washing; the water was heated by an Ascot that tended to explode every time you turned on the hot tap in the chipped, enamel bathtub – but I was in my element there. With the surrounding woods and the River Thames right at the bottom of the garden, I was transported into the world of *Swallows and Amazons*.

I spent most of the 1959 summer holiday, after leaving St Ann's, at Shiplake. I passed my time exploring, climbing trees, picking mushrooms, my imagination running wild. Sometimes I was in a Far Eastern jungle, an escaped prisoner-of-war being hotly pursued by my Japanese captors. Each dog-walker who appeared would unwittingly take on the role of a Japanese soldier. I whiled away whole days in my dreamland, just popping home at lunchtime to pick up rations of cold meat, a few tomatoes and some lardy cake, which I would transport back to my jungle hideaway.

Other days I'd go out on the river in my grandfather's old army blow-up liferaft. No one worried about things like life-jackets then, and there were no adult interruptions, just hours of pleasure with my fishing rod or my catapult, with which I fired stones at the rats running in and out of their holes on the riverbank. I would wait quietly for ages for their little heads to appear, and I was a good shot: whack, another one bit the dust; another notch on the catapult. Fishing didn't come quite so easily to me. I was trained by my mother's cousin Mark, who lived next door with my great-uncle Roger and great-aunt Morna and his younger brother Paul and little sister Kristen. Fishing was Mark's life until he reached his late teens. He was five years older than me, so he seemed very grown up, and he was very stern and quite grumpy. He had been ordered to teach me to fish. Although I didn't realize this at the time, it was clear that he was not at all happy to be saddled with this young whippersnapper, and I don't think he liked me very much. Mark always landed a great selection of Thames fish: roach, tench, pike, bream and gudgeon. Some of them were huge. I caught only tiddlers, usually roach, though I do remember once being chuffed at netting a perch, which wasn't that common a fish in the Thames then.

But what a little shit I must also have been. I constantly sought attention when I grew bored with my own company, and I thought up some corkers. Once, after I'd been eating blackberries from the hedgerows, my grandmother asked me about my red-stained mouth. 'Oh, it's just from some red berries I ate,' I replied casually. 'I found them on the side of the road.'

'What sort of berries?'

'You know, the ones that cluster on the top of a short stem.' I knew full well that I was describing deadly nightshade.

'Show me,' said my grandmother.

I took her to where I'd seen some deadly nightshade growing. Gran started to panic.

'Quickly, we must get you to the hospital!'

'I'm not going.'

'Yes, you jolly well are,' she said, grabbing me.

I managed to wriggle free and ran off, my gran in hot pursuit. I kept darting into some hiding place and lying low for a while, and then popping out so that this sixty-year-old woman would chase me again. I'd let her almost catch me, but, just as she was rugby-tackling me, I'd put on a spurt and leave her sprawling on the grass. My grandmother was in tears. She told me I would die if I didn't get to hospital, but the devil in me carried on torturing my poor gran. I managed to spin out this frightening farce for the entire day. Sometimes I hid in the woods, sometimes I slipped into the river and stayed quietly beneath our landing stage. She never caught me.

Gran called for back-up. First came the gardener, Mr Shepherd, who was equally old, equally feeble and equally unable to bring any pressure to bear on me. Then my great-uncle Bruce was summoned from London, along with my gran's sister, Nancy. Great-uncle Bruce was a shrewd military man, a general in the 2nd Gurkhas. He used his initiative, finally luring me out at about seven o'clock in the evening with the promise of no punishment and a crisp ten shilling note, which was big bucks in the late 1950s. I just couldn't resist that. I emerged from my lair, saying, 'Sorry, Gran, it was only a joke. I didn't really eat the red berries. They were blackberries.' That night, as I gloated over my 'victory', the grown-ups came one by one to lecture me. I couldn't keep driving my gran to distraction; if I didn't improve, I would have to go to a home for bad boys. That threat hit a nerve: things had been bad enough at St Ann's. My conduct must have taken a turn for the better because I wasn't sent away. However, I did end up in a psychiatrist's chair. What else could you do with such a troublesome kid?

In retrospect, the reasons for my bad behaviour seem blindingly obvious. I was fatherless and completely undisciplined. My mother's feeble attempts to bring me to heel usually met with a shocking display of screaming, some thrashing around and a retreat to my room, where I would shut myself in and refuse to reappear for hours. Or I would just generally sulk and be disruptive and unresponsive. I was desperate for attention and, I guess, for the father's love I lost with the divorce, a need that was only heightened by being dumped in a boarding nursery at such a young age and ferried between my grandparents and my mother. Today, hyper-activity in children is often put down to diet, but I wasn't a naturally hyperactive child. I liked my own company, which is perhaps not surprising given that away from school, my only other companions were adults. My life wasn't normal, though as I didn't know any different, it seemed normal to me.

How do you tell a child he is going to see a psychiatrist? You don't. You inform him that he is going to have a chat with a very nice man, a friend of his mum's. I smelled a rat from the start. If this man was a friend of Mum's, how come I'd never met him before? When we arrived at his house in Harrow my suspicions grew. It was quite clear that my mother had never been there before as she had lost her way several times on the journey. We were greeted by a tall, greying gentleman who was smoking a pipe. He seemed nice enough, except that he had terrible BO. It was something I noticed because I was unusually fastidious for a child. I might have loved larking around in the woods or in the river and getting completely filthy, but I had to have a bath at least once a day and a really good scrub in the kitchen sink when I came home, and in between I would often change my clothes. So now, being ushered into a room with a smelly man, the first thing I said was: 'You smell.' The man blushed deep crimson and stammered, 'Oh, do I? I'm sorry.' Straight talking came to me early and never really left me.

Then came a sort of buttering-up session, small talk meant to relax me, I imagine. It didn't. The man produced a book of questions and puzzles, lateral-thinking tests and numerical quizzes. By this time I was thoroughly bored and wondering where my mum was. I failed to answer many of the questions. We moved on to the puzzles.

'You're in a field and you've dropped your purse but don't know where. What's the quickest way to find it?'

'What size is the field?'

'You don't need to know the size of the field. It's rectangular.'

'But I do need to know.'

'Why?'

'Because I can see thirty feet either side of me. So how many times I have to walk up and down the field depends on how big it is.'

'We'll move on to the next puzzle,' said the man, starting to give up on me.

After about an hour he decided I'd gone far enough with my IQ test. He gave me some comics to read while he went into the other room to talk to my mum. He left behind his question book, so instead of reading the comics, I picked up the book and started to answer the questions I had previously chosen to ignore. Not only could I do those with reasonable ease, but I was able to tackle some of the questions he had missed out. I wrote the answers under the questions. When he returned after about twenty minutes he found me with my head stuck in his book. He took it from me, studied my responses and returned again to my mum.

In the car on the way home my mother was smoking heavily. It was my job to light her cigarettes while she drove, which was a disgusting task, but it had its positive side: it put me off smoking – until I was forty anyway. I asked her what the visit had been for. 'Oh, nothing. He just wanted to get to know you.' I was well aware that this was a crock of shit, so I didn't say anything, and we drove the rest of the way home in silence.

As well as noting the lack of love, lack of other kids, lack of a father's influence in my life, the psychiatrist found that above all I was just plain bored. I wasn't being tested enough. I was a bright lad, but nobody was pushing me along. I read a lot – all the Famous Five books, *Swallows and Amazons*; Christopher Robin was my hero (I identified with his ability to go off into his own little world) and I wanted to be a water baby.

My mother was keen to address this problem in her own way but Gran overrode her. Mum was powerless to resist unless she was prepared to lose my gran's handouts, and this wasn't an option. By now Mum wanted out of Chelsea. She planned to buy a small cottage in Putney, and she needed my grandmother to guarantee the mortgage and provide the deposit. The house cost £2,900. It doesn't sound like much today, but Mum's salary was only £800 a year. So Gran won, and I was whisked back to Shiplake and to Gran's initiatives for improving my lot. These included introducing me to some of the local children who, in normal circumstances, would have been far beneath her aspirations as playmates for her grandson. But she swallowed her pride and let me play with the gardener's grandchildren, the cleaner's kids and a boy called Simon who lived on a tented island just above Shiplake Lock.

Simon was the bee's knees. I had always been fascinated by the families living in those tents for the summer. Cool probably wasn't the word I would have used then, but it sums up what I felt about their lifestyle. Simon and I became inseparable that summer holiday of 1959 and I was even allowed to stay overnight at the camp. He taught me to swim and to canoe, and we swung from long, thick ropes in the trees into the river – real *Boys' Own* stuff. He improved my fishing and we even cooked some of the fish we caught, although most of it was repulsively muddy and bony. It didn't matter, though: it was an adventure. The dreams on the inside of my head were now on the outside, too; something I was able to share with someone else.

Our friendship, unfortunately, was abruptly severed towards the end of the summer, when I was forbidden from seeing Simon any more. Among the things he had taught me was the useful art of housebreaking, and we had been caught putting it into practice at the Andrew Duncan House, a home for physically disabled people that had been given by my grandparents to the British Red Cross in memory of their dead son, and which, because of the close relationship between Andrew and Princess Elizabeth, had been officially opened by the future Queen. Luckily for me, the incident was never brought to the attention of the police: my grandmother was on the board of governors and managed to hush up our dastardly crime. To me it was another adventure; to Simon, apparently, it was a hobby, perhaps even an apprenticeship. I've often wondered what course his life took.

For the remainder of the holiday my gran decided to send me to a male childminder, introduced to me as Uncle Eric, who already looked after two older children. He took us boating, to funfairs, on trips to the local open-air swimming pool. It was great: my days were full and active. Until, that is, after swimming one afternoon, Uncle Eric suggested that I shared a bath with one of the other boys. No harm in that, but it was when he told me to remove my swimming trunks that things took a turn for the worse. It was not long since I had been circumcised and I was still quite bashful about the operation, so I declined. He told me I was being silly and pointed to the other boy, who had completely stripped off. 'Look, he's not worried.' He gave the boy's privates a tweak and remarked that bathtime should be fun. I agreed, but insisted that it would be no less fun with my trunks on. Uncle Eric started to get annoyed. He said he would remove his own clothes to show me how stupidly I was behaving. Off they came, only to reveal that he was aroused.

Whether the alarm bells sounded because of my previous experience with Mum's second husband I can't say, but I knew this wasn't right. I shot out of the bath, grabbed my clothes and ran. Outside, as luck would have it, my gran was just pulling up to collect me. I was shaking. She asked me what was wrong. I can't remember now what I said, but it must have been enough to alert my grandmother, because I never visited Uncle Eric again. No more was ever said about the incident.

So much for the development of young minds. My young mind had been far more developed by Simon, who had taught me to be even more mischievous and inquisitive. In his world there were no barriers; mine was stifled by class distinctions. I was never encouraged to mix with normal people, and yet those with whom I really got on well were not my poncey cousins next door, but Simon, Mr Shepherd, the gardener, Mrs Woodward, my gran's housekeeper, and Rosemary at St Ann's. I was, it seems, striving for normality, and in spite of its pitfalls, that summer of 1959 did at least give me the opportunity to break away for the first time from my own little closed society.

CHAPTER FOUR

DURING THE SUMMER I HAD BEEN BACK TO LONDON A COUPLE OF TIMES to be kitted out for my new school. Once again grey was to be the colour: grey guernsey jumpers, long, grey socks, grey shorts. There was sports kit by the bucketload: gym kit, one navy rugby shirt, one navy-and-white-striped rugby shirt (the school colours), navy shorts, rugby boots with big, leather, nailed studs and gym shoes. Then the numerous essentials and accessories: underpants, vests, slippers, dressing gown, pyjamas, leather wash bag (very posh!), sheets, towels, a travelling rug, a trunk, a tuckbox. I was gob-smacked: there was so much stuff, and it all cost so much money. It all had to be new, and it all had to be bought from Selfridges – there were no brothers to provide hand-me-downs.

Going to Milner Court that September was a strange experience. It began with the two women in my life arguing over who would take me down to Kent. My mum won this time. As we arrived at the school our little Austin A35 was surrounded on all sides by Rolls-Royces, Bentleys and Jags. I was bemused but not, at that age, embarrassed. I was far more preoccupied with my terror at the prospect of being left alone again. Tears were welling up in my eyes and I had to bite my lip to keep back the threatening waterfall. One by one, the parents met the headmaster, a Reverend John Edmonds. He looked like a small gorilla: very short and well built with a grey skinhead haircut. He frightened me. He tried to be nice to my mother, but he ignored me, and I wasn't fooled. We were then intro-duced to Matron, a minute lady in a starched white nurse's uniform, the wide navy belt encircling the tiniest of waists. I liked her. Her skin looked like crushed linen, its wrinkles and creases radiating immense warmth. She reminded me of my aunt Daisy, a relative on my father's side.

For my first year I was to live in a magnificent Queen Anne house, which in its days as a private residence must have been something else. Now that it accommodated eight-year-old kids, the rickety wooden servants' staircases were in daily use and the main staircase was out of bounds. The walls were decorated in hospital-style two-tone, an impenetrable, grey-flecked, industrial paint protecting them up to dado level. The dormitories were done out in cream, with red bedspreads. Our first mission, I discovered too late, was to bag a bed. I ended up with the last one, next to the loo, which made for a restless night's sleep as each boy on his way to or from the lavatory would grab its wrought-iron bars to steady himself as he ran past. I was quickly to learn that here it was every man for himself.

When my mother had left I ran into the back garden, a fabulous garden with beautiful flowers surrounded by an old red-brick wall, hid behind a large bush and cried my eyes out. My sobs attracted the attention of one boy, who said to me consolingly: 'Don't cry. I'll be your friend.' His name was Booker. Christian names were out: for the next ten years they might as well not have existed. So I was Worrall Thompson, or WT for short. Brothers were distinguished from one another by adding Senior or Junior to their surname. Booker explained his own composure by revealing that his parents lived in Malaya, as it then was, and that he had already made his tearful farewells at the airport. I was to discover that about 30 per cent of the boys were the sons of expats or rich sheiks or Persians, Fijians – you name it. I was quite jealous of them as I had never been abroad. Poole Harbour was the closest I'd ever been to foreign lands.

In spite of Booker's reassurances, I was embarrassed that I had been caught blubbing. 'Let's go and explore,' he suggested, by way of changing the subject. The grounds seemed massive. Opposite the Queen Anne house was a huge tithe barn that was used as a games and entertainment centre, the venue for school concerts, Gilbert and Sullivan operas, gymnastics, badminton, film shows and end-of-term prizegivings. Up some stairs towards the left of the building was a craft room, where boys made model planes and boats out of balsa wood. This activity was seen as a bit nerdy, but later I did get stuck into a few planes myself and found that I was quite good with my hands.

Booker pointed out the headmaster's house and an oast house

that was home to the art, carpentry and music departments. He seemed very well informed for a boy who was starting school at the same time as me. It turned out that he had already been round the school with his parents to check out the facilities. When I next saw my mum I asked her whether she had visited the school before-hand, and if so, why she hadn't taken me. Amazingly, she told me that she hadn't thought I'd be interested and, perhaps more to the point, that she had feared I might play up and upset the headmaster. What faith. I was not amused.

Opposite the oast house were some fantastic, deeply overgrown wooded grounds, planted mainly with horse chestnuts, which extended to a railway track, and soon, for a short time, I would reveal myself to be the ultimate nerd by becoming a trainspotter. Steam trains fascinated me. I knew every steam engine on Southern Railways, and after Mum moved to Putney during my first term I made the pilgrimage to all the mainline stations with my little book, ticking off all the engine numbers as I came across them.

Behind the oast house, running beside the railway, were playing fields dressed with rugby posts. Booker and I walked on, talking about nothing in particular, just useful, mutually encouraging chitchat that laid the foundations for a five-year friendship. We left the playing fields and headed to our right down a long tarmac path bordered on one side by woodland and on the other by two open-air swimming pools, one shallow and one deep. They were both filled with swamplike water, a legacy of the previous summer term. As the path curved round to the left we came across a small wooden bridge straddling the River Stour, a setting of great significance later in my prep-school career. Over the bridge was a huge playing field where the bigger boys played rugby and cricket, surrounded by a grass running track.

And that was our tour. We paused briefly to take a look inside the senior house, a vast, modern, industrial-looking brick complex, hideous in design, with large classrooms leading off wide corridors to the exterior walls and, in the interior, the changing rooms and the bogs, or the loos, for those who prefer a more delicate turn of phrase. Today it was empty, as the new boys always started a day early. There was a noticeboard and another board where the front and back pages of the newspapers were posted daily. The choice was between the *Daily Express*, a broadsheet in those days, or the *Daily Sketch*, replaced on Sundays by the *Sunday Express* and the *Sunday Times*.

We returned to our house to be told that we needed to report to Matron. I assumed that this would be a registration, but no, it was a physical once-over. 'Get your clothes off,' was the command from Matron's assistant. I slowly took off my kit, hesitating when it came to my regulation Y-fronts as the memories of pervy 'Uncle Eric' came flooding back.

'Come on, make it snappy,' barked the junior nurse. 'We've seen it all before.'

I cupped my privates in both small hands before being persuaded to let go, then quickly glanced up to check for laughter or smirks. To my relief, neither woman batted an eyelid. Instead I was greeted with a puff of powder to my nether regions. Then Matron had a good poke around. 'Turn around. Bend over.' What next? I wondered, but happily there was nothing, just the comforting words, 'Everything seems to be in order.' My ordeal over, I was given a sugar lump, which I later found out was my immunization against polio, and a spoonful of malt extract, which was scrummy, and sent on my way with a motherly hug from Matron. 'There, that wasn't so bad, was it?' she said. And it wasn't, except for the embarrassment.

That night, in my new bed, I just cried. I wasn't the only one. Muffled sobs could be heard from beneath other bedclothes. I wished now I had brought Fred, my scruffy teddy bear, but when Mum had tried to pack him, I had thrown him back, saying that I couldn't possibly be seen with a teddy bear at my new grown-up school. But I counted at least six other boys who had bears, and nobody was taking any notice of them. However, it was only a matter of days before I knew I had made the right decision. Once confidence was built, the boys started to turn on the teddies. Arms went missing, ears were cut off, there were bears blocking the loo and one was even ceremoniously burned. Fred, I felt sure, would have been very disturbed by the behaviour of some of the boys.

I settled in fairly quickly and the first term seemed to fly past. As far as I remember I was well behaved, pretty independent still, but I made a small group of friends, only some of whose names I recall. As well as Booker there was a skinny, blond fellow called Thorndike who, I later discovered, was a nephew of the actress Sybil Thorndike. His famous aunt happened to be a good friend of my grandmother's, and what was more, Thorndike lived in Putney, very near to my mother's new cottage. Thorndike and I were close friends for many years. Then there was Ahmahzadeh, or Mo for

short, who came from Persia – or Iran, as it is now. He was considered to be very exotic as he was apparently related to the Shah.
He was also extremely popular, thanks to the fabulous monthly
food parcels he received from home, which were packed with
delicacies I had never seen before: pistachio nuts, nougat, dates,
fresh pomegranates. Mo shared this bounty with his mates, but I bit
the hand that fed me by nicking pistachios from his tuckbox as
well. I just couldn't get enough of them. The Clarke twins, the sons
of a farmer, were an odd couple, but very friendly. They were
similar to look at, strong boys. I was small, very small, both in
height and girth, with a little toast-rack of a chest. Even at the age
of sixteen I would still weigh only seven stone. I don't know
whether it was down to my diet or something in the water, but it
didn't appear to be hereditary: my father was about five foot eleven
and my mother was five foot four. Grandfather was six foot. I've
no idea what happened to my share of the inches.

Inevitably, there were a couple of boys who disliked me, though
I couldn't understand why, when I was such a small, insignificant
type of guy. True, I was stubborn, and I said what I thought, but I
never really gave anyone anything to dislike about me. One of these
boys was Brown, a big, apelike character, very tall, whose mouth
jutted forward like a chimp and who had gaps between his teeth.
On one occasion we were all playing in the woods, cowboys and
Indians (or perhaps cops and robbers or thugs and neighbours – a
game involving lots of mock violence, anyway), when suddenly I
saw a broken brick coming towards me. I instinctively moved my
head to the left, but the brick still clipped me and I could feel blood
dripping on to my neck. The boys rushed over to find my earlobe
hanging off. Before I was whisked off to the surgery I retaliated
against the perpetrator of the crime – Brown, of course. The claws
came out and carved some deep gouges in his left cheek; then, with
my left hand, I planted a stinger on his nose. I got a good deal of
satisfaction from seeing a trickle of blood escaping from his nostril.
Brown and I were destined to have several more spats over the next
few terms. Small I may be, but there's a smattering of Jack Russell
in my genes and I'm not a quitter. The earlobe recovered, though
the scar remains, but, most importantly, my pride was intact.

Generally, though, my fellow pupils caused me few problems.
From the day I hit back at Brown, I was rarely bothered by any of
the school bullies, in spite of my small stature. The headmaster,
however, was another matter. From the outset John Edmonds

appeared not to like me. He was a hard nut, an ex-Paratrooper, or so he said, though his lack of inches suggested to me that it was more likely he dreamed of being a Paratrooper. He certainly acted the part, and regularly beat boys for misdemeanours. Like many private-school headmasters, he set a lot of store by results on the games field. I was too small to feature in his plans for sporting glory, which was one reason for dismissing me. Another bone of contention was my perennial tendency to answer back. I guess my very independent early childhood had led me to question absolutely everything. As far as I was concerned, I was not put on the planet to be controlled, and this is a belief I've carried throughout my life. Sometimes it has been a burden, sometimes an advantage. Initially, I tried to please the boss by joining the choir and then becoming an altar boy. Neither was my thing, but it was my way of conforming – and perhaps also a bit of attention-seeking.

Although I got on well with many of the other boys, I was still quite lonely. I missed my mum, and my grandparents, too. Visits and post were patchy, we were not allowed phone calls and of course there were no mobile phones then. We were permitted three parental visits a term. Usually just my mum came; occasionally she was accompanied by a boyfriend. I preferred it when she came alone. Then I had her to myself and could feel close to her for a few hours. To my mother these exeat days were a chore. The school was two hours' drive from London, and she was supposed to arrive by 9 am for the Sunday service. She only once made it on time. In fact I counted myself lucky if she showed up before midday. I would be standing there waiting at the gate, ready to hide if anyone approached from the direction of the school – I was too em-barrassed to deal with any awkward questions. One Sunday Mum didn't arrive until two o'clock, which meant that not only did I miss lunch but I didn't have much more than a couple of hours with her, because I had to be back at school for 5 pm. Another time I waited until 12.30 and then gave up and went for my school lunch. At 1.15 I looked out of the dining-hall window and saw her Austin A35 driving up. I excused myself and ran down to inform her that I wouldn't be coming out. She pleaded with me, but I stood my ground. Unfortunately, as so often happened when I dug in my heels, my stubbornness backfired on me. All she could do then was get back into the car and drive off, but as soon as she did I burst into tears. Luckily, all the boys were still lunching, but less luckily, just at that moment the headmaster walked by and demanded to know what I was crying about.

'I don't want to talk about it.'

'I asked you a question: I want a reply,' he insisted.

'Bog off,' I said. Wham! I found myself flat on my back from the impact of his slap. When I got up he sent me off into detention to write out two pages of logarithm tables, an excruciatingly boring task. Another detention he liked to impose was to make the miscreant stand for two hours facing a wall. What a waste of time, don't you think? What about some creative community service: cleaning windows, digging flowerbeds, painting white lines around the rugby pitch, fishing leaves out of the swimming pool or sweeping the driveways?

Getting in trouble always raised your status with the other boys – the fun boys, that is, not the goody-two-shoes – and my stubborn streak earned me the role of a gang leader in a very minor way. I say gang leader, but there weren't really any gangs to speak of; it was more sporty types versus swots or musicians. But our gang, such as it was, stuck together. Whether we were fishing on the banks of the Stour, exploring in the woods or looking for slow-worms in the long grass, we were a unit whose members rarely fell out.

Occasionally would-be interlopers tried to gain favour with us but we didn't admit just anyone and our rules were strict. We would first decide whether we liked the guy, and the decision had to be unanimous, with no dissenters. If he passed that test, he would have to prove his courage by running naked around the main school building or walking 200 yards down the middle of the railway track, again naked, after dark. If he accomplished his task without being caught he was in; if he got caught, he was still in, because then he would be beaten by the headmaster, and either way he had proved his courage.

Only rarely would a gang member defect to another group. If this happened it called for serious action. Itching powder in the bed or black treacle spread on the bottom sheet was just a teaser. The main punishment was being sent to Coventry. None of the gang was allowed to speak to the defector for a set period of time, usually a week, and we stuck to the rule religiously.

Our world was one of adventure and discovery, punctuated by lessons, which were mere distractions from the serious business of growing up in our microcosmic society. Our relationships were characterized by bitter rows, strong friendships, spiteful attacks, either verbal or physical, and extreme secrecy. I hadn't then read William Golding's *Lord of the Flies*, but when I did, it seemed to me to be an accurate reflection, albeit on a very extreme scale, of life among a community of small boys.

The smutty humour and games of doctors and patients (in the absence of any girls to fill the roles of nurses) were par for the course, I guess, for a boys' school. We would sit in a huddle reading a copy of *Parade* or *Titbits* sold to us by some day boy, ogling the semi-naked women, getting excited and comparing the sizes of our miniature erections, or 'roots', as we called them. Investigating each other's bodies was simply a part of learning about them; just comparing notes, really.

Our sexual experimentation took place under the beds after lights-out, in the sports pavilion changing rooms or in the cricket pavilion. Nothing more than hands was ever involved. One early developer, called Hunt, was a particular object of fascination: he had the equipment of a fully grown man. He was about six months older than the rest of us, but he was still only eleven. On the basis of his magnificent member he was invited to join our gang, though he still had to pass the initiative test, of course. It was Hunt who, under a tent fashioned from three beds pushed together with our travelling rugs hung over the edges, first demonstrated to us the art of masturbation. We all went away to practise this new skill on our own. None of us achieved the desired result, but none of us could admit this to Hunt. Instead we all sang the praises of our first encounter with self-flagellation. Each of us in turn then quietly confided our failure to the other members of the gang. We thought perhaps it took a while to get things working, and decided to try again the next night.

After two nights all we had succeeded in doing was rubbing ourselves raw. We were all suffering but nobody dared go to the surgery. I talked this over with Bond, the giggler of the gang, the smallest boy with the smallest member. It was tiny: ten of his wouldn't have made one of Hunt's. But what Bond lacked in this department he more than made up for in others. He was incredibly witty, with a wicked sense of humour, and very brainy, and he went on to win a scholarship to King's, Canterbury. But he wasn't a swot, he was one of us.

We agreed that we would have to go to the surgery and try to get some Germolene from the young nursing assistant, Nurse Elliott.

We intercepted her as she was finishing for the morning and span some implausible story.

'I'd better have a look,' she said. 'Come into the surgery. You first, WT.' This wasn't part of the plan at all.

'It's all right, miss. Just give me a swab of the pink stuff, please.'

'I can't do that, I have to check.'

I blushed. In my infantile way I had a crush on this pretty young nurse. I followed her into the surgery and sheepishly undressed.

'Oh no, this requires something more than Germolene,' she said. 'It's iodine for you.'

'Please, not iodine.' That was going to sting like hell.

'Afraid so,' she chuckled. I looked away as she applied the dreaded lotion and yelped like a dog as the cold liquid inflicted its vicious bite.

'All done,' she said. 'Now, don't go fiddling with it or you'll make it worse.'

'No, miss.'

'You didn't really spill hot tea in your lap, did you?' she said, and smiled.

'No, miss,' I stammered.

'Well, don't worry. I won't tell Matron. It'll be our little secret. Come and see me tonight after bathtime, and I'll redress it.'

'Thank you, miss,' I said, and left the room, happy and embarrassed in equal measure.

Bond wanted to know what happened. I just shrugged and said it hurt. 'Come in, Bond,' commanded the voice from the surgery.

When we met up later we both went into graphic detail as we recounted the discomfort of our consultations. I was puzzled, though, that Bond didn't appear to have been asked to return to have his wounds redressed. Perhaps mine were worse than his.

We had bath nights twice a week, worked out according to an alphabetical rota. I was the only member of our gang in the R–Z group, so I was preoccupied with negotiating my bath without revealing my yellow, blotchy willy to the other boys. I turned myself towards the wall, covering my privates with my flannel. I nearly screamed when they came into contact with the hot water, but I managed to run my flannel discreetly under the cold tap, wrap it around the sore bits and lower myself gently into the bath to reduce the effects of the sudden impact of the scalding water.

That night, with everyone in bed, Nurse Elliott did her rounds, pacing the rows of beds in the dormitory, checking that everyone

had cleaned their teeth. When she reached my bed she bent down
and pretended to pick my socks up off the floor in order to slip a
note under my pillow. I didn't look at it until she had left the
dormitory. It read: 'Come to my room when everyone is asleep.'
Why the mystery? Why her room and not the surgery? I felt a minor
stirring down below.

I waited for the other boys to drift off to sleep or attend gang
meetings, declining my own nightly get-together on the grounds
that I was tired and sore. When all was quiet I slipped out of bed,
stuffed my pillow under the bedclothes and left the dormitory,
silently and slipperless. This is stupid, I thought. I'm only going to
have my willy redressed. And yet still I wondered why Nurse Elliott
was being so secretive. I came to the conclusion that she didn't want
Matron to find out; that she was trying to spare me the
embarrassment.

Nurse Elliott's room, along with those of some of the other
members of staff, was sandwiched between classrooms on the
floor above. I knocked on her door. She opened it, quickly looked
up and down the corridor, put a finger to her lips and ushered me
in.

I went to undo the cord of my winceyette pyjamas, but she told
me to wait. 'I want to talk to you first,' she said. She made me a
cup of cocoa and handed me a couple of gingernut biscuits.

'But I've cleaned my teeth . . .'

'It's not going to matter for one night,' she said. 'Now, tell me
what you were doing to damage your willy.'

I blushed. Then I told her the whole story, not neglecting the
detail of the size of Hunt's member and what happened to it when
it was touched.

She looked shocked. 'But he's only eleven!'

'I know. But you should see it. It's amazing.'

Nurse Elliott stifled a laugh.

'Why are you laughing?' I was feeling pretty foolish.

'It's your innocence. It's lovely,' she said.

I managed a smile. She gave me another biscuit.

'Do you want me to teach you about things?' she asked
hesitantly.

'What do you mean?'

'Well, you know. I can explain things and show you what you are
doing wrong.'

'OK.' I was still embarrassed. But Nurse Elliott reminded me of

Rosemary at St Ann's, and I felt a huge warmth towards her. 'Can I sit with you on the bed?'

'Of course.' I snuggled up beside her, she stroked my hair and I began to relax.

'Ask me some questions,' she said.

'Why is it that Hunt can get his, you know, to work when none of us could, however long and hard we tried?'

'It comes with time,' she said. 'You'll reach what is called puberty, you'll grow hair under your arms and down there, and then you'll need to shave. By that time everything down there should be in perfect working order.'

'So when I'm Hunt's age it'll all start to happen?'

'Not necessarily. It sounds as if he's very mature down there.'

We laughed.

'So it doesn't matter what technique I use? There will be no explosion, just pleasure?'

'Or pain,' she said, 'the way you're doing it. When your wounds have healed, I can show you how to make it pleasurable. If you want.' She was looking down at the bed.

'Oh yes, that would be great,' I replied.

'But it will have to be our little secret. You must promise never to tell the other boys.'

I promised.

So Nurse Elliott was to become my teacher. I saw nothing wrong with our special relationship; on the contrary, it was the most exciting thing to happen to me since Rosemary had taken me under her wing at nights back in Hove. From that day on, I felt different from the other boys, really grown up. And I was true to my promise: our 'friendship' has remained a secret until now. I often wondered why Nurse Elliott chose me. I was not a pretty boy, and what's more I was cheeky, and could have spelled trouble for her. But she judged me well. Probably she felt sympathy for me. I was constantly picked on by the headmaster, who seemed to get a kick out of beating me at least twice a term. I'm not saying that I didn't deserve it sometimes, but I think he took it to extremes. Nurse Elliott also knew about my mother's cavalier approach to my exeat days. Looking back, it seems that she recognized my vulnerability and my need of feminine comfort. 'I like you. I want to take care of you. You need love,' she was to say by way of explanation. But this was a dramatic leap from mother love to a love of another kind altogether.

It sounds strange, but it was almost as if she needed me, too. Perhaps the life of a live-in nurse at a boys' prep school was a lonely one. In the two years of this unusual tuition I don't think I ever inquired whether she had a boyfriend. There were of course times when she couldn't see me, or when she went out. I never asked her where she had been, and she never volunteered any information. I just counted myself lucky to have her as my secret, special friend. I don't think she was doing the same thing with any of the other boys.

Nurse Elliott gave me some of the best education I ever received. My life to date had been totally devoid of any childish female company. There had been no games of mummies and daddies or doctors and nurses, none of the experimentation usually engaged in by little boys and girls. I bypassed that early acclimatization to the opposite sex and went straight from complete ignorance to real, hands-on, grown-up sex education. Since nudity was taboo at home, the most I had seen of a naked woman until then was Rosemary's breasts. So my first sight of Nurse Elliott's body gave me quite a turn, and I don't remember finding it particularly appealing at the age of ten. The reality was, of course, very different from unclothed mannequins in the window of a department store, and quite scary at first.

She gave me a potted explanation of sex and babies, and detailed the mechanics of how I would be able to achieve the sexual act when I was older. It was shocking but at the same time fascinating. It would be many another year before I lost my virginity, but when the time came Nurse Elliott's lessons stood me in good stead. In fact they turned out to be some of the most valuable lessons of my life, and I never forgot them.

Did this have an effect on you? I hear you ask. I honestly don't know. It was obviously wrong for a young lad to be inducted into sexual practices and fantasies by a grown-up, yet I doubt it did me any lasting damage. Probably less than the prolonged ignorance that would otherwise have been my lot. I learned about kissing and massage; how to be rough and how to be gentle. She taught me about women's periods, and how lucky men were not to be burdened with them. She taught me that sex should never be seen as dirty but as a natural and healthy part of life. But I often wonder what would have happened if we had been caught. Nurse Elliott could undoubtedly have been fired or perhaps asked to resign – schools then liked to cover things up. Nevertheless it would have ruined her life. Perhaps the headmaster would have seen me as an 'abused' boy and softened his attitude towards me, though I doubt it. Either way, I didn't feel abused. I participated wholeheartedly, and enjoyed it, once the ice had been broken. Even so, there is no denying the fact that I was a child and Nurse Elliott was an adult in a position of authority and responsibility.

I'm sure my school work suffered, because I was constantly tired. My mother was even advised to start looking for a new public school for me, as I had no chance of getting into King's, Canterbury. She put my name down for Shiplake College, just up the road from my gran's cottage, an establishment with a reputation for taking boys who had failed their Common Entrance into their first-choice public school.

The one thing we never attempted to do was to have full sex. It probably wouldn't have been entirely successful, but in any case she believed that I should lose my virginity to someone of a similar age, someone I might actually love. Of course, it was her I loved, but I didn't say so. We had fun, and we took greater and greater risks late at night, in the school refectory, in the kitchens, in classrooms – even, during the summer, in the swimming pool and on the cricket pitch. And then, suddenly, one day she upped and left, and I never heard from her again.

I still have no idea what happened. All I know is that when I returned for the autumn term of 1963 and my last year at Milner Court, she had vanished. Maybe someone at the school got wind of something and she was sacked; maybe it was simply time for her to move on. I was gutted. For two years she had helped me cope with the lows of being educated by a vindictive man, and I felt lost without her. But, in retrospect, I realize that it was for the best. I look back on these memories now as rather like Laurie Lee's fond reminiscences of Rosie – a book which was a firm favourite of mine as a youngster. Call me a crank, but I do believe that your life is mapped out for you. I've had many disappointments, but just around the corner of every disaster there was a success waiting for me.

So wherever you are now, Nurse Elliott, thank you.

CHAPTER FIVE

MY MOTHER WAS BORN UNDER THE SIGN OF AQUARIUS, AND TO HER the grass was always greener elsewhere. The only trouble was, it didn't occur to her that a nice lawn needs looking after. Having been lured from a successful career as an actress into television, she worked her way up from floor manager to director, and then, just as it looked as if she was about to make it in television, she decided that advertising was the way forward.

One of the programmes she worked on was a show featuring the fearsome Fanny Craddock. Fanny was a formidable introduction for me to the world of television cookery. I was allowed to help on the set of the programme but in truth I only got in the way. Fanny wasn't very good with children. She scared the shit out of me, she definitely scared the shit out of Johnnie, her husband and sidekick, and she treated my mother like a skivvy. Yet as well as terrifying me, this powerful, frightening woman also fascinated me. In the end Fanny and Mum seemed to end up with a reasonable working friendship. Fanny and Johnnie used to come round to dinner sometimes, an event that would throw my mother into a blind panic. My mother was a competent cook, not a wonder cook, but they did have one mutual interest: Fanny enjoyed a good drink with my mother, and that was enough to keep the friendship going.

Ever since the dawn of commercial television, Mum had been a convert to advertising, unlike my grandparents, who would never have dreamed of watching the upstart ITV. Only the BBC would do for them, whether it was television or radio. My grandmother was an avid fan of the Home Service on the wireless, and *Woman's*

Hour and *The Archers* took precedence over everything else. Your life wasn't worth living if you disturbed her after lunch when she was listening to *Woman's Hour*. She would never have approved when it was moved, years later, to a morning slot.

So Mum left television to join an infant advertising agency, C.R. Casson, in Mayfair, and looked after several accounts including Payne's Poppets, Varela sherry and Bush radios. As a result the house was often full of chocolates and sherry.

As for me, it would be fair to say that, until I met my special nurse, I was a very naive young lad. When I first started at Milner Court I had never come across a record-player or even a portable radio. My mother, being a TV-head, didn't listen to the radio, and we never had music in the house. So while I considered myself an Elvis Presley fan, and had just about heard of Cliff Richard, I didn't recognize the tunes popularized by other rock 'n' roll stars of the 1950s and early 1960s that the other boys sang or hummed.

For my first Christmas at school, the Christmas of 1959, I asked my mum for a record-player; for my birthday the following year I requested a portable wireless. I received a blue and cream radio courtesy of Bush. I was thrilled. Now I was able not only to listen to pop music on Radio Luxembourg but to indulge my passion for Test cricket as well. This was the era of Barrington, Dexter, Cowdrey and Trueman, all heroes, especially Colin Cowdrey, who I remember valiantly facing the lethal West Indian pace of Wes Hall and Charlie Griffith with a broken arm. Frank Worrell, later Sir Frank, was another, if for no other reason than that I was a Worrall too, even if the spelling was different.

For me the school curriculum was a mixture of boredom and fun. The boredom was provided by Latin, French and divinity, or religious studies, as it would be known now. Too many of our classes consisted of no more than dry facts read out of textbooks and learned by rote. With no passion and little or no humour injected into the lessons, I found it difficult to concentrate. The fun came in games or PE. We played rugger, as it was called at school. We weren't allowed to play organized soccer: it was considered an ungentlemanly game. I enjoyed all of it, a jack-of-all-sports and master of none, scraping into the house teams but rarely making the grade to represent the school. I was so keen that I volunteered to be scorer in cricket matches or linesman for rugby. I was almost more of a team mascot than a serious contender.

Arithmetic, history and geography were the only subjects that held my attention. Cookery or home economics were not even an option then, of course. Prep schools were breeding centres for real men, guys who would go on to make their mark on the rugby pitch or cricket field, and then progress into the forces, or banking or insurance – suits, we'd call them now, and in those days they wore bowler hats as well. That well-trodden path was never for me. I was always destined to be a black sheep, a nonconformist – in short, a pain in the arse.

I suppose I was a thorn in the flesh of those in authority. Whenever I could lark around, break a rule, create chaos, I would. I was the scourge of the junior school, and my mother received several warnings about my behaviour. But she always managed to charm the head, doubtless by playing to his male ego, hitching up her skirt, flirting, acting the vulnerable woman, and the Reverend fell for it every time. So I escaped expulsion, although an Army school or Borstal would probably have suited me better.

Most of our teachers appeared to be bachelors, in the old-fashioned sense, and lived in tiny boxrooms like Nurse Elliott's. You never saw any of them with women: in the 1950s and 1960s, public schools were male bastions. There were a couple who had a soft spot for me, quiet supporters who tried to get the best out of me. One was Mr Grey, who was short and stocky with a black beard. He taught history and had that ability possessed by too few teachers then to make his subject really interesting. He was also a human being outside the classroom, taking an interest in our other activities. The other was another Mr Edmonds, not related to the headmaster. He had a long, beaked nose and must have been six foot three. The regulation master's gown was far too short for him. Mr Edmonds taught the three maths subjects: arithmetic, geometry and algebra. Both masters were quite young and 'with it', especially Mr Grey, who wore rather swish tailor-made jackets, very Italian-looking in design, which stood out among the tweedy browns and greens and leather elbow pads favoured by most of the teachers, who seemed to wear the same jacket, day in, day out, for the whole term.

The weekday routine began at 7 am, when it was up for a quick wash and brush of the teeth and down to breakfast, which alternated between porridge and cornflakes, followed by greasy fried eggs and even greasier bacon. Occasionally we would get bready sausages with baked beans. My favourite delicacy was a disgusting concoction of fried bread with loads of butter topped with bacon and finished off with marmalade. Tea was poured from huge, aluminium pots, or you could have a glass of milk.

At 8.45 there was assembly, with prayers, and notices for the day. From time to time the headmaster would take the opportunity to single out boys for praise or reprimand. If my name was mentioned it was always for the latter reason. Being small, I was usually able to minimize this public humiliation by hiding behind one of the bigger lads. Sometimes I would titter out of embarrassment, and if I was spotted I would be called to the front and clipped around the head. The main punishment would be either detention or a visit to the headmaster's study, which usually meant a beating. Assembly was immediately followed by lessons. During our morning break we had to drink our government-issue third-of-a-pint of silvertop milk, fine in winter but revolting in the summer because the milk was kept outside the back door of the kitchen to warm in the sun.

Lunch was a noisy affair. We sat on benches at rows of tables, with the headmaster in his gown at the top table, looking like a little Hitler. Occasionally the racket would get to him and he would bash the table with his gavel and call the room to silence. Or he might pick on a particularly voluble boy: 'Bond! I do not enjoy seeing the contents of your meal being masticated at the same time as you entertain the table with your eloquent prose.' Why he couldn't just say 'Don't eat with your mouth open' was beyond me.

After lunch we would all have to rest on our beds for an hour in silence, either reading or snoozing. Prefects were allowed to reprimand us verbally if we misbehaved and if they lost control they would call for Matron, who would make us sit cross-legged in the corridor. In winter terms we would then play sports, followed by tea and biscuits and then two more lessons. On the longer summer days lessons came before sports and we'd have a break before supper, homework and bed. Which was when, as you've already seen, the 'games' began.

On Saturdays there was sometimes morning school for boys who needed extra teaching. In the afternoon we had to watch the first XI or XV playing cricket or rugby and cheer our heads off in support. We were always desperate for Sunday to come around. Even if you weren't being taken out by your parents, this was a fun day, a day for adventures, for building dams or catching eels in the river, swimming in the large, primitive pool or boating in the man-made pond. We built the boats in the craft room, from balsa wood stuck together with intoxicating glue of the type later generations took to sniffing. Model aeroplanes and gliders were also made, some with sophisticated engines, some with propellers driven by elastic bands. Messerschmidts and Spitfires were all the rage – we were obsessed with anything to do with the war. One of the exchange currencies was the small A5 war magazines parents sent their children on a weekly basis, together with comics like *Beano*, *Dandy* and the *Eagle*, which featured Dan Dare, the sophisticated kids' hero. I preferred Desperate Dan in the *Beano*, a more rough-and-ready character. We all looked forward to our weekly letters and packages. However, as you might imagine, I received fewer of these than the boys with more organized parents.

Letters were our only means of communication with the outside world. There were no trips to the local village, Sturry, except for our monthly escorted visit to the barber for our pudding-basin hair-cuts. We wrote to our parents after church on Sundays, an exercise that was supervised by the duty master. Our letters were checked for grammar and spelling mistakes and also for any disparaging remarks about the school. So if we wanted to avoid censorship we had to smuggle out mail via the day boys who, though despised by the boarders, did have their uses.

The day boys were a completely different breed. Since they went home in the evenings, just at the time when real life was beginning for the rest of us, they could never be a part of our brotherhood: of the close relationships that developed, the mischievous fun, the wicked things we got up to. We considered them outcasts. Of course, there were times when we hankered after the freedom they enjoyed. They could watch television or go to the cinema, and they didn't have to attend church on Sundays. But they in turn missed out on a lot. Being a day boy meant never joining a gang, never breaking into the tuck shop after dark, never sneaking down to the kitchen to make doorstep sandwiches with golden syrup, never falling in love with Nurse Elliott. And in spite of the ups and downs of boarding, and even the beatings, I wouldn't have had it any other way.

I can tell you that a few beatings never did me any harm and some crackpot psychiatrist will tell you I'm wrong. My childhood undoubtedly looks like a difficult one to outside eyes, but I reckon I've turned out OK. I'm a stroppy little fellow but I always was, and I guess I will always be outspoken. But for the most part I treat people and animals with respect and I believe that my education and upbringing made me a fair-minded person, certainly not a yes man, but a principled man. Yet there is no denying that I was a handful during my schooldays. How many children would get away with helping to push the music teacher's car into a boating pool? There were teachers who would throw blackboard rubbers or chalk at you if you were talking or not concentrating in class. Some, especially the headmaster, had a deadly aim and would always hit you on the side of the head, which was painful and potentially dangerous. Being the kind of boy I was, on more than one occasion I threw the chalk or board-duster back. This might mean a visit to the head, but sometimes I felt I gained the respect of the teachers.

Not of the headmaster, though. I got myself deeply into trouble with him once after a contretemps with the head boy, a chap called Mount, who was a big lad but, I believed, a lad with no bottle. Mount was despised by my gang. He had not earned the respect of his peers and he knew it. Instead of trying to win us round, he would pick on us, reporting us to teachers, setting us lines, making us face the wall. One day things got out of hand and I lashed out at the head boy with my feet and my fists: a crack in the shins, a fist plumb on the nose. Shocked and bloodied, he stormed off to nurse his wounds. Within minutes he had gone straight to the headmaster, gutlessly blubbing out his story. The head strode around to my classroom in a fury and dragged me from the room by my ear. By the time we arrived at his study we were both shaking. I must have gone very pale, and I had never seen the Reverend Edmonds so angry.

'I should expel you!' he shouted. 'You are the worst boy in the school!'

I'm in for a beating, I thought.

'You wouldn't kick me,' he went on, 'so why kick my head boy?'

A point needed to be made here. I gave him a massive boot to the shins. His expression was priceless. That look of shock will remain imprinted on my memory for ever. It was a gem. His revenge was instant. Within seconds I had taken a thunderbolt to my solar plexus. I vomited, which didn't go down well, either. Then he dragged me to my feet, yanked down my shorts and regulation Y-fronts and told me to lean over a chair. I didn't resist. For a start he was too angry and, besides, I was too winded to put up any fight. So it was time to take my punishment like a man. It was unusual to have your shorts pulled off but I suppose the headmaster wanted to make sure that the full effect of the beating he was about to administer would be felt – I had previously been caught with comics stuffed down my shorts to lessen the pain, for which I had received an extra three lashes.

A normal beating was anything from two for a mild offence to six for a serious one. The punishment could be carried out only by the head or by his assistant, Mr Partington. The head had a selection of canes. On this occasion he decided to use one made up of three lengths of thin bamboo twisted together, which had knotty nodules all the way along it. Now, I know some public-school types get off on being beaten, but I have to tell you that I'm not one of them. I hated pain.

The official ruling was that the cane should not be raised above shoulder height, but I could clearly see in the head's mirror that it was descending from a far higher point than that. As the first whack came down I knew I was in for a severe thrashing. I bit my lip and tried not to cry, but it stung like billy-o. The flexibility in the wood often meant that the cane wrapped itself around your body, and you would find welts and bruising on your stomach and chest. As I was naked from the waist down I felt especially vulnerable, so I cupped my private bits in one hand. After six agonizing strokes I got up to go, but the head pushed me back. 'Six for me and six for kicking the head boy. You've got to learn,' he sneered.

Twelve lashes? It had to be some kind of record. Jesus, I thought, I don't know if I'll survive this one. After nine I sank to my knees, hoping that the head would take pity on me. He didn't. The tenth stroke hit me across the back. As I struggled back up, I felt a wet trickle down the back of my leg. I thought I must have poohed myself, but no, these were drops of blood. His aim was so accurate that several whacks had hit me in exactly the same place. He noticed the blood, made me stand up straight, told me to hold out my hands and delivered the last two to the palms. I don't know which was worse. My hands stung so much that I found it hard to hold a pen the next day.

'Are you going to learn now?' he asked. Lying through my teeth, I managed a reluctant 'yes, sir'. There was no point in making things any worse for myself. He told me to get patched up at the surgery. I just hoped that Nurse Elliott would be on duty rather than Matron. She was.

To say that she was shocked by the condition I was in would be an understatement. In fact she wanted to report the beating to the authorities – in her view it was nothing short of barbaric. She was right – nobody deserves that kind of appalling assault. I may be a believer in discipline, but beatings of that severity are out of order as far as I am concerned. Yet I refused to let Nurse Elliott report it. I had too much pride to want to see the issue taken any further.

Before covering me in sticky Germolene, Nurse Elliott made me take a warm, disinfectant bath, which brought more pain, but she promised it would help. While I sat in the bath she caressed me and I instantly forgot my wounds as she planted kisses all over me. She was in tears.

Before I got out of the bath she ran off to get her Box Brownie camera. The evidence might come in useful one day, she said.

Those pictures never saw the light of day. I wish I had them now, because nobody would believe the extent of that thrashing. There were other beatings, of course, before and afterwards, but none as bad as that one. The only caning that came close took place after a cross-country run. Once a week each class would do a four-mile run which took us across the railway line and up over a hill, through a soft-fruit farm, on through country lanes and back round to the school. One day several of us stopped on the farm to refresh ourselves with some strawberries. I wasn't actually that fond of strawberries so I found a raspberry patch and munched my way through some ripe, plump raspberries instead. We paused for only about five minutes, then set off again at a brisk pace, catching up the goody-two-shoes who had carried on running, and returned to school. After showering, we went to our next class, from which we were unexpectedly summoned to an immediate assembly. We all trooped into the assembly room and waited.

The headmaster walked in with the spineless Mount by his side. 'Will the following boys come to the front of the room,' intoned the head, and read out a list of thirty names, including mine: all the boys who had just been on the run. What had we done wrong? His voice became angry. 'Some of these boys have disgraced this school. They were spotted stealing strawberries from a local farm!' he roared. I was astonished. There were thousands of strawberries on that farm and we'd only eaten one or two. 'Will the guilty boys step forward and wait outside my study,' the head went on. A beating was on the cards. We looked around sheepishly at each other. Nobody wanted to be the first to move. After what seemed an eternity, the head boomed: 'If the guilty people don't own up, there will be no more exeats for the whole school this term, and you'll know who to blame.' Oh, shit, now what? It was an unwritten law that nobody sneaked on their fellow pupils, or did anything else that would lead to a fellow pupil being punished. One by one, ten boys moved forward and left the room, heads bowed, knowing full well what to expect. I stood my ground.

'Worrall Thompson, you have not owned up. I know who stole the strawberries. To me, cowardice is worse than the actual crime.' He glared at me.

'Excuse me, sir, may I say something?' I asked.

'No. Either you are guilty or you're not.'

I was blushing to the roots of my hair, but I stood firm.

'Worrall Thompson, you are a liar, and I won't tolerate liars,' he rasped.

'I am not,' I said indignantly.

'We know you are the ringleader. We know you ate the strawberries,' he insisted.

I decided to go for the killer punch.

'They weren't strawberries, they were raspberries,' I said defiantly. For a split second the laughter of the whole school rang round the assembly hall – only to be stopped dead by the head's icy stare and the volcano erupting from the top of his head. 'Out!' he screamed. *'Get over to my study!'*

I went over to the head's study to join the other boys. I told them what had happened after they'd left and apologized in advance for having made him so furious.

'Here he comes,' whispered one of the boys. And there he was, barrelling towards us, head down, like a miniature steam train or a bull about to charge, as fast as his little legs could carry him, his gown blowing behind him. The bull rampaged past us and into his study. 'All of you, come in here!' he shouted. We shuffled in hesitantly and stood in two rows in his cramped study. 'You will be beaten for your crime. I should have you all prosecuted . . .' His voice tailed off. I was wondering how delirious with excitement the police were likely to be about catching the Great Strawberry Robbers plus one Raspberry Robber. My attention was snapped back by the words: 'You will all receive three of the best, except Worrall Thompson, who will get nine for humiliating me in front of the school and for trying to lie.'

'I didn't lie!' I squeaked.

'Ten!' he screamed. 'And I want Worrall Thompson first!'

The other boys made to leave.

'No,' he said. 'You will all stay and watch.'

So, a public flogging, I thought. Better be brave. No tears.

Remember that Nurse Elliott will be there later to take away the pain. As I bent over the chair I repeated Nurse Elliott's name to myself as a kind of incantation. I felt a movement down below, a movement like a tortoise's head emerging from its shell. As the first stroke struck my arse, the tortoise's head quickly disappeared. As each lash rained down I bit my lip and thought longingly of soothing baths, Nurse Elliott and a Germolene rub. As the last of the ten left its mark along with the others on the surface of my skinny bum, I winced. But I held back the tears and got up, thanking the head, as was the convention. Ridiculous that you always had to say 'Thank you, sir' after a beating. As I left the room, I managed a wink at the other boys, despite my pain. It was my pride, once again, that predominated, and I made a graceful exit, bowed but not broken, which must have greatly irritated the head. As I went I heard him say to the others, 'Wait outside now, and come in one by one.'

Later, in the dormitory, we adhered to tradition by staging a public viewing of our trophies. *Welts and Bruising* by John Edmonds: in today's crazy world, my rear end would probably have won the Turner Prize for art.

The excessive corporal punishment may not have had any lasting effect on me, but my experience of religion at school in general and in the person of the Reverend John Edmonds in particular certainly saw to it that I did not grow up to be a religious person. As far as I am concerned, if there is anyone 'up there', he or she is not going to give a monkey's whether I believe in him or her. That would be far too egotistical. No, he or she would appreciate that I genuinely try to be a good person, and that, surely, is what counts. Keep it simple, don't complicate the issue, and life finds its own balance. I do believe that there is a force governing our lives, but I don't see it as having anything to do with religion. Let's have a dream; let's all live in peace and harmony. The only global religious leader we really need is someone capable of convincing the world that we've all got a place in someone's heart, and we're all entitled to live peacefully on this planet, side by side.

But enough sermonizing. Back at Milner Court, the beatings apart, in general life was a gas. My reports were not particularly good, but I escaped expulsion and I survived, and I was glad to be there. At the end of each term my mother would usually collect me in our little A35 and later a Hillman Imp. I was quite pleased then that she was always late, and that I was invariably the last to be picked up, after all the Rolls-Royces and Bentleys and Jaguars had purred away. As I grew older I became uncomfortably aware that I was almost the poorest boy in the school. If it hadn't been for my grandparents, who were very flush, I would not have been able to go to the school at all, and for that I shall always be grateful. If I had had to rely on my father, I would never have got anywhere. The divorce settlement stipulated that my father should pay my mother the princely sum of £4 10s a week as maintenance for me, but the money never arrived more than about half a dozen times. My mother tried to chase up the payments, on one occasion resorting to my grandparents' lawyers, but to no avail. He just couldn't afford it. The only option was to pursue him through the courts and have him put in prison. Fortunately for him, nobody wanted to take things quite that far.

My father had by this time remarried and had another child, a daughter, with his new wife. His admiration for Henry IV obviously remained undimmed, because they called the baby Henrietta. Sadly, I lost track of Henrietta for many years, though we've recently re-established contact. She went on to become a wardrobe mistress to the Windsor Theatre and Salisbury Playhouse.

My father's second marriage didn't last long. My mother always said that this union, like his first, was doomed to failure by the lure of a particularly persistent siren. This siren's name was Phyllida, and she had chased my father before, during and in between both marriages. Phyllida finally got her man, but you don't always get your cake and the chance to eat it as well. Soon after they married they were involved in a car crash, in which Phyllida was badly injured. From then on she would need constant nursing by my father.

Another thing my mother always said was that my father wasn't really looking for a wife, what he needed was a mother. So when children had come along and the attention of his wives had been distracted from mothering him, the relationships had soon disintegrated. But life has a funny way of turning the tables on you. He got no mothering out of Phyllida; my father ended up mothering her. His life changed completely. Out of the window went the gambling, although he continued to study form, and the alcohol, with the help of AA, and he dedicated his life to this tenacious but unlucky woman. His acting, of course, also had to be curtailed. He limited himself to roles near to home, mainly in local rep. As a child, however, I knew very little of all this, since his name and Phyllida's were mud in our house. She was despised and he was pitied.

CHAPTER SIX

DURING MY TIME AT PREP SCHOOL, HOME BECAME THE COTTAGE IN Coalcroft Road in Putney that my mother had bought with the assistance of my grandmother. It was small, but it was home, and it gave my mum a base from which to launch her forays into her beloved London. I had my own room, well, two in fact, as I had to vacate my official room every time anyone came to stay, or whenever my mother employed the services of an au pair, and move into the boxroom, which measured ten feet by six – barely enough room to swing a cat, or even the pet mice that moved there with me. God, how that room must have stunk. I didn't care, as I was rarely in it, preferring to be outside playing in the streets with my new best friend, Christopher Harrod, who lived next door, another lonely only child.

Christopher was the product of a state education, something that was frowned upon by my mother and my grandparents. But I took the view that I would choose my own friends, thank you. During the holidays we were inseparable, like brothers. We even looked alike, though Christopher had got the better bargain in that department. We played from dawn to dusk, cowboys and Indians when we were small, progressing to more ambitious projects, such as the construction of go-karts from orange boxes, planks and a couple of pairs of pram wheels.

So my home life wasn't dependent on my mother. It didn't matter if she wasn't there, because I entertained myself, and my days were full. My mother's job at the advertising agency was based in Alford Street, just off Park Lane in central London. It was a nine-to-five job, although her idea of five was more likely to be five in the morning than five in the afternoon. She was certainly rarely home before ten in the evening.

She said that she had to work late most nights, but I didn't believe her. One day I cycled up to her office to find the front door locked. Biking around, I found her car outside her mate Valentina Hoolihan's bar, Wilde's Club. I marched in and there she was, drinking at the bar with her boss, Philip. She was shocked to see me and suitably embarrassed, but at least she was graceful enough to introduce us. As I was whisked out the back to watch the television, I heard Philip say, 'You didn't tell me you had a son. Charming boy.' It didn't surprise me that she had neglected to mention me. I knew that being a single mother made things tricky for her and it was quite obvious to me that she had the hots for Philip. I would have loved them to have been closer but it wasn't to be. Philip was a really nice person. The trouble was, so was his wife. But Mother and Philip stayed good friends for many years, and every Christmas we'd be invited around to his beautiful house in Harrow-on-the-Hill for a lavish party. Philip and his wife had some cracking kids. I lusted after one of their daughters something rotten later in my teens, though she never knew that, because I was far too insecure to make any approaches to her.

When Mum went to work she left me with a door key and an arrangement with the neighbours over the road, the Blakes, to feed me at lunchtime, and that was that. Christopher and I spent most of our time with a few of his schoolfriends racing our homemade go-karts down the hills of Putney near Wimbledon Common. On more than one occasion we caused car accidents as we bombed over crossroads without a care in the world. There were not many cars around at that time and we were under the impression that the streets belonged to us. They were our playgrounds, and any other traffic had no right to be there. Amazingly, none of us was ever seriously hurt, though one or two stitches were required occasionally when one of us came off going too fast round a corner. They were magical times. We had the kind of fun today's kids have with skateboards, though with one crucial added factor: a large part of our enjoyment came from having made our go-karts ourselves.

And it is that self-sufficiency that is, I guess, the fundamental difference between the children of the early 1960s and those of the twenty-first century. We amused ourselves; we weren't constantly badgering our parents to take us to theme parks or to buy us

Gameboys or computers. Modern technology – television, videos, computer games and the Internet – seems to have robbed children of their innocence and their imagination. They no longer have to think for themselves; imagination does not appear to be one of the requirements of contemporary life.

Our kids are disadvantaged, too, in that the streets are not a safe playground any more, choked as they are by traffic and haunted by the threat of the pervert. Sexual offences against children appear to have increased, though to what extent this is due to the fact that they are reported and publicized rather than being swept under the carpet as they tended to be forty years ago is a matter of constant debate. Whatever the case, the fear of paedophiles is in itself enough to restrict the freedom of children, and today it is rare to see, let alone hear, kids playing outside together. They are more likely to be glued to the telly, either of their own volition or because their parents are too afraid to let them out. It is so sad.

We created our own cycle paths on Putney Common, hills and jumps and miles of racing track that kept us occupied for hours on our second-hand bikes. Of course, it wasn't all innocence. When the mood took us we were the scourge of Putney households, ringing people's doorbells (not in our street, obviously) and when someone answered the door and said, 'Yes? Can I help you?' replying, 'It says "Please Ring" on the button.' For this we would sometimes be chased down the street. We thought we were being extremely clever. A more serious prank was taking those small cans of Humbrol model paint, loosening the lids and throwing them at London buses. The splatter marks down the side of the bus we imagined to be bullet holes. We were never caught doing that.

Christopher and I used to go canoeing on the Thames at Putney in an old, vinyl-covered canoe we had found on a rubbish heap. With the help of my mother's friend Tony Pelly, who had impressive amateur building skills, we had patched it up enough to make it riverworthy. We used to carry the canoe over a mile from Coalcroft Road down to the Lower Richmond Road and the River Thames, and paddle it around Putney Bridge. We would often deliberately turn it over, hide underneath it in the air pocket and just drift with the current. Passers-by spotting an 'accident' would call the police, crowds would build up and a police river launch with divers would arrive. After we'd been under the canoe for about ten or fifteen minutes we'd pop out and wonder what all the fuss was about. There followed a good old-fashioned dressing-down from a very disgruntled river cop: wasting police time, irresponsible behaviour, strong currents etc. It didn't deter us, for as far as we were concerned it was just harmless fun, but it was of course a stupid thing to do. Not only, as the police correctly pointed out, were the strong undercurrents potentially fatal, but the Thames in those days was horribly polluted.

We took larking about on the river as the norm. Our parents didn't bat an eyelid, we never wore lifejackets and when the police told us off they never asked who or where our parents were. I think we take safety far too seriously nowadays. We nanny our children too much. While some of the things we did as kids were undoubtedly foolish and irresponsible, we lived to tell the tale. We climbed trees, we fell out, we had some hideous prangs on our bikes. If we got lost we would ask a stranger the way, and if we were in distress someone would come up, ask us what was wrong and help us out. It is a tragedy that nowadays caring adults are far less prepared to intervene. We are all too scared that we will be suspected of being perverts.

On Saturday mornings we would go to a children's club at the local cinema. We weren't bothered about the films: this was a chance to pull the girls. We got there early to bag the all-important back-row seats, though more often than not we would be pushed out by bigger boys and forced to move forward a couple of rows. I was keen to put some of Nurse Elliott's lessons into practice. I remember trying out my embryonic chat-up lines on a twelve-year-old girl and finally getting somewhere. As it was all going so swimmingly I ventured an arm around my new friend's shoulder. No resistance. I ran my fingers through her hair, and she nuzzled up closer. I kissed her on the cheek. She turned her face towards mine so I kissed her on the lips – no attempt at tongues, but a real 1930s film kiss. Now it was time for 'outside jumpers', a little grope at her non-existent breasts, keeping my hands in view at all times. She undid the buttons of her blouse. Inside jumpers, I thought; I'm nearly home and dry. I put my hand gingerly on her soft stomach and worked my way up to her flat chest. She kissed me again, and I proceeded with haste, slipping my hands down the front of her pleated skirt and finding the top of her voluminous school knickers. Suddenly she said: 'You won't find my sweeties down there.' Sadly, that was about it for my youthful sexual experimentation, and Saturday-morning cinema would soon be over for me because I was fast approaching the upper age limit for the club.

In my early holidays from prep school my mum discovered au pair girls. We had three before I finally persuaded her that I could be left on my own. I was about ten. One was Swedish and the other two German, and none of them spoke much English. They took me out to do the normal London tourist things: the zoo, the Tower of London, Madame Tussaud's, the Science Museum. I had never been to any of these places before, although I pretended I had. You often find that tourists know London's attractions better than Londoners do. When something is on your doorstep you tend not to get around to visiting it. The only regular London outing I had with my family was an annual trip to Olympia with my grandmother to see the Moscow State Circus. I was fascinated by the circus. A job there was a front-runner on my list of future careers, along with becoming a train driver, which was every kid's fantasy career in the days of steam trains.

It was one of the German au pair girls, Heidi, who unwittingly nurtured my interest in food and cooking. On one of our picnics on the river at my Gran's house in Shiplake I opened one of my sandwiches to discover that it contained raw bacon. I was horrified. I knew that uncooked bacon was dangerous because it could contain parasites. Poor Heidi, who had doubtless used it in the sandwiches in the genuine belief that it was some kind of continental cured, uncooked ham, got a mouthful of abuse for her trouble, but looking back, her mistake did me a great favour, because after that I decided that it would be safest to prepare my food myself whenever possible. On the strength of the unmitigated success of my Instant Whip (butterscotch flavour), I developed a repertoire of the ready meals of the day, which usually had to be reconstituted from dried or powdered form: Vesta curries, Surprise peas and Smash instant mashed potato, which I preferred to make with milk and butter rather than water. It needed extra seasoning, too, I found. I also turned out a mean Betty Crocker chocolate cake and my milkshakes were a great favourite with my chums in Putney.

My first excursion into classic French cooking was duck à l'orange, which I cooked from scratch – and I mean scratch. I was out with Christopher on the Thames in our canoe, feeding the ducks with stale bread, when suddenly I had a flash of inspiration. 'My mum cooked a great dish the other night using duck,' I said to Chris. 'Shall I cook it for you? We could catch one of these.'

It sounded a good idea to him.

'OK, you feed the ducks and distract them, and I'll grab one,' I suggested.

So while Chris had the birds eating out of his hand, I caught a plump-looking mallard by its neck. Hauling it out was easier said than done. The bloody thing flapped and flapped and nearly made me tip the canoe over. With difficulty we managed to secure the duck. With that sick, cruel sense of humour peculiar to small boys, we found the sight of this carrier bag throwing itself around the canoe hilarious. We paddled to the shore, tied up the canoe and ran all the way home with our struggling catch. In the garden, we cut the duck's throat with a Stanley knife. We didn't know anything about pulling its neck. We took it into the kitchen, where I turned on the oven, placed the duck on an oven tray, poured a bottle of Kia-Ora orange squash over it, threw in a couple of cut-up oranges and stuffed everything into the stove. It didn't occur to me at that stage that the feathers should have come off, or that my mother's duck would have been prepared for cooking by the butcher.

After a couple of hours I removed the bedraggled, sticky mess from the oven. Chris looked on with a rather bemused expression on his face as I belatedly began to pluck the feathers from my masterpiece. We then took the naked bird to the bottom of the garden, where I had built a den. We ripped at the flesh with our bare hands, blissfully ignorant of the alarming risks we were taking with our health, and ate with gusto, although the poor duck's fully cooked guts turned out to be a mouthful too far. We both nearly heaved when it came to those and decided to bring our banquet to a swift conclusion.

For me, cooking might have been born out of necessity rather than desire, but I was determined to learn and put together more and more interesting combinations for my lonely lunches. I remember making vegetable fritters by adding eggs and flour to a small tin of Heinz vegetable salad and deep-frying tablespoons of this questionable mixture. These I usually served with fried egg and dollops of Daddies' tomato sauce. It was some years before my taste buds had developed sufficiently for me to move on to the more sophisticated Heinz tomato ketchup.

I look back in amazement at how my culinary interests managed to take root, let alone thrive. As I said, my grandmother couldn't cook to save her life. She had a few – very few – tried and tested recipes that she had learned at finishing school, which I was fed repeatedly. Having relied on servants for thirty-eight years in India and her trusted daily Mrs Woodward on her return, there was very little motivation for her to add to these. My mother could cook the basics pretty well, but I do mean the basics. She dined out a fair amount. For a start it was cheaper, as ladies never paid their way in those days. She did a fairly mean roast, and some of her stews were very tasty, although you could never tell what was in them. In most of her dishes, white sauce, or béchamel, seemed to feature strongly. Soups never came from anywhere other than a tin, and the tin was always Campbell's condensed. We seemed to have hundreds of cans of this around the house. I guess it was one of the perks of having Campbell's as a client in her advertising days. My favourite was the tomato, although their mushroom made an excellent sauce poured over cod or chicken breast. I later discovered that Heinz tomato soup beat all the others hands down. My tastes were very simple. I loved vegetables, though unfortunately most of them were frozen as this 'new' way of preserving food was all the rage then, and eggs. Unfortunately, the only time I had eggs for breakfast – the only time I got breakfast, come to think of it, during the school holidays – was when I stayed with my gran.

From Putney I often went back to school by train. Before a new term it was traditional for my mother to cook me a 'last lunch', and I was gutted if ever circumstances denied me this treat. For years the meal was the same: we started with corn on the cob with loads of butter and black pepper, followed by rump steak, very rare, with peas, grilled mushrooms, tomatoes and frozen chips, and finished with vanilla ice cream, sliced bananas and hot chocolate sauce out of some ghastly plastic bottle. I loved it, and I loved my mother for giving up a day's work to cook for me and take me to Charing Cross Station for my journey back to school.

On the odd occasion that she was unable to keep our lunch date or drive me to the station, I would be given enough money to take the number 30 bus to Trafalgar Square and to buy myself a slap-up lunch at the Lyons Corner House on the Strand. I did this from the age of eight, to the great amusement of the waitresses. But none of them ever asked me what I was doing there on my own. Instead they made a pet of me, giving me lots of little extras free and the biggest-ever banana split to finish with. Afterwards I would struggle with my large overnight bag across the Strand and into Charing Cross. In many ways, going to the station by myself was easier, because when my mother was there to wave me goodbye I would always start blubbing. And whatever I did to hold back the tears, they would always end up embarrassing me. As the train pulled out I would have to rush into one of the loos and splash my face with cold water before facing the other boys taking the train back to Sturry and Milner Court.

One of my favourite puds was trifle, happily among the small number of dishes to which my gran could turn her hand. She used to make me a big bowl of it whenever I stayed with her in Chelsea or Shiplake. As I tucked into a plate of her trifle one day I noticed that it tasted different.

'Gran,' I asked, 'why have you changed the recipe?'

'I haven't,' she said. 'It's the same as always.'

'No, it's not. This one's got a red sauce.'

She looked baffled and came over to have a closer look. Not being blessed with the greatest eyesight in the world, she dipped her finger into the mysterious 'sauce' and tasted it. Her face blanched. Quick as a flash, she whisked away my plate before I had the chance to eat any more of it. It was several years before I found out what had been wrong with the trifle. Apparently, it had been sitting on a shelf in the new gas fridge below a very large rib of beef, which had inconveniently dripped blood on to the pudding. At the time I just thought it was a raspberry sauce, but you'll be pleased to know that my taste buds have improved considerably since then.

You will probably be surprised to hear that I didn't spend days on the loo afterwards. Even our bodies were different forty years ago: our immune systems could deal with all but the worst forms of food poisoning. Before the cottage in Shiplake had a fridge, the food was kept in the larder on a large, marble shelf protected by a wire fly gauze over the window. On that shelf sat raw meat, cooked ham, the leftovers of the Sunday joint, cheese, eggs and bacon. There were no rules about keeping cooked and raw foods apart. Often the daily milk, brought in glass, foil-topped bottles by the milkman, would have been pecked at by hungry birds, but it wouldn't have occurred to us not to drink it. The full milk bottles were stored in a bowl of cold water covered by bottle-shaped terracotta pots which had also been presoaked in cold water. Our only rule was that we washed our hands before meals and after going to the loo, and we washed them with plain soap and water. Surfaces were wiped down, never sterilized, cats would often walk across food preparation surfaces and dogs would sleep in the kitchen. And yet we were healthy. I don't recall ever suffering from food poisoning.

Scientists will say that I am talking crap and that more people died from food poisoning then than do nowadays. Maybe they did, but there were more deaths because we didn't have the drugs or medical knowledge to prevent them. It doesn't necessarily follow that there were more cases of food poisoning in general. And indeed there were not: on the contrary, food poisoning has been on the increase in one form or another every year for the past fifteen years, in spite of the fact that we apparently live far more hygienically, spraying every known surface with antibacterial or antimicrobial sprays. We use disposable paper cloths whereas in the past we had dishcloths which went into the weekly boil wash; we pour chemicals and bleaches down our loos to kill all known germs. Hygiene education is rammed down our throats at school. Restaurants are much cleaner than they were when I entered the profession, refrigeration is far more efficient, packaging of our fresh foods is all but sterile. So why is there more food poisoning? I am sure people are fed up with being fobbed off with scientific jargon and, like me, want some answers from a united body of scientists and doctors. Until then we can only theorize and continue to play with commonsense solutions. All I know for sure is that I didn't get food poisoning until I was eighteen.

The simple answer has to be that our immune systems are on the point of collapse. What else could be causing such rampant food poisoning, the boom in asthma sufferers, the increase in certain types of cancers, the surge of new allergies and food intolerances? We just cannot any longer deal with the minor bugs our bodies used to fight without difficulty.

Perhaps we are now just too clean, living in our sterile bubble almost from birth. Both Sir Terence Conran and myself have got into trouble for saying that a little dirt never did anyone any harm. The Food Standards Agency was incensed at our 'irresponsibility', but I stand by what I have said.

We can't blame everything on global warming and pollution. In many ways the UK is a far cleaner country than it was in my childhood, when we had to deal with regular pea-souper fogs. There are more trees planted now in the UK than there were at the turn of the last century, our rivers are cleaner, fuel emissions from vehicles are less noxious, although admittedly there are many more of those vehicles on the roads. Domestic heating, water supply and power are much more energy-efficient. So common sense would suggest that it's what we are consuming that is destroying our systems, aided and abetted by the unprecedented comforts of our cushy homes with their carpets, double glazing and central heating. But what exactly is it that we are consuming that is causing the problems? It could be all or a combination of a huge range of innovations.

Antibiotics, for example. The fact that doctors seem to give them out like sweets is our own fault. When we go to the doctor's surgery with an ailment we expect to come away with that miracle prescription, even though many of our illnesses can't be cured by antibiotics. Every time we take a course of them we reduce the effectiveness of our immune system and increase our chances of catching something else.

Then there is our obsessive use of antibacterial, antimicrobial sprays, bleaches, disinfectants, fly-killers, air-purifiers. These products kill good bugs as well as the villains. Our bodies need good bacteria. Scientists in America recently announced that antimicrobial sprays could be killing us, but will we in the UK take any notice? Will we heck! And incidentally, other research has also revealed that kids living alongside two or more animals have stronger immune systems. I rest my case.

As for what we eat, the decline in good, home-cooked, solid meals in favour of supermarket ready meals, the burger culture and our fondness for takeaways are almost certainly harmful. Many ready meals contain a huge number of chemicals in the form of preservatives, as well as far too much sugar and salt. The odd burger from time to time doesn't hurt anyone, but there are people I know who practically live on them. Just think about the ridiculously low price of burgers and what that says about the kind of ingredients they must contain and how the cattle that provide the beef for them are raised.

In the years after the Second World War, we spent approximately 30 to 35 per cent of our disposable income on food. Now that nutrition has taken second place to the extra car, the computer, the bigger TV, the exotic holiday, that figure has fallen to 12 to 15 per cent and is decreasing by the year. It is said that you are what you eat, so perhaps we should be giving more attention to what we put into our bodies and remembering that you get what you pay for. How is it that a supermarket can sell you an oven-ready chicken for under £3? The supermarkets have driven prices so low at the farm gate that it shouldn't come as a shock to us if farmers take short cuts. There are plenty of them that are within the law. Those chickens, for example, will probably have been force-fed to accelerate their growth and pumped full of chemicals and water. As a result, farming in the UK is in crisis. Salmonella, listeria, BSE, e-coli, campylobacter, foot and mouth – you name it, we've seen it.

Thanks to foreign travel and air transport, there has been a vast increase in new foodstuffs over the past fifty years, which could be contributing to the increase in allergies. One group of homeopathic allergy consultants believes that it takes the human body two or three generations to develop an immunity to such gatecrashers in our diet. And it's not just different foods, but also modern packaging products like clingfilm and aluminium foil that could be a factor.

The vitamins and minerals we need to fight diseases come from fresh fruit and vegetables, and there can be few of us unaware these days that, as a nation, we do not eat nearly enough of them. The chief medical officer would be happy if we all ate five three-ounce portions of fruit and vegetables (not counting potatoes) every day, but unless you really plan your menus – and how many of us are sufficiently organized to do that? – it is quite a hard target to achieve. Yet it could actually be those very foodstuffs so necessary for good health that are helping to destroy us. For a start it is estimated that, due to intensive farming methods and the heavy use of chemicals, up to nine essential minerals are no longer present in our soil, and therefore absent from what grows in it as well. Even more importantly, the tons of chemicals sprayed on our fruit and vegetables in the form of herbicides, pesticides, fertilizers and preservatives create what is in my view a lethal cocktail that is the main culprit in the deterioration of our immune systems.

While insisting that the levels of chemical residue on fruit and vegetables are safe, successive governments have at the same time advised us to peel fruit, cucumbers and carrots and not to use the zest of citrus fruits. This longstanding ambivalent approach was recently contradicted by the Food Standards Agency, who announced that while we should wash fruit and vegetables for reasons of hygiene there is no need to worry about pesticide contamination. Yet levels of pesticides on a significant amount of fruit and vegetables sold in the UK exceed recommended safety limits, with lettuce, grapes and strawberries proving the worst offenders.

Whatever soothing statements the government chooses to make, the truth is that no one can tell us with any authority whether a lifetime of exposure to all sorts of different combinations of chemicals can be safe, because of course no one has tested all the possible permutations. One day you might eat an apple, a few grapes, some broccoli, a salad and a portion of potatoes. But what did you eat the previous day? Or the day after? Analyse just one product, the dessert apple, and you will find that it may have been treated as many as sixteen times with pesticides containing almost forty separate chemicals. Different fruit and vegetable groups use different chemicals, so the enormous range of chemicals we're digesting in various combinations on a daily basis doesn't bear thinking about.

It is this chemical contamination that worries me more than anything else I have mentioned, and for this reason, as far as possible, I eat only organic produce. It is true that going organic is more expensive – it can add as much as a third to your weekly grocery bill – and I appreciate that there are people who genuinely cannot afford that. But for many who say they can't afford it, it is more a question of priorities than of hardship; of spending only that reduced percentage of their income on food I was talking about earlier. For me, making sure that my body is as free of chemicals as it can be is a priority. My choice has little to do with taste – and if you do decide to go organic, don't be disappointed if you don't notice any difference in the taste of your fruit and vegetables, because often there isn't much of one.

Another good reason for converting is to do our bit towards saving the planet, because as well as damaging us, those same chemicals are also polluting the environment. Unfortunately, at the moment about 70 per cent of all organic produce in the UK is imported, which rather defeats the object of buying it, as the fuel involved in transporting it only adds to the pollution. It also creates a problem for the consumer in that you can't be as certain of its origins. But the more people who buy British and develop the market for local organic fruit and vegetables, the more likely it is that increased numbers of domestic farmers will take up the organic cause.

Although the organic movement still has a long way to go, I believe it is already too large to be policed by independent associations. And it is iniquitous that farmers wishing to go organic have to pay for the privilege of certification, as does everyone else involved in the process of getting the food to the consumer. So ultimately it is the public that pays, of course, which is at least part of the reason for the inflated prices of organic produce. It is time for certification to be controlled by a government body, so that all organic producers are operating on a level playing field.

I am not sure how I got from a few drops of blood in a trifle in the early 1960s to the virtues of organic fruit and vegetables, but as you will have gathered, the contamination of food is a subject about which I have strong feelings. At Milner Court in 1963, however, such debates lay a long way in the future. As I returned for my final year at prep school, I had a more pressing matter on my mind: namely the Common Entrance exam that would determine where I would be spending the remainder of my schooldays.

CHAPTER SEVEN

IN 1963, THERE WAS NO IDYLLIC SUMMER IN PUTNEY OR SHIPLAKE FOR me. After my mother had been warned at the end of the previous school year to find an alternative public school for me, my grandmother rose to the challenge and paid for me to go to a crammer in St George's Square in Pimlico in the holidays. What a bitch that was. While my friends were all enjoying their break, I spent every weekday, from 9 am to 5 pm with an hour off for a greasy-spoon lunch, receiving one-to-one tuition in all my weakest subjects. When there is just you and your teacher there is no slacking, no borrowing your mates' notes, just sheer hard graft. But I went back to school that autumn focused on keeping my nose to the grindstone in the nine months leading up to my exams. There were two voices ringing in my ears as I entered the gates of Milner Court. One was my gran's – 'Don't let me down. I haven't spent thousands on your education for you to end up a failure' – and the other was that of John Edmonds, my hated headmaster, who had told me before he ever said anything to my mum: 'You'll never be good enough to go to King's.' I was determined to make him eat his words.

And by and large, I stuck to my resolution. Sure, I still fooled around and had fun with the gang, but I was a far more studious pupil, and in the mock exams I sat that first term I did pretty well, although the fact that I came top in French was not the triumph it may have seemed: I got the highest marks in that because I cheated.

I have never been sure whether cheats are simply born or whether they develop. Whatever the case, at prep school, cheating in exams appeared to be rife. Prompts were written in code in logarithm tables or in biro on the inside of your arm; notes were slipped into slide-rule cases or taped to the inside of a loo seat (they had to be hidden because if you wanted to go to the loo you were normally escorted, and even the cubicle you chose would be checked). Loo visits were also useful in that they could be organized to occupy a teacher, enabling some candidates to ask the class swots for the answers while he was out of the room. The swots would usually comply for fear of being beaten up later if they refused.

In spite of this culture of academic dishonesty, I cheated in an exam only that once. It was the first and last time because I was caught. And I didn't actually set out to cheat: it was more a case of not looking a gift horse in the mouth. The chance was presented to me on an historic evening: 22 November 1963, the day of the assassination of President Kennedy. When the news of the shooting was announced, an immediate assembly was called for all the boys and teachers to say prayers for his family. I was alone in the school library at the time revising and nobody told me about the assembly. I was curious about some brown envelopes I had noticed on one of the library shelves and, taking advantage of the fact that every-where seemed unusually quiet, I had a quick peek inside them. I couldn't believe it when I discovered that they contained the Common Entrance French and history papers some pupils had been sitting that day. I knew that these were the very papers we would be set as our mocks. It was as if someone was shining a light into the darkness for me. I quickly wrote down all the questions and returned the papers to their envelopes. Now that I knew the questions, I could channel my energy into the right direction as I finished my revision.

When I studied the history questions, I realized I'd done all the necessary revision. But French was one of my weaker subjects, and I was grateful for that shining light in this case. I made notes on tiny scraps of paper, which I concealed about my person, and when I sat the paper the next day I slipped these notes under the legs of my shorts so that they lay on my thighs and I could look down at them when I needed to check on something. Everything was going swimmingly when, towards the end of the exam, I suddenly felt faint and nauseous. The teacher spotted me going white and whisked me off to sick bay. As I left my desk the notes fell out of my trouser leg. I was too groggy to notice, but the boy at the next desk was on the ball. While the teacher was away dealing with me, he picked up the notes and hid them away.

My illness turned out to be measles, and I was confined to sick bay for two weeks. During my incarceration my French teacher came to visit me. 'What happened to you?' he asked.

'What do you mean?'

'You came top of the French exam,' he replied.

I could feel myself blushing. I didn't know what to say because I had no idea whether he knew I had cheated or not. But my guilt must have been written all over my face.

'I can't prove anything,' he said, 'but I think you cheated. If you own up it won't go any further. If you don't, and we discover that you have cheated, you will be beaten and possibly even expelled. What do you want to do?'

'Since you put it like that, sir, I guess I'll have to own up,' I said shamefacedly.

'How did you cheat?' he asked.

'If I tell anyone that, you might get into trouble, sir.' I was well aware that he shouldn't have left the exam papers lying around.

'Why?' he questioned. I explained.

He got up to leave. 'You think you're too clever by half, Worrall Thompson,' he said.

I smiled. No further action was taken and I retained my number-one spot in the French exam to the surprise of all the other pupils, except for one: the one who found my notes. And he struck a hard bargain. I had to give him my complete collection of James Bond first editions in exchange for his silence and my incriminating notes. Never again.

I was generally a healthy lad, and I never had colds or flu, though as well as measles I did get mumps and two doses of rubella, or German measles. There weren't even individual vaccinations against these diseases then, let alone the combination vaccination, MMR. In fact, many parents would deliberately put small children in the way of some diseases, like mumps, that would be more dangerous later on, in the belief that since their offspring were bound to catch them at some stage, it was better to get them over with as early as possible. So when one kid went down with mumps or chicken pox, several of his friends would be brought round to play with him. As I'm sure you're aware, complications can set in if boys get mumps after their balls drop, and these can result in infertility. I met one senior boy at my next school who contracted the disease at sixteen. He could have made use of the proverbial wheelbarrow to carry his balls around in. They were humongous, and very painful.

The debate about the triple MMR vaccination has raged in recent months, with the chief medical officer determined that all babies should have it in spite of concerns about its safety. I can see the point of immunization against rubella, which can be caught more than once, and which can be very dangerous to pregnant women as it can cause deformities in their unborn children. But we only suffered from mumps and measles once, thereafter developing immunity to them, and neither disease was that bad. It is another indication of the deterioration of our immune systems that the medical profession considers it so vital for babies to have the MMR vaccine rather than simply allowing their bodies to deal with these diseases as ours did in the past.

When I had recovered from the measles, it was head down in the run-up to my Common Entrance exams. There was more cramming in the Christmas and Easter holidays. It was going well, but then came two pieces of bad news.

The first was the death of my grandfather. He had been ill for five months. In January of 1964 he had been on a trip to South Africa with my grandmother to visit his sister, Mrs Choleur. This was a biennial event and he always thoroughly enjoyed it, especially the game parks, which reminded him of his shooting days in India. It was while he was out on safari that he had suffered a massive stroke. He had been airlifted to Johannesburg and then flown back to London from there. I remember going with my mother to Heathrow Airport in an ambulance to pick him up and take him to the King Edward VII Hospital for Officers. He looked ghastly. This proud old man had almost reverted to being a baby. He couldn't talk, he couldn't control his bodily functions. In short, he was a cabbage. I wish I'd never seen him like that. I would much rather have been able to remember him as an upright military man, the kind of man all young boys should look up to. But the saddest thing was that, with therapy, he had actually been getting better. And then, just when he had started to talk, started to move again, another stroke had cruelly taken him away.

The second bombshell came from my mother: she was leaving her job and going away for the summer. By now she had switched careers for a third time, once again turning her back on a career she seemed quite good at to take up something completely different. Having decided that she wanted to become an estate agent, she had blagged a job at Ellis Copp in Putney, where she knew one of the senior partners. Female estate agents were a rare breed then, but my mother's philosophy was that it was women who usually had the final say when a couple were buying a house, and another woman would therefore have a better feel for those vital matters that clinched a deal. In her selling strategy she focused on kitchens, bathrooms and loos, and was one of the first agents to advise vendors about the importance of welcoming smells such as the aroma of fresh coffee or newly baked bread. Again she did well, regularly coming top of the sales league, and again, just when everything was going brilliantly, she suddenly decided that she wanted to up sticks and take a three-month job as a hostess on a Greek cruise liner.

Unsurprisingly, she had an ulterior motive for this scheme: she had fallen in love with a Greek steward called Demetrios. The relationship was, of course, doomed from the start, but although she came back without Demetrios, she was still full of the joys of spring. I suppose her decision showed a spirited sense of adventure, but at the time I thought it was a selfish thing to do during my last term at Milner Court, just when I had my big exams coming up. She wasn't even able to pick me up on Speech Day. That was left to the dependable Tony Pelly.

My exams went well in spite of these unsettling developments and I booked my place at King's, Canterbury. But there was still one final major event to occur before I left prep school behind me. We all knew that several boys used to visit a male teacher in his room after lights out, ostensibly for extra tuition. These boys were younger and not from my gang, but I was always slightly intrigued by what they got up to and somewhat put out that I had never been honoured with an invitation to this teacher's room. If you asked the boys about it, all they would say was that, after their extra tuition, they were sometimes allowed to watch television if they were well behaved. This little group – there were about ten of them – kept themselves very much to themselves. Most of them were quite gentle, shy characters. Sometimes they would visit the teacher alone, sometimes in groups of three or four. Whenever they came back they would all get into a little huddle and have a confab about what they had been doing.

From the outside, then, there seemed to be nothing untoward going on. But on the day before Speech Day, the second-last day of the term, in the relaxed, almost festive atmosphere that pervaded the school after the exams were over, one of the group, an ex-pat (let's call him 'Pat'), came up to me and asked if we could have chat.

I was mildly surprised, but since, with the end of term, the old rivalries were all but forgotten and we would soon be going our separate ways, I agreed. He wanted to talk in private, so we walked over to the oast house and went into the woodwork classroom, which we knew would be empty.

'Pat' seemed very nervous but gradually he started to talk about this teacher, recounting how, over three years earlier, he had begun inviting some of the boys to extra gym training. He would help them over the horse or the box and, as he caught them, he would hold each boy close to his body and they could feel the hardening of his penis. There would be mock reprimands if the pupil was not doing his vault properly, which developed into pretend physical chastisement during which the master's hand would accidentally brush against the pupil's member. 'Pat' told me that after a few sessions in the gym, the boys would be invited back to his room, where they were shown top-shelf magazines such as *Titbits*, *Parade* and *Men Only*. They then graduated to pure porn in the form of queer magazines (as they were known then), and slowly the reason for this preferential treatment would begin to dawn on the boys.

'Pat' explained that the group was quite flattered and excited by the attention they were receiving. The teacher would make them frolic around naked, encouraging them to play with each other. This was a normal occurrence, as I have already explained: growing boys making sure they had the same bits as every other boy. What was not normal, obviously, was doing this in the presence of a teacher. The boys knew it was wrong but, as with so many aspects of growing up, wrong is often much more fascinating than right.

At subsequent sessions the teacher would get the boys to unbutton his trousers, remove them and feel his expanding bulge through his underpants. 'Do you want to see it?' he'd say, knowing that the boys would be totally intrigued by the sight of an adult cock in full flight. From there it was a short step to mutual masturbation, and then on to the hitherto unexplored territory of oral sex. The boys weren't too sure about that but the master would manage to persuade one of them to do it, and then everyone would follow suit, not wanting to be seen as wusses. After that there seemed to be no going back. The teacher held them to a code of silence, telling the boys that if they talked about what was going on they would be expelled, their parents would be shamed and they would probably be sent away to children's homes.

I was shocked when 'Pat' went on to describe the one-to-one

sessions during which anal sex would take place. He told me of the excruciating pain the boys suffered, which was lessened only marginally by the master's application of margarine.

I felt sick and also slightly guilty, knowing that my own behaviour with Nurse Elliott had been hardly less shameful. But I didn't reveal this to 'Pat'. I felt even sicker when he told me that this teacher had mentioned me, wondering whether I might join his group. Apparently he had been reluctant to approach me because of my reputation for being troublesome.

'I'm not doing it!' I said, alarmed.

'Of course not,' replied 'Pat'. 'But we want you to tell another teacher. You'll be gone soon, but we're scared, and we don't know what to do. He's making us bleed, and we're worried. It's got to stop.'

'I can try,' I told 'Pat', 'but no teacher is going to believe me. I've got no proof, and they'll think I'm just making it up.'

After some humming and ha-ing, we finally came up with a crafty plan. We needed to lure the teacher into a trap – with me as the bait. I was so appalled by what I had heard that I was prepared to play my part to help 'Pat' and his friends, on two conditions. First, they all had to promise to back up my story and provide full descriptions of what had happened to them. Secondly, there was no way I was going anywhere near that teacher's room.

That meant we would have to entice him outside. 'Pat' said he thought that the master was fixing go-karts on the cricket field at that very moment. We wandered over, and sure enough, there he was. No time like the present. I told 'Pat' to hide in the bushes while I waited for the teacher on the small wooden bridge over the River Stour. I was going to try to get him to take me boating. If it worked out, and the teacher tried it on with me, I would wink at 'Pat' on the way back. That would be his signal to fetch help in the form of the nice Mr Edmonds, the maths master.

Having established our strategy, we moved into position. I stood on the bridge, where the teacher could see me, and after a few minutes he came over.

'What are you doing, Worrall Thompson?' he asked.

'I was hoping to find someone to go boating with, but I'm not having much luck,' I told him.

'I can give you a few minutes if you like.'

'Oh, could you? Thanks, that would be great,' I said appreciatively.

So off we went, with me rowing and the teacher steering. We had been travelling upstream for about fifteen minutes when he made a suggestion. 'Shall we stop and sit on the bank for a few minutes so that you can have a rest?'

I agreed as nonchalantly as I could. My heart was pounding.

We moored up and got out on to the bank, where the grass was really long. There was absolutely no way we could be seen here except from the river. 'Let's sit here,' he said. I sat down nervously and he sat beside me. Although I was the one who had been doing the rowing, he was breathing heavily and his face was very red. I saw that he was playing with a rather large bulge from inside his pocket. 'What are you doing, sir?' I asked innocently.

'On a beautiful sunny day like this, just sitting in a field makes me feel good,' he said. 'Why don't we take our clothes off and get some sun?'

'I'd rather not if that's all right with you.'

'I don't think you quite understand. Let me make myself clear. Take your clothes off. Now!' he snapped. Hastily, I did as I was told. He undressed to reveal a very large, bright red penis. I was terrified. Were all my good intentions going to backfire on me? There's no way that thing is coming anywhere near me, I thought.

'Touch me,' he said. I obeyed, fearing where this was all going to end. He pulled me towards him and started fiddling with me to try to get me aroused. Nothing doing.

'What's wrong?' he asked.

'I'm scared.'

'Don't worry. Everyone is scared their first time. I'm not going to do anything bad,' he said.

This is bad enough, I thought to myself. He started rolling all over me, rubbing himself up against me. Then he turned me over. 'No! Don't!' I said. 'Please.'

'It's all right. I just want to feel your soft skin. Nothing else,' he promised.

Once he'd had enough of that, he rolled off me and finished himself off by masturbating. I watched out of the corner of my eye. It was disgusting. He was disgusting. Nurse Elliott might have been naughty, but this was something else entirely. Nothing could have been as perverted as this repulsive man puffing and panting next to me. I remember the incident as if it happened yesterday: his foul-smelling breath, his sweaty top lip, the hair under his arms dripping with nervous sweat, the stomach-churning smell of his semen.

I hadn't wanted things to get that far, but I had achieved what I had set out to do and had emerged unharmed. The teacher's fate was sealed, and now I just had to get back and spill the beans. In a funny sort of way I almost felt as if I had betrayed him: everything had gone to plan and he had fallen into my trap as easily as a rat baited by a piece of poisoned meat. But my overwhelming feeling was one of triumph. I had done what the others hadn't had the balls to do, and I was chuffed.

The teacher rowed us back while I steered and, with his back to the bank, he wouldn't have seen 'Pat' waiting there for me. I winked in as exaggerated a fashion as I could manage and I saw him run off as fast as his legs would carry him. As we moored up, I thanked the master sarcastically for taking me rowing.

'Remember, you're not to tell a soul,' he said. And then, conversationally, 'If I don't see you before the end of term, have a great holiday.' Forget the end of term: I was hoping I would never have to see him again as long as I lived.

As I ran towards the school I saw 'Pat' heading to meet me with Mr Edmonds. As I reached them the maths master sent 'Pat' away and stopped me. 'Worrall Thompson,' he said. 'I understand you need to see me.'

Looking over my shoulder in case the perve was behind me, I replied, 'Yes, I do. Can I talk to you privately?'

We went to Mr Edmonds's study, where I recounted what had just happened and told him what 'Pat' had told me. He seemed outraged and shocked, but he said calmly, 'Don't worry, you have been very brave. You promise that everything you have told me is the truth?'

'Of course, sir.' I replied. 'All the other boys will talk to you as well if you don't believe me,' I added in a worried tone.

'I believe you,' he said. 'Now off you go.'

I would be leaving Milner Court the very next day: what an ending to an amazing five years, during which I had experienced every possible emotion. The independent spirit and Taurean stubbornness that had often got me into hot water had also seen me through. I just refused to be beaten.

There was one last surprise to come before that chapter of my life closed. As we assembled the following day, Speech Day, for the prizegiving, the perve teacher was, thank God, nowhere to be seen. But this wasn't the surprise, obviously. That came when the winner of the prize for the most improved boy in the school that year was announced. It was a pupil better known as the worst-behaved boy in the school: Antony Worrall Thompson. I was astonished. Although I had buckled down to my work that year and passed my Common Entrance, I still seemed a most unlikely choice, given the headmaster's antipathy towards me, and it did occur to me to wonder whether this might have had anything to do with the events of the previous day.

If I had known how the master who had assaulted all those boys, including me, had been dealt with, or if I had been old enough to appreciate the implications of the way he had been dealt with, I would probably have handed back the prize. As it was, I was dead chuffed. This really was one in the eye for my nemesis, the Reverend Edmonds.

So what did happen to the paedophile teacher? Well, apart from instant dismissal – hence his absence on Speech Day – precisely nothing. He was not prosecuted; in fact, as far as I know, the police were never even involved. Since my mother was not informed, neither, I guess, were the parents of the boys he had raped. Nothing was said to me on the matter by the headmaster, though if he had offered any kind of commiseration, it would have been so out of character that I would probably only have been disgusted anyway. No further action whatsoever was to be taken against the teacher. Instead he was free to walk the streets. God knows how many children he abused after he left the school. But that was how things were: scandal was to be avoided at all costs, and everything was just swept under the carpet.

I came away from Milner Court with one souvenir: the Rev Edmonds's special twisted cane, the one with the knotty nodules on it, which I managed to spirit out of his study. I still have that cane to this day.

CHAPTER EIGHT

WITH MY MOTHER OFF ON HER CRUISE SHIP, I SPENT THE SUMMER AT Shiplake with my bereaved grandmother. True to form, she maintained a traditional stiff upper lip. I think she saw my grandfather's death as a merciful release. She knew how much her formidable husband would have hated living on in such an incapacitated state. My mother returned from her Shirley Valentine experience, in time to take me to my new school, with a wild dream. She wanted to buy a delicatessen and café. This was in 1964, a time when Mr Cohen's Tesco was first formulating its 'stack 'em high, sell 'em cheap' policy, offering Green Shield stamps on the side. Sainsbury's girls still wore cheesecloth hairnets and provided an excellent service from behind wonderful marble counters, and Marks & Spencer catered only for the outsides of people's bodies, not their insides.

Mum managed to borrow enough money from Philip, Frank the Car and a partner at Ellis Copp to set up a double-fronted shop on the Upper Richmond Road in Putney. She called it 'Never on a Monday'. On one side of the shop was the café and on the other the deli. Amazingly, for someone who had no experience whatsoever in restaurants or shops, she created something quite special and well ahead of its time, selling lots of great products that really sparked my interest in food. As its quirky name indicated, the shop closed on a Monday, but the deli was open late into the evenings on weekdays and even on Sundays, which was practically unheard of then.

How she did it was beyond me. Sometimes she ran the place single-handed, cooking lunches out the back and racing through to serve a customer when she heard the bell on the door of the deli ring. She also made a lot of the deli products herself: a Liptauer cream cheese, a rustic terrine, soups, salads, ready meals and a wide range of sandwiches.

Meanwhile, for me, it was time to start public school. Grey shorts and guernseys were replaced by pinstriped trousers, wing-collared shirts, a black jacket and a straw boater. While we undoubtedly looked like snotty little kids, most of us were quite proud of our uniform. The boys on scholarships had to wear black or purple gowns, which was unfortunate as it singled them out for persecution by boys less endowed in the brain department.

My introduction to King's was a startling one. All the new boys were assembled, in alphabetical order, in front of the monitors and some of the housemasters to meet our headmaster, Canon Newell, who moved down the line exchanging pleasantries with each boy.

When he came to me it was, 'Name, boy?'

'Worrall Thompson, sir,' The use of the courtesy was so ingrained into us that it automatically attached itself to the end of each sentence.

'Ah, so you're Worrall Thompson,' he said. 'You came here poorly recommended. But we will change all that, won't we, boy?'

'If you say so, sir,' I replied. Suddenly, he turned into a thermometer dipped into boiling water. The flush started at his dog collar and crept slowly up his face until it seemed certain that steam would emerge from his balding pate. I've seen less colour on a freshly picked strawberry. Trying unsuccessfully to keep his voice down, he raged: 'If it's the last thing I ever do, I will break you. I will break your spirit. You will conform. Do I make myself clear, Worrall Thompson?'

Keep calm, I wanted to say to him. Life's too short to let a whippersnapper of a boy get you down. But it came out as 'Yes, sir.'

Canon Newell flounced out of the room, not once looking back, his gown and his entourage trailing in his wake.

What a to-do, I thought. Why me? And I haven't even done any-thing wrong yet!

The other new boys gathered round and, despite my less than imposing figure and my complete lack of involvement in what had just taken place, I was an instant hero. I felt like one of those free gifts all kids are desperate to find in a cereal packet.

But strong expectations cannot be denied, and within three weeks I had received my first beating from my housemaster. My offence was exploding a stink bomb in a divinity lesson. Those divine scriptures were so boring. I had suffered them at kindergarten and at junior school, and I saw no reason why I should continue to have religion rammed down my throat. I was never going to be religious. I loved some religious occasions, and I still get very emotional over the beauty of a wedding or the morbid passion of a funeral. I loved being confirmed in Canterbury Cathedral because of the church's amazing history and magnificence, but as for the meaning of the ritual, it went in one ear and out the other. I also liked being in the choir, but that was because I thought I was achieving something. The Archbishop of Canterbury at the time of my confirmation was Archbishop Ramsey, a fabulous man who was loved by all; a man of great character, a good man. If all church leaders were like him, maybe I might have been persuaded to change my mind.

In my first year at King's I showed what I could do if I put my mind to it. I came top of my class and received the form prize on Speech Day. Canon Newell's announcement of the award was very grudging: '. . . and to the surprise of all of us, Art Shell C prize goes to a boy never expected to complete the first year at King's, let alone come top of the form – Worrall Thompson.' There was polite clapping all round and I went up to collect my prize as if I were floating on a cloud. A mini miracle had just been achieved, and a two-fingered salute delivered to Canon Newell and the school elders. It was a great day: my mother even made it to the awards, and for once she made me proud and I made her smile. That, however, was that on the school awards front for me: a grand total of two, one for being sexually abused and one for being a determined little shit.

My mother tried a little harder on her monthly visits. Often she would bring a man with her. On several occasions it was an old actor chum of hers from America, Ed Begley, who, I later discovered, had appeared in several movies, usually as a bad guy or an army general. He bored the pants off me, though. He reminded me of the pig-like characters my mother had mixed with when I was a toddler. Because Ed was an American, when he came it was obligatory for us to take English tea at the Chaucer Hotel in Canterbury. This followed a dull traipse around the cathedral, which was the last thing I wanted to do because I saw quite enough of it already: we went there twice on Sundays with the school, for Morning Service in the main body of the church and Evensong in the crypt.

Far more exciting was when Mum brought down Frank the Car, because, among the fingers he had in many pies, he owned Dreamland in Margate, probably one of the largest funfairs in the south of England. So Mum and Frank would drive me up to Dreamland, where no ride remained untried and, candyflossed out, I would stagger back for Evensong, having enjoyed every indulgence known to man, or rather, child, all at the expense of Uncle Frank. Sometimes I took a schoolfriend with me, which, as you can imagine, earned me serious brownie points with my lucky companion.

But my main love on most parental visits was going out for lunch. My foodie tendencies were maturing now, and I was desperate to learn more. Looking back, Canterbury probably wasn't the best town to develop my taste buds, but it was a start. One of our regular haunts was a Greek restaurant called the Cosmopolitan, where I had my first experience of dolmades, stuffed vine leaves, and kleftiko, the slow-roasted shank of lamb. To me the waiters were extremely soigné in their starched white monkey jackets. Had I studied them more closely I would doubtless have discovered black trousers shiny from the constant wiping of greasy hands on their arses and black shoes in serious need of a little spit and polish.

In my second year at King's I moved down to my senior house, the Grange, which had a housemaster of frightening reputation, one Mr Garwood. As I was to find out very quickly, he was a strict disciplinarian, but at the same time he was human. As soon as I arrived at the house, in September 1965, I was booked in for a session. No, not a beating, just a genuine heart-to-heart. He told me that he was there to help me if I wanted to help myself. I asked him in what way he thought I needed help. He appreciated ballsy pupils, he said, but there was ballsy and there was ballsy, and my balls were of the wrong kind. He wanted me to channel my mischievousness into sports and lessons rather than into rebellion. He likened me to a Tarzan-type character, a free spirit used to the ways of the jungle who had never been trained, had been allowed to run riot at home and reacted against control and discipline. He saw nothing wrong with that spirit, he said, as long as it was taking me in the right direction. He assured me that he would do his best to help me with that.

I was surprised at Mr Garwood's perception and honesty. I had been anticipating the usual diatribe, but this seemed to me more

presents

BRIGADOON

18,000 miles baby

Since he was one month old he has been on tour with his mother and he has already travelled 18,000 miles. Anthony, now 15 months, has a dressing-table view as his mother, Joanna Duncan, member of the cast of "Brigadoon," makes-up at Plymouth.

Graphic, Monday, August 25, 1952

What the well-travelled baby wore –
on tour with Mum. Note the reins.

Clockwise from top left: Grandmother as a deb; Grandad with batman; Father in character.

Clockwise from top left: Mother as Juliet; as Eliza Doolittle in *Pygmalion*; in a 'luvvie' pose; ever the actress . . .

Opposite, clockwise from top left: Moi; the family; Brighton seafront – my sleep-walking friend; decorating in Putney; a slow learner; time for a haircut. **Right, from top:** Swallows and Amazons; my first non-pc pet – a tortoise; camping – a few years later.

Left, top: Those were the days – the cross-country runner in action. **Left, bottom:** I look like a right bastard. **Below:** An attempt at school rugby – I'm in there somewhere.

Top right: Drainpipes, winkle-pickers and fashion guru – with Mum. **Above:** Looking a little camp at Restaurant Rosemary in Sardinia. **Bottom right:** Before and after my facial surgery – a slight improvement.

Top left: From Brigadier to male model – Grandad. **Above left:** Another ad – I never knew this bird. **Above right:** Grandfather taking a more servile role. **Left:** Proud Grandfather with Herself.

like a father-to-son talk which, of course, was something I had
never experienced. While asking him not to expect miracles, I
promised him I would do my best, and I meant it. I came away from
that meeting shocked, but pleasantly so, and determined to turn
over a new leaf. I was to be saddened when he suddenly left mid-
term. We were never told the full story but his abrupt departure
made our imaginations run riot. His wife was a real doll whom we
lusted after and when another housemaster left at the same time
we put two and two together, and probably made five.

At King's in those days there was a system of fagging. The
younger boys were either school fags or private fags to individual
senior boys or monitors. School fagging meant being on call to take
chairs from A to B, or to collect rubbish from around the grounds.
It was a bore, a waste of time. If you had any sense you wanted to
be a private fag. I should point out that I use the word 'fag' here in
the British, not the American sense, although it must be said that
occasionally it was difficult to tell the difference.

'Fag ownership' was the privilege of the school and house
monitors, who would select their fag from the boys in their
house of less than seven terms' standing. Whether or not Mr
Garwood had had a word in anybody's ear I don't know, but for
whatever reason I was one of the five private fags chosen from the
Grange. My fagmaster was a boy called Nick Scott, a sporty guy,
whose brother Steve was captain of rugby and head of house. The
Scotts were Italian. Steve was short and muscular with classic
Mediterranean good looks: thick, black hair with a large quiff,
broad shoulders, slim hips; a lad who walked with attitude. He was
a sort of Fonz-type character, very cool, and he knew it. Nick, on
the other hand, was tall and slightly awkward-looking, a gangling,
six-foot-two gentle giant with mousy hair and a slender frame. I
was very lucky to have been picked by Nick. He was a great guy,
and he didn't take the piss. Some of the private fags were constantly
called upon by their 'bosses' to make toasted sandwiches, run
errands into town, polish and repolish shoes, but Nick was fair and
civilized. Incidentally, the Scotts had a sister with whom I was later
to work: the famous cook and presenter Valentina Harris. It's a
small world, isn't it?

I did the normal fag's duties for Nick, making his bed, cleaning
his shoes and so on, but I organized a house-duty rota with the
other private fags so that during the afternoons we didn't all have
to be poised to do the monitors' bidding. Instead we would take it

in turns to serve any or all of our five monitors in their study as required.

I was lucky in the house I had been allocated, too. Grange, it seemed, had cultivated a fairly ordered society. I heard from private fags in other houses about some of the things they did that went well beyond the call of duty: warming the loo seats for their fag-masters' use was a favourite. Then there was warming the bed by lying in it before the 'boss' retired for the night. Some fags were made to stay there with him until he'd gone to sleep; others were even asked to perform acts of indecency. None of them ever let on to a teacher. Many of them complied because they hero-worshipped their fagmasters. In a funny sort of way, we all considered ourselves privileged to be working for these senior boys, most of whom were champions in one sport or another.

I can't say I was a natural at any sport, but by dint of sheer application and hard work I was OK-to-good at everything. My build was still very slight, but I was nippy, strong for my size and very tenacious. Although I never achieved much in sport at school, I was in pretty well all the house teams going. I probably did best at water sports, often winning my swimming races, especially in the crawl and the butterfly. I was quite a mean water polo-player, too. I am often credited in the press as having swum the Channel. Well, I have and I haven't. Later, when I was about fifteen or sixteen, I did do a charity Channel swim with the youth club, though I didn't cover the whole distance in one hit. About six of us worked in three-mile stints to cross the water six times over three days, and by the end of this marathon each of us had completed the equivalent of a Channel swim.

Surprisingly, considering my size, I was good at basketball, captaining the house and even making the school team. My strength was in my forward and shooting skills. With my team-mates protecting me, I could shoot from near the halfway mark, popping the ball straight in the net without any rebound. I know it sounds trivial, but I was desperate to achieve, and I knew I didn't have the dedication to be a scholar, even though I was hardly thick. So instead I channelled my energies into sport. I was also desperate for the recognition of my peers.

And then, of course, there was cooking. I whiled away many afternoons experimenting with a couple of gas burners, a saucepan and a frying pan. I spent a good deal of my pocket money on food and loved cooking for my mates. Soon the word got out and

I found myself the hot property in a bidding war between monitors eager to secure my services. I stuck with Nick, although I did manage to push up my rate from £1 10s to £6 a term. There's money in this food lark, I thought to myself.

During my time at King's I was fortunate enough to meet a couple who were to have a major impact on the development of my cooking skills and on my subsequent career. John and Ulla Laing came to Canterbury from London, where John had run the Guinea Grill in Bruton Place in the West End, to open a pub-restaurant at Pett Bottom, five miles outside the city, near Bridge. After the Laings arrived, whenever Mum came to visit me on a Sunday, we had lunch at the Duck Inn.

John was a large, Pickwickian character with ruddy cheeks whose ample girth testified to his enjoyment of food and drink. His wife, Ulla, was a Swede – an incredibly gorgeous Swede, petite, blonde, tiny waist, voluptuous chest. The food at the Duck Inn was magnificent. Ulla produced dishes I had never seen or heard of before: to start with there would be *brandade de morue*, a Provençal dish of salt cod cooked with olive oil, garlic and cream; a great prawn salad made with jumbo prawns, celeriac, apple and mustard mayonnaise; home-pickled, marinated herrings with soured cream, onion and horseradish; a gutsy, tough country pork terrine that knocked spots off the one my mum made in her deli, which Ulla served with spiced oranges or preserved gooseberries; a fish soup that I could only dream about, presented the French way, with rouille, Gruyère cheese and croutons.

The main courses were equally delicious, based mainly on classic French cooking, but on Sundays there was always a great rib of Scotch beef, too, roasted rare and served with tiny French beans, beetroot in a cream sauce, roast tatties and Yorkshires. There was a chicken breast in a velvety white-wine sauce with wild morel mushrooms; a loin of pork with a parsley, prune and breadcrumb stuffing; turbot steaks presented plainly with steamed potatoes and hollandaise sauce. It was at the Duck Inn that I first encountered offal. One of Ulla's dishes was a whole roast calf's kidney in a mustard sauce; another was calf's sweetbreads, meltingly tender, in a cream sauce with baby vegetables. And then there was the best meat of all: a great Scottish sirloin steak, cooked to perfection. She also produced a slightly better version of duck à l'orange than I had so far managed. And hers had the feathers off.

Ulla went to Calais once a week to buy spectacular cheeses from an *affineur*. No other restaurant had cheeses like that. At the same time she stocked up on her Disque Bleu cigarettes and, more than likely, some duty-free booze to bump up the profits in the bar. Her puddings were usually quite simple: a chocolate mousse, fresh strawberries with unpasteurized cream, a thin apple tart liberally doused with Calvados and set alight.

After I got to know the Laings from our regular Sunday lunches, I asked them whether they might let me come and work for them on Sundays after church. This would of course be against the school rules, but as we were pretty well left to our own devices on Sundays, I reckoned it was unlikely that anyone would know where I was going. Ulla was only too pleased by my suggestion. Sundays were her busiest lunchtimes, with the clientele swelled by King's parents. So, most Sundays when my mother wasn't visiting, I cycled out to the Duck Inn, where to start with I was put to work on the washing-up. In the kitchen I would be sampling the leftovers that came back on the plates like a hungry street urchin. It wasn't long before Ulla gave me my chance to help with the starters and within a year I had progressed to assisting with the mains.

During my Sundays at the Duck I witnessed the full array of human emotions in my beautiful Swedish cook: smiles and praise; the screaming abdabs when food was taking too long to prepare; tears when she fell out with her husband, who controlled the restaurant. I learned about Ulla's strengths and I learned from her weaknesses. For the first time I realized that cooking was a passion that demanded dedication. But I was tremendously excited by it. Even seeing both John and Ulla drunk in charge of a bottle didn't put me off. At the Duck I made up my mind that this was the life for me. I wanted to be a chef.

After lunch service I always joined John and Ulla for their Sunday lunch. I felt privileged to be allowed into their own private space, their inner sanctum, and I learned that sitting down at the end of a busy service and enjoying some food and drink was what the cooking life was all about. From food and drink oozed conversation. Communication skills are honed around the table. It's a lovely world, and an even better one when all the customers have left.

The Duck gave me a valuable and eye-opening all-round education in the running of a restaurant. I picked up front-of-house skills from John, a seasoned professional who had the ability to make his customers feel special even if behind the scenes he was cursing like a trooper. Mutterings were the order of the day. 'Table Fourteen are complete morons. They haven't a clue about wine.' 'Why can't Mrs Whigham just bugger off? Can't she see I want my lunch?' 'Yes, Mrs Jones, up your flaming bottom, Mrs Jones!' 'Table Eleven want their steak well done. Throw it in the fryer for all I care. Spit on it. Their taste buds wouldn't have a clue any-way . . .' Out front nobody would have had the faintest idea all this was going on. There everything was sweetness and light.

John also taught me about the finer things in life, especially red wines. I was allowed to sample a different wine every Sunday with my lunch – very French, very educational.

After lunch, feeling wonderfully full and slightly inebriated, I had to get back to school. John would put my bike on the back of his convertible vintage Bentley and return me to Canterbury at break-neck speed, under the influence of a fair bit of the red stuff himself. He would drop me unobtrusively in a side street near the school and I cycled the rest of the way back. Then it was a dash over to the cathedral crypt for Evensong. I was in the choir then, and my fellow choristers usually gave me a fairly wide berth because I would be reeking of garlic from Ulla's *brandade de morue* – delicious, but lethal to the breath.

How I looked forward to my Sundays at the Duck Inn. I was learning so much, and I was in love, just a little, with Ulla but mainly with her beautiful food. Its quality was recognized when she was awarded a coveted Michelin star. I didn't appreciate the sig-nificance of that at the time, but it must have been about the only one in Kent. After that the restaurant was often full of French visitors over for the day just to sample what was a rarity in Britain then: good food. John and Ulla became like a real family to me. And, never having had any children of their own, they treated me like a son.

I was gaining good experience, too, during the holidays in my mum's deli. For the first time in her career I was able to be a genuine help to her, and suddenly, I was transformed from a hindrance in her life into a useful person to have about. I loved cooking, of course, and I enjoyed serving in the shop as well. From being a shy lad, I was starting to develop confidence by talking to the customers and exchanging pleasantries with the regulars.

It was sad and worrying, though, to see my mother looking that little bit more haggard, a little shakier and a little more tense every time I came home. She was always so tired that after the shop closed she would spend the rest of the evening unwinding in the local pub, the Arab Boy, and alcohol, which had for so long been no more than a convivial incidental to her, was fast becoming her best friend. The long hours and responsibilities were ruining her social life, and the former belle of the ball was increasingly ending up drinking with wasters, destroying both her looks and her reputation. Gradually the drinking sessions grew longer and her temper grew shorter, and in the four years she had Never on a Monday she aged twenty years.

So when I was home I tended to do the morning shift, which gave my mother a lie-in after her nightly assignations with the bottle. But at times, when just the two of us were working together, we became a real team. Not that we didn't have our disagreements: I liked to get my own way – my Taurean controlling streak coming to the fore – and she would sometimes arrive to find that I had changed all the shelves around, made new salads or introduced new suppliers.

In the January of her second winter season at the shop, my mum contracted pleurisy, which made it impossible for her to work. She was resigning herself to having to close the shop when I volunteered to stand in. At first it was obvious what she was thinking: a fourteen-year-old boy running the shop? Out of the question. But my determination won the day. So there I was, organizing the housewives who assisted her for pin money, placing orders, setting the café menus and cashing up the tills. It was a real baptism of fire for me, and doubtless something of an experience for everybody involved. That spring term I went back to school a week late pleading tonsillitis. My caretaking role had been much too important for me to worry about school. This was the moment I had waited for all my life: at last I was an essential cog in the wheel of my mum's life; I meant something to her, even if it was in a commercial context.

It didn't stop Mum finding fault with my management of the business when she returned, but I didn't care. I had succeeded in running her café and deli almost single-handed and I was over the moon. That fortnight was a further catalyst in my choice of future career. Mind you, it was fortunate for me that health and safety issues weren't too high on the agenda in those days: I think today's regulators would have taken rather a dim view of a schoolboy manhandling a meat-slicer, wielding very sharp knives and juggling a chip pan.

The benefits of my developing culinary skills were clearly

appreciated at King's, because after I had diligently served my statutory seven terms of fagging for Nick, he asked me whether I would stay on for his final term at the school. This left me in a bit of a quandary. After more than two years of metaphorically tugging my forelock, it was my turn now to be a senior boy; my turn to enjoy a spell of freedom. My allegiance to Nick, however, was strong, and after giving the matter some thought I agreed – though for a consideration: my price was a whopping £10 for the term.

It was traditional for fagmasters to take their boys out for a meal once a term, and for some reason we always went to the Castle Restaurant, a grill house. It was a nice thank you, most appreciated, and it emphasized our privileged role. I would always have a rare T-bone steak with all the trimmings, followed by dreamy chocolate mousse. A blind eye was turned to an accompanying pint of beer or, in my case, a couple of glasses of red wine. Although the others took the piss out of me for not drinking my beer like one of the lads, they were all curious as to where I had developed my wine-quaffing habit. I couldn't possibly tell them about the Duck Inn, so I simply said that my mother had brought me up in the French style, introducing me at an early age to wine by allowing me a small glass mixed with water. There was at least some truth to this story!

When I was fourteen I began to widen my restaurant experience at Borscht 'n' Tears in Beauchamp Place in Knightsbridge, where I worked in my school holidays, sometimes as a kitchen assistant, sometimes as a commis waiter, until I was sixteen. I thought Borscht 'n' Tears was the height of sophistication, a top London restaurant: it was dark and mysterious; it had sexy waitresses, spring onions and soured cream on the tables and live music, and each customer was given a free glass of sherry on arrival. Dead exclusive. In truth Borscht 'n' Tears was very well known and popular in the mid-sixties, and it probably was quite good then, but it never evolved with the times.

My mentor there was Benny Taylor, a larger-than-life personality. Borscht 'n' Tears was a Russian restaurant, and I can't remember whether Benny actually was Russian or whether he just pretended he was, but he did the tables in a Russian sort of way. The chef was a cliché character too: he was certainly foreign and yes, he was fat. I really looked up to him. He could bone a chicken in under a minute, which was deeply impressive – and he could do it fag in mouth, sweat dripping from the hair under his arms and seeping into his white, blood-stained vest. When I look back on it, his kitchen was the pits, as many were in those days. It was home to several unwanted visitors: cockroaches, mice and even the occasional big boy, Ratty. But in those times, before the cleanliness of kitchens meant anything to me, I loved it.

I left Borscht 'n' Tears on the insistence of my mother and grand-mother after Benny had some trouble with the law – I don't recall exactly what, or how serious it was: all I remember is Mum and Gran putting their collective foot down. Instead they arranged some alternative work experience for me at a restaurant called Casse-Croute on Chelsea Green, round the corner from my grand-mother's house. It was a romantic sort of restaurant that lacked the passion of Borscht; much less fun but with much better food. I wasn't allowed to do a great deal in the kitchen – the trust of the French was not easily earned by a diminutive sixteen-year-old from a posh English family – though they looked after me because my gran was a regular customer. But I missed Borscht, where they had taught me butchery, and how to make the perfect chicken Kiev. It's a recipe I still use today, though I have changed the butter filling in the intervening years.

By now, cooking was well and truly in my blood.

CHAPTER NINE

FAGGING WAS A STRANGE CONCEPT. IT DATED BACK, I SUPPOSE, TO THE days when servants were the norm in the families of public schoolboys, and its continuation not only was a tradition but also served as a reminder that we were still members of a privileged class. As my experience of fagging had been reasonably civilized, I had no problem with it. One of the positive elements was the opportunity it gave you to mix with the older boys, because outside the fagging system it was generally frowned upon, even by teachers, to have friends outside your own age group.

I had two or three friends in the year beneath me. Shock horror. One of them, John Lloyd, was in School House, and when it was observed that I often popped over for a chat, John was warned off me by his housemaster, Mr Goddard. It didn't make a blind bit of difference, of course, except that it made our friendship look sinister because we had to conduct it furtively in snatched conversations and secret rendezvous in the Norman Library or near the gym.

The fact that John was quite a pretty boy might have had something to do with Mr Goddard's worries. But he was also highly intelligent – he was a scholar – and creative, with a wicked sense of humour, which was why I liked him so much. John went on to great things, starting *Not the Nine O'Clock News*, *Blackadder* and various other cutting-edge comedy programmes. Our friendship continued regardless of the attempts to discourage it. I once stayed with him for a few days in the school holidays, during which we took in a performance of *Hair* and he was forced to go and watch my football team, Tottenham Hotspur.

Then there were Barlow and Barratt, an apparently inseparable pair a year or two younger than me. I remember trying to get them fit by taking them on early-morning cross-country runs. I was even called in for a meeting with my housemaster, Mr Boorman – who'd replaced my nice Mr Garwood – over this friendship. He wanted to know what was going on. I was so enraged that I hit back with sarcasm. 'Well, sir,' I said, 'it's like this: I'm in love. I can't help myself. And Barlow and Barratt are in love with me. But don't worry, sir, none of, you know, that, goes on.'

'What do you mean, Worrall Thompson?'

'You know, sir. Penetrations. We just all sleep together. But there's no tongues, just boyish fun.'

His face reddened with embarrassment. 'This is very serious,' he stammered.

'Oh no, you believe me!' I gasped with simulated horror. 'Relax, I was just joking. We're all just good mates and, as it happens, I resent your suggestion that anything else is going on.'

He wasn't amused.

'Out!' he shouted. 'Come and see me at six o'clock this evening. I need time to consider what action to take.'

Oh shit, I thought to myself. My big mouth has got me into trouble again. Why don't any of these teachers have a sense of humour?

By 6 pm Mr Boorman had decided to beat me for being rude and showing a lack of respect. I bet that decision took a lot of thought.

'Why is it, sir,' I asked him, 'that we can't choose our own friends? Why can't you understand the principle of friendship? Age differences shouldn't come into it.'

'Younger friendships are not encouraged,' he replied, 'but that is beside the point. That's not why I'm beating you. I'm beating you because you were disrespectful.'

'Tickle my arse with a feather,' I muttered. It was an in-joke at the time.

'What did you say?' he boomed, not believing his ears.

'Particularly nasty weather,' I replied.

'Can't you ever take life seriously, Worrall Thompson?' he sighed.

'Why should I? Life should be fun. Nothing is worth taking too seriously. I'm happy. I'm always happy.'

'Well, let's see how happy you are after a beating,' he replied.

'If you knew what I went through at Junior King's, sir, you'd realize that what you're about to give me will be a walk in the park,' I told him. It was, too. Four pathetic lashes with an ordinary cane were neither here nor there to me – especially as I had taken the precaution of putting on a couple of extra pairs of Y-fronts. If I had shown him the Rev Edmonds's twisted willow cane, he would have understood how fruitless his punishment had been.

Beatings were not that regular at King's, but I got another for being out on the town with Barlow after the school gates were locked. Normally we bribed the gatekeeper to let us in and out after dark, so what happened that night I don't know. What I do know is that it was only me who suffered. My crime was 'leading youngsters astray'. Perhaps the concerns of those in authority were motivated by the fact that Stephen Barlow, like John Lloyd, was a creative genius, in his case in music. He had a beautiful voice and was a dab hand with anything that made a pleasant noise. He went on not only to become a brilliant conductor but also to marry the actress Joanna Lumley, *Ab Fab*'s Patsy, every mature man's fantasy lover. What a great couple they make.

At least those punishments were for things I actually did, even if I didn't see anything wrong with them. One beating I took was for an offence of which I was totally innocent. After the tell-tale out-line of a packet of cigarettes was clearly seen through my games bag, I was given six strokes, one for each of the cigarettes found to be missing from the box. I didn't smoke; having been given the job of lighting up my mother's ciggies as a child, I hated smoking. These weren't my cigarettes and I was not guilty. It was like going to the electric chair for a crime you hadn't committed. I fought back, screaming my innocence, and had to be held down by a monitor. Between each stroke I protested, promising revenge. For days after this miscarriage of justice, I sulked and worked to rule, refusing to be pleasant to anyone in authority.

I knew who had put the cigarettes in my bag: a brute of a lad called Charles Short, who wasn't. He might have been my age but he towered over me. He was built like a classic back-row forward, and constantly picked on me. Fights were continually breaking out between us, but I would not allow him to get the better of me. I confess that, due to the disparity in our sizes, I was forced to resort to underhand tactics: grabbing him by the balls and squeezing, gouging at his eyes, biting his hands or fingers or scratching his face. For my pains I suffered a broken nose – for the second time – and severe bruising from his club-like fists. Nick Scott tried to protect me, but unfortunately, as Short's elder brother was a monitor, his colleagues had a tendency to turn a blind eye to our fights.

When one of the house monitors suggested that I channelled my aggression into a legitimate form of fighting, I took up boxing. The training was boring but the competitive boxing was satisfying. At that time, no protection was provided for young amateur fighters: no headgear, no box to protect the wedding tackle and no bandaging of the hands. You went into the ring for three three-minute rounds, during which you either beat the shit out of your opponent or had the shit beaten out of you. I progressed well in the school competition and fought through to the final, although my method owed more to streetfighting than to the Marquess of Queensberry. For the most part I was a good ducker and weaver, and while my punches were accurate, they were more like clubs than direct bullets.

In the final I found myself up against an old friend from junior school, a day boy named Christopher Collins. He had always been brilliant at sports, and I knew this was going to be a very tricky fight. From the start Collins showed cold, clinical efficiency, picking me off easily with his longer reach and height advantage. I felt inhibited because he was a friend, and as a result my performance lacked the killer punch. I knew it was all over when I heard the crunch of brittle bones – mine – succumbing to a straight right-hander. Blood was pouring from my shattered nose. Break number three. But I wouldn't give up. I accepted a cold compress between the second and third rounds and carried on. Still the punches rained in. Collins couldn't ease up because by this time there was no stopping me. I was like a mini-bulldozer, relentlessly driving on. I lost, of course. Collins's skills were far superior to mine. But he was graceful in victory, in every way the gentleman. He told everyone that he'd been in a real fight.

That night I thought I would die. My whole skull throbbed. It was bruised, it was swollen – I had never known anything like it. Never again, I told myself. As things turned out, the decision was made for me. After that competition there was no more boxing at the school. It was felt that it was too dangerous.

It was around this time, when I was about fifteen, that, reading the local paper one day, I stumbled across a review of *Murder in the Cathedral* which was being performed in the cathedral itself. The headline was: 'SPELLBINDING PERFORMANCE BY MICHAEL INGHAM'.

When I saw that name my stomach lurched: it was my father's stage name. So, after all this time, there he was, performing less than 200 yards from where I was living. The play had one more night to run. Straight away I phoned the booking office to see whether I could speak to him. I was told he wasn't there, but that he would be back later for the last show. So I left a message for him, telling him where I was and asking him to come and see me.

A few days later I received a letter with a Herne Bay postmark. It was from my father. He said he was sorry and all that, but he felt too guilty to visit me in Canterbury. I couldn't believe what I was reading. If he felt bad about not paying my mother maintenance, or never having seen me, then surely this was the perfect opportunity to make amends? Two hundred yards away and he couldn't be bothered. I later discovered that in fact he could easily have come to see me at any time if he had chosen to: unbeknown to me he had already been living in nearby Herne Bay for a couple of years. I hadn't seen him since I was three, and I felt cheated.

But life went on, of course. School was hard, but I made it fun for myself and, in the process, no doubt hell for those in authority. There was my cooking for the boys and at the Duck Inn; I tried my hand at drama, not particularly successfully given my thespian roots. I couldn't get my head round Shakespearean language, and as for other languages, French and German were definitely my weakest subjects. Molière, Camus and Goethe were not for me. My favourites were economics and politics, rather unusually for someone who wanted to be a chef.

In those days Harold Wilson and Anthony Wedgwood Benn were my political heroes. Perhaps my socialist leanings were a two-fingered salute to my family traditions. I may have been hooked by Peter Sellers in the movie *I'm All Right Jack*, or maybe it was Hugh Gaitskell, the Labour leader whose life was tragically terminated before he came to power. I was a bit of a fan of his. I liked real, earthy characters, which were hardly thick on the ground in the Tory Party. Barbara Castle, the flame-haired Labour temptress who wasn't scared of anyone, beat the wimpish Sir Alec Douglas-Home and Harold Macmillan hands down. You only needed to say boo to them, it seemed, and they would take offence. Theirs was a pampered life of 'please wipe my bottom, nanny', a legacy of the Victorian and Edwardian upper classes. Mine was a world of ideals, devoid of practicality. Give me a strike, a political disruption, some action. 'Go for it, my son' could have been my motto.

My socialist values remained with me until Edward Heath's disastrous government of the early 1970s. Yes, I know that was a Conservative administration, but the disastrous bit was the three-day week, which I blamed on the miners. I hated missing my favourite TV programmes because of the power cuts, and now I wanted to crush the unions. I needed a political fairy godmother, and along she came in the shape of Maggie Thatcher. Besides, the Labour Party after Wilson was not the force it had been. It was becoming weak and ineffectual. Callaghan, Foot, even Kinnock, what planet were they on? It certainly wasn't this one.

So I became a Tory. The Liberals were not an option, although I did think Jo Grimond was a gent. Then along came Jeremy Thorpe, and all the baggage he kept in his closet. No way, José. Politics was exciting in those days. Parliament was made up of true individuals who had a say. Today we are left with a faceless house full of 'yes' people and a megalomaniac prime minister who wants to rule the world. Tony Blair clearly admired Margaret Thatcher, though his politics are more those of Benjamin Disraeli, apart from the fact that Blair's empire-building fantasies will always remain unfulfilled. What Parliament needs is powerful politicians, politicians prepared to be orators, politicians of standing, politicians of character.

And now? Well, today I'm a lost soul. I want to be a Tory, but I'm painfully aware that the party is out of touch with the real world, with real people. New Labour is Old Tory, there isn't yet a New Tory and as for Charles Kennedy, he's a nice boy, but it's easy to be nice when you know you haven't a cat in hell's chance of being elected. He can formulate all the idealistic policies he wants, safe in the knowledge that they will never come to fruition. The way things are going, I can see the gap being filled by a Popstars-cum-Big Brother television programme in which the viewers are asked to create a new political party.

But I digress. At King's, probably my best friend was a guy called Stuart Warren-Stone. When I left, his was the friendship I retained. He was in the year below me, so that was another friendship condemned by one and all. I once spent a whole summer holiday with Stuart in Dublin, where his father was a director of Watney's brewery. It was one of the best holidays ever. We hitch-hiked around southern Ireland, camping, mainly, drinking ourselves silly on pints of Guinness or Beamish and finding weird and wonderful Irish barn dances where all the girls would be lined up on one side of the barn and all the boys on the other. Eventually one of us – and it wasn't me – would pluck up the courage to ask one of the girls for a dance. They all loved the gorgeous Stuart. Me? I was cripplingly insecure. I'd pretend that I wasn't feeling well or that I'd hurt my ankle until eventually, some girl with National Health glasses and pigtails would take pity on me and I'd be forced to dance and to act as if I liked her.

For a time Stuart's parents were like second parents to me, especially his mother, who was a dream. I was really pleased when they moved to England, into a house near Ascot. I was always round for the weekend and later, after I left school, Stuart and I would often go on pub crawls in Windsor or London. The girls were on to Stuart like bees round a honeypot. He did his best to introduce me to his cast-offs, but at that stage in my life I was a hopeless case as far as girls were concerned.

You may think it was hardly surprising I was insecure after the strange upbringing I'd had, and I'm sure the psychiatric profession would have plenty to say on the matter. But neither my rather unusual childhood nor the fact that, like many only children, I had always been a fairly shy lad was the main cause of my difficulties. It was not something hidden away in the recesses of my psyche but a problem that could be seen by everyone I met: a horrible injury to my face.

In my school holidays I used to play rugby for some of the kids' sides at various London clubs. I turned out for one of them – Merton, London Irish, Streatham and Croydon, I don't remember which, as I played for all of them at one time or another, as well as for a youth club in Putney – one morning during the Christmas break when I was sixteen.

It was a cold day and the ground was quite hard. I was playing either wing forward or hooker. In the opposing team was a redhead – freckles, translucent skin, kind of awkward-looking, probably a couple of stone heavier than me – who needled me throughout the game. Eventually I decided it was time to show him I'd had enough. As he powered towards me, intent on scoring, I raised a straight arm which he happened to run into, neck-first. He was dead meat, poleaxed, flat on his back. Satisfaction was mine. Hiding my smug grin, I asked him solicitously whether he was OK, affecting a brotherly concern. At first he couldn't answer me, my straight-arm tackle having dented his windpipe as well as his pride. When he got his breath back a tirade of streetwise Sarf London abuse tumbled from his mouth, 'It was just an accident,' I told him innocently.

'Oh, yeah,' he retorted. 'Don't worry, I'll 'ave you. Just you wait.'

'Oh, I'm shaking! I'm really scared!' I yelled as I ran off to join my team-mates.

Later in the game, when I was at the bottom of a loose scrum, I felt three or four boots in my face. I'd taken so many over the years that I didn't think anything of it until the bodies peeled off me and I looked up to be greeted by a host of shocked expressions. I will never forget those terrified faces. It was as if the other players had discovered something from outer space in the scrum. I tried to say 'What?' but my mouth wouldn't work. I was so cold that I was in no pain, but when I put my hand to my face all my bravado deserted me. I could feel blood. Someone threw a blanket round me and helped me to my feet, and I was put into a car and taken to the hospital.

There I was mopped down by proficient nurses before being seen by the duty doctor. He had just started his shift after playing a game of rugby himself, so he was very sympathetic. He gave me some painkillers and sent me off for an X-ray, which revealed fractures to the nose (again), the lower jaw and the upper jaw (breaking that was quite an achievement, as it is a fixed part of the skull), and a crushed orbit or eye socket. This last injury was the one that had so scared my fellow rugby players, because my eye had slipped out of its normal position.

I was patched up in theatre. It's amazing what they can do: they gave me a plastic eye orbit and wired up my jaw. They couldn't do anything about my nose because of the other injuries, hence the rather novel nose I've been left with. It would be further modified anyway, as I was to break it seven times in total. I've often thought of having it rebuilt, but in a funny kind of way, my nose is me, and I'd feel lost without it. It earned me an affectionate nickname at school, 'Smudge', which stuck for many years.

I was kept in hospital for six days. The day after my operation the consultant who had been brought in to perform it came to see me. He explained that because the bones were still growing he'd been able to do no more than running repairs. My cheeks would look quite concave and the bite of my teeth was going to be out of sync. I had had slightly protruding lower teeth to start with, but now they were awful. Funnily enough, I didn't lose any in the skirmish. The consultant told me that when my bones had developed fully I could have more surgery to improve matters, but they wouldn't be able to operate any more until I was twenty-one. Almost five years like this! It was unthinkable.

When the swelling had eventually subsided I sneaked a look in the mirror. The person staring back bore very little resemblance to me. I was appalled. I didn't go quite as far as insisting that my mother removed all mirrors from the house, but I only ever went near one when I wanted to scare myself. I could see a future auditioning for Punch and Judy on the Brighton seafront or, with a prop hump, for *The Phantom of the Opera*.

No prizes, then, for diagnosing the cause of my complete lack of confidence. Having to wait nearly five years for an operation like that would be bad enough at any time, but for it to happen at such a formative stage of my life was a crushing blow. The years from sixteen to twenty-one are so crucial, especially as far as caring what the opposite sex thinks of you is concerned, and I spent them all totally incapable of even looking at a girl, let alone talking to one. If a girl ever came over to chat to me, it could only be because she felt sorry for me. I would think, 'Patronizing bitch!', make an excuse and hurry off. So while all my mates were out on the pull, losing their virginity and generally enjoying themselves, I was restricted to spying on beautiful females from afar, quickly averting my eyes whenever I was spotted gawping. To outside observers, I must have seemed like a right lecher.

You would have thought that my injury would have put me off the beautifully aggressive game of rugby, but not a bit of it. Now that I had no looks to lose, I became even more of a scrapper. We were always taught that if you went into a tackle like a wimp you'd end up hurt, whereas if you tackled like a man you'd be safe and sound. I'm not sure that philosophy holds true every time, but in broad terms it seemed to work. It wasn't as if there were any budding Jonah Lomus at my school. So tackling became my game. Kicking or punting, however, was not my forte, and it was while I was trying to kick for touch one day that I was dealt my next body blow. As I released the ball and simultaneously took aim with my right leg, confident that the ball was where I believed it to be, for some reason I ended up directing a splendid kick at thin air, and my right leg appeared to come loose at the hinges. For one awful moment I thought it was my leg I could see flying towards the touchline instead of the ball. As it turned out, it was my boot, happily by now detached from my foot, but the horrendous click I heard as I fell flat on my back was less reassuring. As I lay there I watched my leg ballooning as if someone was pumping helium gas into the knee. Once again I was stretchered off the field, this time into the school sanatorium and on to the Casualty Department at the Kent and Canterbury Hospital. When an X-ray revealed nothing untoward, they just bandaged me up to await the consultant. He wasn't much more definite. 'Water on the knee,' he pronounced. 'It'll get better.' Well, it did and it didn't. It would be perfectly OK for a while but then suddenly, during a match, the knee would just go, with no warning, reducing me to a useless heap of jelly. I tried knee supports, ice baths, bags of frozen peas, you name it, but the problem would go away for a time only to re-surface with increasing frequency.

Eventually, my grandmother decided that I should have the knee seen to privately, and sure enough, it was discovered that I had torn a cartilage and there was a fragment of bone floating around in the water on the knee. I was booked in for surgery at Queen Mary's Hospital in Roehampton during the school holidays. In those days cartilage operations were quite a big deal. I had read of footballers being out of action in plaster or heavy bandages for six weeks after this kind of surgery. Queen Mary's was famous for its prosthetic limb factory, which I remember thinking would come in handy if things went wrong.

After I awoke from the op, I couldn't believe the pain. To make matters worse, I came round to find myself gazing into the face of my mother. How uncool was that? At my age it should have been the adoring face of one of my many girlfriends, or failing that, some beautiful nurse. But at least my mother had come, bearing the obligatory basket of fruit and chrysanthemums. 'Darling! Are you all right?' she asked anxiously. I looked around, worried that some-one might have overheard this eighteen-year-old being thus addressed by his outwardly doting mother. To my relief, nobody seemed to have noticed.

'No,' I replied. 'I'm in absolute agony. What have they done, removed the leg?'

'I'm sure you'll be fine,' she said, tidying up my side table. What would you know, I thought to myself. You're not the one lying here with a hole in your leg, bursting to go to the loo and unable to do anything about it.

'I need to go to the loo,' I told her.

'I'll get you a nurse,' she replied. A young nurse appeared, bed-pan in one hand, piss bottle in the other. 'Which is it to be?' she inquired.

'You're having a laugh, aren't you?' I said.

'Well, it's up to you. I can't decide for you.'

'Neither,' I said. 'Help me to the loo, could you? I'm not using either of those.' Well, have you ever tried sitting on one of those horseshoe-shaped things? They're lethal. And I couldn't even bend one of my legs.

'You're not allowed out of bed yet,' the nurse said.

'Want to bet?' I managed to manoeuvre myself to the side of the bed.

'Do as you're told,' Mother hissed.

'Time for you to go,' I hissed back. 'And by the way, I'm not ten years old.'

Seeing that I meant business, the nurse helped me to swing one of my arms around her shoulders and shuffled me towards the loo. I heard muffled laughter coming from the ward. It wasn't until later that I discovered what had amused the other patients. I was still wearing my operating gown and as I made my way out of the ward my very white arse was on public display. But at the time I had only one thing on my mind.

'Need a hand?' asked the nurse.

'On your bike, Nurse, I'm more than capable, thanks.' I didn't realize that she was being sarcastic. As it turned out, after completing my ablutions, I found I couldn't get myself off the seat. I was left there until the nurse thought I had done enough penance for being so cheeky.

I got my own back. A couple of beds away from me was a guy who was a drummer for the singer Cat Stevens. He had a broken leg, and we had got talking and become friends in the way you do in hospital. One evening Cat Stevens came to visit him and found us sitting in our wheelchairs in the TV lounge. He suggested that we all went off to the pub.

'We can't do that!' I exclaimed in my innocence.

'Oh, don't be a wanker,' he said, or words to that effect. So we quietly wheeled ourselves out of the French windows and headed towards the main entrance. St Mary's is not a difficult hospital to get around. Presumably because it caters for those with missing limbs, it is laid out on one floor with no stairs. In fact, it is like a racetrack for wheelchairs.

'How do we get past the gatekeeper?' I asked. We looked a bit suspicious in our pyjamas and dressing gowns. Cat, or, as I was addressing him, Mr Stevens, said that he would distract the security man while we sneaked past. It worked like a dream, and off we bombed to the Earl Spencer in Roehampton, where we remained until a couple of nurses came in after their shift. We were having such a laugh that we'd completely forgotten we were in our night-clothes. Nobody seemed to mind. I guess they were more interested in the fact that Cat Stevens, who was at the peak of his career then, was in their pub.

The nurses, however, immediately rumbled us. They feigned shock and pretended to tell us off, but in truth they were just as impressed as the pub regulars by our famous companion and ended up sitting down and having a drink with us. At closing time they helped to wheel us back up the hill, though they refused to push us back into the hospital for fear of getting into trouble themselves. The main door was closed so we went in via the Casualty Department. Back on the ward we were given some dressing-down by the night sister, who couldn't have cared less if we'd been out with the Queen and the Duke of Edinburgh. The next day we were also disciplined for good measure by the hospital matron and administrator. But nobody minds a good telling-off in a worthwhile cause.

Queen Mary's Hospital was to become a bit of a home from home for me, because it was here that I would live for twelve weeks when I finally had my face-rebuilding operation, and before that it was the venue for the removal of my wisdom teeth, which had to be taken out to enable me to have that surgery.

My public-school career had now drawn to a close, and my rebellious streak showed itself right to the end. I played my final trick on my last night at King's, in the summer of 1969 – the night before all the parents came to collect their little or big Johnnies and to take tea with the headmaster on Green Court, a large patch of lawn in the centre of the school.

At about 2 am about five of us crept out of bed to execute our prearranged prank. We went over to the school dining room, posting one of our number to keep an eye out for the nightwatchman, removed every single dinner plate, side plate, cup, saucer and sugar bowl and put the lot upside-down on the Green Court grass. This magnificent work of art was garnished with saucepans (cutlery escaped our attention as we thought that would be just a little too mean). Can you imagine the look on the faces of those who found it the next day? Over 3,000 pieces scattered over a massive area.

Nothing was mentioned during the headmaster's speech, but a couple of teachers quizzed me afterwards.

'You had something to do with this, Worrall Thompson, didn't you?'

'With what?'

'You know perfectly well what I mean. The plates on the Green Court.'

'I don't know what you're talking about. Why would I want to ruin my impeccable school career for the sake of a prank? Anyway, thank you, sir, for everything you've done for me. I've had a ball.' And with that, and a cheeky grin, I turned on my heels.

I had survived ten years of King's and Junior King's and I hardly regretted a moment of it, in spite of its less enjoyable elements. I had served my grandmother's sentence and now my schooling was complete. I hadn't shone at anything in particular, but thanks to her, I had had an excellent education. Now it was time to try life as an adult.

CHAPTER TEN

BEFORE KNUCKLING DOWN TO REAL LIFE, I FOLLOWED THE WELL-trodden gap-year path of backpacking around India. For me, though, the continent had a special significance. As my mother's birthplace and the home of my grandparents for thirty-eight years, it held many of my family's secrets, and I was looking for connections. I returned from this *Heat and Dust* experience to the more mundane world of present-day family relationships. I had seen many guys come into Mum's life and disappear just as quickly. Apparently I was the reason they didn't hang around. I couldn't understand it. Me? I was a harmless young lad, if a bit chippy in my late teens because of the face factor. But I was giving them such a rough ride it was not surprising that they didn't last the course. They would try their hardest to win me over, but by this time I was acting like a jealous husband or a father vetting his daughter's boyfriends, except that in this case the woman in question was my mother. The bottom line was that I didn't want these men around. Mum was the only woman in my life then, and I didn't want any competition.

This was not, of course, a healthy situation, and it got worse before it got better. Not only was I playing the possessive husband or father to other people, I was even rowing with her like one. When we argued she was theatrical, dramatic and could turn on the tears like a tap. Out would come her whole armoury of hurtful barbs.

'I never wanted to have you in the first place. You were a mistake. You've made my life hell from the moment you were born.'

My responses were equally poisonous.

'You might as well not have bothered because you've been a shit mother. You're a selfish person. Life's all about you: you and your career, you and your pathetic men. You've never had time for me!'

Confrontations like this were regular and repetitive during my late teens. I know what I said was cruel and that I shouldn't have said it, but as a hot-headed youth I couldn't help myself. I had a wicked tongue, and it was to get me into serious trouble over the next few years. I know, too, that I shouldn't have interfered with my mother's love life. But I had standards for a potential stepfather, and none of her men met my demands. And so as one man exited stage left, another would appear, only to face a hard time from me. She had it rough, and it was partly my fault. Sorry, Mum.

By the time I left school, my mother had sold her deli café and returned to estate agency. It was the best decision she could have made. This time she had what her Putney colleagues considered to be the hare-brained idea of setting up business in Battersea. In those days, Battersea, Wandsworth, Clapham and Clapham Junction were very downmarket parts of south-west London, but she became one of the first estate agents to make the Shaftesbury Estate fashionable. When other estate agents started to flock to the area, which became known as South Chelsea, they dubbed my mum the Queen of Battersea. So, despite her financial, personal and alcohol problems, once again she bounced back. She was a good estate agent and she enjoyed dealing with her clients. We moved, too: she bought us a great house just off Clapham Common, a three-storey terrace in Altenburg Gardens. We'd outgrown the Putney cottage, so this was perfect; what was more, with Clapham yet to become popular with middle-class house-buyers, the new place cost less than the £7,500 she had sold Putney for.

Although Mum was much happier, she carried on drinking and I carried on lecturing her. In the street behind us was a wine bar called Just William's, which became her hang-out during and after work, and next door to that was an excellent restaurant, Pollyanna's, which became mine.

I was in no doubt as to what I wanted to do on leaving King's: I was determined to become a chef, and that was that. There was, however, a sizeable obstacle to be overcome in the shape of my grandmother's continuing opposition to the idea. 'That's no job for a gentleman, darling,' she would say. Looking back, I can see why she was so horrified. In 1969, with the exception of a certain Mr

Trompetto at the Savoy Hotel, well-known cooks were as rare as hen's teeth. Chefs crept in by the back door, changed into whites, checks and toques, did their job, sweating a lot, and then changed back into their civvies without washing and sneaked back out into the night air smelling like the local chippy. And the hours were exhausting. There were no shifts then: you worked from 9 am to 2.30 pm, and from 6 pm until you finished for the night. It was considered a downmarket profession usually confined to 'foreigners'; not a very British kind of thing to do for a living.

So our horns were locked.

'I didn't pay for you to be educated at a top public school for you to become a chef,' Gran would insist.

'Oh, come on, Gran. It's my love. Please let me.'

'Enough. I don't wish to talk about it any more. You cannot train to be a chef.'

Eventually a compromise was reached. It was decided that I should study hotel and catering management at that dinosaur of catering colleges, Westminster, an establishment with a classy reputation. I was lucky to get a place as, with all the toing and froing over the matter, I left it very late to apply. My mum had to pull a few strings with a boyfriend of hers, an executive with J. Lyons called Charles, who apparently ran a couple of upmarket cafés for the group (one, I remember, was the Contented Sole in Knightsbridge). Charles was very useful to me and to my catering education and, unlike most of her other boyfriends, he seemed to have staying power. So I became one of the first students to take the new HND (higher national diploma) in hotel management. I didn't want to be a hotel manager of course – most of them reminded me of smart penguins, and were far too 'yes, ma'am, no ma'am' for my liking – but this was the deal I had struck with my grandmother and it had to be honoured.

It didn't take me long to get into the swing of things. Our course was split into two groups, and I got the good one. Or perhaps it would be more accurate to call it the bad one. The very bad one, in fact. For some reason – and it can't have had anything to do with me, can it? – we were incredibly badly behaved, while the other set was a dream crew: normal, hard-working and sensible. I immediately fell in with a few of the guys in my group, a marvellous South African called Wayne Morris, Brian Murphy and Laurence Court. Wayne loved his drink, loved to entertain and appeared to have plenty of money – he rented some amazing house in north London.

He was a real bon viveur with a big gut (and before you start thinking that is the pot calling the kettle black, I should add that I was still quite a lightweight then). Wayne, who was to become my cookery partner, seemed very grown up to me, but as he invited me to some of his excellent dinner parties I considered him a mate. However, I'm sure he thought me extremely immature. And if he did, he was right.

I don't know what it was about me, but I couldn't resist playing the prankster. Perhaps it was something to do with my lack of experience with the opposite sex, because relationships with girls do encourage young men to grow up a bit. Not that I would have owned up to my innocence among my new mates. The chances of enlightenment at college were slim. Apart from the problem of my non-existent confidence, there were only three girls on our course, all of whom were quickly spoken for.

My co-troublemakers were Brian and Laurence, two equally diminutive students. Brian was outrageous, a great wit. I still regret losing touch with him after college. He had me in permanent stitches. He pretended to be dumb, the class idiot, and perhaps he was, but if so it didn't matter. He was a chum with charm who loved the ladies and, immediately seeing through my posturing bravado, he always did his best to set me up with girls. Funnily enough, there were one or two who showed an interest, but when they did my pathetic lack of self-assurance invariably shot me in the foot. I would come up with the most ridiculous excuses as to why I couldn't go out on a date, and eventually they would give up on me. Some of them, however, did become friends.

Brian, Laurence and I worked together in the evenings after college on the banqueting circuit. We needed the money to finance our drinking habits at the Duke of Clarence, the college local, and also to run my motor. I had passed my driving test at seventeen in Canterbury, and for my eighteenth birthday Mum had raided the piggy bank to buy me my first car, a Minivan. I instantly became a boy racer, customizing the van with wide wheels, tiny leather steering wheel, bank of fog-lights, go-faster black-and-white-chequered stripes down the side. I thought it was fabulous, and even if it didn't quite pull the birds, it made me a lot of friends, as few of my contemporaries had their own cars.

We worked like beasts on the banqueting circuit, picking up four to five jobs a week at the Hilton, the Dorchester or, if we were desperate, the Charing Cross or Park Lane hotels, which didn't pay as much and whose standards were not nearly as good. We got to know which were the right functions to do, but to start with we were competing with old banqueting warhorses, professionals who did their best to make life hell for any newcomers. There were quite a few old grumps like the two old hecklers who sat in the gallery in *The Muppet Show*. To them it was just a job. You arrived at six and left at nine-thirty after the pudding had been served. To us it was experience, an exciting evening job that more than covered our monetary needs for the week. I think we were paid £3.50 per shift when we started, rising to a fiver after a year.

It was a cut-throat business. First of all you had to invest in tails, waistcoat, wing collar and bow tie, and then you had to schmooze the Italian banqueting head waiters to convince them that a couple of young whippersnappers could do the job. In those days it was silver service, and you had your own table of ten or twelve to look after. So you had to be good. Well, perhaps good is not quite the right word, but fast, certainly. More often than not the starter would be soup, so down went the plates and then you had to rush back to the huge kitchens and queue for the silver tureens. Serving soup from a tureen can be a messy business. It wasn't so bad if you dripped it on the guys as they never felt a thing through their black jackets, but all hell broke loose if you spilled boiling-hot blobs of mulligatawny on the delicate bare backs of the ladies.

Some of the customers were complete shits. Those dinners were always tight on space – at the Hilton there were often sittings of over 1,000 – and the guests, chatting away, would totally ignore you as you tried to come in over their left shoulder.

'Excuse me, sir.' Firmly but gently at first. You raised your voice a little with each request then finally you would deliberately bash them on the back of the head with a plate or the soup tureen. 'Oops, sorry, sir.' But in your head you'd be thinking, move out the fucking way, you arsehole. Such was the language of the Italian waiter mafia. You soon learned from them that banqueting was no graceful art. It was more like dog-eat-dog.

If a particular warhorse of a waiter made things difficult for us, Brian and I would gang up on him to retaliate. There was the accidental trip to send his plates flying, or leftovers on returned plates somehow finding their way on to his back. If he was dealing with a service of ten steaks, one of them might mysteriously disappear, and then there would be hell to pay when he went back to the kitchens for the extra serving. In this hostile atmosphere we developed and honed our skills, ending up as the fastest banqueting waiters on the circuit. The secret was rising to the challenge of clearing twelve main-course plates and twelve side plates in one hit, because if you couldn't do that you would have to make two journeys to the kitchen, which would put you back in the queue of waiters.

What we all aimed for was to be promoted to wine waiter. They worked longer hours, but they made far more money. Not surprisingly, they were possessive of their jobs. What an eye-opener it was to watch them operate. The scams they got up to were amazing. At the reception before dinner, gin and tonic was the drink of the day, with perhaps the occasional Scotch or gin and bitter lemon for the ladies. Champagne was out of vogue, or at least out of the price range of many people, and vodka hadn't yet become a trend. Rows and rows of 6oz wine glasses would be lined up to await the customers. I once had to stand in for someone on the bar and almost started a riot. I couldn't understand what I was doing wrong. I was pouring proper shots of gin and half-filling the glass with tonic, always Schweppes, and then topping up the tonic when the waiters were ready to take the tray. What could be more efficient than that? Yet I was hastily moved to stacking dirties. The problem, I discovered, was that I was being far too cavalier with the booze. The seasoned 'professionals' would merely rub the rim of the glass with gin before adding the tonic. The customers never complained because the first taste that hit their palate would be the gin. In fact, people would often ask for a top-up of tonic because the drink was too strong!

The wine waiters would have a good half-dozen bottle-sized pockets sewn into their tails. These were for the surplus wine. At most of these functions the ticket just covered pre-dinner drinks and dinner and the wine would be paid for separately at the end of the evening. Often the host of a table would ask the waiter to make sure he kept it flowing through the meal, so when he came to settle the bill he wouldn't have a clue how many bottles had actually been consumed. The wine waiter would therefore stick two or three extras on the bill and snaffle them himself. The same went for after-dinner brandy or whisky, especially if the customer ordered it by the glass. Often the guests would be carrying rolls of notes – credit cards hadn't yet arrived and cheques were not an option at these dos – and, especially at functions such as boxing evenings, these guys would buy whole bottles of brandy to be put on the table after coffee, together with clutches of monster cigars. Sometimes most of the bottle remained untouched, cigars went missing and the bill was topped up. It was a very lucrative business. I, of course, would never have dreamed of ripping off my customers. Seriously, I was content with the big fat tip you got at the end of the night, and I built up a good relationship with the boxing fraternity, most of whom were regulars. They nicknamed me Son of Jimmy Hill because of my unfortunate facial shape. At first I took offence, but I soon realized that it was meant affectionately and accepted it in the same spirit. On one occasion I found myself actually serving Jimmy Hill. Everyone was ribbing him about having this illegitimate son – me – and he took the joke in the same good humour.

After pudding service we would all troop off into the night and either go home to sleep or head off to the bars and clubs around Park Lane to spend our hard-earned wages. I made enough to maintain a ridiculous wardrobe furnished by the hippy Carnaby Street hang-outs. From 1966 through to my college days I was obsessed by clothes – mind you, they were never the kind that suited me. The existence of a catering-management student was not conducive to long hair or beads, and yet I wanted all that; I loved the flowery shirts, and I wore a daft full-length Afghan coat, complete with full flower design and the famous foul smell in wet weather. Nothing was too outrageous. I suppose I should thank my lucky stars that punk chic still lay some years in the future. The only elements of the hippy culture I couldn't get my head round were the sex and the drugs. The sex was only temporarily off the menu, but I never got the hang of drugs. I tried hash but it didn't like me. I would collapse, the legs would go, then the head, then the stomach, and it was throw-up time. Why, I have no idea, and it was very frustrating when everyone else seemed to enjoy it on a regular basis. The way I dressed gave everyone the impression that I was into free love and flying high. If only I had been.

Another piece of window-dressing demanded by this swinging lifestyle was a bachelor pad, and when I was nineteen Brian Murphy and I moved into bedsits, which we rented from a sweet old lady for £3 a week. This was not the bold bid for freedom it might sound, because the house was in Altenburg Gardens, Clapham Common – right next door to my mother's, in fact. And as a severance of the apron strings it was hardly a roaring success, because I rarely slept there. I didn't have any girlfriends I needed to entertain privately, and I much preferred my own double bed next door to the single one in my bedsit. And then there were the creature comforts such as my mum doing my washing, my mum's booze cabinet and telly, not to mention the fact that the little old lady didn't appreciate loud music, joss sticks or tenants who stayed up late.

My off-duty image, then, was in stark contrast to the look required by my waiter training at college – black trousers, starched white shirt, dicky bow and neat hair – not to mention the etiquette we were taught. I just wasn't cut out to be a penguin, and I guess that's the trouble with the Brits as a race: we don't do serving very well. It's about time we realized that we don't have an empire any more. It doesn't matter whether you collect rubbish, sweep roads, cook or wait on tables as long as you do your job to the best of your ability, and the future employment in our country is in the service industries. For too long we have relied on French, Italians, Spanish and Portuguese to do our waiting; the British will only do it while they're waiting (excuse the pun) for another career to come along. But waiting is a proud profession in its own right. Front-of-house skills aren't something that can be learned overnight. Waiters have to be efficient, logical, and well mannered, and in many ways the most important part of their job is their ability to communicate. We chefs often fail to appreciate just how difficult their work is.

At Westminster, I was thoroughly bored by the course. It was a three-year struggle made bearable by some great classmates. There was so much on the syllabus that was not of any interest to me. Every last area of hotel management was covered, and you couldn't specialize. I didn't think I needed to learn about the warp and weft of a carpet, how many bloody tufts it had per square inch. That's why you employed a carpet specialist. I didn't need to know how to make a bed. I'd learned hospital corners at public school, and in the unlikely event that I went on to manage a hotel I would employ a housekeeper. I recognized that accountancy was important, but the way it was taught was impractical and unrelated to any context in which we might end up using it. The science of food was interesting, though again this was taught without any passion for the raw materials or alchemical wonders we were dealing with.

Thank God for the cookery, and for Graham Leedom, a nice lecturer with a dry wit, a sense of fun and excellent knowledge of his subject. We had a laugh but I got a solid grounding in the basics and we handled real food, expensive food: lobsters, Dover sole, there were no short cuts. Nowadays, because of budgetary restraints, pupils rarely see pure excellence of product. I've been to some colleges where they are not even shown how to use a knife correctly, or even the right knife for a particular job.

The only problem with the course as far as cookery was concerned was that there wasn't enough of it, and the fact that we were taught only French cookery. This still happens in many colleges, and yet French food has been out of fashion for the masses for years. In my day at least it was in vogue, so you could appreciate the reasoning behind this emphasis, but still many of the dishes we cooked would never have been seen in a living, breathing restaurant, even then. Who would have dreamed of eating monkey gland steak, even if they knew it had nothing to do with monkeys? Or veal zingara, which had a caramelized sauce with pickled tongue, ham and mushrooms and occasionally chopped gherkin – French meets sweet and sour? Yuk. I suppose it gave you a grasp of the fundamentals, but we were all in for a shock when we did our practical training out in the real world.

For mine, I was sent to the Grosvenor House, first of all in the role of a commis waiter, the lowest of the low, a tray-carrier, shuffling food from kitchen to waiter station, dirty plates from restaurant to plonge (washing-up). No way was I allowed anywhere near the customers. I suppose I was receiving some kind of training – I was observing, taking everything in, after all – but essentially I was just a dogsbody. Eventually I took the bull by the horns and confronted my chef de rang (section waiter). I told him I needed to be waiting tables, not standing around like a lemon. He was an Italian of the old school, who didn't believe young college Brits had any place in his world. 'I don't like you, little man,' was the gist of his reply.

'I don't care whether you like me or not. I'm not interested in going to bed with you, I just want to be a waiter,' I said.

With that he started pushing me about, in front of the customers, too, and poking me in the chest. 'You are not worthy. You are no better than the food left on the side of the plate,' he spat.

Fuck this for a game of soldiers, I thought to myself.

'If you don't stop poking me, there'll be trouble,' I hissed, puffing out my chest and standing as tall as I could, stretching five foot seven and a half inches into five foot eight. He didn't stop, so trouble duly arrived in the form of a handful of his testicles being squeezed, gently at first, through his long apron. When I squeezed a little tighter, he rose to his tiptoes and there was a contorted expression on his face.

'Say sorry,' I whispered.

'Sorry,' he whimpered.

'Say, "I will train you to be a waiter and I won't poke you any more."'

Before he could reply my grip on the situation was ruined by the intervention of the head waiter.

'Both of you, stop this immediately! Get out of the dining room and report to me in my office.' A little chat in the head waiter's office ironed out the problem, and I was given waiter's duties, albeit heavily supervised. I was even allocated a share of the tronc – the tips – at the end of each week. I tried to remember my college training, to serve from the left, so as not to interrupt the customer's drinking arm, but, strangely, to clear from the right. When we poured coffee the jug must never leave the tray, and we were not allowed to ask, 'Black or white?' It had to be 'With or without milk?'

The chefs had heard about my little fracas with the waiter and had decided to teach the cocky little toerag a lesson – the cocky little toerag being me. All food at the Grosvenor House was presented on oval silver flats (flat dishes), and they put one side of one of these over an open flame. A chef then passed it to me in his bare hand, holding the dish on the cold side. I, of course, took it trustingly on the heated side, whereupon I simultaneously heard and felt the sizzle of flesh welding to the tray. With a scream of pain I flung the dish, food, bits of skin from my fingertips and all, across the kitchen. I had never experienced such searing pain, but I got no sympathy, just a roar from the frightened head chef as he smacked me round the head and ordered me to pick up every bit of the food that was now decorating his walls. Those were the days when chefs were shits and waiters were second-class citizens, at least in the eyes of chefs.

So it was a steep learning curve, but I stuck at it and I was shown the ropes. I was even allowed to do some lamp work, that is, cooking at the tables: steak Diane, beef stroganoff, scampi provençale and a gruesome lobster with Pernod.

I should have been looking forward to my next training stint on location at Grosvenor House, but after the finger-burning incident I was dreading it. It was time to try my hand at being a chef. It would have been more sensible to start in the kitchen, because then

I could have built up a rapport with the chefs before I had to face them on the other side of the counter, but it was too late to worry about that now. Here I was quickly introduced to a lower form of life. It came as a shock to a recent public schoolboy, still sheltered to a degree by living at home, or, at any rate, no further from home than next door, still a virgin, still drug-free. What I encountered was a group of commis chefs, unkempt, spotty, unhealthy-looking youths straight out of school and in at the deep end of the cookery world. Greasy hair, shoes with weeks' worth of food slops clinging to their surface, nails either chewed to the quick or ingrained with grease and grime from preparing food. And there was I, blond, peachy-skinned, equipped with a new set of knives, clean whites and a clean pair of underpants, and speaking with a classic public-school accent ('Oh, la-di-da, who's a pretty boy, then? Coochy-coo!'). A person, in short, to be ridiculed – and I was, relentlessly.

On my first day, I was sent to the Butchery Department for Bombay duck. 'Wrong department. Go and see Poultry.' I was pushed from pillar to post looking for this fucking duck. In the days before everyone was acquainted with Indian restaurant menus, a Bombay duck was a pretty obscure item, and I wasn't to know that it was actually a piece of dried fish. 'If it's a bloody fish, why didn't you send me to the fish section?' I said naively.

'Just a joke, Tone.'

'Very funny,' was all I could say as I blushed from my ankles to the roots of my hair.

On another occasion I was given the 'birthday treatment'. In the fish department, all the guts, scales, heads and fins were thrown into a massive wheelie bin. Yes, you've guessed it. The 'birthday treatment' involved being dumped head-first into all this fish waste. I've never had such a disgusting experience. Every inedible bit of fish clung to every nook and cranny of my body. My ears were full of slime, my hair matted with fish glue, and I stank for what seemed like days. I felt completely humiliated. Something had to be done. I decided that if I couldn't beat them, I would have to join them. So I learned to speak more Bethnal Green than Oxford, and went out of my way to be helpful, doing anything for anyone who needed a hand. I used my brain to counter their brawn, a solution that would prove useful again later in my working life. Before long I was drinking with my new mates after work, and they in turn started to treat me with respect and to instruct me in the finer points of Grosvenor

House cooking. I would stay overnight in some of their pretty miserable accommodation if we were out late drinking as I was the only one with a car and would volunteer to take them home. (How many chefs can you get in the back of a Minivan? Answer: twelve.) Respect has to be earned, and I was determined to earn it. I had to show them that I was streetwise (which, of course, I wasn't) and that I was not the spoiled little public schoolboy they had taken me for. I was lucky: they were a better bunch than some. I learned later that other students on the course spent their kitchen training days doing nothing but peeling onions and potatoes, something you hear of even from today's students. Work experience should be about training, not slave labour.

My next port of call at the Grosvenor House was the Red Devil Bar, another education. I think it's always a good idea to be aware of the scams that are practised if you intend to go into business for yourself. I was already familiar with quite a few tricks from the banqueting circuit, including the obvious one of loading customers' bills when you know they have had too much alcohol to notice. In the Red Devil Bar I also learned the subtle art of short-measuring. This was more sophisticated than simply under-pouring. The barmen used to bring in their own measures which had two 1s coins glued into the bottom of them. By doctoring the measure, the barman could easily allay any suspicions from the other side of the bar. If a customer ever complained that he had been given a short measure, the barman would say, 'Impossible, sir. Look, I'll show you.' He would then pour the customer's drink back into the measure – 'See? I knew it wasn't short' – and the punter would go away feeling a bit of a wally.

Another dodge involved the top-of-the-range XO brandy, which wasn't always what it was made out to be. The barman would pour the real stuff into another bottle, which he would take home at the end of this shift, replacing it with ordinary three-star brandy, softened by a couple of shots of sweet sherry to lend it a smoothness and a darker colour. In my time at the bar no one ever noticed and the management never knew about it.

Bringing in your own bottles of spirits, serving them to the customers and pocketing the money was also popular. In those days far more purchases were made with cash, which made this fiddle fairly simple. Security, too, was much laxer than it is today, especially as the cash registers were so basic. Today's tills would connect the sale with the stock, but there was no such link then. It was also much neater than the traditional pub scam of ringing up, say, £1 for a £10 bill and pocketing the £9 difference.

Grosvenor House was an incredible education. I learned more in four months there than I had in the whole of the previous year at college. Theoretical training for management gives you a good overall package, but it doesn't teach you grass-roots systems. Working at the coalface, as it were, taught me a tremendous amount about workplace politics, it taught me humility and it gave me an insight into the working lives of junior employees who, by and large, were and still are, to some degree, treated like shit.

My next foray into the industry was much more sedate and civilized. I was sent as a catering assistant to BP's headquarters, Britannic House in the City of London, to gain a grounding in mass canteen catering. Westminster College had been a bit worried about dispatching a troublesome character like me to such a prestigious company, but because the Grosvenor House had given me a fairly glowing reference, they decided to take the risk. I didn't let them down, returning with the fulsome praise of the catering manager. And I have to say that, while catering on such a large scale was not my cup of tea, the experience was valuable to me in terms of developing my organizational skills, and I was never bored. I learned a huge amount about butchery and, on the business side, about paperwork, budgets, staffing levels and so on. What amazes me, looking back, is that everything was freshly prepared in-house. Nowadays so many companies resort to bulk-ordering ready meals, for which their suppliers do all the butchery, veg and fish prep.

My secondment to Britannic House coincided with the oil crisis of 1970, which was an interesting and busy time to be working at BP. Every night there would be some high-level meeting or cocktail party in the boardroom at the very top of what was in its day a massive skyscraper, at least by London standards. This not only added corporate entertainment to my CV, but provided me with a welcome opportunity to earn some extra dosh, which came in very handy since my banqueting activities obviously had to be curtailed while I was training 'in the field'.

All in all, it provided a fascinating glimpse into another world, albeit one I'd never felt was for me. What I wanted was the cutting edge, the energy, the raw aggression and the excitement of a restaurant. And to my great delight, my first experience of opening one was just around the corner.

CHAPTER ELEVEN

IT WAS IN THE SECOND YEAR OF MY COURSE THAT MY MOTHER'S COUSIN Paul, who lived next door to my grandmother in Shiplake, joined forces with a young British eccentric called George Almond to create a new restaurant on the Costa Smeralda in Sardinia. He asked me if I would like to be part of this adventure and set up the kitchen during my summer recess from college. Did I! I jumped at the chance, and suggested that I brought my friend Laurence Court to help. So Paul and George, and their respective girlfriends, Susan and Melanie, went on ahead to get things up and running – they pretty well had to build the restaurant from scratch before we could start – while we made plans to join them in June.

It wasn't our first working holiday. The previous year, Laurence, Brian and I had been waiters on the cross-Channel ferries for the ten-week summer season, the longest period I had so far spent away from home, which I thought was quite brave of me and which turned out to be very lucrative as well. Today most of the catering facilities offered by ferries seem to be self-service, but in 1970 they were proper restaurants, and they were very busy. We usually did two sittings, sometimes three, between loading and dis-embarkation. Those were the days when Brits driving abroad wanted one last safe meal before having to subject themselves to all that foreign stuff, so the basic gear – steak, fish and chips, grilled lamb or pork chops, southern fried chicken – was the order of the day. We kept our mouths closed about standards. If I'd shown too much interest in the food I'd have been put in the kitchen, which might have given me more shift pay but I'd have lost out on the tips, which were usually about 2s per table, or 1s per person. A typical day's shift was France and back twice, occasionally three times when staff were short, and on a good week I took home the best part of £150, all in coins. Not bad for 1970. When I did have to cover a couple of shifts in the kitchen, I tried hard not to get carried away, but I remember quite often thinking that the garnish of lettuce, tomato, cucumber and cress looked the most appetizing part of the dishes.

Every three weeks we'd have to do a night shift. Although the restaurant wasn't so busy on those, nights paid double the day rate, and the punters were more flash with their cash. Most of the night travellers were lorry-drivers, a good balance of English and French. The French were fairly scathing about the food and usually spent most of the trip drinking red wine in copious quantities (fortunately for them, the drink-drive laws were fairly lax then). Often they would have a mistress or a female hitch-hiker in tow, and what they got up to in the restaurant added to our sex education.

In 1971, with another year's growing up under our belts, Laurence and I set off for Sardinia. We loaded my Minivan to the gunwales, drove down to Dover and took the ferry to France, as customers this time. The car was as good as gold all the way, and we camped for the night in some woods on the far side of the Mont Blanc Tunnel, an overnight stop somewhat marred by our having chosen an anthill to pitch the tent on. By lunchtime we'd made it down to Civitavecchia to take the ferry to Olbia in Sardinia. From there, the trusty Mini headed north on primitive roads, in some cases no more than dirt tracks, towards our destination: Liscia di Vacca, just a couple of miles outside the little, oh-so-cool town of Porto Cervo. George and Paul had rented the premises from the Aga Khan, who was then in the process of developing the Costa Smeralda, and it was becoming hugely trendy.

When we reached Liscia di Vacca at last, I must admit that our immediate reaction was to wonder what we'd let ourselves in for. It wasn't the restaurant itself – it was a great first restaurant. On the outside it was very quaint. The first thing you saw was a picture of a cow inside a cooking pot against a backdrop of the British flag – very patriotic – and the atmosphere inside was M&S with a touch of the Hooray Henrys thrown in for good measure. It was the location, and the practicalities of the location, that worried me slightly. The setting was rustic, to say the least: pot-holed roads, spasmodic electricity, water brought by tanker, a cottage next door with a little old lady dressed in black from head to toe permanently positioned outside, peeling vegetables for the family meals, and to the rear a cow called Rosemary, after whom we named the restaurant.

But on the plus side, the kitchen was small but perfectly formed, if in a domestic rather than a commercial way. There was a large Calor-gas cooker, a couple of domestic fridges, a tiny worktop and a manual wash-up, and most of the food was to be cooked outside on a barbecue in a wonderful back garden overlooking the sea. Besides, who was I to complain? It was a terrific opportunity; my first chance to get to grips with a commercial kitchen of my own. And in spite of my initial reservations, I was tremendously excited.

First of all I needed to get a sense of the place. I asked the boys about the customer profile they were aiming for. This marketing-speak, coming from a twenty-year-old, must have amused them, but at least I was finally getting to make practical use of my college theory. George, Paul, Susan and Melanie had done plenty of net-working in England before coming to Sardinia. They all had excellent pedigrees and were rather la-di-da, but they mixed with the jet set, so the word was out among all the rich yacht-owners that a little bit of Chelsea could now be found in the Mediterranean playground of northern Sardinia.

And sure enough, during the season, they came flooding in: Lord Forte (as he was then), Michael Pearson, even Princess Margaret. Most nights the restaurant ended up pretty full. The customers were eating pretty primitive dinners cooked by two twenty-year-olds, but the food wasn't the point. It was all about the circuit, the scene, and we were getting the crowd George and Paul were after. We all worked like dogs, but we were happy dogs. The wine flowed and hangovers were frequent, but we slept well and generally we all got on like a house on fire, though, just occasionally, the fire needed damping down, and when it did, it was usually me who was the problem.

At times I would get completely out of hand and go on a com-plete bender, which would result in me trying to cook completely pissed. I'd be abusive to the other members of the team and, once or twice, to customers as well. Paul would get angry with me, the girls would be embarrassed and Laurence just kept out of the way. George was the one who really flipped his lid. One tantrum, during which I smashed several plates and glasses, ended up with him pinning me to the floor.

In my late teens and early twenties my temper did often get the better of me. I suppose I was giving vent to the usual seesawing emotions of youth, sharpened in my case by sexual frustration and the depression I felt about my damaged face. In Sardinia these problems were heightened by the presence of so many glamorous women everywhere. And initially I was sometimes needled, too, by the attitude some of these beautiful people adopted with me purely on the basis of what I did for a living.

The women arriving in Porto Cervo on the yachts were absolutely gorgeous – well-spoken, sweet-smelling with bodies to die for. They were also completely out of my reach. Even if I had been able to break free of the shackles of my insecurities, they would have been far too expensive for a catering student to entertain. They came from a different planet from the girls I knew in London. However classy the reputation of Westminster College, a catering course is not exactly a finishing school, and most of the girls entering our profession would have been at home wrestling with Mick McManus. These Sloanes were something else.

A tiny doubt began to tickle the back of my throat. Had I chosen the right career? Because when girls like this were introduced to me at the restaurant, they would look me up and down, usually down, and almost sneer. An unspoken question hung in the air. It was: 'Why are you introducing me to a cook?' It might have made me even more chippy, even less confident, if such a thing were possible; it certainly made me despair of my own kind. Sure, they had good breeding, but they had absolutely no manners unless it suited them. It taught me how much first impressions mean to shallow people. I thought about this a lot, wondering whether my upbringing and education were going to be a problem for my job, or vice versa. I always came back to the same view: image is complete bollocks. I am who I am, grease-stained chef's jacket or Savile Row suit. I might have been 'brung up proper', but that counts for nothing if you can't mix with all classes, all creeds and all religions. Once I'd sorted that out for myself, I felt happier. But it still amazes me how many people will refuse to talk to you unless you wear a suit and talk posh.

So what did I cook for these charming arseholes? The mood of the times stretched my repertoire to include vichyssoise, chilled carrot and coriander soup, Parma ham and melon, artichokes with hollandaise sauce and the occasional gazpacho. Avocado with prawns or seafood was popular, although I peeled, sliced and arranged the avocado rather than just cutting it in half and serving the cocktail in the hole vacated by the stone, as was the convention then. I supplemented the main courses from the barbie with a mean chicken Marengo, coq au vin, shish kebab, paella, beef stroganoff or au poivre and moussaka. Spag bol made the occasional appearance, though by demand rather than by choice. The puds were mainly sniffed at by the stick-insect model types, but if anything was eaten it was usually cheesecake, Black Forest gâteau, profiteroles, caramelized oranges or even, despite the heat, bread-and-butter pudding. I did attempt some of the local dishes, but as the British were still conservative in those days, the likes of octopus didn't go down a storm.

All in all, the season went very well. We got on famously with both the locals and the people who ran the exclusive hotels in the area. Most of my afternoons off were spent sunbathing or satisfying my appetite for swimming and snorkelling at one of two local hotels which have been described as the most exclusive on the Med, the Pitrizzia and the Cala di Volpe. Even in 1970, these were arm-and-a-leg jobs: if the Aga Khan wanted exclusive, he got it. Some of the architecture in the region was out of this world. There were villas which had a mountainside as one wall. Imagine, a mountain in the sitting room. And Signor Olivetti, of typewriter fame, had a villa there built in the shape of his brainchild. Porto Cervo itself was similar to the set of Patrick McGoohan's *The Prisoner*. Yes, I know that was in Wales, but this was similar in that it was twee, toytown and very expensive.

It was all very overwhelming for me, the untravelled one, but it was not only character-forming, it also helped to bolster my resolve to carry on with this cooking lark. And if a proper girlfriend was still not on the cards, I got on well with the two girls at Liscia di Vacca, Susan and Melanie, especially Melanie. She was an impish girl, very similar to one of Charlie's Angels, the bright one with the straight, dark hair. She had a baby-doll body, and a cheeky grin and was full of fun and laughter; head in the clouds but feet on the ground, that was Melanie. She was also a great listener. I would pour out my grief and woes to her and, like an older sister, she'd do her best to reassure me that I was perfectly normal, if a late developer; that it would all come good in the end. I wish I'd believed her.

I'm sure that Melanie, despite her zest for life, had her own problems. She was in love with a *Boy's Own* type. George was tall, good-looking, intelligent, fun and adventurous, but just slightly barking. A man to take risks, a man it was very hard to pin down. I'm sure her heart wanted her to stay with George, but her head told her it wasn't a good idea, and there was another man-in-waiting, a potato-farmer, the sensible option. Sense won in the end, but only for a time, and I'm sure her spirit waned.

Susan, Paul's girlfriend, was a different kettle of fish – the ultimate Hermès girl, tall and blonde and a tad more Rubenesque than Melanie. At first she was a bit cold towards me, and she took a lot of warming up, but eventually we became friends. In fact she has cause to be forever grateful to me for some novel first aid on a swimming expedition when she slipped on a rock and landed bang on a sea urchin. I'd had a couple of encounters with these horrible spiky creatures myself, but at least mine had only involved the feet. Susan had got the nasty spines all over her bum, which must have been like having twenty tetanus injections simultaneously.

It was not only painful, but very tricky to get them out. All you can do is feel your way round. Remembering my manners, I offered to help and, even though I was only the cook, my assistance was graciously accepted. The unbroken spines were fairly easy to deal with, but some of them had broken off and lay just under the skin. There was only one solution: suck and spit. I made discreet inquiries as to whether she required this additional service and was surprised to be given the go-ahead. I can assure you that my mind was so focused on the job in hand, or rather, in mouth, that there wasn't even a twinge of excitement in my loins. Afterwards Susan swore me to secrecy, though we had a good laugh about it later and a big drink to help us get over the ordeal. And up till now I have kept her secret, but I think thirty years' silence is enough for anyone. I'm telling it now as a warning to other women always to carry a pair of tweezers in their bags in case of emergencies.

Susan was a lovely lady though I never thought she was right for my cousin. I'm sure they were devoted to each other at the time, but Paul was a ladies' man.

He and George were great mates and quite alike: they were both endearing rogues. They kept the restaurant for several seasons before selling it as a going concern. Paul went on to do some modelling and ended up flying helicopters in South Africa, where he married the wonderful Karen. We still keep in touch, although distance means we don't see much of one another. As for Susan, she landed on her feet: she went on to marry Major Ronald Ferguson, whose daughter Sarah was to become the Duchess of York. George remained an adventurer, inventor and innovator. The last I heard of him, he was planning to fly over Mount Everest in a plane he was building himself.

My own Sardinian adventure was terrific fun and another stepping-stone towards my goal of becoming a chef. I can't believe my cooking was much cop but, as I pointed out earlier, the food wasn't really that important. So perhaps the significance of Sardinia was that it was my first shop window: my first chance to see and be seen.

The summer over, it was back to London, my final year at college and the looming six-million-dollar-man operation that I hoped would make everything right for me. The surgery I was to have had been developed in the five years since my injury and had never been performed before. I was booked into Queen Mary's three weeks before the end of the Easter term, and would need to stay there throughout the Easter break and for another three weeks into the summer term. Having to be away from college for so long at such a crucial time could have been a bit of a blow to my finals, but they were good enough to agree to send my coursework to me in hospital.

Everyone from my mother, my grandmother and other relatives to the family doctor pleaded with me not to go ahead with the operation, but my mind was made up. I couldn't possibly explain to them all that I was pinning my hopes of ever having a girlfriend on this surgery. I'd never discussed sex with my mother, and nobody since Nurse Elliott had ever tried to give me any advice about it. For all I knew, the image I presented to the world – the flamboyant dress sense, the loud music, the wild friends – had given them the impression that I was already sexually experienced.

So, on the appointed date, I arrived at St Mary's loaded up with reading material and a clean set of jimjams, all new and very M&S, and was shaved from top to toe. They were going to be hacking a chunk out of my hip to graft on to the back of my top jaw, bringing my whole face forward. To my alarm, I also learned that they would be drilling four holes into my skull to hold a halo of scaffolding which would keep the jaw together.

Before I went under the knife I'd been given all sorts of disclaimers to sign carrying warnings about circumstances in which the operation couldn't be performed. One of these stated that the surgery shouldn't take place if I had a cold. You've guessed it: on the very morning of the op I had come down with one. I decided not to mention it to anyone. It was a big mistake. When I came round from the anaesthetic, jaw wired up, head drugged up, I couldn't breathe. Because of the countless times my nose had been broken, breathing through it had never been exactly easy, and now all vital air channels were effectively defunct. And I couldn't even blow my nose – my face was far too sore for that. I started to panic. My mother, who was by my bedside, tried to quieten me, to no avail.

My hip was killing me where they had taken a hammer and chisel to it and I couldn't turn my head to the side because of the Meccano halo that was now embedded in my skull. I thought I was going to die. No, it was worse than that: I *wanted* to die. I indicated to my mother that I needed a pen and paper. On it I wrote, 'I'm dying, call a doctor.' Then she panicked as well, and did the hysterical mother bit, screeching for help. A nurse rushed in, took one look at the state I was in, rushed out again and rushed back with the consultant. He gave me a jab of something that knocked me straight out once more.

When I came to for the second time, things went from bad to worse. My cold had really got going now, and all the nasal passages were completely blocked. The consultant explained to me that my only option was not a nice one. I would have to have a tube rammed up my nose and down my throat, presumably in the direction of my lungs. I didn't care. Anything was better than this feeling of being suffocated in a polythene bag. I put my hands together in an attitude of prayer to indicate that I was ready to take my medicine like a man.

He was right, it wasn't nice. I hate having things stuck up my nose at the best of times. I gripped so hard on to the nurse who was holding me down that I must have drawn blood from her fragile wrists. Up the tube went, and down the other side, and then a second one, and suddenly, air flushed into my lungs. It felt so good that I just hugged the nurse really tight, nearly blinding her with the scaffolding poles sticking out of my head. I will survive, I thought. I probably even managed a little smile.

Had I made the right decision? The answer the first time I looked into a mirror was no. My face was a kaleidoscope of colour from purple through to greyish-brown, and then some yellow, scary bits. My twelve weeks in hospital were punctuated by daily visits from my mother, bless her, and the spasmodic appearance of college friends. Two of the girls, Brigid Tangney and Corinne Travers-Healy, came regularly to try to nurture the seeds of my confidence. Brian and Laurence made the occasional visit, remarking on my huge weight loss. It might have been a beneficial side-effect later, but I'd gone into hospital at an already modest ten and a half stone and left weighing a pathetic seven and a half. You can't eat a lot with your teeth wired up, and there's only so much you can do with a liquidized banana. As for the other pulped food I was able to eat through a straw, you could keep it. I've eaten better baby Organix. So, generally, I chose not to eat much. Instead I had to drink several glasses of carbohydrate or protein drinks a day, and they are hardly to be recommended, either.

After a couple of weeks I was allowed out of bed. I was very sore as the giant hole in my hip was still releasing pus, gross but apparently normal. I spent my time revising, walking – or rather, limping – around the grounds, watching the telly or chatting up the nurses. As I recovered, the psychological boost of having at last got the operation out of the way kicked in, and my confidence began to build, insofar as it is possible for confidence to build when you have a metal scaffold round your head. It was enough for me to decide that this was a good time to practise my chatting-up technique. I'm not sure it was very polished, but the nurses, who found it 'sweet', humoured me. I was smitten by one particular nurse, called Kay Weaver, who was a tiny little thing, and lovely in a cheeky sort of way. It turned out that she lived in the nurses' residence just around the corner from my college. I got to see her a few times after I left, and managed a few clumsy kisses. Practice makes perfect.

I was in hospital for my twenty-first birthday. A few friends came to help me celebrate, but of course it wasn't the real thing. You need to get pissed on your twenty-first. So I had a belated party later, in June, at an excellent Chinese restaurant in Putney. My mother had sold the premises to Peter, the boss, and he owed her a favour, so he laid on a real Chinese banquet (well, it was good for 1972). This was followed by a visit to the Playboy Club on Park Lane. Bunnies everywhere, and not a shotgun in sight! This was it: I had grown up. My confidence was returning, so much so that I managed a good snog with the girls at the party.

And my finals? Well, I passed my HND and, surprise, surprise, left college with a report that read: 'On no account should this boy be let loose near a kitchen.'

So what next? A job, I guessed.

CHAPTER TWELVE

MOST OF MY CLASSMATES FROM WESTMINSTER HAD JOBS UNDER THEIR belts by the time they left college: Savoy this, Connaught that; some went to Trusthouse Hotels, others to the Hilton, one or two into industrial catering. None of it appealed to me. As it turned out, I ended up launching my career with James Paget, a good friend from college. Jim was a lovely guy, and one of the few students who was married. He was renting a flat very close to me, off Clapham Common, and I practically lived there during our latter college days. He loved his food and adored his wine, and we used to give some great dinner parties together.

I was obsessed with cooking. Sad person that I was, every Thursday for about three years, wherever I was living, I'd be outside the newsagent at 5 pm waiting for the *Cordon Bleu* cookery partwork to come in. As soon as I got my hands on it I'd be devouring every word, planning what I was going to cook next. And I learned a lot from it – it was a great course in its day. I also lapped up any cookery book by Elizabeth David. They were compulsory bedtime reading. Many of our dinner parties were based on what we picked up from these books and partworks.

In fact it wasn't long before Jim and I were deciding to take up a job together. My mother had joined forces with Ian Deal, a roguish guy who owned an estate agency on Northcote Road in Clapham. He'd recently bought a big Victorian stack in Warley, near Brentwood in Essex, and wanted someone to help him and his wife to run it as a country-house hotel while my mum looked after his estate agency. I suggested Jim and me, me on food and beverage,

Jim on front-of-house, and he snapped us up. It was a recipe for a nightmare: two youngsters with no experience and a man with a dream.

But we were quite happy. The wages seemed good – I think they were £5,000 a year live-in, which meant in the hotel to start with, then tiny rooms in a stable block that Ian converted for staff accommodation. Jim's wife Sarah left the pharmacy where she worked and the three of us decamped to Warley.

The stack was to be called the Coombe Lodge Hotel. To the right of an impressive entrance hall and reception was a private dining room, which became a gambling den, and a large bar with rather primitive loos out the back. To the left were sofas and a big, country-house-type ballroom which doubled as the restaurant and, on Friday nights, a disco. On Saturdays there was usually a wedding or other function. The ballroom overlooked lovely grounds with rhododendron woods at the bottom of a hill, and sets of French windows opened on to a terrace with a veranda for al-fresco dining and frolics by the pool.

Managing this lot without allowing it to degenerate into Fawlty Towers was a frightening prospect. Suddenly, I wished I'd paid more attention to my housekeeping studies at college. First things first: we had to get some staff. Interviewing potential employees at the tender age of twenty-one was, I discovered, a tricky business. Everyone looks at you quizzically, as if to say, 'Nice meeting you, but now can I meet your dad?' That, of course, ruffles your feathers, dents your ego and you don't give them the job. Days went past and I hadn't taken on anyone. Jim, on the other hand, had managed to recruit a whole front-of-house team. But with his glasses, short haircut, suit and height advantage, he looked older and more authoritative than I did. I was short, had a baby face and longish blond hair, and wore jeans and a T-shirt. I couldn't think where I was going wrong.

Eventually, I did find two very efficient chefs, who were friends (a bad move as they stuck together and outnumbered me). I was so dazzled by their expertly starched chef's jackets, tall white toques and clean shoes that I completely forgot to ask them if they could cook. As it turned out they weren't bad, though as my grounding in cookery was still very amateurish I was hardly the best judge. I desperately wanted to do the menu, but my chefs were not the type to be impressed by my *Cordon Bleu* magazines or my love affair with Elizabeth David, and I was too scared to show them my ideas.

So what I got was the results of their 'classical' training. For the hors d'oeuvres: juices, various; grilled grapefruit with brown sugar; melon in white port or melon boat (it was a toss-up and the boat won); smoked trout with horseradish sauce; soupe du jour (usually Maggi tomato); pâté de la maison (whose house, I'll never know) and, of course, the ubiquitous prawn cocktail. And for the mains it didn't get much better: grilled sole meunière or mornay; scampi-in-the-basket, scampi provençale, scampi mornay; trout with prawns and almonds; chicken Maryland, chicken Kiev; veal cordon bleu (made with chicken legs), veal Holstein; beef stroganoff, steak Diane and, of course, fillet steak garni. Puddings, or should I say desserts, were the normal trolley fare: caramelized oranges, trifle, Black Forest gâteau, crème caramel, chocolate mousse and profiteroles and, from the kitchen, ices, various. Yuk and double yuk. But at the time it was what was expected, and the good people of Essex seemed to enjoy it. So we had ourselves a kitchen.

Ian Deal was around most of the time. Like most enthusiastic amateurs (hark at me), he loved playing mine host. James and I acted as duty managers while Ian swanned around, quite often in a pretty pissed state. I enjoyed the customer contact, too, and made a point of befriending the locals. In some cases this was not the wisest move, because many of the likely lads can only be described as hoods. They would boast openly about their day's work hijacking lorries or robbing post offices and the odd bank, and protection rackets seemed to be a popular sideline. They would cheerfully show you their stab or bullet wounds and brag that they worked or had worked for the Richardsons, the Tibbs or the Krays. It was all over my head and I had no idea what I was letting myself in for, but I enjoyed it. I loved living on the edge, and I soon became 'friends' with the villains, to whom I latched on like some kind of mascot. Most of them were around the forty, forty-five mark, and purported to be car-dealers or horse-breeders, with the occasional farmer thrown in for good measure, but they all appeared to be involved in crime. They were also always accompanied by stunning Essex girls. As for me, I didn't realize what a minefield I was treading.

One of my chefs, who was a whizz with motors, suggested I traded in my Minivan for a Mini Cooper S. I took his advice and he transformed the engine of my new car into something frightening. Don't ask me what he did – I'm not mechanical. All I can tell you is that this Mini suddenly became lethal. It was also flash. The roof was painted with a Union Jack, the body in midnight blue, and it had a leather interior. The perfect pulling car. Now all I had to do was pull.

One of my first serious missions was Rosie. When it coincided with my time off, I used to get down to the Tiger Tavern near Tower Hill, where they had a bit of a rave on Thursday nights. They had a couple of go-go dancers who gyrated in cages suspended from the ceiling to the music of the moment, all Alvin Stardust and Slade, and perennial anthems such as Jeff Beck's 'Hi-Ho Silver Lining'. I was entranced by one of them, Rosie, a girl with a magnificent body, silky skin, silver thigh-high boots, the skimpiest silver bikini, long bottle-blonde hair, Julie Christie lips, piercing blue eyes and the most magnificent, firm chest.

One night I plucked up the courage to ask the barman to send her over a drink. When I saw her take delivery of a pint of bitter I felt a thrill go down my spine. Clearly this was a no-nonsense kind of girl. As she picked up the beer, she looked over in my direction and mouthed, 'Thanks.' Then she was wandering over. I seemed to be rooted to the spot. Oh shit, now what do I do? I thought. Stay calm, don't shake, try to be cool.

'Hi,' I said. 'What do you do?' Possibly the dumbest question ever, since obviously what she did was dance at the pub. I laughed nervously. She smiled. She had a great set of teeth.

'Shall we start again?' she said. Her accent was Hackney-meets-Bow. And so we did. I told her, somewhat implausibly, that I was a researcher on a movie and that I was looking for female talent to feature in it. It was probably the crassest line I've ever used. Mind you, that's not saying much. I never really perfected a successful chat-up technique. When confronted with a girl at close quarters, somehow my brain lost the power to communicate with my tongue.

Not surprisingly, that conversation didn't go very far, but over the next few Thursday visits I persisted. Finally, Rosie was the one who took the bull by the horns. 'Aren't you going to ask me out?' she asked. I was startled.

'Yes,' I replied inadequately.

'Well?' she prompted.

'Where would you like to go?'

'Up West.'

'When?'

'How about next Thursday? I'll call in sick. I'll meet you outside the Leicester Square Odeon at six-thirty.'

The following week we met as arranged. 'Where would you like to go?' I asked Rosie.

'To a Soho strip club,' she said. I thought this was strange, not to say sleazy, but I was anxious to please. Besides, it would be a new experience for me, and at least it would be marginally more respectable for me to go there with a girl on my arm rather than a dirty raincoat. In the club I asked Rosie why she was interested in these rather dog-eared strippers. She told me that she liked to study the way they danced. I didn't think they had much to teach her in the dancing department, especially as in those days the girls weren't allowed to move an inch once they had discarded all their kit, but I didn't say so.

Afterwards I took Rosie to the Villa Caesari on the banks of the Thames in Pimlico, which was very grand. It did some major damage to my modest bank balance but I thought it would impress her and that it would be worth it in the end. We had dinner, though I might as well have given her budgie food for all she ate. I guess she was concerned about keeping her figure. We danced, but with the regulation six inches between us, and she chatted in an 'I-haven't-got-anything-to-talk-about' sort of way.

When we left the Villa Caesari I drove Rosie home. She lived in a Parachute Regiment barracks that was conveniently on my route back to Essex. She invited me in, and I thought, Yes! I'm in here! She made us a drink and came and sat down next to me on the sofa. I put my arm round her. She seemed uncomfortable. I tried to kiss her. It was a definite no-no. 'What's the matter?' I inquired.

'Nothing, really. I do like you. You're not like the others. You seem kind and you don't try to rush things.'

Only because I lack confidence and don't know what the hell I'm doing, I thought to myself.

'I want you to be my friend,' she went on, 'but I don't want the sex bit.'

Great. 'Why?' I probed.

'There's no point in trying to hide it any longer,' she said. 'I'm a lesbian.'

It all fell into place. 'So why did you go out with me?' I asked.

'Well, I meant it when I said I liked you, and I do want somebody to go out with. It's my dad, you see. He's all man, a sergeant-major in the regiment, and he'd kill me if he knew. So I need someone to make me appear normal.'

But after that weird start to our relationship, Rosie and I became great mates. The subterfuge wasn't all one-way traffic, because she was just as good for my image as I was for hers. It was terrific for my ego that people assumed I had a girlfriend at last, and such a stunning one, too. One of our regular haunts was the Embassy Club off Piccadilly, where the clientele was predominantly gay, but that didn't bother me. We had a laugh and it gave Rosie the chance to pursue the kind of relationship she was really after. So that I fitted into the scene, she got me to dress the part by buying me a pink leather catsuit with a zip that ran from thigh to shoulder. Viewed from behind, with my long, blond hair and slight figure, I was often taken for a girl, and there were some shocked faces when I turned round to reveal my beard. I can't see myself in a pink leather outfit nowadays. Perhaps we were all a bit more daring then.

Yet however much fun I had with Rosie, it was not, of course, as much fun as everyone thought I was having, and it wasn't getting me any nearer to what I so desperately wanted, which was to relieve myself of the increasingly heavy burden of my virginity. As luck would have it, after my unceasing efforts to impress the girls, in the end I was the one who was pulled rather than the other way round. Even so, it was by no means plain sailing.

I was picked up in a pub called the Hayden Arms, which was very close to Ford's main offices in Brentwood and was regularly used by some of the company's directors. The young lady in question was the daughter of one of them. She was well spoken, well dressed and she drove a flash, bright-red RS 2000 Escort. Our relationship began with a race through the country lanes between her Escort and my Mini, which she won. We stopped in some woods and she produced a bottle of vodka and some lemonade, which we drank in her car. Then she pulled out a joint. As I've said, dope and I didn't get on but, carried away by the heady atmosphere, I thought it would be churlish not to have a couple of puffs. I was fine, so a couple of puffs became a couple more. She made the first move. It was a wet smacker. I was overcome with excitement. Then, suddenly, something made me retch: the sudden impact of the grass. I pulled away and threw myself in a rather ungainly manner out of the car door just in time to puke up my guts. That's blown it, I thought. I could not believe what had happened. Director's Daughter turned on the motherly charm, and then decided that she would take me back to her flat.

We left my car in the woods. I was feeling terrible and my face must have been green. I slumped in the passenger seat of the Escort with my head out of the window. By the time we arrived I was out for the count. Apparently, she dragged me into her bedroom, undressed me and put me to bed, though I don't remember a thing about it. When I awoke the next morning to find her lying beside me, I thought, Jesus, have I had sex? What a disaster! Virginity gone and I have no memory of what happened. As Director's Daughter stirred I made discreet inquiries. My innocence, I discovered, was still intact. My feelings were mixed. I was relieved that I hadn't been denied the experience, but disappointed, too, to have made no progress.

I jumped out of bed. Big mistake. My head was having difficulty sitting on my shoulders and my mouth tasted like the bottom of a baby's pram. A gargle, a tooth-scrub and a hot shower seemed the only option. Having abandoned myself to the downpour, I nearly leaped out of my skin at the sound of the Director's Daughter's voice in my ear. 'Move over,' she said, and immediately began to tease me with her taut tongue, rubbing her wet hair and her breasts across my body. I started to shiver despite the heat of the water. My legs trembled. Every part of me was standing to attention, not daring to move, not knowing what to do. Her hands were everywhere. She seemed quite happy, though I was fearful she might drown. I tried to remember what Nurse Elliott had shown me, but my mind went blank. Thank God Director's Daughter was in complete control. And then, just as my virginity was about to hit the shower floor, we were rudely interrupted once again. This time it was the doorbell, which it dawned on me had been ringing for some time. 'Shit, shit, shit!' she muttered. 'It's my dad. He's come to give me a lift to work.'

I slid down in the shower, defeated. Will this ever happen? I wondered.

The long-awaited life-changing event did finally happen, but not until I had just turned twenty-two (I can't believe I just admitted that), and it was at the hands of Director's Daughter. She invited me to the British Grand Prix at Brand's Hatch (she had pit passes – Daddy, you know). We got fairly well trollied in some corporate tent before watching the race and we were getting on like a house on fire. Fire was the word for it, too: we were all over each other. Eventually we left the crowd in search of a comfortable grassy bank before we were arrested. Then we let rip. I was dizzy with nerves. As she guided my fumbling fingers I was looking around to make sure there was no one within striking distance. Suddenly, to my horror, I spotted a rubbish-collector with his paper spike advancing in our direction. I whipped my hand from under her skirt.

'Behave yourself,' I said. 'Someone's coming.'

'Let's go and find somewhere more private,' she said, pulling herself to her feet. It was all right for her, but the evidence of my excitement was all too obvious. 'Sit down, quick,' I yelped (my jeans were very tight). 'I can't go anywhere. Look!'

She screeched with laughter. 'I'll walk in front of you,' she suggested. I stood up very awkwardly, trying to cup my manhood in my hands and at the same time to yank her in front of me. It was like trying to walk in a three-legged race. We shuffled over to the pits area, where everything was quiet. The cars had been loaded on to transporters and there was hardly anyone around. We sneaked into what must have been a servicing area. Director's Daughter tugged at my belt and started to unzip my jeans. 'Careful,' I said. This was the point where I wanted to turn off the lights, but it was broad daylight and there weren't any lights to turn off. She jumped up at me, arms around my neck, legs encircling my waist, taking me completely by surprise. I staggered, just about managing to support her. I've never quite worked out how ballet dancers do that so gracefully.

I was now entering uncharted territory. Or, to be more accurate, I wasn't. Do they find their own way in? I wondered. I was trying to juggle her on to the firing pin but, embarrassingly, I wasn't having too much luck. You can't blow it again, I said to myself. There was only one thing for it. 'I'm a virgin,' I blurted out.

A faint glimmer of a smile twitched at the corners of Director's Daughter's mouth. Then she let out a raucous laugh. 'How sweet! You're my first virgin. This is so exciting!'

She removed herself and laid me down. 'Don't worry. I'll treat you gently.' She sat astride me and manoeuvred herself on to me. I didn't know whether to scream 'Eureka!' or burst into tears. Now I was terrified that it might all be over too quickly. I had heard stories from girls about three-second wonders. How did you stop it happening? I needn't have worried. I was so nervous that all my muscles tensed up, and I not only stayed the course but went on so long that Director's Daughter expressed doubts as to my purity. 'I haven't done this before, I promise. I'm just nervous,' I explained.

'Don't be nervous. Just have fun.'

Easier said than done, I thought, as I became aware of how sore my backside was. When I inspected it later it looked like an oil slick.

But in spite of the discomforts, it was certainly worth waiting for. It might have been no more that a casual sexual encounter, but it meant a lot to me. There are any number of clichés I could pick to describe how I felt – the heaven, moon, earth and stars on one big collision course, or a trip to heaven and back – and they'd all be true. A small tear ran down my cheek and she licked it off.

Director's Daughter didn't hang around long. Well, to be fair, she did, after all, have a perfectly handsome, and rather imposing, boyfriend already. From time to time she popped back for the occasional bonk, which helped my confidence no end, and for that I'll always be grateful to her.

CHAPTER THIRTEEN

I FELT SETTLED IN ESSEX. I HAD NEVER BEEN SO CONTENT, AND AT THAT time I thought my future lay there. I decided to buy a house. I scraped together a deposit and took out my first mortgage, for £5,000, which was a big deal for me then, and soon I was the proud owner of a three-bedroomed, fully carpeted (in bright orange) terraced job in Brentwood. I was in my element. I furnished it from a few bits and pieces donated by Gran, who had finally come around to my new life – initially she'd refused to even write to me because I was living in Essex! But there was one brand-new luxury I just had to have: a waterbed. They were a novelty then, and a bit of a talking point, and I thought one of these would be the icing on the cake of my recently acquired status as a ladies' man. I even put a few goldfish in it, but unfortunately they died.

The waterbed too, was a great idea in theory: no pressure points, good for the back. But it didn't come with any instructions. I'm not talking about putting the thing together and filling it, I'm talking about trying to have sex on one. I checked several sex manuals, including the *Kama Sutra*; I spoke to several of my mates, none of whom was able to help. The problem was that when she was going up and you were going down, a serious clash of heads or even worse was on the cards; when you were on the up and she was heading down, you were in danger of slipping your mooring. Try it on your side and you started a tidal wave that was quite likely to throw you out of bed. With a regular girlfriend you'd get used to the ebb and flow, but if you were playing the field – next on my hit list was Essex girl Valerie – it could be an absolute nightmare, and just plain impossible if you were pissed.

Having my own house gave me a feeling of stability and a sudden desire for responsibility which I satisfied by getting a dog. Two dogs, in fact, German Shepherds called Kim and Shane. I'd wanted a dog since I was a kid but had never been allowed one. The best I'd managed until then was a Persian cat called Bianca, who wasn't exactly mentally stimulating even if she was a bit of a princess.

But now I could go around looking really butch with my two bruisers. Kim was slim and elegant with lovely light colouring. Shane must have had a difficult puppyhood. I inherited him as a fully grown young dog and he was chippy, a dog with attitude. He would get exceptionally annoyed when Kim rejected his advances, so they fought like dog and dog. Once, wading in to separate them, I was unfortunate enough to get my hand caught between several large teeth, and it was punctured in several places. That was it. One of them had to go. Because I had a soft spot for the girls, the loser was Shane. He ended up happier, though, because he went to a great home, a farm in Wales. Kim remained but, typical woman, she pined for Shane so badly that a substitute had to be found, and along came Fonzi, another gorgeous Alsatian with a magnificent head. Fortunately, this time Kim fell in love immediately.

I would take the dogs to the hotel every day, and they entertained themselves, running around the expansive grounds. Everything was fine until one day Ian Deal decided that resident dogs, especially German Shepherds, were not in keeping with the image he wanted for the hotel, and asked me not to bring them any more. What was I to do with two big dogs all day? I couldn't leave them cooped up on their own in a small terraced house in Brentwood.

The cavalry arrived in the shape of my villains. I was talking to a couple of them one night about the dog problem and they offered me the use of a stable one of them owned just half a mile from the hotel. The two girls who rode their horses, they said, would let the dogs out from time to time. It was a perfect solution: not only would Kim and Fonzi be well looked after, but I would have the opportunity to make friends with the girls – I knew who they were, and they were both real crackers. There's something about a girl in a pair of jodhpurs that makes me go weak at the knees.

I was naive enough to think that these girls just rode the villains' horses. It didn't occur to me that they might also be their bits on the side. But as I got to know them from my daily visits to deliver or collect the dogs, it became clear that Girl Number 1 was very attached to her villain. I thought she was mad living such a dangerous, dead-end life, but she wasn't to be swayed. Girl Number 2, on the other hand, seemed happy to flirt with me, and the flirting soon developed into frolics in the stable.

The two girls rode their villains' horses at showjumping events around southern England. Showjumping was a strange mix of the rough and the smooth. It is undoubtedly a rich man's sport if you want the best horses, but rich doesn't necessarily mean posh in any walk of life, and especially not in eventing. Some of the guys were as rough as a bear's arse, definitely not the sort to be crossed after a few drinks.

This was a lesson I learned to my cost on a number of occasions, most spectacularly one evening when, returning to Brentwood after a competition, we all went out to dinner at a local Italian. Everything was going swimmingly until Girl Number 2, who was sitting beside me, all touchy-feely, said of a recent trip to Egypt: 'The women over there have to walk in the gutter two paces behind their men.'

I don't know what made me say it. I suppose I was just unthinkingly making the kind of teasing response any guy might make. 'Quite right too. The perfect place for them,' I said.

Suddenly the table went quiet. I was immediately alert to Girl Number 2's villain, who looked as if he was about to burst a blood vessel, but it was Villain Number 1 who moved. He picked me up and flung me across the restaurant, then marched over and started pummelling me about the face and body. Then he smashed a chair over my head. As he attacked me, he said to me under his breath: 'Tony, just pretend I'm hurting you, because if Villain Number 2 gets you, you'll have no chance.'

'What do you mean, pretend?' I spluttered through the blood that was now filling my mouth.

'When I've finished with you,' said Villain 1, 'just get up calmly and return to the table. If I were you, I'd apologize first to Villain 2, for insulting his girl, and then to her.' All I wanted to do was run, but I took his advice and apologized, emphasizing that my comment had just been a joke.

The reception was pretty frosty. 'Apology accepted, but it was a joke in bad taste.' I agreed, then ordered drinks for everyone. Villain 1 was right: a show of bravado was the only option. If I had crept away like a scalded cat I would never have been able to face them again.

But I was hurting quite badly. Blood was still oozing from cuts to my lip and cheek, and I drank about twelve double whiskies to calm my nerves and dull the pain. I don't know which was worse, the beating or the stinging effect of the whisky on my slashed mouth. It was an absurd situation, almost surreal. Here I was, moments after receiving a serious duffing, laughing and larking with the mob.

As I was driving home, a distance of all of half a mile, I was stopped by the police, breathalysed and arrested for being over – well over – the limit. Not only was I very pissed, but I must have looked a complete wreck with my bashed face and bloodstained clothing. All I could say was, 'Please let me go. I've just had a beating from Villain 1.' They questioned me thoroughly and asked me whether I wanted to press charges. I didn't. So they had the police doctor check me over and drove me home. I was never prosecuted for drink-driving.

The next morning, I awoke at 7 am to the sound of the doorbell being pressed repeatedly, a mad thumping on the door and the dogs barking. I dragged on my dressing gown and opened it. Villain 1 charged into the hall, knocking me flying. The dogs recognized him and lost interest. 'Hi,' I said. 'What's the problem?'

'The problem, Tony, is that you've been bleating to the police.'

Suddenly it dawned on me that these boys were in cahoots with the police. 'I was scared,' I whimpered. 'I didn't want to lose my licence. I didn't know what else to do.'

'We don't like squealers. You thought last night was bad? Just you wait.' He dragged me into the kitchen. 'Sit down,' he barked.

'Coffee?' I said nonchalantly, trying to defuse the situation.

'Shut it.'

I took that as a no.

He told me to remove my dressing gown. I saw no point in arguing. Then he wrapped clingfilm all round me, starting at the feet and working up. When he reached my face he said, 'Time to take a deep breath.' He covered my head in the film. I started to panic. I couldn't move or even breathe for what seemed like ages, and I must have been going purple. Through the blurry window of the clingfilm I saw him pull out a knife. I felt a warm sensation down my leg as I pissed myself. To my relief he merely made a slash in the clingfilm over my mouth. I gulped in air, tasting the blood from the lip he'd cut along with the foodwrap.

Villain 1 hadn't quite finished. He delivered a few heavy blows to my body, but not to my face, thank goodness. What I was most worried about was a whack that might undo the good work achieved by my operation. Then he stormed off, taking my house keys. 'I'll be back,' he said over his shoulder as he slammed the door.

Have you ever been wrapped in clingfilm? It has incredible strength and if you don't have any leverage it's unbreakable. I had already been clingfilmed naked to a lamp-post after some student night out, and I had discovered then that it was impossible to wriggle out of. So I had no choice but to sit there and wait for him to come back. Various thoughts passed through my head. While my chief preoccupation was that I was going to die, more mundane observations circled on the periphery of that icy core of fear. Would anybody give the hotel some excuse for my absence? Who would feed the dogs?

It must have been a good couple of hours before I heard the key in the lock and Villain 1 reappeared. He seemed to be in conciliatory mood. He started to tell me how much he liked me, how he was just trying to show me how things worked, that he was teaching me a lesson so that I wouldn't get it wrong again. He put the kettle on. 'Cup of tea?' Unable to speak through the layers of clingfilm, I nodded. He smiled. 'I suppose you want me to release you?' I nodded again. This time he was more gentle with the knife. As the clingfilm fell away he gave me a playful punch on the arm that nearly knocked me off the chair.

As we sat there and drank our tea I didn't know what else to do but apologize.

'Tell you what,' he said. 'I need a driver.' It was not for bank heists, apparently, but for his horsebox. Would I like to do it at weekends? Well, what do you say after such a nice man has wrapped you in clingfilm and almost killed you?

'Yeah, that would be great,' I found myself answering.

So, for a short period, I became the villains' driver – HGV meets GBH. I didn't have an HGV licence, of course, but as far as the villains were concerned that was a minor detail. It meant being closer to my girl, learning something about horses and sharing the cab with Villain 1 and Villain 2.

However, it appeared that Villain 1 was not totally convinced I'd got the message after the clingfilm incident. One Sunday night we were all in the local pub in Warley. It was a warm summer evening and the beer was flowing, or in my case, the lager top. We'd all had lunch at a rather dodgy café in Brentwood, and my stomach was playing up a bit. At about seven o'clock a big white van pulled up in the car park, and Villain 1 and some of his cronies went out to speak to whoever was in there. While they were talking I decided the time had come to make a dash for the loo. There I spent the best part of fifteen minutes contemplating what it had been that had given me the trots. At one point my reverie was interrupted by the wail of police sirens. I walked back into the pub just in time to see Villain 1, the van-driver and half a dozen others being bundled into the back of a Black Maria, along with rails and rails of fur coats which had clearly fallen off the back of a lorry.

Feeling better, I had a few more drinks with the horsey girls before returning home where, at about 1 am, I was woken by a banging and ringing at the front door. When I opened it, there was Villain 1 again, and he was in as ferocious a mood as he had been the last time he'd called. This time I was not about to hang around to see what he wanted. I ran upstairs to the bedroom and bolted the door. Seconds later, the door fell from its hinges and Villain 1 came crashing in. 'You've snitched again, you fucking grass.'

'That's bollocks,' I said indignantly.

'You phoned the police from the pub!' he shouted.

Obviously he had put two and two together and made five. While I was in the loo losing my lunch, he thought I'd been calling the law. I pleaded my innocence. I didn't blub, but by this stage I was shit scared. He was pushing me around the bedroom, and each push was more aggressive. Finally, he knocked me flying on to the bed with an ugly blow to the stomach. I didn't retaliate. I was too small, too weak and too sensible.

Next he jumped on top of me on the bed, turned me on my stomach, and put me in a painful armlock. He must have realized pretty quickly that it was a waterbed as he was finding it very hard to keep his balance. It gave him an evil idea. He removed his knife from his pocket and cut a two-foot slash in the plastic casing that held the water. Then he pushed my head inside it, under the water, and held it there as I flailed my arms around trying to get out. After about thirty seconds he pulled me up by the hair. 'Tell me you phoned the police!' he yelled.

'No,' I replied, and down went my head again, this time for longer. The ducking was repeated at least half a dozen times, but still the answer to his question was no. I imagined the headlines in the local paper: 'WARLEY CHEF DROWNS IN WATERBED'. If I lived I was going to have to deal with some mess in the sitting room below. Would the ceiling withstand the water, or would we both go crashing through it? Then, suddenly, he just walked away. 'OK, I believe you,' he said.

'Thanks a bunch. What about my bed?'

'That's your problem.'

'Shall I call the police?' I quipped. He turned to give me another jab.

'Only joking,' I said hastily, and he was gone.

I ran downstairs to get a hose, stuck one end into the leaking bed and the other out of the window, ran outside and started sucking. Soon the water was coursing away into the garden. I went back inside and fell asleep on the sofa with the dogs, contemplating whether this was really the kind of life I wanted. I came to the conclusion that although I was stupid mixing with the sort of 'friends' who made enemies superfluous, I liked living on the edge. There might be the odd hiccup, but generally things were pretty good. I had a reasonable job, after all, and my love life was on the up.

The partnership between Villain 1 and Villain 2 was, however, shortly to come to a sticky end. I was driving the horsebox for them one day when their horses were competing at Harwood Hall in Essex. In the cab on the way home, both the worse for wear on the drinks front, they started having a furious row. Villain 2's girl (and mine) had won her event and Villain 1's had come second on a technicality. Villain 1 was accusing Villain 2 of having cheated. Although I was asked my opinion, I knew better by now than to venture one.

When we pulled up in the yard I went round to the back and helped the girls unload the horses and get them back into their stables. Villain 1's girlfriend, seeing that the row was escalating, then made herself scarce. Villain 2's girl and I took advantage of the situation to grab a few minutes for ourselves in the stable. We could hear the guys screaming and shouting outside, and it soon became obvious that the slanging match had degenerated into a fully fledged fight. We decided it would be advisable to leg it across the field.

We heard the news the next day. The word was that Villain 2 had taken an axe from the horsebox and laid into Villain 1, almost severing one of his arms. Villain 1 had ripped a fencing bar out of the ground and smashed it over Villain 2's head, causing a severe fracture. Villain 2 was in hospital, Villain 1 had been treated by a doctor he knew. The rumour was that Villain 2 was pressing charges, a definite no-no in the gangsters' code of honour.

Before it went any further, a stranger in a pinstriped suit and bowler hat walked up to Villain 2's house one day saying that his Jaguar had broken down outside. Villain 2 went out to help and his six-year-old son tagged along behind, teddy bear in hand. Neither of them was ever seen again.

Villain 1 was an obvious suspect, and the police held him on several occasions, but Villain 2 seemed to have upset everyone he'd ever met. I heard that the police dug up Villain 1's entire garden, checked quarries and even investigated building works on the new M25, but they never came up with any evidence, and he was never prosecuted.

A few years later I read in a red top that a hitman known as Big H. had been arrested for several murders. Villain 2 and his son were listed among his victims. Apparently, the boy had been shot in front of his dad in a warehouse in the East End. His father had then been similarly disposed of and both bodies had been dismembered and burned in the grate of a small house in east London. I was questioned by the police at the time, and after the clingfilm incident I was hugely relieved that I hadn't witnessed the fight – or the false breakdown. Even so, it wasn't until the hitman was caught that I fully appreciated just how lucky I had been not to be more involved.

With all this going on, you could be forgiven for thinking that my life consisted of no more than drinking and hanging around with hoodlums, but I was working quite hard as well. I found the management part really dull, though, and still yearned for the kitchen. It wasn't long before I got my wish. My two chefs walked out on me after a bit of a ding-dong and I was left holding the baby. It was a big baby, too: on the Saturday after the chefs' departure we had a function for 120 people and all I had in the kitchen was me and one commis. The menu was pretty straight-forward: cream of tomato soup, trout Cleopatra and Black Forest gâteau. The trout was easy enough – it would be pan-fried whole to seal it, then popped in the oven for twelve minutes, and sprinkled with prawns, toasted almonds, lemon butter and parsley – and the gâteau would be bought frozen, which was just as well, as I hadn't a clue how to make a cake. It was the soup I was worried about. I hated the powdered version my two chefs had always used, and the fresh tomato soup I had learned to make at Westminster College wasn't any better. What was needed, I decided, was that unique tomato-soup taste of childhood, and that meant canned Heinz variety. I shot down to the Cash and Carry to pick up a couple of cases and served it with diced fresh tomato, some chopped, crispy bacon, butter-fried croutons and a dollop of soured cream. It went down a storm, and several of the guests were raving about it. This cooking lark wasn't as hard as I thought, even if my soup was a delicious con.

On the basis of the success of that evening, I decided not to replace my two chefs directly. Instead I covered two jobs – food and beverage manager and head chef – employed a reasonable sous-chef, or second chef, told him what to do and then watched how he did it. And that, in a nutshell, was more or less how I learned to cook. From then on the Coombe Lodge Hotel built up a fairly strong clientele. My mother even persuaded my grandmother to set foot in Essex, and they would come and stay, usually for Christmas, when we laid on the classic turkey and all the trimmings: ghastly entertainers, crackers and cheap hats.

I was meeting lots of girls, some at disco nights at the hotel, others on trips to the Zero 6 club by Southend Airport, which was a regular hang-out after work. Some nights there ended up in the traditional bar brawl. The trouble with me was that, with my newly acquired confidence, I would just chat to anyone. If I wanted to strike up a conversation with a girl I did, regardless of the possibility that she might have a boyfriend in tow. My pint-sized aggression was a bit of a feature of my early life, at work as well as socially. It wasn't directed at chefs or waiting staff, though – usually it was the boss who caught it. Other chefs and waiters were regularly treated to a tongue-lashing, but never physical aggression. It was not uncommon in those days for head chefs to rule by scaring the hell out of everyone, and woe betide anybody who crossed them, but I have no time for that attitude. What is the point in putting the fear of God into a young chef, or, for that matter, a waiter? As a senior member of staff, you should be encouraging them.

That's one reason why I'm no great fan of Gordon Ramsay, although he is a brilliant chef. His television series *Boiling Point* was an embarrassment to everyone in the catering industry and tarred us all with the same brush. It might have made good telly but it's hard enough to get chefs in our business, and even more difficult to get youngsters to enter the trade in the first place, without

Gordon giving the impression that we are a bunch of psychotic dictators. It's exactly the sort of behaviour the industry is trying to drive out, and there is absolutely no excuse for it. It's time the *Michelin Guide*, the paranoid chef's Bible, made a stand against it by removing the offenders from the guide completely. Only then will they realize that it's time to grow up and calm down. Many of the chefs who work in this abusive way today were themselves abused as commis chefs or chefs de partie, and feel it's their right to dish out similar treatment when they reach the top. It's a cycle that needs to be broken.

I'm sure Gordon will mellow eventually – we all do. He is simply following in the footsteps of Nico Ladenis and Marco Pierre White who had been there before him and who were famous not only for their food but also for their antics in, and often outside, the kitchen, and they are pussycats now.

My own belligerence was the main cause of the parting of the ways between Ian Deal and me. There were other factors, not least a bone of contention over my concentration at work, which was not all it should have been. The reason for this was that I had fallen in love. The girl's name was Jill Thompson (no relation), and she was to become my first wife.

When I met Jill, a stunning youngster barely out of school uniform, she was dating David Chipping, the manager of a Brentwood restaurant where I would later work. She used to come to the hotel on Friday nights with her sister and a couple of the waiters from the restaurant. She had long, straight, reddish hair and a long, straight, slim body, and for me it was lust at first sight. I can't remember how we first got talking – perhaps we chatted about my dogs, or horses, which she was very keen on – but it wasn't long before conversation turned to canoodling (away from the eagle eye of her young suitor, of course).

Jill lived with her parents round the corner from my house in Brentwood, which was highly convenient for clandestine rendez-vous. We'd arrange to meet when I was walking the dogs, or she'd pop round to my house after her parents had gone to bed. As the relationship developed, I no longer saw her as another conquest, but as someone special. I knew it was more than lust when I got those butterflies in my stomach every time I saw or spoke to her.

Whether I was infatuated, in love, or whatever you want to call it, it had a detrimental effect on my job and Ian Deal and I were forever rowing. During one argument I finally flipped my lid and it escalated into a full-blown fight. Ian, who wasn't a particularly big guy, wound up on the wrong end of some serious welly and his wife had to hit me over the head with a milk bottle to separate us. There is no going back once fists have been raised, so I was on my bike. Now I had a home, a girl, and two dogs – but no job.

CHAPTER FOURTEEN

AFTER A FEW DAYS I GOT SOME RELIEF WORK AT THE RATHER UPMARKET restaurant above the pub where Director's Daughter had once been a regular. It was posh nosh, silver service, that sort of thing, and I didn't stay long. I have to admit I was a bit out of my depth – no souped-up Heinz cans here. Next I became the chef-manager of a carvery in a pub called the Golden Fleece, which was part of the Queen's Moat House group. It was not exactly a glamorous career move, but when you haven't saved any money, needs must. And in fact I learned quite a lot on the management side, and how to slice meats paper thin and to incorporate leftovers into dishes on the salad bar, and generally my profit margins were very good.

People often complain about restaurant prices and suspect that they are being ripped off. If they see a bottle of wine in a supermarket priced at a fiver and then find it on a restaurant wine list for nearly £20 they are outraged. Yet the same people will happily go into a shop and pay £30 for a designer T-shirt that probably cost the retailer £6. The problem for our industry is that most people have an idea of the price of a steak at the butcher's or a bottle of champagne or beer from the off-licence. What they don't see are the overheads involved in putting that steak on their plate or that champagne in their glass in a restaurant.

Just compare what has to be paid for from the mark-up on a bottle of wine and from the mark-up on a designer T-shirt, and you will see what I mean. If a small fashion shop buys well there is little wastage and their overheads, aside from the rent, are far lower than those of a restaurant. They might have two to five staff, whereas most restaurants have upwards of fifteen, including washing-up staff, waiting staff, bar staff and chefs. The fashion shop's customer comes in, selects an outfit, pays for it and takes it away, wrapped up and packed into a fancy bag. The restaurant's customer stays with us longer and will be served by several different people. He or she needs a constant supply of clean crockery, cutlery and glasses, plus loos and loo paper, candles and lighting, printed menus. Staff uniforms, chefs' whites, napkins and tablecloths must be laundered, wastage of food taken into account. And then of course there is all the expensive equipment required, the huge utility and insurance bills . . . the list goes on and on. In effect, then, each chair in a restaurant has to be seen as a space being rented out that must show a return. Don't get me wrong: I am not whingeing, but it is not an easy business to be in.

But I digress. At the Golden Fleece life levelled out on to a fairly boring plateau, but it was a steady job, it paid the mortgage and it allowed me a fair amount of free time. I was desperate to spend that time with Jill, but an awkward situation emerged. She was still try-ing to choose between me and her other boyfriend, David Chipping, who managed the ridiculously named Ye Olde Logge on Shenfield Common in Brentwood. He was younger than me, taller, scrawnier, good-looking and a lovely guy. But lovely guys don't always come up trumps with women, and I was happy to let Jill make up her own mind which of us she wanted to be with. I didn't put any pressure on her. Apart from anything else, I wasn't really in any position to do so as I also had a couple of girls on the side.

Jill suggested that I took a part-time job in David's restaurant. They needed a waiter on Saturday nights and occasionally a relief chef in the kitchen. Ye Olde Logge was owned by an Italian, Gino Appierdo, and his wife, Elizabeth. Gino was never seen without a penis-extension cigar in his mouth and his shirt unbuttoned to the waist. He was the original medallion man. He was a flash git, but I liked him. He admired my flamboyance as a waiter and I became the flambé king of cooking at the tables. Steak Diane, beef stroganoff, scampi provençale, scampi in cream and mushrooms; lots of alcohol and flames, pure theatre.

Gino's restaurant was a money-making machine. Some Saturdays we would cater for two weddings, one at eleven in the morning, one at three in the afternoon, then do two full services of seventy in the evening. He did for Essex customers what Terence Conran learned to do in the West End several years later: he treated them like products. It was ship 'em in and ship 'em out, but they loved him for it. I was very impressed. To me, this was the biz.

After a while, Gino offered me a full-time chef's job. He explained that he wanted me to work alongside his head chef, Norman, creating new dishes. He didn't want to lose Norman, because he worked like a dog and he was 100 per cent reliable. Suits me, I thought. I would have the pleasure of cooking and creating without the responsibility. The only problem was that Dave Chipping would be my immediate boss. It was obvious that taking orders from someone whose girlfriend I was seeing behind his back and badly wanted for myself was going to be a bit delicate.

Yet somehow things seemed to work out, and I ended up with David as my boss and got the girl as well. At work I had the advantage of my college management experience and of having been food and beverage manager at the Coombe Lodge Hotel. Dave used to strut around like a peacock. I flattered him, buttering him up and generally brown-nosing, but at the same time I was charming Gino's wife Elizabeth, making regular suggestions to her as to how we could improve the restaurant in the knowledge that these ideas would get back to Gino. I even named a radical chicken dish after her: supreme de volaille Elizabeth, which was a version of chicken Kiev stuffed, instead of garlic butter, with shellfish in a crab mousse and served with a lobster sauce. It was an excellent dish that proved very popular, and quite a departure from the norm in an era when all menus seemed to offer the same things.

Slowly, slowly, I won Gino's confidence, and whether he liked it or not, Dave had to take notice of that. Being a competitive soul, I relished my two victories: establishing my superiority at the restaurant and winning Jill. David dealt with it by remaining aloof and refusing to mix with me and the other staff. In our afternoon break, the rest of us would either play football on Shenfield Common or snooker at the snooker hall in Brentwood High Street. After work at night we would either shoot off to the Zero 6 nightclub in Southend or play cards. Luigi, the head waiter at Ye Olde Logge, was the boyfriend of Jill's sister, Gail. He was a keen gambler, passionate about Italian football and often held late-night card schools. Cards and booze: many a caterer's downfall.

I was totally infatuated with my gorgeous young redhead and for the first time in my life, but not the last, I started to become obsessive. My obsessions were to take a variety of shapes, but in this case I was fixated on the need to become more successful. Don't ask me why, but I decided I wanted to own a discotheque. A friend of mine knew of a building going cheap in Hornchurch, a double-fronted freehold property in a bit of a derelict state. My mother introduced me to a designer who drew up the necessary plans, and I cobbled together a business plan, sold my house to raise the deposit and some cash for the builders, and off I went to sell the idea to potential investors. Since I had no experience whatsoever in the club world, money was not easy to come by. Nothing was forthcoming until I met a fairy godfather called Mr Burchett, who saved the day. As well as pledging loads of dosh himself, he even arranged a loan for me from a merchant bank.

It was going to be an amazing club. Good food, racy cocktails, ultraviolet lights, sloppy sofas: something Essex wasn't used to. On the ground floor there was to be the dance area, bar and restaurant, and upstairs a kitsch romping room where couples could do their thing. I would have a fleet of branded minicabs to shuttle people home. Joe Putney, my builder, was going to be the general manager, and he would deck out the club with the right sort of dolly birds.

As the building progressed word got round and then the visitors starting coming. They were more East End than Essex and they came every week. 'If you're running a club, you'll need protection,' they said.

'No thanks,' I told them. 'I'm not going to be running that sort of club. My bouncers will be beautiful girls, braless, tight T-shirts, you know the sort of thing.'

'You don't understand,' they'd say. And I didn't, of course. This wasn't my world. Public schoolboys didn't get involved with protection rackets. So I ignored their advice and their it'll-be-worth-your-while-type comments.

The club was taking shape. Furniture had been ordered, key staff were in place, and it was all systems go. We made plans to announce the opening. Because of cashflow problems I decided to keep on my job at Ye Olde Logge and let Joe Putney run the operation. I would go over every night after work. Then one evening I got a phone call out of the blue. It was like a thunderbolt hitting me in the back of the head.

'There's a fire at your club,' was all the caller said. I don't know who he was but I imagine it was one of the 'friends' who was so keen for me to buy protection. I raced over. The Fire Brigade were already there. It was too late to salvage anything. The interior was a blackened, soggy mess. My club days were over before they had even begun. The building was insured, but not the fittings, and I couldn't afford to start again. I couldn't even afford to keep up the repayments to the bank, and nobody wanted to put any more funding into the project, so the building was repossessed.

I was broke. I moved into one of Gino's flats a few doors down from the restaurant. I sold my Mini Cooper and bought a Volkswagen campervan, just in case I ever became homeless again. I hate relying on handouts. I was at a really low ebb and I badly needed Jill. I asked her to move in with me and, in the face of the strong objections of her parents, she agreed. I was so glad she did, because it was Jill who pulled me through.

It was the summer of 1976, a very hot, dry summer, and a period of calamity after calamity for me. In the afternoons we'd go to the swimming pool in Brentwood for a swim and gossip. I was asleep in the sun by the pool one day when two jerks from the restaurant decided to throw me in as a joke. Of course I awoke immediately they tried to grab hold of me. I'm not good when roused suddenly from a deep sleep. Somehow, in my befuddled state, I managed to lift both the jerks off the ground. My body took the weight without any problems but one of my legs decided to snap on me. I was in agony. I thought my knee had gone again but the pain seemed too severe for that, so I dragged myself over to my Volkswagen, affectionately known as the Fuck Truck, and drove to Harold Wood Hospital. Sure enough, the leg was broken. Now I was sentenced to eight weeks in plaster in the hottest summer for years. I remember the sweat constantly trickling down the inside of the cast. I tried to carry on working, but it was hopeless. The kindly Gino continued to pay me, saying he would claim the money off insurance, but it was only sick pay, hardly enough to feed Jill and myself. By this time she was working as a nurse at a local psychiatric hospital, but her wages were hardly lavish. Gino asked me to help out part-time, but I was frustrated by my immobility. Jill suggested that I went down to Shiplake to relax and give my leg a complete rest while it healed. So off I went to my grandmother's house. Jill came down for a couple of weekends and then she went quiet on me. Something was up. I called Luigi to check up on her. He was Mr Discretion. All he would say was that he thought I should return to Brentwood. Immediately I smelled a rat.

So I took the train home and walked into the flat to find Jill there with a mutual 'friend', who beat a hasty retreat. I forget his name, so I'll call him Snake. All I remember is that he was small, even smaller than me, with blond hair that he wore in a curly, uncared-for sort of style and that he was a modest builder. That description might sound a little bitchy, but hey, this guy was trying to steal my girl. Even so, I was glad I hadn't gone steaming in as further research revealed him to be a black-belt karate kid, more than a match for my brown belt with broken leg.

Instead I confronted Jill. I let rip; she pleaded her innocence. I let rip some more, she prepared supper and I smashed the plate out of her hand as she offered it to me. Yes, I know it was immature, but I wasn't hungry and I wanted to get to the bottom of the story. It didn't work, though. She pushed past me, dumping me flat on my arse with my gammy leg floundering in mid-air. I struggled to my feet, blaspheming, and my temper got the better of me. I lashed out with the back of my hand. Wrong, very wrong and I knew it. No excuses. She charged out of the front door, yelling that I had chipped her front tooth. I ran after her, not an easy task for a man on crutches. I used them like a pole vaulter's pole. With every pace I took off and landed about ten yards further down the pavement. I wasn't exactly catching her but she wasn't gaining much ground, either. We must have made a ridiculous sight, but I wasn't about to lose my girl to some poxy builder. Eventually, though, my armoured leg got the better of me. I crashed in a crumpled mess on the pavement and she got away.

In a sorry state, I made my way back to the flat. I was experiencing emotions that were entirely new to me. Up until now I hadn't ever been jealous. There hadn't been any need for me to be. The other girls had simply been points on a learning curve. Jill was different. I was not happy about contracting the disease of jealousy, but there wasn't going to be any instant cure for it now. I was hell-bent on destruction, namely the destruction of Snake, the builder. As he wasn't a man to take on physically, I had to exact my revenge in an underhand way. I began by removing the spark plugs from his van. It turned out that he was a whizz with mechanics so that hardly had him in racking sobs. Next I tried the slashed tyres. Not bad. I was getting to him. Then came the brake fluid over the paintwork. Not too effective, as Snake's van wasn't what you would call the Rolls-Royce of builders' vans, more Del Boy than McAlpine.

It wasn't a part of my plan, but I ended up going out with Snake's ex. She wasn't the most attractive girl in the world, but she was pissed off with him and I felt the same and this mutual feeling threw us together. Then I started to put myself about a bit, making sure that Jill was around when I did. She kept company with Snake and I pretended I was having a whale of a time with whoever I was with. A few nights of her seeing me with other women started to get to Jill. I affected not to notice that her wicked eyes were throwing daggers at the innocent third party with me, but inside I was chuckling. It wasn't a deliberate strategy but it was such a success that it might as well have been.

Within a couple of days Jill was round at the flat to try to remedy the situation. I insisted that it was all over and that I had moved on. It was a terrible lie, of course, because I worshipped the ground she walked on. I didn't hold out for long. She soon had me back in the sack and I soon had her up the aisle.

The other disaster in the summer of 1976 occurred while I was still incapacitated with my broken leg. One Sunday I got a call from my gran, now trucking along into her eighties. She seemed agitated, which was most unusual for her. 'You'd better get up to town quickly,' she told me. 'Your mother's gone mad.'

'What do you mean, gone mad?'

'Well, apparently she's up a tree, naked, ranting and raving.'

If anyone else had said this to me, I would have thought it was a tasteless prank, but coming from Gran I knew it was on the level. I told her I'd be there as fast as my one and a half legs could carry me. The journey, by train to Liverpool Street and then on by tube and a bus, took me two hours, and by the time I reached my mother's house (she was now living in Bolingbroke Grove on Wandsworth Common), she was nowhere to be seen. I went to her neighbour's door and was told that she'd been carted off in an ambulance. She'd been taken to St George's Hospital in Tooting. Off I hobbled again, in search of a cab. It was a blazing day. I couldn't work out whether I was cooking or rotting. Whatever it was, it was not pleasant.

At St George's I found myself amid the usual National Health mayhem. All I wanted to do was find my mother, but it seemed I was asking the impossible.

'What's your name?' barked a receptionist.

'Antony Worrall Thompson.'

'We don't have anyone here by that name,' she said, closing the register.

'Well, that's because I'm standing in front of you.' I checked myself. Sarcasm was unlikely to get me too far. 'My mother's name is Joanna Duncan,' I said more politely.

'She was here, but she's been sent to a mental home.' She didn't say anything more than that. She just wrote down the address of the institution.

A mental home? I thought to myself. What is going on? She was perfectly all right the last time I saw her. I took another cab to what looked like a Victorian fortress, all grey, rectangular buildings, lifeless buildings that frightened me. I had once been to the hospital where Jill worked and had been appalled at the way their patients were dealt with. Jill was young and idealistic, and tried her best to do things the right way, but some of the seasoned minders treated the patients as if they were a load of cabbages. I sincerely hope that things have improved since then, because in those days it seemed that people were just dumped there and forgotten about. Any medical treatment seemed to be the exception rather than the rule, and cruelty the name of the game.

I saw nothing at the fortress to convince me that this was not a general attitude in the so-called care of the mentally ill. I was taken through several prison-type doors that were kept firmly locked before I finally got to the ward where my mother was being kept. The duty nurse explained that she had been discovered wandering down Bolingbroke Grove stark naked. The police had been called and had taken her, kicking and screaming, to St George's, from where she had immediately been transferred to the psychiatric hospital. While the nurse was out of the room I glanced at her notes. From what I could gather she hadn't even been seen by a doctor yet. It seemed that she had simply been dosed to the hilt to calm her down.

Eventually I was taken through to see Mum. The sight that greeted me shocked me to the marrow. She was lying there completely comatose and completely naked, except for the bedclothes. Around both wrists were two large, leather straps which secured her to the bed. As if that wasn't bad enough, my fifty-four-year-old mother looked more like an eighty-four-year-old. Her face was as wrinkled as an old prune, scored by deep lines, and her hands were withered and twisted. This was a merely middle-aged woman who, despite her love for the bottle and the fags, always took a pride in her appearance. She used every cream known to woman to stave off old age.

'Has my mother seen a doctor?' I stammered.

'No.'

'Why not?'

'Well, we thought she had just lost her marbles, had a break-down. That's why she's here.'

'But she's sick,' I said. 'I'm going to get her doctor now. Please order me a cab.'

'That's not allowed. A doctor from the hospital will see her in the morning. You can't bring in your own doctor.'

'Just try and stop me!' I shouted. 'Look at her! She may be dead by the morning!' I really thought that was a possibility. I had never ever seen anything so disturbing in my life.

I stormed off, shot back to my mum's house and picked up some nightclothes, some day clothes, some juice and her toothbrush and beauty products. I had already phoned our family doctor and the local bobby and arranged to meet them there. The doctor drove us both back to the institution. Getting back into it was easier said than done. At first they tried to argue that visiting hours were over for the day. 'You've got my mother in there against her will,' I said. 'She has not been committed, so she's free to leave at any time.' Our policeman had to flash his badge before they backed down.

When we reached the ward, the doctor couldn't believe his eyes. He was horrified not only by my mum's appearance but also by the nightmarish scene. The patients were allowed no modesty, no dignity. The doctor pulled some screens around my mother's bed and went through the routine of taking her blood pressure and temperature and listening to her chest. He concluded that she wasn't mad at all, but was suffering from an attack of the DTs brought on by massive dehydration, which had in turn developed into double pneumonia.

He was outraged that nobody had so much as taken her temperature. It was 105 degrees. He called a private ambulance and had Mum transported to the King Edward VII Hospital at Hyde Park Corner, the building that now houses the Lanesborough Hotel. This hospital, the one where my grandfather had been treated on his return from South Africa, was usually reserved for officers of the services and, for some reason, the Royal Family, and I knew my mother was now in safe hands. And so it proved. Within ten days she was back on her feet and acutely embarrassed by the scene she had caused back in Wandsworth.

Once she was compos mentis we pieced together what had happened. She had made one of her trips to Menorca, her favourite holiday destination, which she visited two or three times a year. She loved the island, and would have moved there if she had been able to pluck up the courage to make the break with England. She knew loads of people there, she loved the sun and she loved the cheap booze. She also loved walking, and would spend hours rambling round the countryside. On one of these walks she had developed bad blisters which had become infected. With walking off the agenda, she spent the rest of her holiday sunbathing in extremely hot temperatures and hitting the cheap wine without counteracting the dehydrating effects of both of these pastimes by drinking water.

Her illness, then, had started in Menorca and had been exacerbated on her return to the UK by that scorching summer. She had carried on soaking up the rays and the wine at home and her body had turned bronze and wrinkled – a plum transforming itself into a prune. Her brain had been affected and had taken on an aggressive character. Fortunately she made a full recovery, and I'm pleased to report that most of her wrinkles disappeared once she was forced to drink some reasonable quantities of water.

It should be a lesson to us all. We're told we need to drink two litres of water a day, and I can offer this conclusive evidence that it gets rid of wrinkles, too. I hate water. Fishes swim and do other things in it, and unless the weather is very hot, it doesn't slip down easily. But I'm getting better at drinking it. I'm up to a forced litre a day since I had a filter system fitted to my tap.

By the autumn life had returned to what passed for normal. My mother's health was restored, my leg had healed, I was back at work at Ye Olde Logge, and Jill was home at the flat with me and my Alsatians once again.

The restaurant was going from strength to strength. It was almost always packed, and the reputation of our food was growing all the time. The kitchen was still run by Norman, me and Raoul, the kitchen porter, with schoolboy help on Saturdays. One of the schoolboys was a guy called Chris Galvin, a kid who showed real promise. He was to work for me again briefly later in my career and from there went on to do wonderful things, ending up as executive chef for Sir Terence Conran at the Orrery restaurant in London. It's fabulous when youngsters you've helped to inspire go on to become a success. The sense of pride I get from that gives me more pleasure than almost anything else in my career. It's an attitude in which modern chefs differ from their sixties counterparts, who tended to be jealous of the achievements of their protégés rather than proud.

They were so protective of their recipes that youngsters then had to fight much harder to learn anything than they do today.

At home Jill and I settled into a comfortable domestic routine. My jaunts to pubs and discos were curtailed, Jill, who proved to be an excellent cook herself, made me some great meals and our life together seemed rosy. After the rift in the summer we felt that our relationship was strong, and at the beginning of the following year, 1977, we got married.

CHAPTER FIFTEEN

MY EARLIER BOAST ABOUT GETTING JILL UP THE AISLE WAS JUST A FIGURE of speech, because in fact there were no aisles involved. We planned a quiet wedding in the unlovely surroundings of Brentwood Register Office. And a quiet wedding it was, although it was remarkable for the fact that it saw my grandmother, my mother and my father assembled in the same room for the first time in nearly twenty-five years. It was strange that, given the fragmentation of my family and the more conventional structure of Jill's, both my parents should be present while hers stayed away. But sadly, the deterioration in my relationship with her mother and father as a result of our earlier split was such that they chose not to attend. They had never really forgiven me for that fight I had with Jill over the Snake.

It was Jill who was determined to get my father to come. She knew that I hadn't seen him since I was three and she felt, quite rightly, that this was absurd. We managed to establish that he was still living in Herne Bay with Phyllida, his third wife, and one day Jill persuaded me to pay him a visit. If she had discussed this with me beforehand I might well have bottled out, but she gave me no advance warning – we just jumped into the campervan and set off for Kent. There were several points during the journey when I wanted nothing more than to turn for home, but Jill was a forceful type and once she'd made up her mind about something, that was it. We must have been crazy. We didn't even know whether or not he was going to be at home.

When we arrived Jill said she thought she ought to stay in the van until the ice had been broken. So I approached the small, well-kept semi on my own. I cast a glance back at Jill for reassurance, then I rang the doorbell and waited. My father, a tall, grey-haired man with grey goatee beard, answered the door.

'Yes,' he said. 'Can I help you?'

He didn't recognize me. And there was no reason why he should have done. As far as I knew, my mother hadn't sent him any photos of me. His sister, my Aunt Margie, kept him in touch with my progress, but she wouldn't have sent him any pictures, either. I guess I had changed a bit since I was three. Now I had long, blond hair, I was several feet taller and several broken noses flatter, and I was sporting a pathetic attempt at a beard. So it is perfectly understandable that he wouldn't have known me from Adam, but even so, it still comes as a shock when you are not recognized by your own dad.

'Let me introduce myself,' I said. 'I'm Henry Antony Cardew Worrall Thompson, your son. How are you, Dad?'

The colour drained from his face. 'Come in, come in,' he said weakly. I explained that I had my future wife in the car, and beckoned her over.

Inside the house, my father introduced me to his wife, Phillida, who seemed pleasant, overawed and frightfully, frightfully. I suppose I viewed her with suspicion as my mother had been less than flattering about her. We chatted, rather uncomfortably at first, slowly warming to each other. Phillida kept her distance, which, to be fair, was probably her way of giving me the chance to talk to the father I hadn't seen for the best part of twenty-five years.

I discovered that he had given up drinking and gambling and, unfortunately, most of his acting. He was still passionate about horse racing and cricket, and his shelves were crammed with all sorts of books on both subjects. It was obvious to me that he had fallen on hard times. His life now was looking after Phillida, who had been left with minor but permanent disabilities by her car accident. He seemed a gentle, charming man. Later, he was to devote his life to the Church by becoming a lay priest at Leintwardine in Shropshire. I liked him. As we left he promised to come to our wedding. He honoured that promise, and thereafter we vaguely kept in touch, but the absence of any basis of a father–son relationship throughout my childhood was a gulf we were never really able to bridge.

On our big day the appearance of Brentwood Register Office was enhanced by snow. It could have been a romantic occasion, but it wasn't, it was very matter-of-fact. It was also a little tense, because I hadn't told my mother that my father would be coming. Fortunately, after she and my grandmother had got over the shock of seeing him, things were OK. My grandmother, who always blamed my mother for everything, was actually rather fond of him, and later, after a few drinks, the three of them finished up at one end of the table chatting companionably.

After the formalities we had the usual photographs taken, outside in the snow. What a disaster. The photographer hadn't a clue. In one picture the line-up suggested that it was my father who was the bridegroom. Both Jill and I appeared to be having a bad hair day, though that could be attributable to the fashions of the time. Mine – gag and double gag – was curled under at the back, and there was not a hair out of place. Jill's long locks were almost orange, and crimped, giving the impression that she was wearing a wig.

The wedding breakfast took place at Ye Olde Logge. It was a soberish affair. My mother and my father were initially placed at opposite ends of the table, and the absence of Jill's parents was keenly felt. Luigi, Gail's boyfriend, was serving us with Jill's ex, David Chipping. Looking back it was not the best way to get married. Every girl deserves romance, a little pomp and ceremony. Her wedding day should be a day to remember. I don't know about Jill, but my memories of it are pretty dim. I have no idea what we ate or what presents we received, and my best man was a mate at the time whose name I forget.

Impulsiveness, desperation, rebellion are the three words that sum up my marriage to Jill. Impulsiveness because I thought I loved her. Jill was lovely, but she was not the one for me. We were like two shooting stars heading towards each other in the solar system. At some stage there was bound to be an explosion.

The desperation I am talking about was mine, not Jill's. Having had all the confidence knocked out of me by that rugby accident and waited so long to regain it, when a really beautiful girl came into my life, subconsciously I must have been thinking, Fuck me, I'm never going to find a bird as gorgeous as this again. I'd better marry her. Or something along those lines.

And then there was rebellion. In my case it was an unconscious one, but marrying an Essex girl was a rebellion against my family. I know the Christian faith doesn't do arranged marriages, but in my gran's eyes I was marked down to marry one of those 'finished off' girls. I should have been doing the circuit, chatting up a Sophie or an Annabel. But that wasn't me. I needed a girl I could throw into the snow or into a haystack and who wouldn't cry over smudged make-up or a chipped nail. I needed character, passion; a girl with attitude, someone prepared to say no, someone who would fight their corner.

Jill's rebellion was more obvious. She ignored the sound advice of her parents not to touch me with a bargepole. She was a strong-minded girl who wanted and often got her own way. It wasn't long before she, too, realized that she had made the wrong decision. She had been impulsive and rebellious, if not desperate.

Our marriage began in a cosy, cutesy sort of way as Jill got to grips with domesticity. New man had yet to be invented so I was more than happy to let her do the cooking, the washing, the cleaning and the ironing while I handled the decorating, pasting hideous, loud wallpaper on to every wall I could find, shopped for furniture and did the gardening.

Then one day I woke up wanting more. It wasn't Jill I was dissatisfied with: this was about my career. I had a cushy little job, a great girl and a pleasant enough home, but cushy never did it for me. I started getting arsey with people at work. I became short-tempered and prima-donna-ish and began to believe that I was the best thing since sliced bread for Ye Olde Logge, which of course I wasn't. One summer's day I picked an argument with the boss, Gino. God knows what it was about, and it doesn't really matter. The point was that it escalated until things got completely out of hand and we ended up fighting, alley cat and top dog, crashing about the restaurant, breaking chairs, overturning tables, smashing glasses. Gino was totally gobsmacked by my aggression, and the staff just looked on in amazement and horror. Finally one of them had the brains to call Raoul, the kitchen porter, who tried to separate us. I was furious. I threw a powerful punch that landed plumb on Raoul's chin and he went down as if he had been poleaxed. There he was, out cold, in the middle of the restaurant. I was shocked, Gino was shocked and we both stopped fighting. I liked Raoul. He was a friend and bloody hard worker. I couldn't believe that I had just decked him.

The fist is a deadly weapon. I can vouch for the power of a single blow to the face. In the days when I had my Mini Cooper, I was stupidly driving it too fast once in London, overplaying the exuberance of youth. I was overtaking a white van in Streatham when suddenly a car turned left out of a side road, the driver looking to the right but not looking left. I had to cut in front of the van to avoid a collision. At the next set of red traffic lights, the van driver jumped out and, with no cursing or swearing or other preamble, let rip a punch straight through my window on to my eye and nose. The result was a broken nose (again) and fractured cheek: an early example of road rage, circa 1969.

After the restaurant rage incident, I was, of course, sacked on the spot. Having lost my job, I then stubbornly refused to leave the flat Gino had been kind enough to rent to me. At first he tried the traditional Italian eviction method: threats and harassment. I responded by dispatching some market lads to have a quiet word in his ear. The harassment stopped and Gino had to revert to the law to get me and Jill out of his property. It took him nearly nine months. Free accommodation gratefully received. Thanks, Gino.

In the meantime, alternative employment had to be found. But who would have me, a street-fighter with a public-school education? I did a few nights as a casual in local pubs, and then I had a stroke of luck. My friend and fishmonger, Lee Hicks, mentioned to me that one of his customers was in urgent need of a head chef. The only hitch was that the restaurant was an Italian restaurant, and I knew nothing about Italian food.

'Does that matter?' asked Lee. 'You can cook, can't you?'

'I know I can cook, but this is different. This is proper foreign food, and I only know French.'

'Go for it. He's desperate. Just read some books and do your homework,' advised Lee.

The only book I had that dealt with Italian cooking was one of my trusty Elizabeth Davids, *Italian Food*, still a favourite. It gave me a grounding that might impress at the interview. I went along to the Adriatico in Woodford Green, on the outskirts of east London, to see the owner, Mario, a tallish, slimmish guy of uncertain years with that classic Italian nose. I found that my bullshit was not really required, as the interview was brief. 'Lee tells me you're a good cook. Can you start on Monday?'

'Yes,' I replied, without much confidence. Mario showed me a small, rather grotty kitchen, and that was that.

I explained that my knowledge of Italian cookery was not extensive. I looked at the menu. It was long, and it was definitely Italian, but one of the dishes on it gave me hope. Pollo sorpresa

was, I knew, the Italian name for my old standby, chicken Kiev. I
often wondered whether they called it pollo sorpresa because of the
unwelcome surprise you got when you cut into it and ended up
with a spurt of very garlicky butter on your Italian designer shirt. I
never found out. But I took the job, though not without a certain
amount of trepidation.

What I learned at the Adriatico served me well for many years.
The first lesson was that a man who is friendly at your interview is
likely to turn out to be a right bastard when you work for him.
Mario ruled the Adriatico with a rod of iron, ably backed up by his
Irish wife who controlled the finances and, I have a sneaking
suspicion, wore the trousers as well. Secondly, it taught me that
having an Englishman in charge of an Italian kitchen is not something a restaurant is inclined to boast about. It was tantamount to
having an Englishman running the Italian national football team. It
was obvious that Mario hated having me in his kitchen, but he
needed me, and it must be said that both the standard of cooking
and the customer numbers rose after my arrival.

Once I got to grips with the change in nationality, the cooking
itself was a piece of cake. The main courses mainly revolved around
three big pots of sauce sitting in a bain-marie (literally Mary's bath
– what she had to do with it I've no idea, but basically this is a
trough of simmering water in which sauces sit in a separate container, happily multiplying their bacterial count). To the béchamel
you would add white wine, cooked mushrooms and onions for a
white wine and mushroom sauce; grated Gruyère or Emmental for
a cheese sauce; parsley for parsley sauce, or mustard, brandy and
cheese for a thermidor sauce. Then there was a vat of tomato sauce,
from which stemmed another half-dozen combinations, and a pot
of brown stuff known in its various guises as gravy, jus, sauce
espagnole and so on.

My cooking went from strength to strength. Mario even allowed
me to put some specials on the menu. But all he was doing was
lengthening the leash, not letting go of it. The new dishes were a
roaring success. The customers liked them so much that Mario was
finding it harder and harder to criticize me. So he reined me in
again. He called me into his office and explained that while my
food was excellent, it was not what he wanted in his restaurant and
that I would have to go back to the original concept. He wouldn't
be swayed by any of my protests so I had no choice but to comply.
I needed the job and I wasn't at this stage prepared to bite off the

hand that was feeding me. It was utterly frustrating because the basic menu bored me to tears. By now I had learned all the Adriatico had to teach me.

Then Lee Hicks the fishmonger came up trumps again. He told me that some acquaintances of his, one of whom was a regular at the Adriatico and a fan of my food, were opening a restaurant about half a mile away, on George Lane in South Woodford. They were looking for a chef, so I arranged to meet them.

There were three guys involved in the project. Barry Jackson was a short, good-looking bloke, very flash, very smiley, but he didn't like to look you straight in the eye. His warmth appealed to me, though, and I felt I could work with him. Ray Brown looked like a conman, which was what he turned out to be. He was full of false charm and as slippery as an eel. And then there was a quiet one, Peter Goring, a bit of a cool cat, stylishly dressed. He was rather aloof and did not have much to say for himself. These were my first impressions of the trio, and they weren't far off the mark. In fact, both Ray and Peter later did a little stretch for their mischievous ways.

When I got to know them, I learned that Barry, the resident smoothie, was in the wedding business – cars, photographers, that sort of thing. He was a legitimate businessman and very successful. He had a big house in an upmarket local suburb, a flash car and a flash wife called Bunny. The other two, Slippery and Cool, had made their money in a Robin Hood kind of way, except that they forgot to pass it on to the poor. Peter was the mysterious one. He kept himself to himself and allowed the others to do the talking. While he undoubtedly had a 'past', he now lived contentedly with his gorgeous lover, Christine, in Brighton, where he spent most of his time. He was the one I ended up liking and trusting.

At our initial meetings, the desperation on both sides was palpable. I was desperate to be out of the Italian's hair, and the boys desperate to find a chef in time to open their restaurant, Hedges, three weeks later. I took the job and resigned from the Adriatico. In spite of having done his level best to frustrate me, Mario seemed disappointed, and he gave me some advice that I should have heeded but, as usual, didn't. 'You watch those boys. They're nice enough on the surface, but they're not to be trusted. They'll suck everything out of you and then discard you.' In a roundabout sort of way, he was proved quite right.

But by now you know what I was like then. As I've said, I

relished living on the edge, and I was dazzled by my bosses' lifestyle. It was great being wined, dined and driven around in flash cars. It was Barry who provided all these trappings. He also invited me to use the pool at his palatial house. I'd always loved swimming, but the only place I'd ever been able to do it even half privately was in the small section of the Thames at the bottom of my gran's Shiplake garden, where I'd first learned to swim as a small boy. I had been taught in a weir stream there by my grandmother's best friend, the actress Margaret Rutherford. What a marvellous old eccentric she was. She didn't seem in the slightest bit bothered about what people thought of her. There she'd be, dressed in a bathing suit that came down to her knees, having races with me across the Thames, much to the amusement of the boating fraternity, who, on spotting her, would snap away on their Box Brownies.

I might have been impressed by all this ostentation, but Jill certainly wasn't. She took an instant dislike to the boys and especially to their women – apart from Christine, who was rarely seen – with their Essex airs and graces and jewellery dripping from every bare bit of flesh. Jill was appalled at their showiness. Personally, I thought they were very sexy, but I was still influenced by the idea of the perfect body and the labels attached to it.

In the busy run-up to the opening Jill and I had a pressing problem to solve, which was that we needed to move out of Gino's flat before we were thrown out. There was an office over the restaurant where we could stay while we sorted ourselves out, so we decided that we would move in there as soon as Hedges had been launched.

The day before the restaurant opened, something happened to me that had never happened before and has never, thank God, happened since. I had a panic attack so severe that it was almost a breakdown. Suddenly, I was convinced that I couldn't do the job. I couldn't concentrate, I couldn't focus, I just wanted to jack it all in. Belatedly, it dawned on me that the responsibility for all this was mine. I was opening a restaurant for the first time as a head chef. It was my menu, I had chosen the staff and it was my neck that was sticking out. The boys couldn't be relied upon for any serious support because they knew sod all about restaurants. Sure, they ate out regularly, they were great at design and they knew their customers, but that wasn't the same thing. The front-of-house staff weren't much better. They had all been employed on the basis of their looks rather than their ability or experience. The final nail in the coffin was an unforeseen disaster of the kind that could easily push you over the edge.

On our test-run night there was no gas pressure. Eighty guests and no fucking gas. I wanted to cry. I had taken it for granted that the restaurant had been designed properly but now I discovered that the pipework was geared to a domestic gas supply as opposed to a commercial one. This hadn't been noticeable when we were testing the dishes, but when you turned the gas on full blast it was a different story. If ever there was a time when I wanted the ground to open and swallow me, this was it. The boys pulled out the stops, and somehow – don't ask me how – they got the Gas Board to work overnight to change the pipes.

When I got home that night I couldn't sleep, which was very unusual for me. Normally I could sleep on a pinhead through a heavy landing on Olympic Airways. I can tell you for nothing that counting sheep doesn't work, and as for sheep jumping over two-bar gates, sheep just don't do that. I must have dropped off eventually because the next thing I knew, Jill was shaking me. 'Wake up, you've got a restaurant to open.' As I rolled over to face her she said, 'God, you look like shit.'

'No need to call me God,' I replied weakly, trying to make light of it. Then I blurted it out. 'I can't do it, Jill. I can't go in. I can't cope.'

'Bollocks, don't be a wimp. You're going in, and I'm coming with you.'

Without Jill I couldn't have done it. I realized I hadn't eaten for days, so she drip-fed me glucose and milk as I worked, and somehow it all went off without any serious hitches.

Within three days we had moved out of Gino's flat – in the nick of time, as it happened, because our departure coincided with the arrival of the court order evicting us. The office above the restaurant which we were to occupy temporarily was bedsit land at its worst. There was no sound insulation from the restaurant, so we could hear the clink of every glass, every note of music, every ring of the till, every Cockney accent. It was three months of hell. We started looking locally for a flat to buy, but by the time we found one and the deal was completed, it was too late.

Living on top of the restaurant, Jill saw at first hand all the beautiful, braless waitresses and a feeling of insecurity began to set in. Her jealousy, combined with our stressful living conditions and our inability to cohabit in domestic bliss, all accelerated the break-up of our marriage. But the fault was totally mine. I was completely blind to her anxieties, an immature man who showed no respect to a wife who was a virtual prisoner in a grotty room above the restaurant. It's true that I was working incredibly hard, but after lunch, and again after dinner, I would sit in the restaurant drinking with the boys, usually surrounded by a bevy of Barry's beautiful birds, all fresh from their facials. The restaurant and its attractions were my life to such an extent that Jill was ignored and even made to feel unwelcome in the restaurant. I wouldn't have blamed Jill if she'd thought that I was bonking everything that moved in the restaurant, and ended up hating any female that was even half attractive. In fact I was not having any affairs, but for all the consideration I showed Jill, I might as well have been. I was too wrapped up in my own little world to notice that she was slowly slipping away from me.

As the arguments grew more and more frequent and the tension built, I would slide into bed when she was asleep and slide out again before she awoke. We were soon leading very separate lives. After work I would go to the Chigwell Country Club with the girls and party until late, and on my days off I would spend time with my new best friends, a family called the Tugbys who had three gorgeous daughters, one of whom was very interested in Peter. It was through these three sisters – Anne, who worked for us on front-of-house, Sarah and Janet – that I became much closer to Peter. Although he was a quiet guy, I quickly discovered that he was an incorrigible flirt.

I can fully understand Jill's paranoia. While I was not actually being unfaithful to her, I'm sure I was mentally undressing every girl I spoke to and imagining what it would be like to sleep with her. In short, I was an arsehole. It was obvious that I was not grown-up enough to have got married. I wasn't being fair to Jill, and in many ways I wasn't being fair to myself, either. I enjoyed the security of marriage, but I loved women and I wasn't ready to settle down. I wanted it both ways, and of course that wasn't possible. On the surface Jill appeared to be content with life, but deep down, she wasn't ready for it either. I knew that we had to end it but I didn't know how, and I was a coward. I needn't have worried. Jill had obviously had enough, and she brought matters to a head in a pretty dramatic way.

The boys saw that my marriage was breaking up and they were worried that it was affecting my work. They thought that if Jill got

to know their wives a little better she might feel more included, so
Barry invited us to lunch one Sunday, along with Ray and Peter and
their other halves. Jill, however, had other ideas. We'd been told to
bring our swimsuits, and after lunch we all retired to the pool. As
the drinks flowed a piggyback fight was suggested, husbands
carrying the wives. At first all was hilarious and jolly, but then it all
turned sour and it became clear Jill and Maggie, Ray's wife, were
no longer playing a game. As is their wont in confrontational
situations, the men retired, trying to pretend that this wasn't
happening. The hostess, Bunny Jackson, was having none of that.
She was in there like a shot, but unfortunately the whole thing got
out of hand. She steamed into Jill and one of the guys was at last
forced to break up the mêlée. Barry had a quiet word in my ear. 'I
think it might be sensible if you took your wife home.' I agreed.

Jill drove, as I'd had a fair amount to drink. In the van we had a
blazing row. I was outraged that she could have embarrassed me so
thoroughly in front of my bosses. I had little understanding of
where she was coming from. It was very much a case of me, me,
me. Quite rightly, she wasn't impressed. Neither was I when we
pulled up outside the restaurant and she tore into me. I got out of
the van and told her to fuck off. She obliged. Later that evening she
called me to say that she was leaving me and that she'd collect her
things the next day.

And that was that. The end of marriage number one. Regardless
of whether or not you want out of a relationship, when the split
finally comes it's still gut-wrenching, and I shed a few tears. But all
you can do is try to learn from your mistakes – it would be some
while yet before I got the hang of that. I'd been with Jill for three
years or so, and I keenly felt the loss of the security that having one
special relationship brings. Now it was just me and the two
Alsatians again.

Once the usual hostilities of breaking up were over, Jill and I did
keep in touch, and over the twenty-odd years that have passed
since, we have remained friends. Jill went off to lead an incredibly
exciting life, but I don't think it's my place to go into that. She is
still a gorgeous, glamorous lady. I hope one day she'll find the
happiness she deserves.

CHAPTER SIXTEEN

JILL AND I HAD BEEN IN THE PROCESS OF BUYING A TWO-BEDROOMED flat off George Lane, just round the corner from the restaurant. By the time the purchase was finalized she had gone, so I moved in on my own with the dogs. Upstairs lived a beautiful Cher lookalike with whom I whiled away many an idle hour. I was desperate to get her into the sack. Jill's departure had knocked my confidence for six, and having been with her for so long I felt as if I had forgotten all the moves. But Cher was in any case in a relationship already, so we became good mates instead, and she helped me through a bad time.

I already used the restaurant as a base for my social life, but now I had no woman in my life it was all I had. I spent even more time with the Tugbys, especially Sarah and Anne, and fell hook, line and sinker for Anne. She had no idea how I felt about her and I didn't push it because she had a boyfriend, Simon, who was an aggressive carrot-top with a black belt in karate. So all I did was flirt with her, and whenever Simon was around that small pleasure was brought to an abrupt halt. Even I wasn't prepared to challenge this fitness freak for the prize of a night of passion with her.

While my marriage had been disintegrating, Hedges had been coming on in leaps and bounds, with many nights yielding 180 covers. I even managed to get a glowing review in the now-defunct London *Evening News*, which must have been a first then for a restaurant on the outskirts of the East End. The clientele was very flash, very Chigwell Country Club; the girls were blonde and the guys were tanned. The restaurant was *the* place to go in sunny

South Woodford. The music was loud, the cocktails came adorned with every decoration in the book and the food was above average for a trendy venue. It was all about seeing and being seen, keeping up with the Joneses, spending more money than the people on the neighbouring table. On Saturday nights we sometimes sold five cases of Dom Perignon.

My menu was typical of the seventies – hardly state-of-the-art, but then, nothing much had changed on menus in twenty years. For the Essex borders it was quite radical, though, and I did have a few interpretations of my own: some great ribs, in addition to the ubiquitous Parma ham and melon, and lots of prawns in one guise or another. Lobster, sea bass, the regulation well-done fillet steak and, of course, scampi featured strongly.

But just when we all thought we had it cracked, disaster struck in the form of a very old grumpy lady who lived upstairs, who complained to the council about the noise. They monitored the situation and made Hedges spend thousands of pounds on sound insulation. But that wasn't enough for our neighbour. This old dear had a real bee in her bonnet, and she wasn't going to rest until she had closed us down. The boys even offered to rehouse her, but she was having none of it. Eventually our late-drinking licence was rescinded and all the customers had to leave by 11 pm. It was the kiss of death. Trade dropped off and the boys panicked. They began to nit-pick, coming down like a ton of bricks on the tiniest problem. They were starting to get up my nose.

Then they decided that my relationship with Anne was unhealthy, and put pressure on her to leave the restaurant. At the root of this, I suspect, was the fact that Simon, the black-belted boyfriend, got on very well with Barry, and doubtless he was applying a little pressure of his own. Faced with this united front, Anne had little choice but to bow out. I was gutted. I had a word with Peter Goring, with whom I was more friendly than I was with the other two. He said that his hands were tied. Although he was a partner, he didn't have any say in the day-to-day running of the operation. But he reassured me that all that was about to change. He wanted to keep a closer eye on things, so he was going to move up from Brighton and divide his time between Hedges and his father's pub, the Queen's in Buckhurst Hill.

Clearly he didn't trust his partners, so I became his little spy at Hedges. Barry, it seemed, was as good as gold, apart from his tendency to drink the profits. Ray was another matter. One night I watched him cashing up and became suspicious that he was fiddling the books. I asked him about it and suddenly he turned nasty. Basically he told me to fuck off and mind my own business. My hackles rose and, like the Jack Russell of old, I sank in my teeth and demanded to know what he was doing. Ray was an arrogant pig of a man who was not about to be challenged by some whipper-snapper of a chef. Without warning there was the flash of a fist which, by chance, I managed to avoid. His rage was written all over his white face in patches of blood-pressure red.

That was it. You know me: a scrap was my kind of game. I responded with a couple of hard punches that sent him crashing over two sofas positioned near the front windows of the restaurant. Then I threw myself on top of him. We rolled over several times before I pinned him to the floor with one hand around his throat. I was, in a sick way, rather enjoying the battle. Ray was a greasy git who lived behind an image of false breeding. He might have had a posh voice, but underneath he was a street urchin.

My hand tightened around his throat. His face was now beetroot red, his eyes bulging. God knows what might have happened if I hadn't suddenly been treated to an unexpected explosion of stars. Maggie, Ray's missus, had somehow managed to separate us. That didn't stop Ray delivering a couple of blows into my body followed by a brace of well-aimed boots to my back. Maggie was screaming hysterically for him to stop. He obeyed. Thank you, Mags. The fracas over, Ray screamed at me: 'You're finished! Get out and stay out!'

'Don't you believe it,' I retorted as I left the restaurant, slamming the door behind me.

I stalked off home. As I opened the door of my ground-floor flat and turned on the light there was a pop as the lightbulb gave up the ghost. Walking in the darkness towards the kitchen, where I kept the new bulbs, I trod on something soft. Shit, I thought. One of the dogs has done something it shouldn't have. And indeed one of them had, but it wasn't what I was expecting. My Alsatian Kim had just given birth to twelve puppies. All things considered, it had certainly been one of those days.

I'd thought Kim was getting a bit fat so I had put her on a diet. It never crossed my mind that she and Fonzi, the best of pals, would actually mate with each other. How naive can you get? The pups were gorgeous, but it must be said that they were a slight in-convenience, especially as there was every chance that I had just lost my job.

I'm sure Peter and Barry privately thought the incident with Ray was hilarious. Neither of them could picture the 'toff' Ray Brown fighting, and as for Maggie getting involved, well, that took the biscuit. Peter was more concerned about the suspicions that had led to the scrap. Publicly, however, they had to support Ray, and the three of them presented a united front. They said they would have to officially caution me, give me 'a verbal warning', to use the industrial-relations vernacular. To which I replied: 'Bollocks. Either you want to get rid of me or you don't. We're grown men. You don't need to give all the legal crap. Besides, it's a bit rich coming from two gentleman villains.'

'We don't want you to go, we just want you to apologize,' they said.

I thought about my new family of dogs, about how much I needed the job, at least for the time being, and for once I bit my tongue and gave in. I shook hands with Ray. It was like shaking hands with a frog, wet, clammy and cold. What was even worse was his smug grin. How I wanted to wipe it off his smarmy face. But I kept my cool.

Hedges had been a major success, but because of the tenacity of one old lady upstairs the goose that had laid the golden egg was dying and the boys were beginning to lose interest. The appearance of a trendy bar called Jets a hundred yards down the street was another nail in its coffin. Overnight we lost our bar trade. Jets was, to put it crudely, wall-to-wall totty, which attracted the high-rollers. There wasn't a credit card in sight, just wodges of wonga. The owner, Phil, was raking it in. I used to go there after work and he and I became friends.

So the writing was on the wall for Hedges and for me. I think I lasted about two months after my fight with Ray Brown before he got his way and had me squeezed out. Trade was bad, and my wages were high, so it was described as a 'business decision'. Despite all the ups and downs, I was sad to be leaving the restaurant, especially as I had nothing else in the pipeline.

It was a mysterious fire that finally put paid to Hedges, about a month after my departure. After my fight with Ray Brown, I was petrified that he might try to blame me. I shared these fears with my mother, who had never liked Ray, and she made me go to see a lawyer, Simon Bowen, to discuss my worries. He asked me why I had come to him. 'My mum sent me,' I replied lamely, feeling like a schoolboy facing the headmaster. Simon was able to swiftly dismiss my concerns, but that meeting was the start of what was to be a lifelong friendship. Even now I sometimes feel as if I am in front of the headmaster when I am with Simon. If I am a Jack Russell, then he is a bulldog, and he has saved my life on more than one occasion.

I decided it was time to hit the big city. I applied for several jobs from the ads in the London *Evening Standard* and was rejected out of hand for most of them purely because of my Essex-based CV. London restaurants can be very up their own bottoms. Their attitude was one I've always tried to avoid. When I interview a prospective chef or waiter I don't pay any attention to college diplomas and very little to their CVs, unless it is a head chef I am after. What I am looking for is passion and enthusiasm. You can teach the basics, you can teach the systems, but you can't teach someone to be in love with the job.

Eventually I got an interview, with a Mr Cooper, who owned a restaurant in Covent Garden called Russell's and was seeking a head chef. This was at a time when Covent Garden was known only for its fruit and vegetable market and for the Opera House. It was still very *My Fair Lady*, a mixture of toffs and discarded cabbage leaves, but long-term plans to relocate the market to its current site, at Nine Elms, were already being discussed. There were very few restaurants there then, apart from the rather grand Inigo Jones, and of course Joe Allen, and a place owned by head chef Antonio Carluccio in partnership with Terence Conran, which is now called The Neal Street Restaurant. Carluccio was one of the guys who had turned me down without seeing me.

I got the job at Russell's. Mr Cooper, it transpired, was desperate: his was a one-man kitchen with extra help on Saturdays. It turned out to be a nightmare, but it was work, and it was in London. Although I had been brought up in its suburbs, the city itself was scary. The chefs I knew by name were like gods to me, and I wondered whether I had it in me to compete with the best.

I certainly wasn't going to find out as head chef of Russell's. Apart from on Fridays and Saturdays, customers were a rare sight. Lunch attracted maybe a dozen and the evenings were dire. There would be one or two before the opera and painfully fewer afterwards. My hours were 10 am to 2.30 pm and then 5 pm to 11.30 in the evening, six days a week, with Sundays off. If that wasn't bad enough, every afternoon I had to jump on the tube at Holborn and shoot back to South Woodford to walk and feed the dogs and the puppies, which were now living in a kennel I had built in the garden. Some nights I would miss my last tube and have to take the night bus, which didn't get me home until 1 am.

Eventually the dog situation became ridiculous. Reluctantly, I found a farm willing to take Kim and three of her pups, sold the rest of the litter and convinced my mum that she needed Fonzi to protect her in an increasingly dangerous city. My mother never took any ideas or suggestions of mine very well but on this occasion she said she'd give it a go. This was a relief because I had tried giving her a dog once before and things had gone badly wrong. It was a Jack Russell, a snappy little number. We left it at my mother's house one evening while I took her out to dinner, and when we returned I noticed a lot of fur in the hallway. The Jack Russell had ripped our twenty-one-year-old cat Bianca into about six pieces. Not a pleasant way to end an evening. Mum made me bury the bits of Bianca at the bottom of the garden at Shiplake and find another home for the Jack Russell. Happily, Mum and Fonzi got along much better. He became her best friend, after the bottle.

Mum was one of Alcoholics Anonymous's failures. She had her good days and she had shocking days. She told me to call and let her know in advance whenever I wanted to visit her. I soon realized why she didn't want me to drop in unexpectedly: she needed time to pull herself together before I arrived. Every cupboard in the house contained discarded bottles, usually empty halves of Teacher's whisky. It made me sad that such a proud lady had to turn to drink for comfort and ended up so lonely. I sometimes blamed myself. As a tiresome kid and a troubled adolescent I was impossible to handle, and once I was an adult I did little to help her. It sounds selfish to say it, but the unpalatable truth was that she'd become an embarrassment to me. I rarely introduced her to my friends, because I never knew what state I was going to find her in.

Russell's, meanwhile, was not proving to be a good move. I tried hard, but old boy Cooper was very fixed in his ways and there was no room for my experimental methods with food. It was a sleazy restaurant, a basement dressed in red that smelled of stale tobacco and spilled beer. Old smells, old menu, old customers, old owner – a restaurant that should have been consigned to the graveyard long before I arrived. But for the reward of being head chef in my first London restaurant I endured the pain. The hours were killing me, but after my early track record running kitchens with a cleaver instead of a brain I was determined to stick at it.

Saturday was the one day I was allowed to employ an extra chef, since on Saturdays all the restaurants in the centre of London were chock-full. Russell's would have three sittings, so we might end up cooking for 160 people. My regular Saturday chef was Max, a very upright German – immaculate whites, polished shoes, very precise. He was extremely efficient, very fast and had obviously had a classic training. I looked forward to seeing him every week. In only one day out of six did I have anyone to talk to, and he was it. The rest of the week I would study the same boring faces as I travelled backwards and forwards on the tube. I would read two papers a day, the *Sun* in the mornings (all young chefs read the *Sun*) and the *Evening Standard* on the way home at night. Afternoon journeys were spent reading the latest cookbook and occasionally trying to seduce a woman without saying a word, just undressing her with my eyes. It never worked, except once when, to my astonishment, a girl spoke to me. 'Ten pounds for a blow job, twenty-five for the full works, no kissing,' she said. I was mortified. And no, I didn't accept the offer.

One weekend Max came to work and told me this would be his last Saturday at Russell's. He had got a head chef's job in Fulham at a new restaurant, opening in three weeks' time, called Brinkley's. I was pleased for him but it was depressing news for me. I would be losing my only mate and having to find a new sparring partner for Saturdays. I didn't think I could stand the pressure any more. I thought about it as we worked and had an idea. I asked Max if he had a second chef for the new restaurant.

'Why, do you know someone?'

'Yes. Me,' I said.

He laughed. 'But you've been my boss for four months. I couldn't possibly ask you to work for me.'

'But it makes sense. You know how I work, and I respect how you work,' I grovelled. I could see he was tempted.

'OK, let me talk to John Brinkley, and I'll call you next week.'

The next week I gave old boy Cooper a week's notice. He was stunned. He liked me, and he liked my cooking, and actually I was fond of him in the way you might be fond of an elderly uncle. But Russell's wasn't my whole life, as other restaurants had been, and I had no future there. Mr Cooper offered me more money, but my mind was made up – I was off to Fulham.

What a contrast. Having worked in Essex and the East End for half a dozen years, Brinkley's came as a bit of a culture shock to me.

It was a return from the gorblimeys to the mwah-mwah land of my heritage. I was still living in South Woodford, of course, but the distance was no obstacle. There was free parking in Fulham so I was able to drive to work and kiss goodbye to the interminable hours on the tube and the mad dash for the last train at night. And compared to Russell's it was a cushy number – there was no day work, just evenings. Brinkley's was opposite St Stephen's Hospital in Hollywood Road, which was home to several other independent restaurants, including Bistro Vino, Jake's and the Golden Duck – local restaurants for local people. It was a restaurant of tasteful design, a ground floor and a basement with a private room for friends in the know on the first floor. On the top floor were storerooms, one of which was later converted into a bedsit for me.

When I first met John Brinkley I found talking to him like talking to wet cardboard. He absorbed everything I said but seemed to have difficulty responding. He was a man of few words, and those he did utter were short, usually of only one syllable. But he was very well spoken when you could get anything out of him. As I got to know him, I realized that his reticence was due to shyness, not a great attribute in a front-of-house operator. And for a man who showed such style when it came to design, I thought his personal appearance was abysmal. Most days he'd wander around in a red or claret V-necked sweater with what we'd later call Jeremy Clarkson jeans or country cords. In fact, I was to discover that this was quite normal in Hooray country. It was just that I was used to the mutton-dressed-as-lamb Essex folk. While John was the public face of Brinkley's, the real power behind the throne, it was believed, was a gorgeous, classically beautiful older woman: his mum, Dr Diana Brinkley.

This guy's got to be gay, I thought. He had very effeminate and mincing mannerisms, full, red lips and neat, short wavy hair. How wrong I was. This dark horse turned out to be a bit of a stud. On the surface, we did not appear to have that much in common. We were like chalk and cheese to look at, for a start. John was tall but unassuming in his understated Fulham clothes, whereas I was short with long, blond hair and went around in flip-flops, shorts and a sleeveless T-shirt. But we were practically the same age, we both came from quite posh families and he had taken the same catering management course at Ealing as I had completed at Westminster College. And in his own way John was passionate about food and his restaurant, it was just that his was an inner passion. There was nothing he wore on his sleeve. Sometimes you wanted to shout, 'For fuck's sake, John, lighten up! Show us your heart instead of a brick wall!' He was something of a boiled sweet with a soft centre.

John had left the initial menu to Max. It was quite classical, as befitted a man of Max's training. I'm sure John had input – he was that sort of a guy – but Max was in charge. For the first couple of weeks after we opened, there were nights when the restaurant had no customers whatsoever, which was very depressing. I would say to Max, 'Can I come in late tomorrow, as there is nothing to prepare?' But my friendly Saturday second chef had turned power-mad overnight. 'I don't care if you have to stand by your work table doing nothing, you will be here at four, do you understand?'

Bollocks, I thought to myself, but I said nothing.

After a couple of weeks Max began to take the odd night off, but when he wasn't there his mate Karl would hover around the kitchen pass, watching my every move, and report back to Mein Führer. Max would then reprimand me for not doing things his way in his absence. 'Bite your tongue, Tone – you need the job,' I told myself. But it soon became impossible. One night, after Max had come in on his evening off just to stand there watching me cook and we'd had a blazing row, I asked to see John Brinkley. 'John,' I said. 'I can't take any more of Max's shit. I'm giving you a week's notice.'

'Don't be too hasty,' he replied. 'Come and talk to me tomorrow.'

When I arrived the next day I found to my surprise that John and Max had parted company and I was to be in charge of Brinkley's kitchen.

The way things panned out, that first month at Brinkley's was the only time in my whole career I ever worked as a second chef. My management training had allowed me to con, waffle, bluff and bull-shit my way into all my suburban head chefs' jobs. But now here I was with the real thing. This was the real London, and I was ready to tackle it. If I could crack it here, I could crack it anywhere.

CHAPTER SEVENTEEN

DON'T ASK ME WHAT I PUT ON MY FIRST MENU. I CAN'T FOR THE LIFE
of me remember anything about it except for one pudding that
wasn't mine: Dr Brinkley's chocolate bombe, deliciously moreish
and deliciously simple. John wanted relative simplicity, and to start
with I gave it to him. I wanted to cook properly, and I recall hanging whole sirloins of beef and boning out 'proper' fish like turbot.

It wasn't until we received our first restaurant review, in of all
publications *World Medicine* on 30 June 1979, that the restaurant
started to take off. The piece was written by the famous gourmet,
foodie and raconteur Derek Cooper. What a brilliant man. Looking
at it again over twenty years later, it reminds me of the rather inauspicious start to my London restaurant career: he begins by
describing how he entered an empty restaurant. On offer were
terrine of chicken breasts, deep-fried mushrooms stuffed with crab-
meat, crudités with dips, prawns wrapped in smoked salmon and
cream cheese (at Hedges I had called these prawns in nappies, but
I didn't think Dr Brinkley would approve of that), and the soup of
Sloanes, carrot, orange and coriander. The average price for starters
was £1.40. Main courses, at an average price of £3.35, included
chicken stuffed with shellfish in a lobster sauce (the dish I had
invented at Ye Olde Logge for Gino's wife, Elizabeth), Scotch beef
fillet with chicken livers and grapes (sounds pretty grim), guinea
fowl roasted with juniper, thyme, parsley and lemon. And for
pudding, apart from the chocolate bombe, there was brown bread
and rum ice cream and strawberry delight. Derek Cooper wrote,
without mentioning my name (chefs were unmentionables in those

days): 'The menu is short and well balanced . . . Brinkley's deserves to succeed.'

After that other reviews came thick and fast and, as I remember it, most of them were favourable. Those were the days when reviewers wrote about food and spared us the psychobabble. Brinkley's soon began to fill up very quickly. I even had to employ a team in the kitchen. I managed to find a very talented Kiwi chef called John Campbell, whose weird and wonderful little sister also helped out. They were a brilliant pair, and I loved them to bits. Front-of-house was John Brinkley's domain. Originally there was a German head waiter, but he was dispatched fairly soon after Max. John then resorted to the raw talent of a gorgeous Irish girl called Harriet Bunbury, who was very posh with little trace of the Irish lilt until she was well oiled. As well as being particularly attractive, Harriet was a bit of a hothead. She had an incredibly fiery temper which reared its head on several occasions in the kitchen. Here there is an unwritten rule that the chef is always right, even when he's wrong. Harriet was unable to grasp this simple concept. I was no soft touch, as you might expect, but Harriet was not cowed by any tongue-lashings of mine. On one occasion she hurled a sugar pot at me, though her accuracy let her down – it smashed into the wall just behind my head.

This fierce side of Harriet was very sexy, and I began to lust after her. Unfortunately for me, so did John Brinkley. The boss won. After she got together with John, Harriet tended to leave us alone in the kitchen, concentrating her energies on meeting John's demands or on throwing herself into the blazing rows they used to enjoy. It was one of those high-octane relationships that burn out very quickly. I guess we've all had romances like that, and they're intoxicating, but the flames that burn the brightest rapidly die out. While the volatile relationship between John and Harriet was not destined to last, she and I remained firm friends.

At the restaurant I was gaining in confidence every day. I wasn't cocky, because I never forgot that this was London, the UK's centre of gastronomy, although in the 1970s gastronomy was probably not the right word for it. By and large the customers at Brinkley's were a nice bunch, quite well-heeled and usually pretty cool. My early misgivings about John proved unfounded. For all his reticence, he was an excellent networker and it was obvious that he and his mother moved in quality circles. Saturdays could be a bit of a problem, however. Most of the regulars would decamp at

Right, top: I can't believe my hair! Wife number one: Jill Thompson. **Right, bottom:** We lost one of the families – my father, mother and Jill.

Above left: Benny from Abba? No: AWT. **Above right:** More big hair from wife number two – Militza. A couple of drinks had been consumed. She was cute.

Above left: Happy days? **Above right:** Militza with our two sons, Sam and Blake. **Below left:** Sam and Blake aged two and three, and, yes, I used to be slim. **Below right:** Blake and Sam aged sixteen and fourteen – Aussie hunks.

Right, from top: Ronda and me
. . . catering for a party; Ronda
at rest; Annie Foster-Firth in
Mustique; Annie F-F at play.

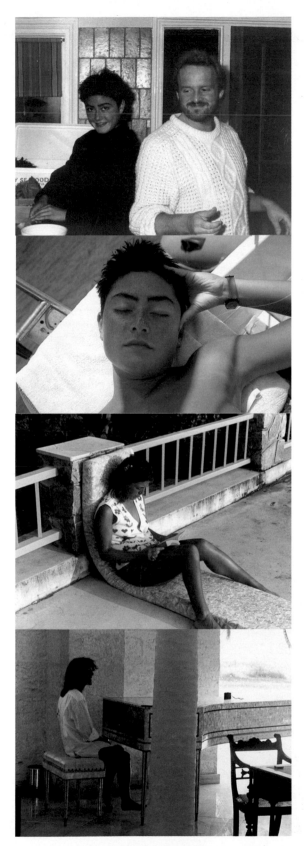

Above: Ménage à Trois – top left, with front-of-house team Jim Dunn and Eddie Knoo. **Below left:** My sassy waiting team at Ménage à Trois. **Below right:** At Ménage à Trois with Fay Maschler. **Opposite, main image:** In MOGB whites on a promotional tour of Australia in 1987. **Opposite below:** Three generations: Mother, Grandmother and me.

Right and far right: With Peter Stringfellow at the Oxford Union Debate; with my mate and right-hand man David Wilby at our restaurant at London Fashion Week. **Below, from left to right:** My right-hand girl Francesca with sleepy friend Mark; with Rory Bremner in Zimbabwe; Darina Allen at Ballymaloe Cookery School; with Fay Maschler on holiday in Greece.

Far left and left. AWT and friends: Michel Roux with Blake Worrall Thompson; with Tony Tobin, Ainsley Harriott and one of my head chefs, David Massey.

worrall thor

One of the best meals of my life at a beach shack in Jamaica: fish still alive and kicking go well with Red Stripe!

weekends to their country seats, or somebody else's, and in their place would come out-of-towners, the odd few of whom could sometimes become a little overawed by their night on the town. Give them a few drinks and they would start getting arsey, making loud remarks, winding up the waitresses, pinching their bums. Hilarious for the perpetrator of the offence perhaps, but for the waitresses it was at best a big yawn, and if it got out of hand it could be distressing. But if John Brinkley didn't like confrontation, Harriet did, and she had a marvellous way of making the guilty party feel very small indeed.

Essentially it was all about showing off. One Saturday, for instance, on a table of eight we had one complete tosser. You know the sort: has to be the centre of attention, only laughs at his own jokes, insists on Dom Perignon and smokes a cigar at least four inches longer than his willy. After his main course, the Tosser called Harriet over. 'If that steak was fresh, then my granny lives under the ice,' he said as he returned a half-eaten steak. 'Tell the chef to stick the rest of it up his arse.'

The message was conveyed to me, and it made my blood boil. I took real pride in the beef I bought, and I still do. I bought only meat on the bone, which I hung for twenty-eight days before personally butchering it into steaks.

I told Harriet to clear the Tosser's table. When she had done so I removed a 35lb sirloin on the bone from its hook in the walk-in fridge and marched out with it to confront him. I threw this massive piece of bull on to the table. 'If sir thinks this is frozen,' I said, 'then sir can stick it up my arse himself.' The whole restaurant, including most of his table, burst out into spontaneous applause.

You might be thinking that this incident was yet another example of my aggressive behaviour. But there's a difference between acting the prima donna and putting up with abuse. Life's too short to have to tolerate completely and utterly unjustified insults. For the most part, I do believe that the customer is always right, but there will be the exceptions of whom this is patently not true. All the same, I would react differently now. When you're young you tend to be more impulsive, more quarrelsome, more adventurous and more stubborn. I certainly was.

However, as I've said, the majority of our customers were gems. It was at Brinkley's that I met a wonderful couple, Kay and Jimmy Nissaire, with whom I've remained friends ever since. Jimmy is godfather to one of my children. I first knew them as regular customers who were obviously foodies with a love of excellent wines. They got the best out of the restaurant and I suppose the restaurant got the best out of them. In my view, to get the best out of a restaurant you need to make it your club. You get to know the owner, the owner makes friends with you, and both parties benefit. Nowadays, people tend to be more fickle and transient, moving from one restaurant to another and never forming a lasting relationship with any of them, which is a real lost opportunity. It's important that a restaurant owner or manager forges a bond with his customers. To some of the mega restaurants, you are just a number, whereas when you visit a favourite place regularly, the boss will get to know you by name and get to know your likes and dislikes. He'll offer you dishes that are not on the menu and the occasional drink, and you'll become friends. Regular customers, being familiar with the standards of the restaurant, are more tolerant of the odd mistake or meal that is not quite up to scratch. They will see it for what it is – a rare slip – rather than as evidence of poor-quality cooking or service.

One of my all-time favourite restaurants is Riva, which is to be found in a row of shops in Barnes in south-west London. It's a small place, seating about forty people, and it's not pretentious. There are no inflated egos flying around, and it's not about some named chef, although the northern Italian food is very good, and head chef Francesco has been there since it opened. No, the real secret of its success is that Andrea Riva is always there, behind a massive display of flowers on his cash desk. It's about Andrea Riva being the perfect host; about the way he retains his staff, Doro, Sandra and Robert, plus, of course, Francesco. The restaurant business is about personalities, especially front-of-house. For too long the host, the maitre d' and the restaurant manager have lived in the shadow of the chef. It's time to appreciate who is really important, and that person is the one who looks after you: the boss.

Brinkley's was a lovely restaurant to work in. It felt like a part of the local community. A lot of that was due to the neighbourliness of Hollywood Road, which was like a little village. Everyone would be in and out of each other's restaurants, mainly after work, for a restaurateurs' lock-in. There was no real rivalry, since each had a different concept, and if you ran out of something there would always be a willing lender. Annie and Donald Foster-Firth, who owned the Bistro Vino, were very supportive of Brinkley's and would often spend fortunes on Sunday lunch there, more often than not getting extremely pissed in the process.

Annie was Hollywood Road's matriarch. Whenever anyone had a problem, they would go to Don or Annie, but mostly to Annie. She had a special knack for solving anything. As a couple they would have been more at home running a country estate. Don was all game and shooting and Annie would have been the social queen, opening the village fête or flower show. They were the perfect couple. Or so it seemed.

It was after one Sunday lunch, about five months after Brinkley's had opened, that a strange and exciting thing happened. Annie, Don and a bunch of other regulars were all having a very late session. I tended to stay away from front-of-house, feeling a little out of place in my usual shorts, skimpy T-shirt, and flip-flops when most of the clientele were dressed in their glad rags. So after I finished work I would slope off back to my dull flat in South Woodford. On this occasion, however, as I emerged from my kitchen, knife pack under my arm, Annie called me over. In an apologetic way, I shuffled over. 'I don't really know you,' she said. 'You are the mystery man of Brinkley's. Why don't you join us for a drink and get to know the team?'

I was a bit taken aback. 'I can't possibly, looking like this,' I mumbled, but John gave me the nod, so I accepted Annie's invitation. That one decision was to change the rest of my life. We all became merrier and merrier, and then one of the girls, the sister of my sous-chef, John Campbell, said she was having a little gathering at her flat and asked me if I'd like to come over. I don't often attend staff parties. I've had my fill of drunken student sessions in flats or bedsits reeking of chefs' dirty washing, where you know the wine is going to be undrinkable and the only thing to soak up the alcohol will be a plate of crisps. But before I could say no thanks, I've got to get home, Annie piped up in her plummy voice: 'Can I come?' We were all gobsmacked. Here was the Queen of Hollywood Road, dressed to the nines in a flowing skirt, outrageously wide belt and lacy party blouse, bedecked with pearls, wanting to go to a revolting staff party. I immediately changed my mind. It wasn't because I fancied her – she was a dumpy little thing, and I would never in a million years have thought that she fancied me – it was because she was confident, strong and a little outrageous.

By the time we all set off for the party, Don had already left to sleep it off. We decided to walk as it was only half a mile. The flat was pleasantly clean, though the liquid refreshments were as expected. There were no crisps. Several of John and his sister's Kiwi mates were also invited, and before long spliffs were being passed round and everyone was flying. Annie and I abstained. After a couple of hours, Annie said, 'I'd better get home. Don will be wanting his supper. Will you walk me back?'

'Of course. Anything to get me out of here.'

We said our goodbyes and beat a hasty retreat. As we walked, Annie talked. I don't remember what about. I occasionally grunted, trying to sound vaguely intelligent. I was more worried about my state of intoxication and how I was going to drive home. Suddenly, completely out of the blue, Annie grabbed hold of me and thrust her tongue down my throat. Of all the situations I might have got into on my way home, this was the last thing I had expected. It was beyond comprehension, like being mugged by a Duchess. Jesus, what do I do now? I thought. When I finally disentangled my mouth I said lamely, 'Annie, are you OK?'

'I've wanted to do that for several weeks,' she replied. 'You have this raw appeal. Rough but exciting. I just love your shoulders.'

Before you dissolve into mocking laughter, I was still slim in those days, with a thirty-inch waist and, yes, quite good shoulders.

As we arrived back at the Bistro Vino, I was still in a state of shock. 'You can't possibly drive home,' said Annie. 'Come and have dinner at the bistro and then you must stay with us tonight.'

Was it the drink talking or was she being serious? I wasn't sure, but I agreed anyway. 'That would be great. I was envisaging spending the night in the campervan.' Don, now awake from his slumbers, was working in the Bistro. He gave us both a warm greeting. I felt guilty.

'Tony is going to stay with us tonight, he's had too much to drive home,' Annie told him.

'Great, marvellous,' said Don in his effusive way. He was full of well-bred charm, the perfect gent.

'Let's have supper. Then we can have a nightcap in the flat.'

We talked about the party. There was, of course, no mention of the mugging. Annie sat next to me during dinner, from time to time rubbing her ample thighs against mine. I'm sure I must have been blushing throughout.

'Come upstairs and I'll show you your room,' said Annie, when the meal was over. By this time I was a nervous wreck. I was shaking. Whether it was from fear or anticipation, I don't know.

'Is Don coming?' I asked feebly.

'Oh, he'll be up when he's locked up.'

Oh shit, I thought. I'm going to be alone with this vamp. Annie was definitely not my type. She was far too sophisticated, far too round.

Don and Annie's flat was above Bistro Vino. I could tell immediately that they were a couple with immaculate taste in a Nina Campbell sort of way. There was wonderful antique furniture and some bold artwork, including a magnificent Elizabeth Frink. But all that was neither here nor there. I felt I was about to be raped, but I couldn't say whether or not I was a willing victim. My fears were not realized at this stage. All I got was an extra tongue sandwich and the promise that there was more to come. Crassly, all I could say was, 'Lovely.' Why did I say that? What a great big plonker. Don arrived, and drinks were served. He was a bit of a malt whisky man, having a dose of Scots blood in him. I wasn't, but I didn't have the gumption to ask for wine. Instead I said, 'I'll have the Talisker.' I hadn't a clue what it was but I had spotted it among some other whiskies. As I took the first sip – no water, no ice – I felt the searing, peaty liquid attack the back of my throat. I had an immediate coughing attack. 'Must have gone down the wrong way,' I explained. Annie provided me with a glass of water and a knowing look. As a couple, she and Don reminded me of younger versions of my grandparents. Awfully, awfully perfect on the surface, but with hidden depths.

Annie showed me to my bedroom, which had a massive double bed. She supplied me with a new toothbrush and toothpaste. A girl prepared for every eventuality. I showered and went to bed. It was so comfy that I was asleep before my head hit the pillow. I awoke with a start in the middle of the night, to find a hand attached to my private parts. I established that I wasn't dreaming. Through the darkness I could make out the silhouette of a small, curvaceous lady. Annie, of course. She had her finger to her mouth, indicating that I should keep quiet. I whispered, 'You can't do this! What about your husband in the next room?'

'Don't worry. As long as he's snoring, we'll be fine.' She jumped in beside me and continued on her mission. I felt like I had in the last days of virginity. I didn't know what to do. Annie was unlike anyone I had ever encountered in my Essex days. I always had dreamed of bonking a society girl, to honour the spirit of my grandmother's wishes. But in my naivety I had pictured a lady who needed to be treated with kid gloves, handled like a fragile piece of bone china. Never in my wildest dreams had I imagined a wolf in Hermès clothing. It was all a bit overwhelming for a country boy.

We didn't go the whole hog that first night. She just smothered me with nips and kisses and I just had to lie there and take it like a man. It was a tough job, but someone had to do it, and it looked like Don wasn't. Over the next few days Annie was to explain the ground rules for this new relationship, the main one being that no one must ever know. We needed somewhere to meet, so I suggested my mother's house in Wandsworth Common, which became a trysting place on several occasions while my mum was at work.

With Annie, I discovered real sex. I soon realized that my experiences so far had been amateurish. My crash course in the pleasures of the flesh was fast and furious and very demanding. For Annie it was raw sex, and her appetite was insatiable. She was like the mistress of the manor showing a farmhand that there was more to life than straw in the mouth and dung behind the ears. As she got to know me and discovered my often hidden enthusiasm for design, antiques and gardening, the relationship changed from pure sex to pure sex with a little culture on the side. When we could sneak away and visit antique shops, galleries and exhibitions, she enhanced my knowledge with her impeccable taste. Annie was my real introduction to London life. Until I met her, I was like a closed book. Outsiders saw only the cover, and nobody had succeeded in opening it and leafing through the pages. Annie more or less ripped the cover off. Without Annie, I wouldn't be where I am today. She gave me my first real break in the restaurant business and for that I will be forever grateful.

Nobody knew of our affair. I suppose we made an unlikely couple so fortunately everyone assumed we were just incredibly good friends. I imagine many of Hollywood Road's resident restaurateurs couldn't understand why Annie had taken such an oddball under her wing, but once she had, I was accepted into the Hollywood Road mafia and began to feel more at home with the Fulham scene. I persuaded John Brinkley to let me have one of the storerooms on the top floor above the restaurant. I rented out my Essex flat and moved in. It was clean and convenient, if a little like returning to student accommodation. Now, instead of driving back to South Woodford, I'd go to the Bistro Vino when I finished work and drink late into the night with Annie, Don and their great bunch of girls. No one there suspected anything except for a big, buxom waitress called Caroline. She was to end up, much later, in the sack with Don. It's a funny old world, isn't it?

In the kitchen at Brinkley's, I was desperate to expand my know-ledge. When you've been lucky enough to be a head chef for all but four weeks of your career, it makes it hard to learn anything new. Being self-taught has its advantages and disadvantages. On the plus side, you don't get tunnel vision. You're not pre-programmed into a college form of cookery and you can let your imagination run riot. The drawbacks are that you become very difficult to work for, your kitchen management skills are limited and there's no one master from whom you can learn and whose experience you can absorb on a daily basis.

My streak of gourmet inspiration came from one book, *The Great Chefs of France* by Quentin Crewe and Anthony Blake, a compendium of all the Michelin three-starred restaurants in the country. I read this book over and over again and, in the summer of 1980, it inspired an extended holiday. John Brinkley agreed to give me the time off, so I sold the VW camper, replacing it with a rather flash VW Scirocco and, with *The Great Chefs of France* under my arm, took off on a tour of all the restaurants listed in the book.

My journey took me nearly 4,000 miles and to the north, south, east and west of France. I had pre-booked my complete schedule and saved nearly £3,000 to finance the trip. Annie had wanted to come with me, but I told her I thought that would be a little too obvious. Instead it was decided that both Don and Annie would join me for two legs, covering the south of France and the eastern Alsace region.

For me, at the age of twenty-nine, it was the trip of a lifetime. I was totally amazed, completely starstruck. The food was, for the most part, unbelievably good. I would spend part of my day at a restaurant, observing the service, marvelling at the number of chefs, the precision of the cooking, the spotless kitchens and the immacu-late decadence of the dining rooms. All the great *chef-patrons* were perfect gentlemen, hospitable, understanding and informative. Impressed by my foodie pilgrimage and my thirst for knowledge, they were also incredibly generous. When I was dining alone, several of them gave me a free meal, which was a wonderful gesture.

The most imaginative food came from Alain Chapel in Mionnay, Michel Guerard in Eugénie-les-Bains and Jacques Pic in Valence.

My personal awards for the most beautiful settings were to Roger Vergé at Le Moulin de Mougins, Françoise Bise at L'Auberge de Père Bise in Talloires and Raymond Thulier at L'Oustau de Beaumanière. And the most hospitable *patron* was the king of French chefs, Paul Bocuse, with the Troisgros brothers in Roanne running him a close second.

It was Bocuse and the Troisgros brothers who provided me with two memories of my tour that stand out from the rest. I have many happy recollections of that summer in France, but what made these exquisite and completely different experiences all the more special was the fact that they were totally unexpected.

Bocuse's restaurant, in Lyons, was the one place I was wary of going to. I had been warned that he was not a friendly man and could be very pompous and dismissive. But I couldn't miss out the star who had inherited the mantle of arguably the greatest chef of the twentieth century, Fernand Point, on his death. I arrived at the appointed hour, presented my copy of *The Great Chefs of France* to the restaurant manager, and asked if Monsieur Bocuse would autograph it for me. The book came back unsigned. Bastard, I thought. They were right. This man is an ignorant pig. I was enjoying my meal nevertheless. I had chosen the soupe de truffes, the pigeonneu en terrine au foie gras and the assiette Bretonne aux petits legumes, all of which were top notch, and was waiting for my final course, volaille de Bresse en civet, when Paul Bocuse himself came out of the kitchen and sat down at my table. He picked up my book and signed it on the appropriate page, had a chat with me despite my pidgin French, shook me by the hand and rose to return to the kitchen. As he walked away, he looked at the waiter's slip, waved briefly and was gone. The waiter appeared, and instead of my chicken he brought me a grilled escalope of foie gras. This was followed by a small salad of haricots verts with crayfish, then an escalope of turbot and a half-bottle of 1961 Château Haut Brion. By the time the puddings started arriving I felt like a stuffed pig.

As I was about to have my coffee and thinking about getting back to my hotel, Paul (excuse the familiarity) returned. In good French and bad English, he said, 'No time for coffee. You must come with me and see my other operation.' By now all I wanted to do was to lie down and digest my brilliant feast, but of course there was no question of declining. So Paul whipped me off to his other establishment, the Abbaye, which he used for '*jours de fêtes*' – weddings, private parties and other functions – and which was dominated by his private collection of steam organs and old horses from fairground carousels.

I was overwhelmed. It was amazing that someone like Paul Bocuse – a man who had been awarded the Chevalier de la Légion d'Honneur, one of the highest honours in France – should show such kindness and hospitality to a young, unknown chef from Fulham. But he hadn't finished yet. After a few drinks, he said: 'It's too late to return to your hotel now. You must come and stay with me, and in the morning you can join me in the market.'

By then it was 2 am. Later that morning, at 5.30, there was a knock on my bedroom door and a shout of *'Allez!'* I crawled out of bed, my stomach still overloaded with the indulgences of the previous evening, and we drove to the market in Lyons, a magnificent flagship for the culinary capital of France. Paul knew everybody. It was like walking beside a god, and yet here he was mixing with all and sundry. We took breakfast in a market café where the air was thick with cigarette smoke and red-wine breath. It was packed with ruddy-faced market traders, many of whom were already hitting the cognac with their morning coffee. One by one, each of them came up to say, 'Bonjour, Monsieur Paul.' The chef introduced me as his little Chinese friend, a joke at my expense that produced great hilarity. I didn't care. He could call me anything he liked. I was lapping up every minute of this irreplaceable experience and filing it away so that I could bring it out and savour it again in years ahead. I vowed that if I ever became successful, perhaps even grand and powerful, I would try always to remember to make time for others just stepping on to the lower rungs of the ladder.

La Maison Troisgros, the restaurant run by the Troisgros brothers in Roanne, was the least ostentatious establishment I visited. Their hotel-restaurant opposite the local station had no particular claims to glamour, but the larger-than-life *patrons* were perfect examples of great but unpretentious chefs – never precious, never unwilling to serve their customers what they wanted – and their staff were the friendliest I came across in all the three-star restaurants of France.

I spent a day in their bright kitchen, joined in with the kitchen lunch around a large table and then played football in the car park overlooked by the kitchens. After showering in my hotel room above the restaurant, I went down to dinner. 'There's more to life than food,' Jean told me. 'You must have company when you dine.'

As if on cue, a beautiful French girl appeared and sat down at my table. She was studying English, so I was able to share some shy conversation. After dinner Jean suggested that I joined him and two or three of his staff for a few drinks at a local bar. I felt honoured to be invited into their inner sanctum. It was so obvious that their working environment was a happy one.

I returned to England inspired by my magical and hugely educational summer. The dishes I had tasted had captured my imagination, and I was fascinated by this nouvelle cuisine. No longer were chefs tied to tradition. They had been freed to express their own creativity. I wanted to soak up every droplet of this new knowledge. I would have loved to stay on to serve an apprenticeship with the Troisgros brothers, but there was a kitchen in Fulham waiting for me.

CHAPTER EIGHTEEN

BACK AT BRINKLEY'S, I COULDN'T WAIT TO SHOW OFF MY NEW-FOUND knowledge. But first I needed to see Annie, who was rapidly metamorphosing from godmother into temptress, if a rather Rubenesque temptress. I returned to her bed with a confidence that I think surprised her. Suddenly, I was taking the lead. We were always very honest with each other, so one day I decided to broach the subject of her weight, though after my culinary adventures in France I was beginning to notice the first signs of an expanding waistline of my own. 'Why don't we go on a diet together?' I suggested. I thought it sounded more pleasant and supportive than bluntly saying that she had put on weight. She agreed.

Annie's appeal was in her face. She was bold, she had the most beautiful eyes, she made me laugh and she made me feel good about myself. She also had a great brain, she was self-assured, she had lots to talk about and I liked her tremendously. But her figure wasn't my usual cup of tea. Annie wanted to please me, I wanted to please Annie, and over the next year she lost over two stone. She was delighted with her new shape, so we were both happy.

John Brinkley, meanwhile, was not so happy. After my trip to France, the menu at the restaurant changed beyond recognition. In came the foie gras, poulet de Bresse, wild mushrooms and truffles. Out of the window went John's profit margins. The restaurant was full, but my new food was creating a major economic headache for the boss. Time after time he demanded that I pulled in my horns, but I was dead set on exploring the new possibilities that had opened up to me. The only solution I could see was to abandon ship.

It was while I was in this unsettled frame of mind that opportunity came knocking, this time in the shape of a guy called David Whitehead, who owned a restaurant in Sydney Street, Chelsea.

When Dan, the name by which both he and his restaurant were known, rang me one day, I agreed to go and see him. We got on well. I was falling into another Hooray enclave: Dan was a man with an impeccable accent. He talked like the Queen did in the early 1950s, though in a slightly gruffer voice. He had a girlfriend who had clearly been moulded at Heathfield or Benenden. Their restaurant was, to put it bluntly, a shithole. It was towards the King's Road end of Sydney Street in a row of Georgian terraces. It looked quite quaint from the outside, but on the inside it was in serious need of an injection of taste. It was a kind of Sloaney greasy spoon: lino on the floor, loos with no hot water, awful décor and a grubby kitchen, inconveniently positioned on the first floor, with less refrigeration than I had at home.

On the plus side, Dan was willing to almost double my salary and prepared to spend about £10,000 getting the restaurant half attractive. He needed help. He'd worked in the City, and had a romantic idea of how it would be to own his own restaurant – a common fault among the British. He had modelled his menu to some degree on that of one of London's most successful tatty miracles, a restaurant called Foxtrot Oscar in Royal Hospital Road, which was more like an Old Etonian club than a restaurant. Dan envisaged his numerous friends from his school and City days filling his restaurant and making him rich. That, of course, is easier said than done. He had no trouble packing them in to start with. But although friends will come once, they won't keep coming if the product is not up to scratch, and in Dan's case it was pretty dire. So in a very short space of time the restaurant was empty.

Brinkley's had proved to me that London was not as tough a market as I had believed it to be when I'd been looking at it from Essex. Dan seemed quite a lad. He was more personality-led than John, and I saw him as a useful foil to some good cooking from me. He also had a strong Romanian restaurant manageress who wouldn't take any shit from anyone, and some great waiters. So the key infrastructure was in place. They just needed some food to be proud of. I was ready for such a fresh challenge, and I wanted out of Brinkley's and to be fair John wanted me out. I accepted the job.

There was one minor hitch. The week before I was due to start, Dan's had been paid a visit by Fay Maschler, the restaurant critic of the *Evening Standard*. From what I heard from the waiters and from Dan himself, it had clearly been a disaster. The timing was terrible. Fay had a wide readership and was highly respected, and the bad publicity generated by an unfavourable review would have a lasting effect. What was more, unless we changed the name of the restaurant, it would be impossible to coax Fay back so soon after her first visit. If I didn't do something drastic, I would be left with a much bigger mountain to climb than I'd bargained for.

I told Dan that I would write to Fay Maschler. She didn't know me from Adam in those days, though she had reviewed Brinkley's, so it was quite a formal letter. I threw myself on her mercy. I began by saying that I understood she had recently visited Dan's and hadn't enjoyed the experience. I explained that I was about to accept the position of head chef at the restaurant and that I would very much appreciate it if she were to hold off on her review. I told her that if she published an account of her meal there, which, of course, she had every right to do, I would have to decline the job offer. I concluded by expressing the hope that she didn't mind me writing to her like this, but her decision could make a massive difference to my career.

Within three days I received a reply. In it Fay Maschler confirmed that her experience at Dan's had not been a particularly pleasant one, but said that she would happily agree to my request. She asked me to let her know when I felt that Dan's restaurant was ready for another visit. I took the job.

John Brinkley was not distraught to see me go, but we parted on amicable terms. Of course, I not only had to leave the restaurant but also my storeroom accommodation on the top floor. So unless I turfed out the tenant renting my South Woodford flat and tried to commute to and from Sydney Street from there, I would be homeless. Annie had thought of that. She offered me a room in her flat, presumably with the blessing of her husband.

My affair with Annie was in full flow, although I still felt I had to pinch myself from time to time to make sure that this weird situation was not a dream. I told Annie that if I moved into her house I would need to have some kind of separate social life, and ought to be seen to mix with other girls, to avoid arousing Don's suspicions. Still nobody had rumbled us, but even if they didn't, I was worried that I would appear to be gay, asexual or just plain strange if I didn't put myself about a bit. I hooked up with four lovely girls who were regulars at Brinkley's. They all worked for an advertising jingles company called Airedel, which was owned by former Beatles producer George Martin. They were a cool bunch, very alternative. Maggie 1 was the boss, a very peaches-and-cream type of girl who seemed out of place and always remained slightly aloof. Maggie 2, very loud, very frightening, very American, was a few years older than the rest of us, but a very young, good-looking American boyfriend kept her youthful. Liz was the weirdest, distant, arty, tall, skinny and the one I found hardest going. Susie I fell for straight away, but she was hooked up with a very talented musician, Richard Harvey.

With the exception of Maggie 1, the girls stuck together as a real team. They drank together, ate together, almost lived in each other's pockets. They accepted me into their gang. I was often bemused by my new friends. I guess in many ways I was the outsider, but I enjoyed every minute of their company. It was great that they had nothing to do with catering. That made them all the more interesting to me, and gave me a real break from shop talk. I was the quiet one, the dark horse. Being such a loner, I had never really had that many friends. Sad, I know, but I quite liked my own company. With this musical team, life suddenly became different, fun. I remembered again what Jean Troisgros had said about there being more to life than food. The part of my life that wasn't taken up by Annie and Dan's was totally dominated by these friends. We ate out, went to racy bars, enjoyed good wines and for the first time I began to develop the confidence to have a life outside the catering world. It felt good.

The relaunch of Dan's was marked by a bit of a Sloaney bash, a second hit at Dan's friends. It was a great success, producing many promises to return and give Dan another chance. We would see. I knew only a handful of the guests, among them Rex Leyland and Michael Wickes, who owned Foxtrot Oscar, and Michael Proudlock, who had been brought into the team to rescue the ailing fortunes of their Royal Hospital Road establishment. Foxtrot Oscar, named for an Etonian euphemism for 'fuck off', was effectively a tuck shop beyond the school gates, a playground for public schoolboys who didn't want to grow up. Over twenty years later, it's still going.

On the first real night of trading Dan's was pretty busy. Halfway through the evening, Dan rushed into the kitchen exclaiming that he thought Fay Maschler was in. Oh, shit. That's all I need on day one, I thought to myself. It's amazing how the rumoured presence of a food critic can reduce you to a shambolic heap of quivering jelly. I often wonder whether they enjoy the power they wield. The other customers suffer terribly as you stupidly throw all your energies into four or five dishes for the critic. Yet the last thing a chef should do is overgild the lily by sending little extras to the table or, worse, going out and suggesting choices. The reviewer must want to tell him to bog off, or at the very least be wondering why he is so desperate to push these particular dishes. Might there be something not quite right with the others? If you are confident enough of your own ability, it's better not to know that a critic is in. It would certainly save a lot of stress. But I guess most chefs have masochistic tendencies, otherwise they wouldn't be in the job in the first place.

At the end of the first evening's service I popped down to see this all-powerful lady whose writings I had digested on a weekly basis from the *Evening Standard*. 'Hi, I'm Antony. I hope you enjoyed your evening.' Was there a tremble in my voice? Quite possibly. Then I decided to go all bold. 'It was a bit mean of you to come on the first night,' I said, remembering the letter in which she had asked me to let her know when I was ready.

Her answer lives with me every time I open a new restaurant. 'Not at all. You aren't having a dress rehearsal, are you? As far as I'm aware, you're charging full prices.' She was right, of course: this wasn't a dress rehearsal, and yes, we were charging full prices. At every other restaurant I've opened since, I've either offered half-price on food for the opening week or, even better, if I could afford it, given the food away for nothing. That is a gesture that has often worked in my favour on the publicity front, especially when it wasn't just invited guests who were being treated to a free meal.

I have only a vague recollection now of Fay's review, but it was a fair one, and it helped fill the restaurant. One detail that has stuck in my mind is her description of my garden vegetable terrine, inspired by the Troisgros restaurant. It was not so much a garden terrine, she wrote, as something from a children's playgroup. After that the terrine was renamed on the menu 'Fay's Garden Playgroup'.

Other reviews were generally good, and I had put my name on the London restaurant map in a minor way. I even featured on the front cover of the *Sunday Express* magazine as one of the exponents of 'modern British cuisine', a label I loathed. In the beginning Dan was very pleased by the way things were going, but soon we hit exactly the same problem as Brinkley's: a packed restaurant but no profit. I wanted what I'd seen in France, I wanted the best, but in pursuing that ambition I had lost sight of the gross profit margins. The lessons of my management training at college had gone out of the window, and I was indulging my passion on poor old Dan's money. We had many a barney.

Working with me in the kitchen at Dan's was a girl called Linda. She was a friend of my mate Susie's who needed a job, and I'd managed to get Dan to take her on to help me even though she couldn't actually cook. I guided her through and she picked things up quickly, including me. Linda was blonde, attractive without being beautiful, and had a wicked laugh and a terrific sense of humour. She would stand very close to me when I was instructing her on some dish or other, electricity would be created and the light would go on. A few beers at the end of service were enough to get her going. It wasn't a merger, it was a takeover, I was smitten. I discovered that she had a weekend boyfriend, but she had set her mind on a midweek dalliance with me and nothing was going to stop her. So our affair was off the record, but I enjoyed being with her. She was great fun, and she was, well, normal. She had none of Annie's sophistication or, for that matter, her airs and graces.

Annie knew about my little flings, but she didn't seem to mind. She even asked me if Linda wanted to move in with me at her flat, which she did for a while. Annie always assumed that my girls weren't serious, that they were just decoys to conceal our affair. To some degree they were, but on the other hand I never saw Annie leaving Don, their life seemed so perfect, their bond seemed concrete. Annie wanted her bit on the side, and that was all I was. Linda was now starting to grow on me, and Annie realized this. I sensed that a little jealousy was beginning to creep into our relationship.

Annie arranged for us to spend a couple of days together at the Ship Hotel in Brighton. She told Don she was going to stay with friends. My story was that I was visiting my father in Shropshire. The plan was for Annie to go on ahead and warm up the bed. There was one slight hitch. On the night I was due to drive down to Brighton after work, I found that my car had a flat battery. Don, bless him, found jump-leads and got it started. This one act of kindness played on my mind, and on the journey my anticipation was marred by a strong feeling of guilt.

At the hotel, Annie had organized all the trimmings in her usual immaculate style. There were flowers and vintage champagne, and she had even scoured the Lanes for two antique champagne coupes. It was a wonderfully romantic setting, but I let the side down. For the first and, I'm glad to say, last time, I couldn't get it up. I just couldn't get the thought out of my head that Don had been helping me on my way to betray him with his own wife. It brought home to me just how deeply I was stabbing him in the back. I suppose the physical reaction was understandable but it was mortifying all the same. Annie was disappointed, but tactful and sympathetic.

Such was life. By now the rough edges of my Essex days had been smoothed down and I was becoming a more rounded person. I was already fairly streetwise, and thanks to Annie I was developing some sophistication. I guess I needed to grow up and stop hating the world. My childhood and adolescence could always be cited as the cause of that, but you can't blame your shortcomings on difficult circumstances for ever. At some stage you have to come to terms with the fact that it is you who may be at fault, and take responsibility for yourself and your actions.

The overemotional side of my temperament came to the fore when Linda decided to end our affair. She broke the news to me over lunch at the Ebury Wine Bar, and I got a bit tearful. I had really grown very attached to her but she saw in me too much raw ambition. She felt that I would slip away from her. I tried to convince her otherwise, but if I am honest, she was probably right. It didn't make the parting any easier. There are some girls you allow to walk away without a backwards glance, and others you don't. But she was in charge. I'd still never instigated a relationship with a girl, or finished one, either. I'd always let them do all the hard work.

But I was annoyed with myself for having let Linda slip out of my grasp, so I was not in the mood for one of Dan's ballistic rants a short time later. When he started in the middle of lunch one day he took the brunt of my frustration. 'Bollocks. I can't take all this shit. You cook the fucking lunch.' I stormed off. I decided to drown my sorrows over a good lunch cooked by someone else. I went round to Beauchamp Place and plumped for a restaurant called Sabatini. At the end of a perfectly average meal washed down by plenty of perfectly drinkable wine the owner came over. 'You look like you're carrying the troubles of the world on your shoulders,' he said. 'Let me buy you a drink.'

'Thanks, that would be great,' came the slightly pissed reply. He sat down with me and I poured out my heart to him. Unburdening yourself on a complete stranger is like going to Alcoholics Anonymous. You can say things you'd never dream of sharing with anyone close to you. The owner was a good listener, and I felt better.

'I've come to the conclusion that I'm not cut out for working for others,' I told him after I'd got everything off my chest. 'I need a restaurant of my own.'

'This must be your lucky day. I have just put this restaurant on the market.'

It was if my life had been mapped out. Although I am not religious, I do believe in fate. This was great news. But how could I ever find the £70,000 he wanted, not to mention the money to meet the refit costs? When I told Annie about it she was excited. She said that she and Don had been thinking for a long time that I should have my own restaurant. 'I'll have a word with Don, and fingers crossed, if he agrees, we might be able to come up with the finance.'

I've always said that to raise any money a young chef needs either a willing lover or an understanding bank manager, and preferably both. I was doubly fortunate: I had a great lover and Don had the understanding bank manager at the Royal Bank of Scotland. I don't think it ever crossed my mind that I should feel guilty about accepting his money when I was screwing his wife. I was just too caught up in the idea of having my own restaurant.

The money was in place, but Don wasn't particularly keen on the basement site in Beauchamp Place. Instead he came up with a restaurant in the West End, Le Caprice, and another on Chelsea Green. We went for Le Caprice, which offered a wonderful site together with the dilapidated grandeur of a once-famous establishment. We started planning our layout, designing the décor and researching the area, but then we lost the site. Joseph Ettegui, of the Joseph fashion shops, had stepped in with the same amount of money plus a much better covenant. So Le Caprice went to him, though it was a short-lived victory as he closed down his restaurant three months after opening it. Chris Corbin, his restaurant director, and Jeremy King managed to raise the funds to restart the operation and went on to make history. Chris came to me asking if I would invest in the new company. Declining that opportunity proved to be one of the biggest financial mistakes of my life.

So we were stuck with Sabatini, my original choice. It was a honeycomb of basement rooms with nothing like the glamour of Le Caprice. But you can't dwell on what might have been. I had great fun with Annie trawling junk shops for decorative pieces. My ideas were quite radical. I wanted a restaurant geared towards women. They were, I felt, a burgeoning sector of the market whose preferences were not being catered for. Many girls I'd eaten out with had commented that they would rather eat two starters and a pudding than a heavy main course. In those days this was a choice discouraged by head waiters. There was a big price difference between starters and main courses, so if you allowed a diner to order two starters, the restaurant's revenue would fall and so would the percentage service charge or tips.

I'd learned from talking to other restaurateurs that women eating alone or with a girlfriend were not considered good for business. They were seen as lousy tippers and lousy drinkers. As a result they were usually allocated tables near the kitchen, the entrance or the loos. One fast-food chain even banned women from eating alone after nine in the evening, a mind-boggling rule that effectively branded them as hookers. Apart from being sexist, these attitudes did not seem to me to make commercial sense at a time when more and more women executives were having business lunches and women generally were increasingly using restaurants as meeting places.

I was sure that there would be mileage in a restaurant targeting this new breed of power girls. Don, who was very much a meat-and-two-veg man, took some convincing that my idea for a restaurant serving only starters and puddings was a winner, but Annie saw the point immediately and was right behind me. What finally confirmed to me that I was on the right track was my first club-class flight on British Airways, a luxury to which I treated myself on a trip to the States to do some background research. I estimated that about a third of the club-class passengers were women, and yet the extras offered to the people paying these higher fares were all aimed at men. The travel packs contained razors, shaving foam and aftershave, and the magazines on the racks were all male-orientated – there wasn't a single copy of *Homes and Gardens* or *Cosmopolitan*, for example. On my return I wrote to Lord King, then the head of British Airways, to point out the error of his ways. To give him his due, he wrote me a very nice letter in reply in which he said that while the company tried always to be alert to these matters, sometimes executives can't see for looking, and assured me that the situation would be addressed. His response made me feel that I had caught the mood of the moment.

With plans for the new restaurant well under way, I handed in my notice to Dan Whitehead. We remained friends, but he was definitely another boss who was pleased to see the back of me. As he once said, 'All I wanted was a fucking burger bar,' but he was stuck with posh nosh. My replacement was a chef called Philip Britten, a bit of a culinary genius who went on to become a success at the Capital Hotel. He now runs his own company, Solstice, supplying restaurants, and provides me with top-of-the-range prepared vegetables. As I've often had cause to observe, the food world is a pretty small one.

CHAPTER NINETEEN

WE HAD THE CONCEPT – ALL WE NEEDED NOW WAS A NAME. NONE OF us could come up with one that all three of us liked. Eventually it came to me, out of the blue, on a plane returning home from Italy. I had skipped off with Annie for a naughty weekend at Harriet Bunbury's mother's house in Porto Ecole. Harriet, my great friend from Brinkley's, had finally parted from John Brinkley and had been in Porto Ecole with her new man. She was the only person among our circle who had been let into the secret of the affair between Annie and me.

I had told Don I was going sailing, and the deception was worked out with military precision. I had even bought some sailing gear that I manhandled a bit before we went back to the flat so that it would look as if it had been used. It was a wonderful weekend of great sex (Annie and I managed to break our bed), great food and great fun.

On the plane back I had a brainwave. 'We'll call the restaurant Ménage à Trois,' I said to Annie.

'Why?'

'Well, I guess it stems from my sick sense of humour. Me, you and Donald are a kind of *ménage à trois*, even if he doesn't know he's in one.'

She laughed.

It was cheeky of me, but it had a certain ring to it.

Preparations for the restaurant went reasonably smoothly. We interviewed potential staff at the flat. We were after personality and youth, not polish, and a predominantly female front-of-house personnel. As for the waiting staff, I didn't want slick, pepper-grinding Italians or surly, professional French – neither Annie nor myself had the necessary experience to deal with seasoned waiters. We needed people who would be an extension of Annie's fairly outrageous personality. We employed two contrasting manageresses with totally different characters and attributes: Dorothy, a tiny, young Scottish girl who showed an amazing amount of energy and enthusiasm, and Hazel, who had overlapped with me at college and also turned out to be the sister of one of my new musical mates, Graham Prescott, a brilliant musician who paid his mortgage by creating advertising jingles.

I say preparations were going smoothly, but there was one incident that nearly put a stop to the whole proceedings. One evening, alone in her flat, Annie and I had a row – probably our first – and suddenly I saw a completely different woman. I can't even remember what it was all about. All I remember is, I started to walk away and then turned to say something (and, knowing my sharp tongue, it was probably something quite mean, cold and cutting), when – wham! – a heavy lead crystal whisky tumbler smashed on my forehead, knocking me off my feet and out cold. I crumpled into a heap at the top of the stairs.

I don't know how long I was out, but when I regained consciousness my head was lying in a puddle of blood. I staggered to my feet, felt the egg on my head and realized that blood was still pouring from the wound. I made my way down the stairs and out of the flat and headed for St Stephen's Hospital. I have no qualms about putting my hand up a chicken's backside and wrenching out its guts, but when it comes to my own blood, I can go a bit girlie, and as I weaved down the road I could tell this was a bad cut because the blood was hitting the pavement some distance in front of me. Projectile bleeding. When I reached Casualty, I made a right mess of their floor. I apologized to the receptionist and a nurse rushed round and whipped me into a cubicle. No long waiting time for me. She tied a bandage really tightly round my head. 'Careful, nurse, there may be glass in there,' I protested. Then I passed out cold.

The broken glass had hit some vein or artery, I can't remember what they called it, but it was something serious. Apparently, if I hadn't come round when I did and got to the hospital, Annie could have been in deep shit. I didn't dwell on that at the time, but when I look back, it sends a shiver down my spine. When I came to again, a doctor had stitched up the right bits and Annie was at my side. My mum's theatrical genes came to the fore. 'That's it, Annie,' I said. 'It's all over. No more me, no more fucking restaurant. You're on your own.' She pleaded, cried, begged, apologized and I gave in. It was a bad decision in the long run, but the right one at the time. I felt then that there was obviously something in my make-up that provoked extreme reactions in people; that either brought out great passion in them or caused them great pain. It had happened before, and it would happen again.

We put that episode behind us and Ménage à Trois opened to great acclaim. Almost from day one we were full. Fay Maschler actually rang to ask whether I wanted her to review us or not, because she had been unable to book a table. The reviews on the whole were pretty good, but they didn't seem to matter: the restaurant was the only one of its kind and one of the first British restaurants to serve 'nouvelle cuisine', and the customers flocked to it.

We were almost overtaken by our own success, but Annie did a brilliant job with her team out front. They were all girls, except for a Burmese barman who had come to me from Anouska Hempel's hotel, Blake's. An ex-policeman with a more-to-it-than-meets-the-eye past, he was brilliant at cocktails and over the years he also built up a fabulous knowledge of wines. In the kitchen my main man was a Czech called Vasclav, a mighty guy of six foot three with a hairstyle like Bobby Charlton. He cooked with his chef's jacket undone to the waist, pouring buckets of sweat. Not an attractive sight, but he was a gentleman and a gentle man, a philosophical bloke and a natural cook. I loved him to bits and he was my life support in such a busy restaurant. The remainder of my staff was made up of Moroccan students and the Portuguese mafia. They all shared a quality you don't find much nowadays: allegiance. They were good people.

The first hiccup came after three months. It was a review in one of those monthly glossies. I nearly choked on my Weetabix when I read it. I felt as if a dagger had been plunged into my heart. I know now that you have to take reviews in your stride, but in the early days I took them all personally. A single review was capable of making me feel like either a million dollars or a sack of shit. I still remember this one very clearly. It was bad. One line read: 'Perhaps the low standard of food can be attributed to the fact that Mr Worrall Thompson was sitting at the next table drinking all night.'

Or words to that effect. Lies, damned lies. I may have done that later in my career, but for the first six months at Ménage à Trois I never left the kitchen during a service. It wasn't quite yet the fashion for chefs to mingle with the customers.

I was really aggrieved. I showed my insecurity by phoning anyone and everyone and asking them what I should do. I even phoned Fay Maschler for her advice. She very sensibly counselled that I should probably take it on the chin. And anyway, she pointed out, it was only a monthly glossy, and hardly a great authority, so there was no need to worry. But as you know by now, I'm a stubborn shit. I phoned my lawyer, Simon Bowen, who I had still only met on a couple of occasions but who I would see a lot more of over the years.

To my surprise, Simon took the issue seriously. He decided to raise it with some senior guy at the glossy, and as a result, I was awarded an apology in print and promised an independent review, which was carried out a couple of months later by the famous foodie Paul Levy, one of the most respected food writers of the day. His report was extremely favourable, singing the praises of one of my best-known, non-profit-making successes, whole truffle wrapped in foie gras and Parma ham en croute – an exceptional dish at a ridiculously low price. Meanwhile, I tried to find out why the original reviewer had been so uncompromisingly critical. Although nothing could be proved, I've always suspected that he had been bribed by our main restaurant rival to put the boot into Ménage. It's a rough game, this restaurant business.

After the glass incident my relationship with Annie returned to normal, although there were tensions created by her jealousy of a friendship I had with a woman in Brighton. This was Christine, the longstanding girlfriend of my old boss Peter Goring from Hedges. There had been no difficulties when I had first taken Annie down to Brighton some months earlier to meet Peter and Christine and to acquaint her with my Essex past, although the evening could hardly be described as a roaring success.

Peter and Christine had recently had a new baby daughter, and the four of us had gone out to dinner at a restaurant on the seafront to celebrate. Annie was dressed to kill in a skimpy little number that flattered her new, slimline figure. As was the case more often than not in the early 1980s, the place was no great shakes – cold food and warm Dom Perignon – but that didn't really matter: the outing was more about the company, and we were good punters, drinking well and generally enjoying ourselves. To round off the meal, we ordered Hennessy XO brandy for everyone.

As soon as I tasted the brandy, I suspected that it was not what it was meant to be. It was crude and very sweet, and not of the quality you would expect from the top-of-the-range XO. I guessed that we were being treated to the old scam: the three-star stuff doctored with a couple of slugs of sweet sherry. So I asked to see the bottle our drinks had been poured from. Surprise, surprise, it was finished. I asked to see the empty bottle. Apparently, it had been broken. By the time the bill arrived, my hackles were up. Apart from the substandard brandy, two of the main courses had been inedible, so I decided to knock £15 off the bill and to give it instead to the waitress as a tip. None of this, after all, had been her fault, and she had tried her best. As the tip was discretionary, I wasn't actually paying out any less than the bill amounted to; I was simply reallocating the money.

But the owner came over and refused to accept my revised figure. An argument ensued, voices were raised and things turned a bit nasty. Peter, Annie and Christine all wanted me to drop the matter, but I had the bit between my teeth. The owner threatened to call the police. 'Feel free,' I said. 'They won't be interested – this is a civil issue. If I walked out leaving my name and address, you would have to sue me for the money. And that's exactly what I'm going to do. And by the by, I'm also going to take this brandy with me and have it analysed.'

As we got up to leave, in marched a constable who announced that he was arresting us for bilking under some act or other. Law had been one of my strong subjects at college. 'You can't do that,' I told him. '"Bilking" is when you go to a restaurant or buy some goods with the intention of not paying. That is patently not what is going on here. Look, here's my cheque proving my intention to pay.' He tried to grab the cheque, but I quickly withdrew it. I explained what had happened and showed him the brandy I was taking away with me. The unfriendly arm of the law knocked it out of my hand, spilling the contents and smashing the glass. 'That wasn't very nice,' I said. His response was that unless we paid the bill in full, we would be arrested.

By this time the rest of my team were giving me stick. They just wanted to forget the whole thing and get home. But I was deter-mined that this crooked restaurateur was not going to get the better of me. I suggested that they left me to take the flak, but they didn't want to go without me. Once again I pleaded with the bobby, 'Check with your superiors, you're making a big mistake.' This got right up his nose, and instead he called for assistance.

The next thing we knew, we were being pushed into a police van and driven round to the nick, to the accompaniment of rantings and ravings from me about what a big mistake the bobby was making. At the police station we were stripped of all our belongings, including belts and socks, just in case we did something silly like hanging ourselves. Oh, please. Over a restaurant bill? Christine was pleading with the police to be allowed to phone the babysitter, who would be worried sick. Not only that, but the baby needed breastfeeding. She wasn't permitted to make the call until 5 am. Now, that's the sort of thing that gives the police a bad name.

We were put into different cells. Mine was already occupied by some out-of-sorts football hooligans, and smelled of vomit and urine, not the most attractive cocktail at two o'clock in the morning, or at any time of day, come to that. I didn't sleep. I was concerned for the girls, and especially about Christine, who was by now frantic about her baby. I needn't have worried about Annie, though. She may have been a posh bird, but she was ballsy. Nothing really fazed her.

We were eventually released, without charge, at noon the next day. A grovelling inspector said that there had been a terrible mistake. I agreed. I told him that he would be hearing from my lawyer. And he did. Simon Bowen, the bulldog, loved a challenge. Within a week we had received £2,000 in compensation for the police error.

Nobody likes to be arrested, especially normally law-abiding citizens, but once I had calmed down I did feel some sympathy for the policeman who had been at fault. How on earth a young constable can be expected to know the finer points of the law inside out I can't imagine. I was aware of the details of that particular legal area because it was one that was relevant to my profession, but it would constitute only a tiny fraction of what a police officer needs to keep between his or her ears. It's a tough job.

It was after Peter had to 'go away' for a year that the green-eyed monster reared its head in Annie. I had promised him that I would take care of Christine and the children. I honoured my promise, although there were times when I wanted to take care of her more than Peter had envisaged. But I kept myself in check. I'm not that much of a bastard. Before the Ménage à Trois opened I visited her most weekends, and once we were up and running I went as often as I could, and we became very close. I looked forward to my trips to Brighton. I felt very protective of Christine and the kids, especially Amy, to whom I became surrogate godfather, and if for any reason Peter hadn't returned, I could easily have made my life with Christina. To me Brighton was an island of sanity amid the madness of London and Annie. Nevertheless, Annie remained a very powerful magnet.

At the restaurant, Vasclav had to leave to do his national service at home. He kept in touch. Remarkably, he went on to become an actor, and apparently a good one. He was replaced at Ménage by a Frenchman, Philippe Roy, a classical chef who was very bemused by the way I ran a kitchen. If you were asked to imagine a caricature of a Frenchman, you would come up with Philippe. He was small, with dark hair and a black 'tache, a cross between a gendarme and Inspector Clouseau. Very 'Allo, 'Allo, and a great character. He was a terrific right-hand man, friend and all-round good guy who went from strength to strength in his own right and is now based in Bath.

As for me, I was getting lots of press and enjoying the limelight, but occasionally it would all get the better of me and I would turn into a right little prima donna. One night I threw a complete fit. Annie was bombing in the checks and we just lost control in the kitchen, which can happen. I told her no more checks for half an hour. She ignored me. So I pulled out all the chefs and we went and sat on the steps outside the restaurant on Beauchamp Place. Five minutes later, Annie had rounded up all the floor staff and sent them outside equipped with buckets of water. We were duly soaked from head to foot. Defeated, the chefs returned to work. All except me. I stayed there sulking. Eventually Annie persuaded me to return and, to show there were no hard feelings, in front of all the customers, she poured a bucket of water over herself. The customers' irritation at having to wait for their food rapidly turned to astonishment at Annie's cabaret act. She liked to wear designer T-shirts with no bra, so there she was, bold as brass, taking orders and controlling the room as if she was competing in a wet T-shirt contest. At the end of the evening, over a bottle or two, we all saw the funny side of the incident, and because of her antics the customers left happy. Outrageous could have been Annie's middle name. I can't remember who said, 'The quality that first attracts you to a person often ends up being the quality that you most dislike about them.' And so it proved.

Ménage à Trois was all the rage. Ninety per cent of our customers at lunchtime, as we'd foreseen, were women who appreciated the small portions. With nouvelle cuisine overtaking London, I considered my restaurant honest and accurate in its description of the dishes we offered. In essence, my main-course-style starters were no smaller than many other nouvelle restaurants' main courses, but we called them starters. Those were the days when everything had to be the best: fillet steak, lobster, sea bass, turbot, truffles, foie gras, and there was always an abundance of caviar flying around, usually made to go further by the addition of some sauce or other being smeared over a sea-bass fillet. Half a dozen mouthfuls and it was gone.

When you remember it now, the food always looked as if it had passed through ten pairs of chefs' hands. Out went flour-based sauces, in came reductions made from stocks with so much cream that it was hard to discern the flavour. If it was a meat-and-wine-based sauce it would be so reduced that it was like eating liquid caramel. But I'm not embarrassed about having produced that style of food. It was what the customers wanted then, and I gave it to them. I have always been a bit of a slave to fashion. I keep my ear to the ground and try to be there or thereabouts when a food fad strikes. And I have to say that, although in all honesty I prefer good, gutsy, wholesome food, I did enjoy nouvelle cuisine. For a young chef it was a way of expressing himself on a plate. I accept that it was not always done in the best possible taste, but it was a first tentative step for the British towards believing in their ability to cook without constantly looking over their shoulders at the French. Ten years later, the French, embarrassed by the monster they had created, had retreated into their escargot shells while chefs in Britain, their confidence increasing in leaps and bounds, were blossoming. The UK was no longer a country that had to be apologetic about its food.

The biggest problem spawned by nouvelle cuisine was that it made the tradition of the waiter redundant. The chef had become king, and the waiters were demoted to servants. The chef's ready-plated designs were works of art and the waiter had only to set them on the table in precisely the way the chef decreed – 'Kiwi at two o'clock' sort of thing. Into the shoes of the professional waiter stepped students and antipodean travellers. Staff turnover was high, customers rarely recognized the same faces and many restaurants lost their personality. I'm sure we chefs didn't realize what we were destroying, but I guess it was our fault. What the country gained in the quality of its food it lost in the quality of its service. Fashions tend to be cyclical, so I hope that one day we will make front-of-house service a profession that we can be proud of once again.

As Ménage à Trois put down roots, I bought, with Annie's financial backing, a ground-floor flat in Nightingale Lane just off Wandsworth Common. It was a great little flat: two bedrooms, a spacious kitchen, a large sitting room and a decent-sized garden. While Annie helped enormously by buying me some bits to furnish it with, including a massive double bed, I was dead set on designing it myself. It was as if I needed to prove to her that I had good taste of my own. At the time I was going through my old-pine-and-potted-plants period: tastefully tame.

Exactly six months after the restaurant opened, Annie decided that her relationship with Don was over. She plucked up the courage to come clean with her husband and to leave him. Don must have seen the writing on the wall as it was obvious to others that he was having a fling with Caroline, my buddy and his waitress at the Bistro Vino. Annie (though she would never admit it) was jealous of Caroline, and Don was now jealous of me. I had no one to be jealous of, so I just went with the flow. Although Annie and I had been having an on-off affair for the best part of two years, it had never occurred to me that she would ever leave Don. But the impossible had happened: the cook had stolen the mistress from the Lord of the Manor.

On the day Annie moved into my flat, we experienced every emotion imaginable: elation, love, anger, sadness. That evening, we decided to celebrate six months of Ménage à Trois and her move from king to pawn by having our first official night out together. We dined at Langan's, which was great fun and had great atmosphere, and then had the idea of going on to the Embassy Club. We wandered towards Piccadilly like two teenagers in love, larking around and playing tag in and out of some scaffolding over the shops opposite the Ritz Hotel. In the distance I spotted two police constables walking towards us in that classic, 'evening, all', way, their feet pounding the beat in perfect harmony.

As they approached, I saw that they were both very young. The older one must have been about twenty; the other was still a flat-cap, a student policeman. 'Better behave,' I said to Annie. When they reached us, for some stupid reason – put it down to the general mood of hilarity and our sense of release – I said to the elder one, 'Officer, can you tell this woman to go away. She's been following me all night.'

'That's not how I saw it,' came the reply. 'You've been abusing this woman. I'm arresting you for breach of the peace.'

Oh dear. A young copper trying to impress his cadet. 'Oops, sorry,' I said. 'I thought you would have a sense of humour. Sorry I spoke.'

I tried to walk away, but he grabbed me by the shoulder. My temper began to get the better of me. 'You don't have to touch me to talk to me,' I said through gritted teeth. 'Let us go on our way, or explain to me whose peace I'm breaching at one o'clock in the morning in the middle of Piccadilly.' I moved off again. He grabbed me again. 'Don't touch me!' I shouted.

'You are under arrest. You are not obliged to say anything . . .' he recited.

'Knickers,' I retorted. I thought it funny at the time, but he was not amused.

Annie was laughing her head off, not quite believing what was happening. Again I tried to reason with this rookie, but it was like water off a duck's back. He was not going to budge. He wanted his moment of glory. When I attempted to walk off a third time, and for a third time he seized me, I flipped. I turned on him, interlocking my fingers with his and lifting him up. There was a clicking noise which, I assume, was a couple of his fingers dislocating. Then we were bundling around, out of control.

The cadet and Annie just stood there, aghast. As his hat went flying, the grappling bobby yelled at his cadet to call for back-up. The cadet panicked. Clearly his mind had gone blank. 'I've forgotten what to say over the radio,' he replied falteringly. If I hadn't been so angry and preoccupied with his colleague I would have been in fits of laughter. When he finally got to grips with the technology, I have to say that back-up was swift to arrive. Within a minute there were two vans with police dogs on the scene. Outnumbered, I surrendered gracefully, and was cuffed and manhandled unceremoniously into the back of one of the vans. Annie was warned to stay out of it or she'd get arrested, even though she'd left her handbag in the back of the van where she'd tried to join me. She remained on the pavement, but as the door closed on me and the van pulled away, she tried to stop it by throwing herself on to the riot grille that protected the front windscreen. The law grabbed her and pushed her into the back with me.

'I don't believe you just did that,' I said.

'I have to stick with my man.'

I laughed. Neither of us could believe what was happening to us. We still thought, as most basically law-abiding citizens would, that any minute we would wake up and everything would return to normal. But it didn't.

As we were led into Vine Street Police Station I was still in handcuffs, ranting and raving. After about half an hour, a nice sergeant came over and asked if I had calmed down enough for him to remove the handcuffs. 'Oh, go on then,' I sighed in mock capitulation. While Annie was taken off to a cell by a couple of women PCs, I was left sitting on a bench behind an office desk with a typewriter on it, given a cup of tea and told to behave.

Five minutes later the unmistakable sound of Annie screaming her head off reached my ears. In an instant I had turned the desk upside down, sending typewriter and tea flying, and charged into the open door of Annie's cell. I was greeted by the sight of two policewomen beating the shit out of Annie. She yelled that they were trying to steal her jewellery. I jumped into the fray, and tried to pull the constables off. I was quickly restrained by a burly bobby. 'She'll be all right,' he assured me.

The handcuffs were reapplied and I was returned to my bench. A hooker came over. 'Don't make a fuss,' she advised me. 'We're in here all the time. It's best just to go with the flow.' Another fifteen minutes passed. I watched the world go by until one of Annie's muggers emerged, clutching her arm. 'The bitch just bit me,' she hissed, showing me a juicy circle of horsey teethmarks from which blood was starting to ooze. Good on you, girl, I thought.

'Constable!' barked a sergeant. 'Take this man down to a cell.' I had so far refused to give my name. I stood up from the bench but immediately found myself flat on my back courtesy of two well-timed blows to the stomach and jaw. The sergeant came rushing over and helped me to my feet, removing my handcuffs. 'We don't want any of that in my station,' he told the constable.

'It's a bit late for that now,' I pointed out. I was feeling distinctly shaky.

'Take him away,' said the sergeant.

As I went through the door leading to the cells, I knew I was in for a hiding. Remembering the warnings of my face surgeon about getting involved in fights, I wondered how I was going to get out of this awkward situation. Perhaps calling his bluff would defuse it.

'Come on, copper, hit me,' I said as we reached the door of the cell. 'I know you want to. Come on. Hit me. Hit me!'

'Sonny, I wouldn't give you that pleasure. Now, get in there.' He sneered. 'I suggest you get some sleep.'

Phew. Not the brightest pebble on the beach, he had taken a sucker punch like a good 'un.

I didn't sleep, of course. I kicked at the door all night, shouting obscenities and demanding the phone call I had a right to make. At 5 am I was finally allowed a call, four, in fact. They were being nice to me by this stage. But instead of ringing my lawyer – I was too scared of Simon to wake him at five o'clock in the morning – I placed my food orders with my greengrocer, butcher and other suppliers. The policeman who was standing by looked on in amazement. I suppose it must have seemed a strange thing to do, but even though I had injured a policeman while resisting arrest and spent a night in the cells, I still believed that the nightmare would be over when the morning proper arrived. Unfortunately, it wasn't.

As I was treated to the privilege of having my mugshot and fingerprints taken, the sergeant had a fatherly word in my ear. 'Son,' he said, 'I've had murderers in here, rapists, muggers – you name it, they've all been in here, but never have I had anyone who has caused so much disruption. You would probably have got away with a verbal warning, but now we're going to have to charge you, especially after what your friend did to my female officers.' He was right, of course, but there was a principle at stake. Morals and principles, alas, have often been my downfall. So here I was, in deep shit, and all because I had defended myself against a stroppy little rookie trying to prove his manhood. The police didn't seem to see it that way, because they charged me with breach of the peace, resisting arrest and actual bodily harm.

When I saw Annie I was shocked. She was black and blue. There were bruises all over her face, arms and body. When we were finally released we went straight to see Simon, who immediately sent Annie off to be photographed. I had no visible bruises. There might have been some under my beard from that sock on the jaw, but I drew the line at shaving it off.

When Annie and I appeared at Bow Street Magistrates' Court we both pleaded not guilty and were bailed to appear at a later date. I never understood why we didn't go for trial by jury, because I'm sure it would have been the best option, but Simon advised otherwise and we went along with his directions. Annie was charged, as far as I remember, with the more serious crime of grievous bodily harm because of the business with the WPC's arm, but her case was thrown out after the police refused to allow the photographs of her injuries to be produced and our brief then blocked their photographs of the WPC's arm.

As for me, I was found guilty. The beak wouldn't take my word against that of the police, even though all the police notebooks contained conflicting accounts. That was when I knew I should have chosen trial by jury. I received a big fine and a six-month sentence suspended for two years, which was later reduced to six weeks on appeal at Knightsbridge Crown Court. But I was still a criminal, a label that weighed heavily on my shoulders.

There were two interesting postscripts to this incident. A month or so later, a couple of officers from the Police Complaints Office came to see me at the restaurant. They said they had had several complaints about Vine Street nick, but they had never had enough evidence to take a case forward. They listened to my story sympathetically and reassured me that in the future I would have no hassle if I were to apply for a visa or a liquor licence, both of which can be affected by a criminal record. And sure enough, to this day I have never been denied either a liquor licence or a visa.

The second really rubbed salt in the wound. Years later, I was watching breakfast telly one morning in bed, an item on an awards ceremony. And there he was, receiving a gong for holding back 200 crazed football supporters single-handedly with only his dog for protection. Yes, it was none other than the policeman who'd knocked me down that night. Sometimes there's no justice in this world. Personally, I would have given the award to the football supporters for beating the shit out of him.

I wasn't a complete stranger to the inside of a cell, though. Back in my college days, one of my pals was given a brand-new and extremely flashy open-top Mustang as an eighteenth birthday present and we decided to celebrate by heading off to the sun. We got a ferry to Spain and then another over to Morocco. Just as we were approaching Marrakech, we were pulled over at a police checkpoint and the car was searched. Miraculously, given the fact that neither of us touched the stuff, a bag of marijuana appeared in the glove compartment and we were thrown into a jail cell which made Vine Street nick look positively luxurious. A rough straw mat on the floor was all we had to sleep on. To make matters worse, very little English was spoken and we couldn't make our requests to contact the British Consulate understood. Eventually (after a couple of weeks!), we were told that we could leave if we paid a fine. Of course we didn't have enough cash with us and the next problem was that for some reason we weren't allowed to go to the bank we could see across the road through the cell window to arrange a money transfer.

Eventually we persuaded them to escort us to the bank and give us the Mustang back. But while we'd been doing our time, the Chief of Police had been driving it round town and clearly having a pretty good time – the car was trashed. Needless to say we got out of Morocco as quickly as possible after that, having seen nothing at all of the country except the inside of a cell!

CHAPTER TWENTY

I OFTEN WONDERED WHETHER THE PRINCESS OF WALES KNEW OF MY criminal record when she began to come to Ménage à Trois. Before her first visit we were, as was usual, checked out by her private detectives. It was all very exciting. Although I didn't know it at the time, she had chosen our restaurant for a rendezvous with Camilla Parker-Bowles, presumably to lay her cards on the table. I don't know whether she deliberately picked Ménage à Trois because of its name, or whether it was pure coincidence. If she was aware of its appropriateness, she obviously had a cheeky sense of humour. At the time the press were hounding the poor girl about her weight and speculating that she was suffering from anorexia, so perhaps she was trying to kill two birds with one stone.

When word got out that she had been to Ménage I had every newspaper in Fleet Street on the phone. What had she eaten? What had she been wearing? Who had she been with? I, of course, was a model of discretion, but unfortunately some of my staff weren't, and the reporters found out everything. Even so, I can't say it was bad publicity for us, and it didn't seem to harm the Princess, either, because she soon returned and before long we became known as 'Princess Di's favourite restaurant', which brought the Americans flocking in. The accolade wasn't strictly true, because San Lorenzo, a few doors down on Beauchamp Place, was definitely her number-one choice, but I wasn't about to knock it.

We remained *the* Knightsbridge watering-hole for smart ladies for a few years; unfortunately, we eventually became so popular with Americans, who tend to book up months in advance, that the

Brits began to give us up as a bad job. We ended up attracting many foreign dignitaries, too, all of whom wanted to have my modest little basement vetted before they came. King Hussein's entourage was the strictest. They managed to clear all the parked cars in the street as well as our 'friendly' tramp, whose regular pitch was the steps of the shop next door – the ideal site for opening my customers' car doors in the hope of a tip. Hussein's security officers advised us that if he were to do that to the King's car, it was quite likely that he would be shot. We got the message, and Friendly was ushered to the back of the restaurant and told to stay there until the coast was clear.

There was plenty of excitement at Ménage à Trois, much of it generated by Annie. On the restaurant's first birthday we held a party for regulars, friends and the press. Everything went swimmingly, and a good time was had by all. By about midnight, many of the guests had left and those who remained were late-drinking mates, so the staff were able to unwind and enjoy a drink or two themselves. One waitress, a raven-haired beauty from Australia called Melinda, perched herself on the edge of my knee in a friendly, quite unselfconscious and insignificant way. When I saw Annie approaching, I thought she was coming over to exchange congratulations with the rest of us for a great party. She bent down as if to kiss me, but instead she bit me. It was an aggressive, un-warranted, jealous act. I flipped. 'What the fuck's wrong with you? That was totally unnecessary.' In an instant, she had ruined what had been a happy anniversary party.

Melinda saw the whole thing. 'I'm out of here,' she said. 'Are you coming?'

'Yeah,' I replied. 'Let's go and get a drink. We'll leave by the back way.' We got out, but not before Annie had hurled a coffee cup in my direction. Fortunately for me, it missed.

Melinda and I found a bar where we could drown our sorrows in peace, though I didn't need alcohol to enhance my awareness that I was in the company of a gorgeous young lady. Wicked, dark Jewish eyes sent shivers deep inside me. She had a smattering of freckles in a bridge across her perfect nose. I love freckles. There's something extremely innocent but challengingly naughty about sun-kissed freckled flesh. Enough, enough: you get the message. Bad thoughts were tearing at my self-restraint. Melinda's full, in-viting lips parted to say, 'A penny for your thoughts.'

'Oh, I don't know.'

'Yes you do,' she countered.

She was right. I loved Annie in a strange way, and I hadn't even dreamed of double-crossing her when Melinda was sitting on my lap. We had been really settled once we moved in together. But her aggressive, possessive behaviour was not only becoming boring, it was chipping away my self-esteem.

Now, however, buoyed by alcohol and the attentions of a beauty ten years my junior, I was floating on a cloud. Melinda was flattering my bruised ego. 'I would like you to make love to me,' I said.

'Why don't you make love to me?'

'I'm not like that,' I said. 'I get confused by women. They say no when they mean yes; they say yes and then realize they should have said no. Of course I want you, but you're going to have to do the groundwork. Call me a wuss, but that's how I am.' Phew, that's got that off my chest, I thought. But how would Melinda react?

She played with me a bit, expressing doubts as to the wisdom of bonking the boss, but in the end I spent a guilty night of passion with her. Wild, raunchy sex is great fun, but it can be strangely unsatisfying when there are no emotions involved. This was of-the-moment sex, a dream that suddenly comes true only for the bubble to burst very quickly afterwards. But at that stage of my life I was not going to turn it down, especially on a night when I was questioning my future with Annie.

The next morning I found a note on my car windscreen. 'You can never hide from me. I'll always find you.' Thanks, Annie. I love you, too.

After my night out with Melinda, things got decidedly worse with Annie. Her behaviour became more and more aggressive, our fights passed into legend. I was not totally innocent, of course. There were times when I had to react physically to defend myself. I didn't like what I was doing, but I didn't like what I was suffering. I was the prisoner of her emotions. Like the women you read about who refuse to leave their violent partners, I was drawn back to her again and again. There was something quite special about Annie, she had a unique magic, but there was also something quite awful about her. And in a typically male, cowardly way, I couldn't deal with the problem. I just kept my options open by stringing Melinda along as an alternative, although Annie's hold was too powerful for me to break free. And here again Annie was her own worst enemy. She knew Melinda had a penchant for me, and Melinda was happy to flaunt her disdain in front of Annie, caressing me, grabbing hold of me and flirting with me outrageously at every possible opportunity.

My old friend Harriet Bunbury had asked Ménage à Trois to cater for her wedding reception, which was taking place at a country stack somewhere west of London. So I billeted a team, including Melinda but excluding Annie who unfortunately was a guest, at my grandmother's cottage at Shiplake the night before the wedding. It was a night of riotous student fun, drink for me, spliffs for them, and the night turned into a sexual romp, ending up in a literal Ménage à Trois involving Melinda, me and a Kiwi girl, Tanya. It remains my only experience of three-in-a-bed: something for the CV, perhaps, but not an experience I really got to grips with. It was a bit like trying to rub your stomach and pat your head at the same time, and especially tricky for the uncoordinated and uninitiated. Do you get the impression that I was slipping from Annie's grasp? I wish. However poorly I treated her, she kept coming back for more. I simply hadn't a clue what to do about it, but I wanted out.

The day after Harriet's wedding, Annie and I escorted the happy couple to Mustique for their honeymoon. Exactly why Harriet wanted us along was never explained. It was a holiday of high passion, high jinks, and electricity sparked by hot sun, sand, crystal waters and tropical storms. Fun and frightening are the two words that sum it up. For Harriet and her husband a relationship was just beginning, but Annie's and mine was in its death throes. Opposites certainly attract, but for how long? I realized that if you took the sex away there was not enough left to hold us together. And there were to be no smouldering embers for us. Our fast-burning fire was out. The problem was, how was I to dispose of the ashes?

Back in London, there was a nasty shock awaiting us. In spite of losing his wife to the chef, Annie's ex-ish husband was still involved with the restaurant, where his role was to look after the books. After about eighteen months of trading we were alarmed to discover that, despite the obvious appeal of Ménage à Trois, it had lost about £168,000. The reason we were still able to trade was that these debts were owed almost entirely to the Inland Revenue in tax on our wages.

Neither Annie nor I could believe these figures. I stopped short of accusing Don of cooking the books, but it would have been the ideal sting, the perfect slap in the face for Annie and me. Without any evidence to show who had been at fault, I just didn't know. I do remember being completely incapable of understanding why it had taken so long for me to be informed of these losses. As a director of a limited company, I should, of course, have been au fait with the financial side of the operation, but Annie, Don and I had very distinct responsibilities. Mine was the kitchen, Annie's was front-of-house and Don's was the finances. And somehow, amid the euphoria of cooking for a packed restaurant and the fun Annie and I were having on a personal level, the business element of the operation had passed us by. Even twenty years later I have to accept that it is a mystery I will never unravel. One thing was certain, however. If something wasn't done quickly to rectify the situation, the successful Ménage à Trois would soon be history.

I went to see Simon Bowen to ask his advice, and he agreed to travel down to Cardiff with me to see the people at the Inland Revenue to try to work out a solution. It was in their interests to make a deal with us: Ménage à Trois was, after all, hugely popular. All it needed was the right management. By the end of the meeting we had agreed to pay the Inland Revenue £1,000 a week to clear the arrears. It was a tall order given that we had apparently been losing over £2,000 a week for the previous year and a half, but it had to be done if we were going to get the restaurant back on its financial feet.

Needless to say, this was a stressful time. I had a restaurant losing a fortune and a woman who wouldn't leave me and then, to cap it all, I lost my head chef. Of the applicants for his job only two excited me, one of whom was a youngster by the name of Gary Rhodes. He looked a bit of a wide boy, a bit of a rocker, and he talked himself up well, but in the end there was no decision for me to make, because after expressing his interest in the job he then chose to work instead for a guy who later became both a great friend and a friendly rival to me, Brian Turner, the proud holder of a Michelin star at David Levin's Capital Hotel. As it turned out, it was the right move for both of us. Gary did brilliantly at the Capital and its sister restaurant, the Greenhouse, before accepting the head chef's position with Kit Chapman at the Castle Hotel in Taunton. And the rest, as they say, is history.

I wasn't too downhearted because the other promising applicant, a young sous-chef from Stringfellow's nightclub called David Wilby, accepted the job. David was a classically trained chef from Coventry who had served his apprenticeship at Mirabelle before his nightclub career. I knew the quality of the menu at Stringfellow's as it was one of my late-night haunts. Peter Stringfellow always demanded the best, and at the time it was the only nightclub to offer decent food.

I don't know whether David knew what he was letting himself in for at Ménage. For a start, as I was self-taught, my ways were different from anything he had experienced. There was no formal structure to the kitchen. My band of renegade chefs all just pitched in, in a desperate attempt to keep their heads above water. The menu was massive, several pages long, and every time I changed it it got bigger. I kept adding to it but I found it hard to subtract. The preparation and service were all handled from a cramped, badly designed kitchen, fifteen foot by fifteen foot, with the wash-up and stores located under a staircase. To get in and out you had to squeeze through a narrow, five-foot corridor where the espresso machine was positioned, along with its rather portly operator, Costa, a friendly Portuguese. The girls had to struggle past with their fully laden plates, suffering appalling abuse from David and me and polite abuse from Costa. Hardly the perfect environment in which to serve posh nosh. It was a nightmare, really, and yet we coped with in excess of 140 unsuspecting customers ordering intricate mini-dishes of nouvelle cuisine. When I talk about it nowadays with David we wonder how we ever coped.

David proved to be the stability I needed in the kitchen. He whipped a strong team into shape and gradually replaced my motley little army with more professional crew. One such was a chef called Frank Rourke, a fiery giant of a man who occasionally scared the hell out of me. This was a difficult period for me because I was slowly having to let go of my kitchen and delegate control to my new boys, who were much more professional than I was, even if it was me who had the flair and the creative skills. Frank was a beer-swilling, cigarette-smoking caricature of a chef, belly hanging over apron and low-slung trousers revealing his chef's cleavage. He would have been more at home on a picket line, arm in arm with Arthur Scargill. At the start we clashed something rotten. He was a classic whinger and he took a very scathing view of my ability to organize a kitchen. He had a point, of course, but initially he failed to appreciate that I was a stubborn bastard who, diminutive though I might be, had dealt with bigger fish than him in my Essex days. However, once the pecking order had been established, we ended up becoming quite good friends. To challenge these professional chefs I often had to bluff my way through their arguments. Very occasionally I felt like a mouse saying 'Don't fuck with me' to a giant rat.

If I say so myself, the food was great, and as each year went by I was extremely disappointed not to receive an entry in the *Michelin Guide*. My early ambition was to become England's first British holder of three Michelin stars. That ambition soon waned when I realized that the British edition of the *Michelin Guide* was so stuck up its French parent's arse that it could have cleaned its teeth from the inside. It became clear to me that, at that time, to some degree even today, the guide was not particularly interested in the customer enjoyment factor. Escoffier and Carême were its gods, and it was far too élitist to countenance giving houseroom to a cocky English chef.

Perhaps you think I'm just a bitter, jealous man who's pissed off because he didn't get Michelin recognition. If so, you'd be right, at least as far as the early part of my restaurant career is concerned. But since then I have spent a fair amount of time studying the Michelin standard and it didn't take me long to come to the conclusion that the customer enjoyment factor was not taken into consideration. Off the top of my head I can name three outstanding chefs of my era who were not recognized by Michelin: Alastair Little of the eponymous restaurants, Simon Hopkinson of Bibendum and Rowley Leigh of Kensington Place. All three of them produce, or produced, food that had heart, passion, depth and, above all, flavour. They didn't have any truck with poncy designer dishes. Theirs was a triumph of substance over image, not style over substance. Others, too, were ignored by the guide, but you need only look at these three to see what I mean about the Michelin standard. They blow it out of the water.

Much as I care about food, there is far more to the enjoyment of a meal in a restaurant than food alone. It is the package that makes everything fall into place. So what are the components of my 'customer enjoyment factor'?

First of all, there's service, which is very important. And I don't mean waiters standing like a row of soldiers anticipating an order, then lifting the silver domes and hovering, domes in hand, for the customers' oohs and aahs. As I've said, for too long we in the UK have tended to ignore the importance of this skilled profession and consequently we put up with very average service skills. It's time for a change. Then there is ambience – the lighting, design, comfort of a restaurant mean a lot to people. I've eaten in some cold, badly lit, uncomfortable restaurants where the food has been excellent but where I haven't been able to relax, and therefore I've been in a hurry to leave. Japanese restaurants are particularly bad at ambience. Too many of them look like IKEA meets hospital canteen.

Next, value for money. By value for money, I don't mean cheap, necessarily: you can eat in quite expensive restaurants which still represent value for money in terms of the quality of food or service while some inexpensive trendy burger bars can leave you feeling that you've been ripped off. Wine lists often represent extremely bad value, with many establishments pricing it at three or four times the cost to them. Personally, I would rather see my top-of-the-range wines turning over, so I mark up by the pound rather than by percentage. The bottom line, of course, has to be the cheapest wine, so if a customer chooses a bottle of house wine, he will pay the usual mark-up and I may net a £8 profit. But a bottle of wine costing me £50 I might sell at £70, excluding VAT, and make only £20 rather than the £150 plus I would make if I priced it according to the usual catering margins. But I'm still £12 better off than I would be if the customer who chooses it had purchased my cheapest wine instead. It's less percentage for me, and the accountant will moan, but it's more money in the bank.

Probably the most important influence on a customer's overall experience of a restaurant is his or her dining companion or companions, but of course, that is the one factor I can't do anything about. Speaking from the restaurateur's point of view, I am not very fond of couples. Obviously that is a generalization, but it's true that they can be the hardest diners to please. While groups of four or six are harder to cook for, they tend to be more appreciative of your efforts. Between courses they are usually engrossed in conversation, which covers a multitude of restaurant sins such as how long the food takes to arrive at the table. Couples, on the other hand, fall into several categories. At the risk of being accused of stereotyping, I'd say it's a fair bet that an old couple will have nothing to talk about, and so they will stare around and pick holes in your restaurant while they keep tabs on how long the food is taking. A couple having a row will never enjoy the ambience or the food, and will often leave before pudding or coffee, in some cases even before the main course. If they cause a scene the truculent mood they create can spread like an epidemic through the restaurant. They'll still be in love the next morning, but they might well write and complain that they had an awful time in your restaurant.

A couple on an early date are usually too infatuated with each other to even notice the food, let alone eat it. He is more pre-occupied with having big-toe sex under the table; she is intent on devouring his tongue. They regularly visit the loos, leaving foot-prints on every conceivable bit of paintwork. He wakes the next day having enjoyed his oats far more than the meal and wonders why on earth he paid such a fortune for dinner in a good restaurant when the same result could have been achieved at home with a couple of bottles of wine.

Valentine's Night is a particularly painful occasion for restau-rants. You have dozens of twos taking up valuable space where fours could be seated, and many of them are couples who have to go out to dinner that night whether they want to or not, because if he forgets 14 February his life will not be worth living. Usually the atmosphere is muted – a mixture of love, lust and 'I'd rather be with my bit on the side' boredom and 'I'd better not order an expensive bottle of wine when she'd rather spend it on a new Hoover'. The next night it's all couples again, but the atmosphere is totally different. It's lively, fun and the booze flows. Why? Because the next night is mistress night, the night when people go out with the person they really want to go out with. Am I an old cynic? Of course I am, but in the restaurant world you see it all.

The restaurateur's code has to be to see no evil, hear no evil, speak no evil. On one occasion, after lunch service we found a carrier bag a customer had left under his chair. We looked to see what was in it, as you did in the days before the danger of terrorist attacks, and discovered £27,000 in used notes. My first reaction was, 'Fuck me, that'll pay off a few debts,' but while I was out during the afternoon the customer returned, bold as brass, to collect his loot. Rather stingily, he gave the waitress only a tenner for her trouble. A few days later, the same man returned for lunch. Afterwards I sat down with him and his moll for a drink. After a few bevvies I was brave enough to put the question. 'What would you have done if that money had just gone missing?' Cool as a cucumber, he replied, 'Oh, I don't know. Probably sent the boys in, trashed the place and burned it out.' Fair enough, I thought.

In 1983, Donald Foster-Firth invited me to help him open a new restaurant on the King's Road in Chelsea. It might sound a strange proposal for a guy to make to the man who had nicked his wife, but I got the impression that Don held Annie responsible for that. Maybe he just thought I owed him a favour. Either way, I agreed to help him for a pittance. It seemed only fair. I came up with the name Avoirdupois, after the British system of weights, with its additional connotations of heaviness and stoutness, to emphasize that the new restaurant would be taking a completely opposite approach to Ménage à Trois. There was no nouvelle cuisine here. Avoirdupois served oversized portions of rustic food, plainly cooked; dishes for the public schoolboy. Steak and kidney pud, calf's liver and bacon, shepherd's pie, steaks, a variety of burgers, including the headline-grabbing deal of an 8oz burger with a bottle of 1961 Château Lafite for £69.50, and some good, old-fashioned puddings. If I remember rightly, I think I may have even put on prawn cocktail and Black Forest gâteau.

I based my menus very much on my favourite trashy restaurant, Foxtrot Oscar, run by my two old mates Michael Proudlock and Rex Leyland, which had cornered the market west of the city for public-school food. With so many restaurants jumping on to the nouvelle cuisine bandwagon, I felt there was room for another Foxtrot-type place. I was right. From day one it was packed, much to the annoyance of the Foxtrot boys, but as I pointed out, there was plenty of room for everyone in the anti-nouvelle cuisine market.

There was nothing remotely sophisticated about Avoirdupois. With its black and red décor, loud music, trendy cocktails and delicious young ladies serving its tweedy-jacketed clientele, it was brash. The food and the atmosphere hit the spot, although I wouldn't say that the dishes were among those I was especially proud of. For me, Avoirdupois served another purpose. It was a way of escaping Annie's clutches.

As Annie grew more and more jealous and possessive, I became more and more provocative, openly flaunting other girls under her nose. It must have been torture for her, but however badly I behaved, it seemed, she just wouldn't go. I didn't want to be mean, but I couldn't afford to walk out of my adored flat in Nightingale Lane. Annie would have to be the one to leave. I went off to America for a week, dragging with me the blonde manageress of the boutique above Ménage à Trois, hoping to return to an empty flat. Before I left, I pleaded with Annie's friends to set her up with another man for her own sake. When I got back, it had finally happened. At last, I could end this farce. Pretending to be suitably offended, I asked her to leave the flat. She refused, so I resolved the issue by putting her antique furniture out on the pavement and phoning her to ask her to collect it. It worked. She sent round a man in a white coat with a white van to pick up her belongings. He was a very helpful chap. My car wouldn't start, and he obligingly gave me a lift to the restaurant. It was only later that I discovered that the van man was Annie's new bloke, Eric. He seemed nice enough.

I was free. I couldn't believe it. If we'd stayed together, one of us wouldn't have survived. To be on the safe side, I changed the locks and tried to make sure that I did different shifts at Ménage à Trois from Annie. When we did meet, we managed to be civilized. Eric, bless him, escorted her everywhere. If I thought the whole saga was over, though, I was sadly mistaken. Annie joined forces with Donald once again on the business front, and together they tried to squeeze me out of Ménage à Trois by serving me with an injunction not to set foot in the restaurant. It was a futile gesture. I set Simon Bowen on them. I don't know what he did, but I was allowed to remain. Annie continued to work there for a few months, but only occasionally. In the meantime, I radically changed the operation, closing at weekends, slashing the number of staff and running only one team of chefs and, slowly, slowly, we pulled the restaurant round, enabling us to pay the Inland Revenue their £1,000 a week and to make a small profit as well.

CHAPTER TWENTY-ONE

WHEN ANNIE REALIZED THAT OUR RELATIONSHIP WAS FINISHED FOR good, she said to me: 'You'll never find anyone as good as me.'

'Don't you believe it,' I retorted. 'I'll be married by Christmas.'

It was an idle boast, but I don't like to break my promises. We had that conversation in May 1983, and my wedding took place on 4 December that year.

If you suspect that I married on the rebound, you'd be right – but it wasn't just Annie I was on the rebound from.

I had become a regular luncher at Foxtrot Oscar, and most afternoons I'd get slaughtered with the Foxtrot girls, who weren't girls at all, but a group of rather rowdy, ageing, former public schoolboys, predominantly old Etonians or Harrovians. These guys were all about forty going on eighteen. Their conversation usually revolved around Lloyd's, women and sex, in no particular order. Female conquests were often brought along, even though most of the group were married men. Few of them showed any inclination to work, and for those who did have jobs, the working day seemed to end with lunch. They lived on legacies, trust funds or Lloyd's, some while they were waiting to inherit the family seat. Looking at them, you could immediately see why the Labour Party wanted to abolish hereditary peers. These all-singing, all-dancing, all-spanking socialites were more suited to a bygone age than to the realities of the twentieth century. But it was fun at the time.

Michael Proudlock was the chief whip. He spent his mornings rounding up these reprobates – it was good for business. They would all troop in, as if they were coming into a school dining hall, at about 2 pm, by which time Michael would have finished work for the day. The only duty that remained to him was to push drink down his mates' throats, and his own, and he was bloody good at it, too. Even though Foxtrot was in essence an upmarket burger bar, Michael managed to get us all to part with in excess of £30 a head, pretty good going in the early eighties.

Through Michael's wife, Lena, I met her sister, Maria. The two women, who were Swedish, couldn't have been more different. Lena had embraced the merry-go-round of society and success. She ran a knitwear design company with Edina Ronay called Lena and Edina, and she had a brilliant head for business, especially when it came to property. She had picked up a bargain corner house, a veritable mansion, in Phillimore Gardens in Kensington for next to nothing. Maria, on the other hand, was a penniless actress who merely rented a room in this great mansion. She was introduced to me by Lena in the hope that I might be able to give her some part-time work at Ménage to tide her over between acting roles.

I did take Maria on at the restaurant, and she worked well, with quiet, Scandinavian efficiency. When we had finished for the night I would run her home, sometimes stopping for a drink en route, and we became quite close. She was quite the Swedish ice maiden, very sexy in a melt-me-and-I-could-be-yours kind of way, but I had no intention of trying to seduce her. It was all a bit close to home, with Proudlock being married to her sister. Inevitably, though, one night she invited me in for a drink. There was a separate side entrance to her room at Phillimore Gardens, so I was able to slip in without the Proudlocks knowing about it. The sex just happened. For Maria, it appeared to be just another bodily function, like eating when you were hungry, and for me, this seemed cold, lacking in romance and strangely unsatisfying. I didn't really know what I felt about Maria herself, though I was certainly intrigued by her. To be absolutely truthful, right at the start, I think, as far as I was concerned, there was an element to it of putting one over on Michael, whose lifestyle rather fascinated me in a morbid sort of way.

Yet from these uncertain, not to say inauspicious beginnings, the relationship warmed up considerably in the following months, even if, for the most part, it was still based predominantly on sex. Still, the ice melted and I found it very relaxing, after Annie, to be involved in an affair with a girl who was totally ungushy and non-materialistic. Maria was her own person, with no airs and graces, and we found we had a lot in common on a fundamental level. She loved the ordinary things in life – gardening, animals, food; simple pleasures that nourished her soul – as opposed to its transient trappings.

I began to take more and more interest in Maria's acting, becoming prouder and prouder of her every time I watched her perform. By now I was desperate to be with her at every possible opportunity, but there were times when I wouldn't see her for days, weeks if she was touring. Often I travelled with her between theatres and we enjoyed dangerous sex – on the front row of seats on a cross-Channel ferry, or on the train from Calais to Paris. We'd try to break records for the number of times you could have sex in twenty-four hours. It was all a delicious adventure. I loved her company, I loved our intense conversations, I loved the sex, I loved her ability to be herself. I was falling in love, period.

And then, suddenly, nothing. I last saw Maria in Paris. We stayed on the Rue des Beaux-Arts, enjoying lots of sex, lots of food and behaving outrageously. She had made up her mind to leave her touring theatre company over the next couple of weeks and to return to me and England. But it never happened. Apparently, the company offered her the lead role in the production, but the news never reached me. Maria had sent me a message via Lena telling me of her plans and urging me to hold on for her, but Lena didn't pass it on to me. It was a real tragedy. If I had known I would have waited for Maria, but as it was I thought the worst: that she had simply dumped me. By the time I found out the truth, I was well and truly ensconced with my future wife.

So who was the girl I married in such a hurry? She was an Aussie traveller named Militza-Jane Millar, and yes, she worked for me as a waitress. She was a gorgeous girl, blonde, sexy and un-selfconscious, and I fancied her like mad from the beginning. It all got off to rather a disastrous start. Although I was thirty-two by now, I still hadn't grown up, had still never made the running with any girl. And I can assure you that my first attempt at a chat-up line is not one to be recommended.

I spotted my chance when I noticed Militza – or Mish, as she was known for short – going into the coat cupboard one day. I went in after her, shutting the door behind me. She seemed rather shocked, but not nearly as shocked as she was when she heard what I had to say. 'I suppose a fuck is out of the question?' I asked, without preamble. She almost decked me. Fortunately, I got away with being called a dirty bastard. Undaunted, I decided to try a different tack. I hovered around her, trying to train her to be great at her job, and she seemed to appreciate the interest I took in her work. In the past, at the end of a service I had kept myself to myself and rarely drank with the staff. Now I was down in the well under the pavement that was our bar area along with everybody else, listening to Mish's every word and drinking myself silly.

Mish, I discovered, thought that all Brits were prats. I consoled myself with the knowledge that to date the only British men she had mixed with had been Hooray Henrys and pinstriped City boys. I had the optimistic idea that my flip-flops and long, blond hair might make her feel at home, but I was soon made aware that it was going to take a great deal more than that. How was I actually going to appeal to the heart of this Australian girl who didn't like Englishmen? I decided to take the bull by the horns. Each year I went to Paris to buy the waitresses' uniforms, usually wacky jump-suits that looked great on the slim girls but made the dumpier ones look a bit like delicate elephants. I asked her if she would come with me to help me choose an outfit that would suit everyone. There would be no hanky-panky, I assured her: it would be separate rooms, and she had my word as an Englishman and a gentleman on that. Given her view of Englishmen, this promise perhaps didn't carry the weight it might have done in other quarters, but although she seemed rather taken aback, this time she said she'd think about it.

She put the idea to her flatmate, another Aussie, who told her that if she believed me, she had nothing to lose. She was planning to return to Oz soon anyway, so she wasn't going to end up getting involved. Mish thought she could trust me, and so she could. Almost. So, unbeknown to the rest of my staff, we drove off to Paris together. When we arrived at our hotel, we hit our first technical hitch. I had booked separate rooms but for some reason we got one room with twin beds. Clearly my French had let me down. Mish seemed unfazed by this. We showered, went out to dinner, watched a show at the Moulin Rouge and then went on to a nightclub. We had plenty of drink – Mish liked a drink – and there was plenty of hip-grinding on the dance floor and a kiss or six. I was very aroused, but I had made a promise and I intended to keep it. We returned to the hotel, kissed, and I got into my bed and she got into hers. About twenty minutes later she crept into my bed. 'No sex,' she whispered. 'No sex,' I replied. We fell asleep in each other's arms.

Day two was a great, sunny, Parisian day. We went off to Rue St Denis and bought the staff uniforms, lunched at Brasserie Flo, champagned at the Jules Verne Restaurant high up in the Eiffel Tower, returned to the hotel, showered together and had pre-dinner nibbles. But no sex. We dined at Alain Senderens's small, suede-covered restaurant where he was awarded his three Michelin stars before moving to Place de la Madeleine. The food was probably exquisite, but unfortunately our hands were rarely above the table-top long enough to handle the cutlery. The bill was exorbitant, but I didn't care. It was worth every centime.

The next four hours were spent in what seemed like an endless dance among hundreds of cavorting Parisians. I spent dance upon dance just enjoying the aroma of Mish's body, the sweet taste of her flesh, the rise and fall of her perfectly formed breasts, the nonsensical nothings whispered in my ear but failing to reach my brain due to the level of the Paris decibels. We walked hand in hand back to the hotel, gulping in the carbon monoxide of the Champs Elysées in spring. Not that it mattered where we were. We could have been walking down Walthamstow High Street and it would have been just as romantic. Back at the hotel, we showered again, nibbled again, and climbed into my bed. 'Sex,' she whispered. 'No sex,' I replied.

'I can't believe you!'

'I'm a man of my word,' I said, pained and bitterly regretting my promise. 'As soon as we get home, my promise will have been ful-filled and we can start again.'

Of course, by the time we got back to my flat in Nightingale Lane we were hardly up the garden path before our clothes were off and we were at it like dogs. And from that moment on, we were in-separable. Mish moved in with me, and within three months I had proposed.

Mish wasn't sure about marriage. She wanted to go home to Australia to get her bearings and make certain that she no longer had feelings for her ex-boyfriend there. I talked her out of it. I was terrified of losing her, frightened that if she went home she would never come back. So she didn't go. She stayed, and said yes to my proposal.

Our relationship was rather frowned upon by my staff, especially as Mish was 'only' a waitress and they had been used to Annie being my partner. So I decided to remove Mish from the restaurant. She was outraged, even when I told her that I was making her a manageress at Avoirdupois instead. My theory was that she would be so shocked at losing her job that she would try doubly hard as a manageress, and so it proved. She turned out to be a star. She was great at handling people, whether they were staff or customers, she worked like a dog and she confounded all the cynics who thought I was making a big mistake. I'm not sure my theory should be included in any management manual, but it worked with Mish.

She was a lovely person, very naive to the ways of the big city, but when you mix with hardened Londoners, a little naivety is a breath of fresh air. She was the sort of girl who would talk to anyone. Wandering down a busy London street, she would just chat, Crocodile Dundee-style, to anyone who looked interesting, 'G'day,' she'd say, and then she was off, gabbing away, winding up with an 'I'm sure I'll see you around'. The shell-shocked Brit she'd been talking to, who had most likely been travelling on the same train with the same people for years without uttering a word to them, would stagger off in a daze, probably thinking that Mish should be committed. It was marvellous; a great gift that made everyone love her. And I thought I did, too, but looking back I wonder.

We holidayed that year in Greece, taking a yacht in a flotilla. All the other boats seemed to be occupied by four, but we were on our own. I had taken a two-day sailing course on the Solent, but once I saw all the peak-capped weekend sailors in the other boats I began to have doubts about my ability to sail, especially with just two of us. I asked if one of the sailing tour leaders could come on board and show us the ropes, and was promised that someone would be there once we got out of harbour, but our leader never showed. I panicked. I didn't know how to read a course on a map, I forgot my knots, and tacking seemed like a foreign word to me. In the end I decided I would just copy what the boat in front did, and it worked a treat. Not everything went as smoothly, however.

Militza, bless her, decided to make the cabin homely. She put flowers on the table and laid out our duty-free and glasses. As we motored out of harbour, the sails went up and we hit a wave. Crash. Flowers, booze, glasses all hit the cabin floor. Nice one, darling. We survived the first day and pulled into harbour, the last boat to straggle in. Mish's duty was to throw out the rear anchor when I thought we needed to stop, 'Three, two, one, now!' I called. Mish duly lugged the anchor over the stern, but the boat failed to stop. Crash. Cheers all round from the other sailors. She had thrown the anchor over the side, all right, but had forgotten to tie

it on to a cleat first. So now we had no anchor. Pink with embarrassment, I dived over the side to retrieve it.

That was Mish all over. Her clumsy awkwardness endeared her
to me and to many others, too. In spite of the scrapes we got into,
the holiday was a laugh a minute. We left the flotilla – having won
the regatta, incidentally – and travelled to Rhodes to meet the
outlaws. Mish's father, Hugh Millar, was a top ear, nose and throat
specialist, and he was over in Europe with his wife, Mitzi, for a
conference. Mish had warned me that they were fairly traditional,
old-fashioned parents, and in the course of her phone calls home it
had become clear that they weren't overly impressed that she had
got herself tied up with a Brit. So this summit was a pretty daunting prospect. The parents had arrived in Rhodes late in the evening,
and as they were early-to-bed types, we all arranged to meet for
breakfast the following morning.

We hit it off very well. Hugh was an intelligent, affable man.
Mish's beauty, I saw straight away, came from her mum, an
attractive older woman from a White Russian family with a touch
of the oriental in there somewhere. She seemed convinced that I
was Australian. It must have been the tan, the flip-flops – or thongs,
as they call them Down Under – or the sun-bleached hair. Later in
the day, I took a long walk on the beach with Mish's dad, doing the
correct thing of asking for his daughter's hand in marriage, while
Mitzi gave Mish the third degree. Hugh delivered the time-
honoured fatherly lecture. Mish was a bit of a wild child, very
young with little experience of life. Did I love her? Was she sure she
was doing the right thing? I would have to answer to him if his little
girl was ever unhappy. You know the sort of thing.

Both Mish and I seemed to pass our respective tests, so next
the marriage arrangements were discussed. It was agreed that the
nuptials would take place in South Yarra, Melbourne, over
the Christmas holidays in Australia. There was to be a ceremony in
church followed by a reception at the South Yarra Tennis Club,
where Hugh and Mitzi had had their own wedding reception.
Sorted.

There was only one small problem. Although none of us knew it
at the time, Mish was pregnant. The baby had been conceived, we
worked out later, on the yacht, just days before our rendezvous
with Mish's parents. The pregnancy was to prove to be a bit of an
embarrassment to her folks. What would their friends say? Our
friends back home were excited about it, at least. Life in London

was beginning to take shape. The spectre of Annie receded: now that there was a baby on the way she could see there was no going back, and reluctantly offered us her congratulations. On the business side, things were looking up, too. David Wilby had done wonders in the kitchen at Ménage and at last we were making money. During our financial troubles I had resisted the temptation to sell my pride and joy, our wine cellar, which was worth about £150,000 (luckily, the Inland Revenue hadn't been aware of its existence, or doubtless they would have insisted on it being sold). Slowly it became the pride and joy of my head barman, Eddie Khoo, as well, as he transformed himself from a great cocktail barman into one of the country's best sommeliers.

Nowadays few restaurants can afford cellars of this value, but with me it was an obsession. I would visit the monthly sales at Sotheby's and soon built up a reputation as a serious buyer. Early on I bought some rubbish, of course, but with the help of the great wine buff Geoffrey Roberts, sadly no longer with us, and his mate Anders Ousback, a knowledgeable man on all food- and wine-based matters, I learned the pitfalls of buying at auction. One of the best pieces of advice they gave me was never to buy lots of one case and eleven bottles. This often means that the wine has been tasted by the seller and the quality found to be poor. With the further assistance of Michael Broadbent's book on French wines, I built up a list of 900 bins, a list good enough to win Ménage à Trois the Grand Award from the *Wine Spectator* in America. The *Wine Spectator* flew Eddie Khoo and me over to America to collect the award in front of hundreds of people in a luxury hotel in New York. It was a proud day for our little basement restaurant in Knightsbridge, especially as only two other restaurants in the UK had ever received this accolade.

The cellar also did wonders for our trade from American customers. Bills could run into thousands of pounds when they bought some of our great clarets. For someone who had spent his whole life seeking recognition, first from his mother and grand-mother and then from his peers, it was a much-valued step in the right direction. Recognition is such an intangible quality, and why it was of such paramount importance to me I can't say. It was that persistent insecurity, I suppose. I was constantly questioning whether I was doing the right thing, and yet it seemed that what-ever I decided, some mysterious force determined to deny me satisfaction would always go and blow it for me. And the face I presented to the world belied this serious intent. I was a committed foodie, and yet my attitude to life was so laid back that I exuded an air of irresponsibility.

This much was obvious from the views, usually ill-founded, of other chefs. The fact that Ménage à Trois had received mega-publicity, was always full, and was probably one of London's most successful restaurants cut no ice with classical chefs such as Michel Roux, who dismissed Ménage as a gimmick. To the glitterati of the chef world I was a jumped-up cowboy who had cottoned on to the nouvelle cuisine trend.

Everyone is entitled to his or her own opinion, but not if it is based on ignorance. None of these chefs had ever even eaten at the restaurant. At least Michel Roux, to be fair to him, was big enough to make it up to me later for having prejudged me. His wife-to-be at the time, Robyn, used to come to Ménage regularly on a Sunday and seemed to enjoy it. She was indignant on my behalf when Michel made some disparaging remarks about Ménage and, being a straight-talking Aussie, immediately took him to task. Michel, to give him his due, arranged to have dinner at Ménage one Monday night with a party of six. He left the menu to me. This was scary stuff. What do you cook for one of the greatest chefs in Britain? It was possibly the most crucial moment of my short cheffing life, but do you know what? Twenty years later I can't for the life of me remember what I did finally decide to cook for him. The one dish I can recall sticks in my mind only because it was the first and last time I ever made it – it was very complicated and quite original for its time. Each diner was served three sea urchins on a bed of hot rock salt, one filled with scrambled sea-urchin eggs with a topping of caviar, another with a gull's egg baked in the urchin shell with an urchin cream, and the third with poached quails' eggs on a ragout of urchin roe finished with sorrel hollandaise. Never one to under-gild the lily, me. Why make a dish easy when you can make it complicated? It's a philosophy I grew out of, I promise.

I think Michel and his guests, who included Robyn, enjoyed dinner. I was too nervous to ask, but Robyn gave me a cheeky look as they left which gave me the impression that all was well. And a few weeks later, I received a letter from Michel Roux asking me if I would like to join the Académie Culinaire, a very exclusive association. In those days this was the pinnacle of our profession, and to say that I was flattered would be an understatement. Michel said he would propose me to the Académie with the backing of

Michel Bourdin, the one chef who had attended the opening party of Ménage à Trois. The first proposal was thrown out, but the Michels didn't give up, and a few months later I became a member of this hallowed club.

Going to the first meeting was a bit like going to a new school for the first time and discovering that your mum has forgotten to tell you that you are supposed to wear a uniform. I turned up in my jeans, T-shirt and leather jacket to be met by dirty looks from almost every member in the room. Everyone else seemed to have put on their Sunday best: slacks, white shirts, sombre ties and jackets were the order of the day. Oh dear, not a good start, but conformity was never one of my strengths. The other chefs were mainly either French, hotel boys or the cream of restaurant chefs. I knew who most of them were but to me they were untouchable idols, first-division players. All the big shots were in the Académie: Albert Roux, Anton Mosimann, Richard Shepherd, Anton Edelman, Pierre Koffman, Bernard Gaume, Brian Turner, Peter Kromberg, to name but a few. It was a daunting display of cheffie power. I was so gobsmacked to find myself in such company that I don't think I said a word for the first three meetings.

In the meantime, preparations for the wedding were getting under way. To minimize the embarrassment to Mish's parents of what would be by Christmas a visible pregnancy, we ended up demoting the South Yarra part of the wedding ceremony to a blessing, and officially tied the knot before going out to Australia. I managed to secure a booking at Chelsea Register Office by saying I lived at my grandmother's house in Markham Street. It was convenient for the restaurant and it was a bit of a trendy venue at the time. For some absurd reason I decided to get married in my chef's jacket with an ornamental cabbage as a bouquet. That was me all over: for ever playing the fool. I must learn to take these marriages more seriously.

I was quite happy about it. At the time I was sure I was in love with Militza. She was lovely, great fun, a girl who could do nothing wrong in the eyes of others, a veritable angel. But our married life was not destined to be a success.

It was a weird day. I can't remember anything about the register office ceremony, apart from the fact that Donald and Annie Foster-Firth were there, together with the Proudlocks – I think Michael was my best man – my mother, and my grandmother, though no father on this occasion. Why on earth we had invited Don and

Annie God only knows. When I think about it now it seems a little surreal. Don and Annie never got back together as a couple, but on that day it was as if nothing had ever happened, and it was all happy families again.

I arranged for the Chelsea Fire Brigade to come out and serenade us on their sirens as we left the register office, which was very sweet, and then the party moved on to Ménage à Trois for lunch. I can't remember what we ate; it was more about booze. My grandmother had to escort my mother home before she caused a scene. The next night we held a belting bash at Michael and Lena Proudlock's house in Kensington attended by about 150 of our 'closest' friends. It was an elaborate occasion and a great setting, thanks to the generosity of the Proudlocks. Big buffet, big hair, big booze bill, even though many of my suppliers were generous with the donations. It went on late and there was lots of dancing.

Then it was heads down for the Christmas rush at both restaurants before we left for Melbourne on 22 December for my first Aussie Christmas and my first chance to meet Mish's whole family. Bobby, her eldest brother, was a well-rounded Australian who enjoyed a drink or two, not the surfer type I had imagined, but a property man. He made me very welcome. It was the younger brother, Tommy, who was the good-looking beach babe, blond and lean – and the most opposed to the marriage of their sister to a fat boy from the UK nine years her senior. Mish's younger sister, Eppie, was our biggest supporter. She was herself hitched to a much older man who lived in New Zealand.

Our second wedding ceremony, the blessing, went smoothly. Once Mish's parents got over the discomfort of the shotgun wedding, they relaxed. Hugh was a great laugh, a knowledgeable man with lots of sound advice to offer; a doctor at the top of his profession. Mitzi had a wicked smile and a lovely cheekiness, and she was partial to a drink and a smoke. Our honeymoon, a wedding present from Mish's parents, was a few days on the Gold Coast and a couple of islands on the Great Barrier Reef. It was magical. There were great walks on the reef. I loved rock-pooling as a kid, but the Barrier Reef is a little different from Hastings or Brighton. Instead of tiddlers there were mini sharks, multicoloured clams embedded in the reef replaced mussels and limpets and the huge, fuck-off crabs put our little brown, unassuming ones in the shade, but it still brought back memories. We had a fabulous time and, alone at last, we could relax and do just what we wanted.

CHAPTER TWENTY-TWO

OUR IDYLLIC HONEYMOON AT THE START OF 1984 HERALDED A GREAT year for us. The restaurant was booming, and I was commissioned by Mark Boxer of Weidenfeld and Nicolson to write my first cookbook. Mark, also a celebrated cartoonist, was married to the journalist Anna Ford. His early death in 1988 from a brain tumour was a real tragedy.

I think I'm right in claiming to be the first of a generation of British chefs (as opposed to cooks) to produce a cookbook in the UK. *The Small and Beautiful Cookbook* was on the shelves just at the right time to capitalize on the peaking interest in nouvelle cuisine. Chefs were having fun experimenting, and their customers, too, wanted to try out new combinations, so it caught the wave perfectly. Some of the recipes you wouldn't dream of using nowadays, in fact, a few of them – feuilleté of partridge and mango with a spinach sauce and mango coulis, for example – make me positively retch, but they were right for the moment.

The book sold very well, and the special edition I had printed for the restaurant was a winner with my customers. I also managed to sell a 'translated' version in America, under the rather crass title of *The Elegant Chef's Guide to Hors d'Oeuvres and Appetizers* which, as far as I was concerned, missed the point entirely. But it was a bit of a coup to get a book into the American market at all. This is how I dedicated it: 'To all the young ladies in my past, and to Militza-Jane, my present and future . . .' At the time I had no thought that maybe our marriage wouldn't last.

There was certainly no indication of that when, at the beginning of May, Blake arrived. We had decided to go private for the birth, and on the advice of Lena Proudlock we, or should I say Mish, went to this rather scary guy in Harley Street who clearly thought my wife was too much of a child herself to be having a child of her own. If I hadn't been paying him so much money I'd have called him a patronizing bastard.

When everything started to happen we were down at Shiplake. Mish, like me a keen gardener, had been sitting on the ride-on mower all day, sorting out the lawns, which proved to be an excellent way of hurrying along a child who appears to be a bit reluctant to enter the world. After supper, not surprisingly, she fancied a bath and a drink, but then she wanted another bath, then another drink and so it went on. It was strange behaviour: obviously something was up. We went to bed. I slept, but Mish was up and down like a yo-yo. At about 4 am she woke me up and told me she was having contractions. I reassured her, reminding her that, according to our highly paid gynaecologist, there was no need to do anything until the contractions were coming every five minutes, at which point we were to give him a call. So Mish had another bath and I went back to sleep. I do like my sleep.

She roused me again at 5 am. By now the pain was excruciating, she said. I tried to comfort her, but I felt a little inadequate. So I phoned the doc. I was a bit concerned about waking him up so early but sod it, he was being paid to help. He answered the phone in a voice thick with sleep and told me to get Mish to the Humana Wellington Hospital in St John's Wood. He'd see me there in about twenty minutes. 'No you won't,' I said, 'I'm down in Shiplake. It'll be more like an hour.'

'What!' he bellowed. 'I told Militza not to be far away! What the fuck are you doing down there?'

Ooh-er, I thought. I hadn't heard our highly paid gynae swearing before. 'Calm down,' I said. 'I'll get there as soon as I can. Now, go and make yourself a cup of tea, and stay calm. I don't need you, of all people, to get agitated when you're about to deliver my baby. That's meant to be my job.' And yet I wasn't agitated at all. Excited, yes, but I wasn't a flapping father-to-be.

In times of crisis, my gran was fond of paraphrasing Kipling: 'When all around you are losing their heads, try to keep hold of your own,' she'd say. Remembering her advice, I calmly phoned the police, explained the situation and warned them that I would be breaking every speed limit on my journey. They very kindly offered to have a police car waiting for us at the Hammersmith flyover to escort us to north London. It was all jolly exciting stuff for me, but I'm not sure my wife was as entertained. So we flew up the motorway at speeds in excess of 120 mph, safe in the knowledge that the police were aware of the impending birth. Every five minutes or so there would be screams from the passenger seat. There was very little I could do but keep driving. We men are pretty hopeless when it comes to this sort of thing. After all, pain is something we don't suffer unless we are ill or injured, and the pain of labour is beyond our experience altogether. We'll never really understand.

As I reached the end of the motorway, I saw the blue, flashing light waiting, flashed my own lights and off we went in convoy. I was thoroughly enjoying myself. We reached the hospital in forty minutes, door to door. In we rushed, thanking the police, and first the midwife then the gynaecologist inspected Mish, pronouncing that, despite all the panic, we still had plenty of time. The gynae told the nurse that he was going to play tennis, and instructed her to call him if there were any developments.

At the appropriate time he was summoned from the tennis court and Mish was wheeled into theatre. Being a private hospital, it seemed they had to use every gadget available to science to justify all those steep bills, so Mish was strapped into some stirrups in a very unladylike way. Women always think that we'll look at them in a different light sexually once we've seen them give birth, but as far as I'm concerned nothing could be further from the truth. It's the most magical experience, and I would thoroughly recommend it to all prospective fathers.

Mish was having a bit of a hard time so out came the scissors and a huge pair of forceps that looked like an instrument of torture. That wasn't so nice. Our poor baby. I thought its head was going to come off. But finally, he was out – our first son. All his bits and pieces seemed to be present and correct as far as I could tell. The gynaecologist passed the baby to me while he was still attached to his mother, which I only discovered when I tried to walk off.

I was a little worried when he suddenly exclaimed, 'Oh my God!'

'What's wrong?' I asked, concerned that the doctor had noticed something abnormal.

'I've got blood on my new tennis shoes! Nurse, clean them, would you? Quickly!'

And that was that. He was off back to his game of tennis. Nice

work if you can get it, I thought later as I perused his bill for
£2,000, a lot of money in 1984. It was worth it, of course – anything is worth it if it maximizes the chances of having a healthy
baby – and the private rooms with bathrooms, reasonable food and
unrestricted visits were a nice touch, but to be honest the National
Health Service did just as good a job with my last two babies. They
provided nothing more than a big, safe pair of hands – no forceps,
no snips, just experience – and they were brilliant.

Mish and I were over the moon with our little boy. We both felt
a great bond with him from the start. We named him Blake Antony
Cardew. Why Blake? We both hated names that ended up being
shortened, and maybe there was a gentle nudge from the character
Blake Carrington in *Dynasty* (I know, very sad, but there you go).
Trying to choose a name that wouldn't be corrupted turned out
to be a waste of effort, because if it couldn't be abbreviated it could
be lengthened, and poor baby Blake soon became known as Blakey.
The Antony was my ego, of course, and the Cardew a Duncan
family tradition. Apparently there has been a Cardew in every
generation since the days of Cornelius, the dodgy mayor of Truro
in the eighteenth century.

With Blake I was a fairly modern dad. Given the choice I probably wouldn't want to change too many nappies, but then I'm sure
the same could be said of most mums. I often did the 2 am feed,
which allowed Mish to sleep through from 10 pm to 6 am. My
routine was to idle at Stringfellow's after I closed the restaurant
until it was time to go home and feed the baby. By now I had
become quite good friends with Peter Stringfellow and his right-
hand man, Roger Howe.

Roger had been a regular customer at Ménage à Trois with his
girlfriend, Suzie, during a period that had seen several changes in
front-of-house management. My two original manageresses, Hazel,
who had been at my college, and Dorothy, the magical midget from
Scotland who'd become a great friend, had moved on by this stage.
Hazel had left about the same time as Annie; Dorothy had stuck it
out for a bit longer before taking a job, through one of our
customers, in the new business arena of cable television. I had
promoted two waitresses, Ursula and Lysette, to take their place.
Ursula, who had been with us almost from the start, was a tall
gangly Hooray Henrietta, often described as 'a long, tall streak of
piss'. She was particularly fond of Annie, and was therefore almost
a spy in the camp, but she knew the restaurant inside out and there

was something about her that was endearing. Don't ask me what, as she could be the most annoying person on the planet, and she upset most of the staff, including my head chef, David Wilby, who couldn't abide her. Perhaps his views were influenced by the fact that he was dating my other new manageress, Lysette, a cool, laid-back girl who was efficient and practical, but who couldn't really fathom me.

My new management team saw us through a great period, a new era in which I struck out on my own, without Annie and Don, making my own decisions, and one in which the restaurant finally prospered financially. More success was to follow when I was approached by Camellia Punjabi of the Taj Hotel group to set up a Ménage à Trois in the Taj Hotel in Bombay. It sounds an odd place, I know, for my first expansion, but I was so flattered I just jumped at the chance. With my family connections, I felt a strong affinity with India, and somehow it seemed like my destiny to be running a restaurant there. By an extremely weird coincidence, it was also a restaurant I'd visited many years before, when I was backpacking round India as a student. They'd refused me entry because I was wearing shorts. Ever resourceful, I'd gone and changed into my pyjamas and been allowed to eat. It was to become hugely popular, especially with the Bollywood set. A little piece of London in the heart of Bombay. The Taj group were a lovely company to work for, perfectionists at what they did in India, if a little naive when it came to bringing a London operation to the subcontinent. Many of the products and wines I had in London were impossible to purchase there and difficult to import, because of the complicated Indian import laws and taxes. There were also strict rules about paying foreigners. So you won't be surprised to hear that profit was not the principal manifestation of its success. But the holidays were fab.

Camellia Punjabi was a fabulous hostess. I fell in love with India again, and half fell in love with my tiny Indian head chef, Maria. I was preoccupied by the squalor and poverty; amazed by the wealth and riches. Just absorbing it all was like rubberneck-ing at the scene of an accident. And Bombay itself, a city of 17 million people, where every nook and cranny holds a story. The constant noise of horns blaring, the brightly painted lorries, the ubiquitous Ambassador or Fiat cars, all modelled on Morris designs of the 1950s. A city that never sleeps. A city for ever fascinating.

A world away in London, life was pretty good. Blake was growing fast, and I would pop home from the restaurant most afternoons to have tea with him and Mish. Afterwards we'd take him for a walk on Wandsworth Common. We had taken in a tenant: Roger Howe's girlfriend, Suzie, who went on to work for me as a manageress at Ménage. She also became one of Mish's best friends and godmother to Blake. It was a cosy little life, but one without any particular excitement. I was getting itchy feet.

One day I was invited to award some prizes at a cookery school in Sussex. The outstanding pupil of the year was a young lady of Japanese-American extraction called Ronda Kamihira and she was absolutely gorgeous. It was the eyes. Or perhaps the freckles. No, the shy, delicious smile. Maybe the soft American accent. Oh, I don't know, but whatever it was, I was bowled over. Stop it, I told myself, you're a happily married man. As I politely nibbled on my cucumber sandwiches and made small talk with the principal of the college, Ronda indicated from the far side of the marquee that she wanted to talk to me. I made my excuses to the principal and wandered over.

My guts were churning and I'm sure I was blushing. I was behaving like a pathetic schoolboy. She was blushing as well: there was just a slight rosy tint beneath her tanned, olive complexion. Our conversation was brief and to the point. She wanted a job. 'I'll see what I can do,' I said. She gave me her phone number, and explained that her boyfriend was a guy called Nick who also lived on Wandsworth Common and whom I apparently knew. And that was that. I would have given her any job she'd wanted if my dick had been running my company, but my brain erred on the side of caution. I reminded myself I couldn't buy everything I saw in the shop window, and that one woman at a time was enough, especially when that woman was your wife and the mother of your child. But it didn't stop me having fantasies.

A couple of months later, Ronda's boyfriend invited Mish and me to a cocktail party at his house. Ronda was there, preparing the canapés with a couple of friends, twins called the Lumsdens, who went on to become very respected caterers themselves. Ronda looked even more stunning out of her whites – I don't think chefs' clothes were ever designed with women in mind.

Two big decisions were made that evening. I agreed to set up a catering company with Ronda – her canapés were brilliant – and I bought us a new house, in Jessica Road, again near Wandsworth

Common. Ronda was excited, and Nick was pleased for her; he was pleased on his own account, too, because it was he who sold me the house. Nick and his partner, Jonathan, were property dealers, a bit flash, one with the Porsche, the other with the Ferrari. Jonathan was outgoing, full of himself, good-looking, a girl's guy. Nick was quieter, less confident, not such a looker, Ronda's guy.

I'll return to the catering operation shortly, but as for the house, it was great: an original Victorian three-storey terrace. It was a complete wreck, but all its character was intact, and I relished the challenge of redesigning it myself. A bad move, as it turned out, not because I wasn't up to renovating it or anything like that, but because it took over a year to rebuild. For that year, Mish, Blake and I practically lived out of suitcases, begging, borrowing or stealing rooms from friends and even customers, and, looking back, it's clear that this was when the storyline of our marriage began to fall apart. We lived in a customer's flat in Eaton Square (very nice, but no soul), a flat near Putney Common that had belonged to Rex Leyland's recently deceased mother (fine, but the neighbours complained about the baby's washing hanging out on the veranda), one of the cold, unheated cottages at Shiplake, which my grandmother finally agreed to rent me (her objection, and I quote, had been: 'I think you're a little young to be looking after a house' – I was thirty-four), and lastly, the one that nearly destroyed our marriage there and then, a house on Wandsworth Common which we shared with another couple.

They seemed nice enough. She – let's call her Sharon – was a good friend of Mish's, outrageous and brassy. He, Adam, was a mild-mannered nice guy in property or finance, I can't remember which. I don't think he knew what he had married. Sure, Sharon was fun, but she was also highly dangerous. They were due to move to Australia and Adam, a classic Hooray, went out to Oz to look for a house for them there. Mish was down at Shiplake for the same two weeks with Blake and an au pair. Which left me alone with Sharon, the vamp.

She was fun to flirt with, but that was it, honestly. I would come back from the restaurant knackered and go straight to bed; Sharon would wander in at about 4 am, having been out on the town. A couple of nights before Adam was due back from Australia, some guy must have given her a right good seeing-to, because the next morning her neck was black and blue. 'Jesus,' I said to her. 'What are you going to tell Adam?'

'I'm going to tell him it was you,' she said laughing. I thought she was joking, but that's exactly what she did. Not only that, but then Adam called my wife to ask her out to dinner, where he announced: 'Your husband is having an affair with my wife.'

You try convincing your wife something like that isn't true. As things began to unravel, Mish accused me – among other things – of being fat, which I was. I remembered Nick telling me that he and Ronda were regulars at the Latchmere Leisure Centre, so I gave him a call. He told me that a gang of them did an aerobics class there and invited me to join them. Aerobics was the big thing then, but I couldn't think of anything worse, especially as getting feet, arms and brain in one harmonious motion has always been beyond me. Reassuringly, a female friend once told me that you can't be good in bed and a good dancer. The logic of that escapes me, but it sounds good! But clearly it was what I needed. And besides, underneath my embarrassment there was a frisson of excitement at the thought that Ronda would be there. So I joined.

The gang included Nick and Ronda, the swimmer Duncan Goodhew, an American preppie called Mike and occasionally his wife, who appeared to be a good friend of Ronda's. Our aerobics instructor was a power-packed woman called Joanna. There's a definite pecking order to an aerobics class. At the Latchmere, the beginners started at the back, I guess to save their blushes. Ronda was in the front row, along with Nick. Being a stubborn Taurean, I was determined to work my way up there. It took me about three months, but I did it.

At first I was about three moves behind everyone else. The *Riverdance* lot had it easy: they only had to move their legs, you try doing aerobics to the frenetic beat of 'It's Raining Men'.

After the class, having sweated buckets, it was into the shower, and then our gang would gather for a drink at the club bar. Ronda was looking more gorgeous by the week. I'm not sure it was all beauty in the classic sense: she was simply sexy. Really sexy. It didn't matter what she was wearing – shorts, baggy socks, trainers and a sports bra during the class, or ripped jeans and a skimpy singlet in the bar – she just oozed sex. She had the most marvellous face: those slightly oriental eyes from her father, a well-known Japanese artist; short, jet-black spiky hair; the tiniest arms covered with peachy, soft, tanned skin; the most elegant, slimmest waist; toned, coffee-coloured, hairless legs.

What is sexy? It's certainly not just about beauty, but since everyone's taste is so different, it's almost impossible to define. Girlfriends and wives have told me I'm sexy, something that is not immediately apparent to me when I look in the mirror. When I've asked them what they find sexy about me, the best answer I've had is that it's something to do with acting as if I'm attractive even if outwardly it would be hard to describe me as such; that if you think yourself attractive, that in itself attracts. I'm not sure this was a great compliment, but still.

Ronda knew who she was, she had a strong awareness of herself and a subtle confidence that was without conceit. She was self-assured, and that's sexy. Even before she knew me very well, she looked me straight in the eye with sensuality. She was fleetingly tactile without letting her touch linger too long. And, of course, she was very physically attractive as well. Taking care of her body made her feel good about herself, but she worked at it, often spending six nights a week in the gym. It wasn't long before I was doing the same. Though whether it was fitness that I was obsessed with or Ronda was a debatable point.

At first Mish was pleased that I was getting fit, but her pleasure soon turned to despair as she realized there was more to my visits to the gym than met the eye. I tried to encourage her to join us and get herself fit too, but she was always tired and fed up. Now I can see that it was a classic case of postnatal depression, but neither of us recognized the symptoms then and I was selfishly distracted by the gym or the restaurant.

I used Ménage à Trois as my excuse for not going home, but in fact more often than not I would be dining *ménage à trois* with Nick and Ronda. We made a strange threesome. On the surface Ronda seemed to be perfectly happy with Nick and I was the gooseberry. Yet they didn't seem to mind me being there, and I certainly didn't. Anything to be close to her. My lust for Ronda became an infatuation, almost a sickness, and so did the punishing routine I put myself through at the gym: five or six nights a week and then an hour and a half of circuit training on Sunday mornings. Either my feelings for Ronda weren't obvious, or if they were, Nick was too gutless to confront me. In fact, in some ways he encouraged our friendship. Desperate to make Ronda happy, he was very keen for her to work with me. In a funny and rather guilty way, I grew to like Nick at the same time as I was insanely jealous of him.

By now we were producing dinners as outside caterers from the great flat where Nick and Ronda lived, overlooking the river on Battersea Bridge. It was a little impractical but anything that got me close to Ronda was all right by me. Not only was she a gorgeous girl, but she had impeccable taste. Her style was evident both in the way she dressed and in the interior of her flat. It wasn't long before there was an opportunity for me to be alone with Ronda. When I was asked by an oil magnate to cook for a clients' dinner just outside Aberdeen, I invited her to help me. She agreed. I was over the moon: time alone with the girl of my dreams. I was surprised that Nick allowed her to go on her own, because up until that point they had seemed to be joined at the hip. Ronda and I flew up early on the morning of the dinner, and during the day I acted like a true professional, working closely with her in preparing a meal for twenty people. As the evening drew to a close, we had a drink with the guests then made our excuses and fled. We were staying at a beautiful old country-house hotel called Maryculter House, beautiful when buzzing, that is; spooky when empty. When we returned at about 1 am there was no one to be seen, just a roaring log fire, flickering candles and a bottle of champagne set out on a table with two glasses. My name was on the bottle.

It seemed a pity to waste the champagne, so I suggested we drank it. Ronda agreed. I had done my homework, and I knew it was her favourite tipple. The fire cast uneasy shadows on the ceiling of this great hall which played on Ronda's fears, and to tell you the truth, it played on mine, too. She snuggled up to me on the well-worn leather sofa. Suddenly, and for no apparent reason, the candles guttered violently, as if someone had opened a door. No one had. Ronda snuggled closer. I was nervous, but it had less to do with ghosts than with our situation. When the champagne was finished, it was 3 am. We made our way up to our adjoining rooms. She planted a filmy, fleeting kiss on my lips, wished me a goodnight and was gone.

I was in bed, fantasizing about what might have been, when there was a knock on the door. 'Who is it?'

'It's me, Ronda,' came the whispered reply.

'Hold on a minute.'

I wrapped a towel round my waist and, sucking in my stomach, opened the door. There she was, a vision of loveliness dressed only in an oversized T-shirt.

'I'm scared,' she said in a small voice. 'Can I share your bed?'

She jumped into bed and I slipped in beside her, still wearing my towel. She wriggled close. She smelled delicious and her skin felt like velvet. Oh God, what now? I thought. I hardly dared breathe. I let her make the moves. She kissed my neck and I turned to meet her lips. My head was dizzy, I was in heaven. Simultaneously we searched, pressed, explored; our bodies seemed in perfect harmony. Never had I experienced such a perfect little body with such soft skin.

This was not raw sex. In fact, if you apply the Clinton rule, it wasn't sex at all. This was love. This was tenderness. I was afraid. I didn't want to push Ronda too far, but I wanted more. There was no guilt, no thoughts of Mish, I was totally committed to pleasing Ronda. But she came to her senses, and my dream exploded. 'We shouldn't be doing this,' she said, though it was clear that she didn't entirely mean it. Did that mean yes or no? I never knew. To be on the safe side I took her at face value. 'Shame,' I said.

'I know. I want to, but I have to think of Nick. We're getting married.'

Jesus. This was news to me. 'Can I do the catering?' It was the only thing I could think of to say.

Ronda laughed. 'You're unreal,' she said.

We cuddled for a long while. The moment was gone. But what a moment. If I had never seen her again it would have been worth it: a fleeting visit to heaven.

But of course I did see her again, and there was to be more – a lot more. We became lovers, and in the purest sense of the word. We men sometimes want sex with love, and sometimes just-give-it-to-me-darling, physical sex. With Ronda I wanted to make love, an emotional act that demands the involvement of more than one person; that requires warmth, passion, caring, generosity, unselfishness; that requires the use of all of your senses. One-dimensional, physical sex makes you feel good temporarily; loving is total fulfilment. And for the first time in my life, I felt real, deep love coming on.

But I am getting ahead of myself. The ice that surrounded Ronda and kept her feelings dormant had a crack in it. It would not be long before it shattered completely.

CHAPTER TWENTY-THREE

OVERTAKEN BY MY OBSESSION WITH RONDA AND MY OBSESSIVE attendance at the gym, I was rather neglecting Ménage à Trois, making only fleeting visits there, usually late at night. But I knew it was in safe hands. David Wilby was in control of the kitchen and by this time a new front-of-house team had settled to the job: an American Adonis named Jim Dunne and his second-in-command, Mish's close friend Suzie.

To develop the catering company I had set up with Ronda, I leased an industrial premises from Wandsworth Council and set about converting it into a great kitchen. This, I decided, would be Ronda's baby, a base where she could organize her outside catering and products for delis more efficiently than was possible at her flat.

Since the Sharon-and-Adam débâcle, Mish had been living at Shiplake. So I spent many nights staying over at Ronda and Nick's, lying awake frustrated in the bedroom next door to theirs. The escapade in Scotland had brought Ronda and me much closer, and there was great warmth between us. We'd sneak a lingering kiss here and there, and the inevitable could only be just around the corner. It happened at the food factory, after an aerobics class which, for once, Nick hadn't been able to make. I decided to take her over there to show her the new walk-in fridge. I know, it doesn't sound very romantic, but it makes a change from etchings. Just being alone with her was enough for me, but seeing the new fridge was obviously too much for her, and she lost control.

We weren't quite ripping off each other's clothes the way they do in the movies, but we were naked in pretty quick time, and there she was, in all her glory: a magnificent body, every inch honed to perfection. All that time we'd spent in the gym suddenly made sense. This was physical sex, not quite raw, but definitely blue or rare, and it was perfect: exciting, naughty, passionate, incandescent. Like tight-fitting gloves, we seemed made for each other. With the kitchen setting, the cold stainless steel against warm, showered bodies, it was like a scene from *The Postman Always Rings Twice*.

From then on we took every opportunity we had. Nick had no concerns about our relationship, and why should he have had? His male ego wouldn't have seen what Ronda would want with a short little fella ten years her senior when she already had him, tall, far better-looking and with apparently unlimited amounts of dosh. Well, I've never been able to work out the female psyche, either. I have no idea why a woman chooses one man over another. But I'm sure they are less shallow than the male of the species, and go for substance rather than style. Still, Ronda seemed determined to go ahead and marry Nick. I was beside myself.

And what of Mish? Relations between us were more and more strained. She'd hang out with her friends; I'd hang out with mine. There were occasional flashes of the old togetherness. After a party at Michael Proudlock's one night, both a little worse for wear, Mish and I did have a rare sexual encounter – in my car – and that brief liaison produced our second son, Sam. So both my children were conceived on modes of transport, Blake on a yacht and Sam in a car. I would never say that Sam was a mistake, because he has turned out to be a fantastic boy, and I love him to bits. But it wasn't the right way to conceive. And it was as if that little foetus knew it, because throughout Mish's pregnancy there were nothing but problems, and several times we feared we would lose him.

The most dramatic crisis came about seven months into the pregnancy. Ronda and I had been catering a party at London Zoo, and I was staying at her flat. At about 1 am I received a panicky phone call from Mish down in Shiplake to say she was bleeding heavily. I jumped into the car and almost flew the forty miles to be with her. There was no stopping at red lights, no observing speed limits, but I didn't care if I was caught – in fact I would have welcomed it, because I needed a police escort. But there were no police to be seen. In under thirty minutes I was screeching up out-side the cottage, arriving, in fact, at the same time as the ambulance, which had only come from Reading, seven miles away.

The scene that greeted me made me retch. The kitchen floor was covered in blood, the bed looked like a scene from *The Godfather* and Mish's nightclothes were just a scarlet blur.

Not surprisingly, I was convinced we had lost the baby. There was a tirade of verbal abuse from my wife and her mate Jane, who had been staying with her, and sheepishly I followed the ambulance to the Royal Berkshire Hospital. Against all the odds, Sam was saved, but Mish had to take it easy for the remainder of the pregnancy.

Sam was born on 8 February 1986 and, despite all the problems, he was a healthy baby. The cause of the terrifying bleeding had been the placenta, which was badly damaged. It would appear that Sam had wanted more sustenance than was on offer and had ripped at the umbilical cord. He continued to be a great eater, a boy who enjoyed both eating and cooking.

I wanted to be a good father to Sam, but not surprisingly Mish became incredibly possessive of him. It was as if, after all the perils of the pregnancy, she had decided that Sam was her little miracle, and hers alone. By the time Sam was born, Ronda, despite my pleadings, had married Nick. It was a strange wedding, in which, at Ronda's request, I gave her away, even though her famous father was present.

To take my mind off Ronda I threw myself back into Ménage à Trois. With Bombay Ménage going like a bomb, Taj Hotels invited me to open another restaurant, in their hotel in New York, the Lexington. New York! I was thrilled. The only problem was that the Hotel Lexington had seen better days and its grandeur was of the faded variety. It was a midtown hotel, on 48th and Lexington, which I thought would be a good site as it was within walking distance of many of the city's great hotels. However, I soon realized that this was no advantage because in New York nobody walked anywhere. In the days before Mayor Giuliano cleaned up the city it was too dangerous. Everybody jumped into cabs.

Setting up a restaurant there was a tough business. There is limited scope for shopping around for the best deals: cartels are the name of the game. There's no bargaining for the booze, because the same wine is on offer at exactly the same price no matter where you buy it. You couldn't choose your dairy, because each one had its own patch, and the same went for refuse-collection and laundry. The laundry was something else. On the day we were due to open, the laundry hadn't shown. I called the company every hour from 9 am until 4 pm, and each time the response was the same: 'It'll be there.' Finally, I blew my top, swearing and screaming like a good 'un, and threatening to change laundries. This time the response was a throaty laugh. An hour later, a limousine pulled up outside the Lexington, and five burly guys, all in shades and well-cut suits, swept into the kitchens carrying between them four large bags of laundry. 'Where's the limey who's been giving us a hard time?' one of them yelled. My office was pointed out to him. All five of them stormed in. 'Here's your fucking laundry. Don't you ever give us a hard time again, or someone will find you in one of these laundry bags. You understand?' Blimey, I thought to myself. They don't seem too impressed by an Englishman in New York.

Not only did the Mafia seem to control most of the services, but they also had massive power within the unions. Their rules were strict and the hotel management were frightened of them, which made it extremely expensive to run a kitchen. Had I bitten off more than I could chew? No, I told myself. New York would just take a little getting used to.

The product was right, but the location was wrong and the design was wrong, and the Taj group were unwilling to spend the kind of money that would enable us to make it look anything more than a boring hotel restaurant. I had a good kitchen team, headed by my fiery Irishman from London, Frank Rourke, ably backed up by another of my London boys, a talented youngster called Patrick Reilly. Frank was still a difficult sod, and God knows what the laid-back New Yorkers on the staff thought of him, but he was a hard worker and he was turning into an excellent chef. David Wilby came over for the opening, and for a few months Ménage New York fired on all cylinders, attracting various celebs including Mayor Koch who, like his successor, Mayor Giuliani, was a bit of a local institution.

For the most part we received excellent reviews, including one in the *New York Times* by Bryan Millar, the scourge of the restaurant world. He was like the Pied Piper – when he played, New York followed – and he could make or break a new restaurant. I appeared on many morning television shows and was given the credit by many for starting the 'grazing' trend in America. I even worked with the legendary Craig Claiborne and America's answer to Delia Smith, Martha Stewart. But success is never guaranteed in New York. Its public is far more fickle than the UK's. A new restaurant opens and off they go, like rats up a drainpipe. Ménage New York soon quietened down, and I lost interest. New Yorkers like style, and for a restaurant to survive for any length of time, it also needs a permanent figurehead. We had neither, and the clients moved on.

But not before I had had two years of fun there. It's a vibrant city, and there are some brilliant restaurants in New York. And if they're good, with the right personality in charge, they last. Here's a whistlestop tour of my favourites. For steaks and classic American service, Peter Luger's, Sparks, Smith and Wollensky. For Japanese with style, Nobu, Koruma Zushi, Sushi Yasuda. For over-the-top American, Union Square Café, Gramercy Tavern, Gotham Bar and Grill, Aureole. For power dining, Le Cirque, Four Seasons, Jean-Georges, 21 Club. For French away from home, Daniel, Montrachet, Chanterelle, La Grenouille, Le Bernadin (fish). Stuck for something to eat at 3 am? Florent.

The Ménage à Trois success story was escalating, and in the mid-1980s we opened in Washington, Melbourne and Stockholm. In financial terms, however, the success was more modest. I was naive and I didn't make the kind of money I should have made from these ventures. I hate talking money, as I'm sure do many people whose work is their passion. What I needed was a manager, but it would be a few years yet before I got one.

By this time, Mish, Blake, Sam and I had moved into our newly renovated house in Jessica Road. It was a terrific pad: four bedrooms, three bathrooms, a large through sitting room and the kitchen, at that time, of my dreams – it had a walk-in fridge and a walk-in larder. It was just a shame that it was too late for us to enjoy it as a family.

Things were also rocky between Nick and Ronda. She would often ring and ask me to pick her up, and I would find her crying. We were spending more and more time together, and more and more openly. Neither of our partners could do anything to stop it. I think it's almost impossible to describe real love. It turns your world upside down. The emotions are teased and tested, and nothing can get in the way – logic, reason, understanding of others' feelings all go out of the window. It can be a suicidal path. My relationship with Mish didn't stand a chance now. Not only had the year living out of suitcases created severe difficulties, but those difficulties had put temptation in my path and I'd been too weak to resist it. And once love had taken a hold, I didn't want to resist it.

To others Mish was an angel who could do no wrong, I was always going to be the villain. I have often wondered since whether the situation could ever have been retrieved, if only for the sake of the boys. Could Nick have tried harder to keep Ronda? What if Mish and I hadn't been living such a chaotic domestic life for all that time? What if Mish had been spared such bad postnatal depression? There will always be what-ifs, but in truth I can only blame myself. When it came down to brass tacks, I didn't want Mish and I was prepared to let her go. My second marriage was lurching to a grinding halt. As for Ronda and me, once the honeymoon period of her marriage was over she was back with me whenever she could get away. Nothing mattered apart from our time together. I barely saw my friends, and I'm sure I lost several.

Mish and I tried counselling. It didn't work, not least because I mistakenly turned up three hours late for one of our appointments. That proved to be the straw that broke the camel's back. Mish announced that she was returning to Australia with the kids. There was no screaming, no histrionics, just bland resignation for both of us. I felt very confused. I knew I wanted Ronda, but this was so final. My two kids, whom I loved to bits, were going to be 13,000 miles away. They left after a party to celebrate Sam's first birthday. I drove them to the airport. There were tears from all of us except Sam, who was too young to understand. I cried all the way back to my empty home.

By now Ronda's short-lived marriage was also over, and she had left Nick. I had arranged a flat for her in Battersea, a rented property that suited her. We had agreed that she shouldn't move in with me immediately, but I devoted the next few months to her to the point where I became ridiculously possessive. That is an incredibly destructive disease. I smothered Ronda, gave her no room to breathe, and she quite understandably began to reject me. Men can be such idiots. Because of my behaviour, a beautiful relationship that was meant to be started to crumble.

In a very immature way, I was trying to buy her. I bought a Morgan sports car for her to drive, gratefully received but never sought. I plied her with champagne and expensive dinners at the best restaurants. I lavished designer clothes on her. Outsiders thought she was a money-grabber, but at no time did she ever ask me for any of this. It was all down to my crass stupidity. I wanted her so much that I became blind to her fear of making another commitment so soon after the last one. I should have been much more patient, but instead I was reverting to the insecurity of my youth, a curse that would plague me anew for a good couple of years.

Over in Australia, things weren't much rosier for Mish. She and the kids were living in fairly squalid rented accommodation. I had made a settlement offer via Simon Bowen, which she had verbally accepted, but her father wasn't having any of it. As far as he was concerned, I was rolling in it, and I could afford much more. He hired one of Melbourne's top lawyers, who in turn hired one of the most expensive lawyers in London, Farrers, who, incidentally, handled Prince Charles's divorce. They may have had an excellent reputation, but they seemed to have got the wrong end of the stick. They thought that I was made of money, and despite affidavits from me setting out my finances, they were like a dog with a bone. They just wouldn't let go. I even offered Mish the house in Jessica Road, which would have netted her £180,000 at this early stage of the proceedings, but the offer was rejected. There had to be more, they thought, but of course there wasn't. Most of my money was tied up in Ménage à Trois. My flash cars – a Porsche and a Mercedes – were company cars, as was the Morgan that Ronda drove. There was next to nothing in my bank account.

We had been married only four years, and Mish had brought nothing to the party apart from her lovely innocence. Once the financial flak of the divorce had died down, cordial relations were restored with Mish. For about seven years I made an annual trip to Australia to see the boys, but those visits apart, from a distance of 13,000 miles it was always going to be hard for me to be a great dad.

At the divorce hearing in London, Mish was offered half of what she would have received if her lawyers had accepted the house, and most of that was eaten up by their fees. Even so, when I finally finish paying her, it will have cost me the best part of £1 million of pre-tax income, including legal fees. I struggled to meet her maintenance payments, but I never let her down. I was bitter about the settlement to start with, but you make your bed and you must lie in it.

Talking of bed, Ronda did eventually move into my house, albeit for a very short period. Once we were living together, she caught the bug and became possessive herself. She was jealous of Ménage. She wanted me at home all the time, something I couldn't accommodate, and her demands put an enormous strain on what could have been a fantastic relationship. Now that we were officially a couple, she had this idea in her head that I might fall for someone else and do the same to her as I had to Mish. Nothing I could say or do would convince her that I was desperately in love with her.

I wanted Ronda to be part of Ménage, but she wasn't cut out to be my front lady. She was her own woman, very comfortable in her own company or in mine, but not particularly fond of my friends. It was flattering that she wanted me to herself, but it wasn't a way of living that we could have sustained. You can't be a restaurateur and not like people, and I love people, even if it often takes me a long time to get to know them. But love, as they say, is blind.

In the end she announced that she was going back to Philadelphia. She argued that I was more in love with the restaurant than I was with her; in fact, 'You'll never sell Ménage à Trois', were almost her parting words to me. When she left I was gutted, so gutted that I spent more and more time at Ménage in New York so that I could take Amtrak up to Philly to see her in the hope that she would reconsider. The relationship fizzed and spluttered. She visited me in New York a few times, but she wouldn't change her mind. She refused to come back to England.

For the one and only time in my life – as far as affairs of the heart are concerned, at any rate – I lost the plot. After we said our final goodbyes in Philadelphia, I cried all the way back to New York. I was due to fly home to London that night. At Kennedy Airport everything suddenly became too much for me and I decided I wanted to end it all. Somehow I managed to get through a security door into the airside area. I had made up my mind that I would throw myself in front of an incoming plane, but I hadn't got very far before suddenly, out of the darkness, I was surrounded by headlights and red flashing lights and the booming command to lie flat on the ground with my hands on my head. I was cuffed and escorted back to the terminal. It would have been exciting stuff if I hadn't been so distraught. But the American police softened their approach when they realized that I had cried enough salt water to cook a lobster. They listened to me, decided that I was no threat and turned me over to a doctor, who sedated me and arranged accommodation for me near the airport. And there was me believing I was a rational kind of guy. I resolved from that day never to let anyone break my heart like that again.

CHAPTER TWENTY-FOUR

RONDA'S PREDICTION THAT I WOULD NEVER SELL MÉNAGE COULDN'T have been more wrong. I did so only about six months later. It was extremely fortunate that I did, because a year later the UK followed America into recession. It was 1988, and at the time I hadn't been planning on selling, but a couple of guys made me an offer I couldn't refuse. Bearing in mind the fact that my restaurant was a small, poky basement in a buzzy street not really known for proper restaurants, apart from San Lorenzo; that Ménage was getting a little dilapidated and the kitchen really needed a complete overhaul; that David Wilby had left me to set up 51:51, a Cajun restaurant, with Robert Earl; and that I was going through that expensive divorce, I couldn't really afford to turn down a sum in excess of £650,000, including stock. Simon Bowen handled the sale. There were numerous headaches to be overcome as Annie and Donald Foster-Firth tried to squeeze more money out of me, but in the end the deal was done.

In a way I was sad to let it go, of course, but the time was right. The public was becoming fed up with nouvelle cuisine, the Americans weren't coming over because of the recession and because of the IRA bombing campaign, and to tell the truth, my heart was no longer in it. But it was Ménage that had put me on the culinary map, and its reputation lives on. Recently A.A. Gill honoured it in his top three restaurants that changed the face of London dining and Jonathan Meades mentioned it in dispatches when he resigned as the restaurant critic of *The Times*.

In my last eighteen months at Ménage I also gained the

recognition of my peers when I won the prestigious Mouton Rothschild competition, judged by Michel Roux, and early in 1987 I entered the newly set up Meilleur Ouvrier de Grande Bretagne. This competition included categories for over a hundred manual skills, and the cookery award was contested by the country's top chefs, so it was a kind of chefs' Oscar. The French version had been running for generations, backed by the state. The British organizers had to find private sponsorship, which was an eloquent comment on the importance of manual skills to our government.

I entered the competition as a thank you to Michel Roux and Michel Bourdin of the Connaught Hotel for having supported my entry into the Académie Culinaire. In the initial stages I had to produce a three-course meal in recipe form based on classic French dishes, something I hadn't been trained for. My complete lack of belief in my own ability to compete with some of the best chefs in the country can be gauged by the fact that I forgot to put my name on the entry form. Luckily, Sara-Jayne of the Académie Culinaire recognized my handwriting. I got through the first round of the competition, along with fifteen other hopefuls; the next round involved actually cooking.

I felt I had no chance against the likes of Le Gavroche, the Waterside, the Connaught Hotel and the Savoy, but of course I was going to give it my best shot. Among the dishes we had to produce was salmis of pheasant with fresh noodles, which I had never cooked before. Everything went marvellously with the pheasant but when it came to the noodles I was lost. Fresh pasta had yet to become fashionable, so noodles, to me, were something that came out of a packet. I had a sneaky look at what the other chefs were doing. Eggs and flour seemed to be the order of the day. But then my creative juices started to flow. How about lots of black pepper and some finely chopped parsley in the pasta mix? Let's go for broke. The pasta dough seemed to work, but rolling it through the pasta machine was a farce. There was dough everywhere. I knew I had to get it down to the thinnest setting on the rollers and then cut it into noodles, but what I had failed to realize was that without a dusting of flour or semolina, it would stick like buggery. Eventually, after dumping about half the pasta, I produced enough for the dish, and amazingly, I won through to the final, along with the then unknown Gary Rhodes. The other seven finalists, who included Michel Perraud of the Waterside, Michael Aldridge of the Connaught Hotel and Stephen Docherty of Le Gavroche, were all well heeled and highly respected, top boys. Both Gary and I were thrilled.

In the final, each of the nine contestants would be required to cook a three-course meal. We were notified of two of the courses ten days in advance; for the other one, the starter, we would be presented with a surprise basket of ingredients on the day and left to decide for ourselves what to make from them.

My heart sank when I learned what the two pre-set dishes were. The main course was the ridiculous classic timbale of sole Carême, which consisted of a deep mould lined with Dover sole fillets, trimmed and slightly flattened. The fillets were lined with a whiting mousse, then filled with cooked shellfish, crayfish, oysters, scallops and mussels, set in a crayfish or nantua sauce. I say ridiculous because it would never be offered on a restaurant menu today – the time and money involved simply couldn't be justified. With the price of the ingredients, plus all the labour, it would cost over £30 a portion to produce. But the judges wanted to give us a challenge. They certainly did that, especially as the moulds needed to make the dish for eight to ten people were no longer being manufactured, which meant that we were provided instead with silver-plated soup tureens to practise in. The tureens were much deeper than the proper moulds, which created problems we could have done without.

The pudding was a classic eight-portion tart of pears set in an almond sponge – poire Bourdaloue. Fuck, fuck, fuck – pastry work. I panicked. But a quick call to Ronda, who was a whizz at baking, put me straight.

Michel Roux was a real lifesaver, too. He agreed to check out my rehearsals alongside those of his own chef, Michel Perraud, and allowed me to practise my dishes at his restaurant, the Waterside Inn at Bray. Without his valuable assistance I would never have come close to being ready for the big event.

The night before the final you would never have believed I was facing one of the most important days of my professional life. We all stayed at Cliveden, which was convenient for Slough Catering College, now part of Thames Valley University, where the contest was to take place. What a fabulous hotel: beautiful rooms, great service and wonderful history. Gary Rhodes and I intended to make the most of it. We ate, drank, made merry and ended up playing snooker until about 4 am. I was not feeling like a five-hour cook-off the next morning, I can tell you, but there's a funny thing about a hangover: it can overwhelm all other worries. In any case, if I had gone to bed at a sensible hour, I would only have tossed and turned fretting about the next day. As it was, I hadn't a care in the world, apart from my sore head.

And if I needed an extra incentive, it was provided by a glance through the papers that morning. It was already abundantly clear that Gary and I were the underdogs, and we didn't need be written off by Drew Smith in an article in the *Guardian* that basically extolled the virtues of the grand finalists and dismissed Gary and me as having done jolly well to have got as far as we had. To be honest, I didn't think I had a chance either, but that really got my dander up.

The nine of us were to begin cooking starting at fifteen-minute intervals. I was drawn in ninth place. Not a good start. I was worried that the eminent judges would be bored by the food by the time they got round to tasting mine. The panel included several top chefs from France, including the king of French chefs Paul Bocuse, who had been so good to me all those years before, and Roger Vergé, another star. Among those from the UK were Albert Roux, Michel Bourdin and Richard Shepherd. The kitchen-supervising judge was to be my mate Brian Turner.

In spite of the bad draw, someone up there must have been smiling down on me because the surprise ingredients for the starter were just my thing: Mediterranean vegetables – aubergines, courgettes, peppers, onions – and some cheese and eggs. I knew exactly what I wanted to cook: a delicate baked egg set in a ratatouille mousse in a pastry-cutter mould lined with strips of grilled courgette and aubergine and served on a glazed cheese sauce.

The main course was somewhat more of a problem. On both my practice runs, the bleeding great dome of shellfish-stuffed fish had collapsed when I turned it out of its mould, and the whiting mousse had tasted very grainy. In an attempt to save the situation I had devised a make-or-break plan – which unfortunately I had not had a chance to test – for the actual day. I had decided to flatten my Dover sole fillets a bit more to get more coverage from them. This would also leave me with a little surplus sole, which meant I could discard the whiting and use the excess Dover sole and a couple of scallops to make a much smoother mousse that would be far nicer on the palate.

Now I put my idea into action, steaming the unfilled sole and the mousse lining to set the mousse and enable me to check that there was no shrinkage to the fish. So far so good. Then I deviated from the method again by partially freezing this semi-cooked shell. I could see some of the other chefs glancing over, clearly thinking I had gone mad.

Next, instead of lightly poaching the shellfish as suggested, I decided to pan-fry it in butter, salt and pepper – much more flavourful, even if it wasn't true to the absolute letter of the recipe. I deglazed the pan juices with some dry white wine and made a fantastic crayfish sauce. I coated the shellfish with the sauce and packed it tightly into the partially frozen fish mould, covered it with more sole fillets and put it in the oven to gently cook the fish. My theory was that by the time the heat penetrated the frozen fish and mousse, the sole fillets would be cooked and the already hot shellfish filling wouldn't get overdone and rubbery. It was a bit of a gamble, to say the least, but then, as you know, I've always preferred living on the edge. And it worked.

My tart was as perfect as a pastryphobe could make it, but in finishing it I almost wrecked my starter. To cook the poire Bourdaloue thoroughly I had turned the oven temperature right down and had forgotten to turn it up again. This gave me kittens when I tried to bake my eggs in their ratatouille casings. The bloody things just wouldn't cook, and by now I was late with my presentation. Fuck, fuck, fuck. What did I do now? There were penalties for being over five minutes late . . . There was nothing for it but to coat the whole tray of eight baked (or not so baked) eggs with the cheese sauce and grated cheese and slam the lot under the salamander (the grill) for a final burst and then, very carefully, remove the deep pastry-cutter moulds supporting my concoction. Wow, did they wobble, but they held. Not only that, but, according to reports later, the French judges were very impressed that I had managed to produce such perfectly cooked eggs after five hours of intensive work. But hey, you need a bit of luck sometimes.

At the end of the competition I was totally fucked. Exhausted, exhilarated, nervous, elated, deflated, a jelly on legs. What you need then is a good drink, preferably several, and, thanks to Laurent Perrier, who were one of the sponsors, that was no problem. Brian Turner warned me not to get too pissed, but I didn't take much notice of him. Amid the wealth of talent on show that day, I couldn't see I'd be required to play any further part in the proceedings, so as far as I was concerned, it was time to relax and enjoy myself.

That evening there was a magnificent dinner at the Meridian Hotel in Piccadilly. All the great and good of the catering industry were there, and many other faces besides, and there was much speculation about and gambling on the result. I did a lot of ear-wigging but I didn't hear my name on anyone's lips. It was going to be a long night – the awards weren't due to be announced until after the dinner, at nearly midnight, so until then the finalists just had to sweat it out. I fortified myself with some very good red wine. Halfway through the very elaborate dinner, a waiter knocked into me just as I was about to slurp a mouthful of it, and suddenly my white dress shirt was a red dress shirt. Brian Turner, bless him, spotted the incident. He came over to my table and insisted we swapped shirts. What a nice man, I thought.

At last the awards ceremony began. I looked over to Gary Rhodes and mouthed, 'Good luck.' He reciprocated, and gave me a nervous smile and a thank you. I can't remember who was on the mike – I was pretty pissed by then – Richard Shepherd, then chairman of the Académie Culinaire, Michel Bourdin, the president, or Keith Podmore, the chef organizer, but whoever it was began: 'The judges have decided to only make three awards . . .' The awards all had equal billing, no first, second and third, because all nine chefs were deemed to already have met the required standard of excellence. 'The awards will be made in alphabetical order . . .' The suspense was killing us. The first winner didn't give the rest of us much of a clue to the identity of the others because his surname began with A. It was Michael Aldridge from the Connaught Hotel. Loud applause, and a big beaming face from Michael. Not a hair out of place – he's obviously still sober, I thought. Second out of the hat was Michel Perraud from the Waterside, my co-trainee under Michel Roux. He was a nice guy and his award was well deserved. He's a P, so that's several of the others out, I calculated. In fact, I realized, it left only Gary Rhodes and myself. I looked over at Gary, and he looked back at me. We were both as nervous as each other.

'Finally,' said the announcer, 'Antony Worrall Thompson from Ménage à Trois.'

For a moment it didn't sink in. As it did, my first reaction, unfortunately, was to direct a one-fingered salute towards Drew Smith of the *Guardian*. I can't think what came over me. I suppose I was releasing all the pent-up fury I felt towards those who had written me off before I had even started cooking in the final.

As I walked slowly from my table to the podium, soaking up the applause, I felt my eyes fill with tears. I'm such a damn softie. To me it was like my village football team winning the FA Cup, one of the biggest days of my life. It fully justified Michel Roux and Michel Bourdin's faith in me and their support for my election to the Académie. I was over the moon.

I gave the two Michels massive hugs, very unBritish kisses on both cheeks and then there was an equally big smacker for my hero Paul Bocuse before I congratulated the winners. Now it was clear why Brian Turner had urged caution with the champagne and insisted on giving me his shirt. Obviously he had known the result. But I sobered up very quickly – who needs alcohol or drugs when you're on such a natural high?

As will be apparent from the detail in which I've described this event, winning the MOGB in 1987 meant a huge amount to me at the time and I still treasure the memory, so thank you for indulging me. It opened numerous doors for me. I was asked to join many committees, including those of the Académie Culinaire and the Restaurateurs' Association of Great Britain. There were to be other competitions, but they don't shine in my memory in the same way as this one. Call that sour grapes if you like.

The intense adrenaline highs of the fantasy world of competitions can soon evaporate in the real world. The year that brought me the MOGB also saw me lose Ronda, and the following one, 1988, first gave me the exhilaration of selling Ménage à Trois and moving on, and then took away my ancient grandmother.

Her death was hardly unexpected as by now she was well into her nineties, but it was still a blow. I had, after all, never known life without her. She had had a great innings but she wasn't interested in cracking a ton. She wanted out. For the last year of her life she relied on two saints, my mother and a cousin, Peta Binney, who remained constantly and willingly at her beck and call. And she was very demanding and very crotchety right up until the last few months, when she became almost an angel. Not a cross word passed her lips. She was, it seemed, preparing herself for death.

Before that serenity descended on her, however, the Bette Davis persona was to the fore. She was awful. She would bang her stick on the bedroom floor, shouting for my mother. 'Joan, where's my tea?' I don't know how my mother or Peta didn't lose their rag. In fact, considering how my grandmother treated her daughter for most of her life, she was lucky to have her. My mother was a very forgiving, good-hearted woman. Unfortunately, life had dealt her a bad hand. I didn't help, and my grandmother certainly didn't.

My grandmother eventually died at St Stephen's Hospital in Fulham Road. I was at her side, my mother having left a few moments earlier. I had just flown in from America and rushed straight to the hospital. Although she was weak she was very lucid, and we had a short conversation in which she asked me to apologize to my mother for how badly she had behaved towards her and for the provisions in her will. I already knew what these were as I had escorted her to her ridiculously expensive lawyers in the City a year earlier when she had wanted to make some final adjustments to it.

My grandmother, always very astute, was worried that my mother would drink away her inheritance, so although her will allowed my mother to benefit from the whole estate, it was protected by being put into trust for me. My mother was not amused. My grandmother had known she wouldn't be, hence her deathbed apology. But she had settled matters to her satisfaction, though her will proved to be so convoluted that it cost us over £70,000 to sort out – and that's not including serious sums in death duties, or inheritance tax. This tax is evil. You're taxed all your life and then you're taxed when you die. It should be abolished.

My grandmother's death was the first I had witnessed. She died calmly, and what was remarkable to me was that fifteen minutes afterwards, every line and wrinkle had disappeared and she looked totally at peace. It was a deliverance for a proud woman who hated the indignities of having to be changed and bathed in her final months by a succession of nurses. I miss her still, but she lives on in my memory, through the various heirlooms she left me and through her Shiplake house, where I continue to live. I will always be grateful for everything she did to try to equip me for life, not least that excellent education, which I would never have had without her.

She was a classic old dame, a real British eccentric. For some reason she often chose to confide in me. She would say to my mother: 'Joan, kindly leave the room. I wish to talk to my grandson,' much to my mum's annoyance. I don't blame her for being irritated, but at the same time I was delighted to be the centre of attention, the person selected to be privy to Gran's secrets. As an adult she told me some shocking things: how she had had so much fun in London in her younger days that she had on occasion been tempted to leave my grandfather. She dropped this bombshell when she was trying to persuade me not to let my first wife, Jill, go. She believed that, whatever its ups and downs, marriage was for life, and that when you married a man you also married his job.

I learned that it was on one of her visits home from India that my grandmother struck up a relationship with the famous writer H.G. Wells. She had told me euphemistically that she used to 'take tea with H.G.', and it wasn't until I was in my thirties that she revealed that they had had an affair. She seemed very proud of the fact that she was one of only two of his dalliances not have been outed in his autobiography. She was obviously a naughty young thing in her day, and knowing this, it made me chuckle when she volubly disapproved of some of the things my mother got up to.

The aftermath of my grandmother's death was a difficult time for my mother, especially as she was very upset about the will. She seemed in many ways to lose her purpose in life. She was only sixty-six, but because her sight had deteriorated to the point where she was now classified as blind, she led the lonely and inactive existence of a much older woman. So many pleasures were no longer available to her: she couldn't drive, or read, or even watch television.

It was time for me to build bridges with my mother after years of virtual estrangement caused in part by my closer relationship with my grandmother and in part by my inability to deal with my mother's alcoholism. My family had always been fractured, and I felt I was heading down the same avenue. I had already cocked up two marriages and lost one family, so I was determined to make my peace with my mother and sustain some sort of relationship with her before it was too late. I had never managed that with my father. Although I had seen him maybe a couple of times a year since Jill had dragged me down to Herne Bay to re-establish contact all those years ago, I felt it was too late for us to forge a really close bond. Worse than that, just when my father had needed me on a personal and financial level, I wasn't there for him. In the death throes of my marriage to Mish he had written to me asking for my help and I never replied. He must have been devastated.

I never replied because I never received the letter. Mish, who was furious with me at the time, opened it, read the contents and destroyed it, and I never knew. She did not tell me until he died a couple of years later. I wasn't even able to go to his funeral because I was abroad at the time and found out too late that he was dead. The only shred of consolation I had was that, although he left this world penniless, at least he left it happy. He was content with his modest life and he loved his third wife, Phyllida, more than anything, and those are gifts money can't buy.

Grandmother gone, father gone, Mish gone, Ronda gone, restaurant gone ... suddenly my life seemed very empty. I needed a project. I decided to go into food production and delicatessens, which I have to admit was a move aimed at enticing Ronda back from the States. And it worked. Well, sort of.

Having checked out Paris – I found the shops were too poncy, a show of style over substance – I went off to New York to research gourmet food stores and extended my research to Philadelphia. New York had the likes of Dean and Deluca and Balducci's, brilliant stores with a huge array of the best produce from greengrocery through cheese to wonderful salads and ready meals. I could get very excited about these stores. I still do, in fact. Nothing in London at that time came close to what New York had to offer, and even today it can't really compete, with the possible exceptions of Selfridges Food Hall, Harrods and Harvey Nicks. The only problem was that my site was on Wandsworth Common when it needed to be in Knightsbridge, where disposable income was more plentiful.

I was ecstatic when Ronda agreed to return to London and run the operation on a day-to-day basis. She helped me to design the shop, and together we came up with dishes we would produce and the ingredients we would sell. We called it the KWT Foodshow. The 'K' was for Ronda's surname, Kamihira. We were back together, and I thought I was in heaven. But hell would perhaps have been nearer the mark.

Everything was in place. The printing and design had been produced by our former gym-mate Duncan Goodhew's wife Anne, and we were ready to go. Just one small technical hitch: three weeks before we were due to open, the 'K' of KWT upped and left, just like that. She had a panic attack and wanted out, just as all our dreams were about to come true. And they weren't only my dreams, but Ronda's, too, remember; dreams that her ex-husband Nick had set her towards achieving a few years earlier.

So there I was stuck with a deli that I didn't want, a food factory supplying Harrods and other outlets and no one to help me. I just got on with it, as one does. It was a beautiful little shop, and it did very well to start with, winning a couple of retail awards. But life does have a tendency to kick you when you're down, and the recession began to kick in with a vengeance. Suddenly mortgages

went up to 15 per cent and the upwardly mobile people of
Wandsworth, who had stretched themselves on their house
purchases in boom times, were now deep in the shit with their
mortgage payments. What else would they cut back on but
expensive, luxury foods?

My life was starting to fray at the edges. I lost heart in KWT. My
staff had no passion – some of them were ripping me off at the shop
– but worst of all, my pride prevented me from closing the place
down. All that hard-earned money I had gained from the sale of
Ménage à Trois was being poured into a bottomless pit.

CHAPTER TWENTY-FIVE

AFTER SELLING MÉNAGE À TROIS, AS WELL AS SETTING UP KWT I HAD gone back into the restaurant business, with Roy Ackerman, chairman of the Restaurateurs' Association. He had come up with the idea of a chefs' club at a premises called 190 Queensgate in Knightsbridge and brought in investors from the restaurant world, including myself, to fund the idea. It was in a swimming pool at a mutual friend's house in St Tropez that Roy asked me if I wanted to be the first chef of this new club, running the basement restaurant. I jumped at the opportunity. Restaurateuring was in my blood; shopkeeping wasn't. The thing about restaurants is that, whether your regulars come once a week, once a month or even only once a year, generally they are out for a good time. With shopkeeping you might see your customers four times a week, or in some cases every day, but the social context is different, and there are only so many times you can say, 'Good morning, Mrs Jones, and how's little Johnny today?' with a genuine smile on your face. Familiarity, as the adage goes, breeds contempt, and I wasn't cut out for small talk. I wasn't cut out to be a shopkeeper full stop.

190 Queensgate opened to excellent reviews. The food was posh gear, proper meals, a change for me after serving only starters and puddings for eight years at Ménage. We won the *Time Out* Best New Restaurant award, which came as a bit of a surprise since we were by no means cheap – the average bill was about £60 a head.

Above the restaurant, on the ground floor, was a members' bar. The only problem with that was that we did not have many members, and those we had were obviously predominantly chefs or restaurateurs, and when are they working? That's right, exactly when you want them to be in the club. It was a nice idea, but it had not really been thought through, and the bar was a complete flop.

What changed that was the opening of Bistrot 190, a second, less formal restaurant, about a year later. We managed to persuade Roy Ackerman and the board to relax the membership rules (which upset some of the old farts, but at the end of the day the bar had to survive) and we also opened the bar to the public until 11 pm. The customers then consisted mainly of guests waiting for tables in the Bistrot, which only members were allowed to book in advance. The bar was restricted to members only between 11 pm and 2 am. Suddenly, we had a huge spurt in membership and the bar became a hot little number in that part of town.

When I started the restaurant at 190 Queensgate, I chose an excellent team. Sebastian Snow was the head chef. Prior to joining me he had worked for David Wilby at 51:51. Sebastian had sung from the right hymnsheet at his interview, but when I checked him out with David I was warned that he wasn't particularly keen on hard work. In fact, I seem to recall the words 'lazy bastard' entering the discussion. At his second interview I drew Sebastian's attention to this criticism. He didn't seem shocked, but he thought carefully before telling me that I would never find a harder worker.

And I have to say that he was right. Sebastian rose to the challenge. He worked as hard as any chef I've had the privilege of employing, except for David Wilby himself. He was a great guy, extremely handsome, a classic Hooray whose trademark was a spotted neckerchief he wore to accompany his chef's clothes. In conversation you got the feeling that his brain hadn't caught up with his mouth. But it mattered not, because he was a bloody good chef.

I took on two young manageresses, Melissa and Kate, not so much for their ability, as neither had much experience, as for their brains and, in Melissa's case, her looks as well (sorry, Kate). They were both great girls in their different ways. Melissa was very methodical, and had lists for everything. She had a bit of a temper, well, a massive temper – you knew when she was on the warpath because the eyes turned black – but she was refined with it. Kate was a rough diamond, hard to tame, and she had an attitude problem when crossed. A blunt, northern lass, and rightly proud of it, she had been at school with Marco Pierre White and told me some brilliant stories about him, none of which I can mention here for fear of being sued. She sometimes drove me mad because she never wrote anything down, preferring to rely on her seriously well-endowed head. But she was fantastic with the customers and staff. They were a great team, and we had great times.

It was not long before Sebastian fell in love with Melissa. As you've seen, restaurants are often breeding grounds for romantic relationships – one or two of mine included – but Sebastian and Melissa's love story was one that had a happy ending: the perfect handsome couple eventually got married, and I catered their wedding at the Orangery in Holland Park.

But things were pretty rough all round for me. Six months or so after I started at 190, I had to put my deli company into liquidation. At the time it was reported that I was broke, but I was still intact, though only just. The divorce was costing me dear, all the Ménage money had gone and I couldn't afford to meet my mortgage payments on Jessica Road.

Since Ronda had bolted, various women had drifted in and out of my orbit, but I just wasn't that interested. Some I gelled with, others I didn't; none could replace what I had lost with Ronda, or, if I am honest, what had gone with Mish. These were dark days, but che sera sera and all that, and it's only by experiencing the downs in life that you can really appreciate the ups. So I hung on. Apart from that one aberration at the airport in New York, I am not a quitter.

However, I hadn't quite seen the last of Ronda. Our paths were to cross for a third time, when she called me and told me she wanted to come back and give it another shot. She had already booked herself on a flight to the UK the following Friday. My spirits soared. On the day of her arrival I was due to be in Monaco judging the best luxury yacht chef (it's a hard job, but someone has to do it), so I arranged with Ronda that I would leave her a key. She could let herself into Jessica Road, make herself at home and I'd see her on the Sunday night.

When I got home, all of a quiver, Ronda was nowhere to be seen, and there was no sign of her. No bag, nothing. I called a mutual friend, who gave me the message that Ronda would ring me the next day. That was all she said, but it was obvious something was up. I knew Ronda too well. Sure enough, when Ronda phoned she explained that she wouldn't be staying with me now as she was staying instead with a guy called Hugh. I ought to have been gob-smacked, but nothing about Ronda surprised me any more.

According to her friend, on her first evening in London Ronda had popped into Latchmere Fitness Centre for one of her beloved aerobics classes. The mysterious Hugh, another fitness fanatic, was also at the class. He invited her to dinner afterwards and the rest, as they say, is history. They married. They separated. Ronda went back to the States again. In the US she married for a third time, had kids, got divorced and now is either about to be or already married to a very rich man who flies her around the world in his private jet. Maybe she's finally cracked it. The last time I met her, which was not so long ago, she still had all the old magic and I remembered why I had loved her. But that time I came away unscathed.

The one bright spot of that black period for me personally was the success of 190, and then another light came into my life, albeit briefly. I used to pop round to my mate Brian Turner's restaurant in Walton Street for a late-evening drink, Brian being a hospitable sort. And there was this girl behind the bar, Suzie Halewood. She had fabulous eyes, great head of hair, beautiful skin texture and she was just bursting with sexiness and cheek. Physically she wasn't my usual lean and hungry type, but there was something about her, a magnetic quality. She also had a dry sense of humour and she didn't take any crap. Soon, when I went to Walton Street, I was spending much more time talking to her than to Brian.

Brian was like a father to his staff. When he paid them it was almost as if he was giving them pocket money. But he was such a charmer that he was always rewarded with great loyalty. He saw what was going on. He warned me that Suzie had a good-looking boyfriend, a talented chef, and basically said I'd got no chance. But he agreed that there was no harm in me asking her out. To the surprise of both of us, when I did she said yes.

Suzie and I kept our little liaison secret for a few weeks, first because we didn't want her boyfriend Richard to find out, and also for fear that Brian would go into overprotective father mode. To start our relationship was based on sex and laughter and neither of us took it particularly seriously, in fact I behaved like a prat for the first few months, treating her with little or no respect. It was as if I was reverting to the days when I had kept girls at a distance because I never really believed that they wanted to be with me. I imagine I was also afraid of getting involved again.

Once I belatedly realized, after about six months, that my feelings for Suzie ran deep, the damage had been done. Now I was desperate to build on what had been a shaky start, but by then she no longer trusted me, and it was she who was putting up the barriers. We were together for just over a year, living together at Jessica Road for a good part of that time, and it was like a game of two halves.

Suzie was a wonderful artist, but she lacked self-belief. I have no doubt that I contributed to that, for while I praised her paintings, I undermined her confidence in other ways. By the time it dawned on me what I was doing wrong it was too late for me to make amends, however hard I tried, and God, did I try. But the uneven foundations of our relationship were not strong enough to prevent her from just waking up one morning and thinking to herself, what the hell am I doing here with this old man? I'm getting too set in my ways, and I want my life to be exciting and challenging. I need more than this. And she was gone.

For the next couple of months I made a complete fool of myself, charging around after her like a wounded bull and pestering her on the phone. I would even break into her flat during the day to leave love notes on her pillow, and once in the middle of the night, when I just sat on the floor while she slept. In one of my particularly paranoid moments I forced my way in and assaulted her flatmate, Paul, because I thought she was sleeping with him. Poor Paul. He was a lovely guy. And what was more, he was gay. I just didn't know what to do. I had let another girl into my heart, it had gone wrong and I was at a loss as to how to deal with it.

But in spite of everything it is a year I neither regret nor will forget. Suzie's humour cracked me up, her superior intelligence stretched my brain and her sensual, almost Rubenesque body taught me that there is more to life than skin and bone. From her witty put-downs I learned to laugh at myself and her brilliant creative skills widened my horizons.

During my year with Suzie I took in a couple of lodgers at Jessica Road to try to make ends meet. The first one was Martin, a roly-poly, gay food-lover and a one-time manager at Foxtrot Oscar who got stuck into KWT Foodshow for a while. It's not something you really want to own up to in this politically correct world of ours, but at this point I need to make a confession. My public-school background had made me, I realize now, quite homophobic, so renting a room in my house to a gay guy was a pretty bold move for me. Sure, in my youth I had cavorted round various gay haunts with my lesbian girlfriend Rose, but that was more to do with trying to look avant-garde than anything else. In truth I hadn't really had very much to do with gay men before. I remember being utterly shocked when the DJ and comedian Kenny Everett, who was a regular at Ménage à Trois and became a mate, told me he had 'changed sides', even though he still loved his wife. A few nights at the gay club Heaven with him and his crowd really opened up my eyes. But when Martin moved in, did we have some laughs. He had a wild group of friends, some of whom I knew from Foxtrot, and every night, it seemed, was party night.

Martin's regular boyfriend was a bloke called Sam Kemp, and between them they completely changed my attitude. Well, not completely, I suppose – I am still straight – but prior to knowing them, and later loads of others of like mind, the thought of either of my sons turning out to be homosexual would have horrified me. But I was gradually growing up and learning to accept people from all walks of life, and I felt better for it.

Sam eventually ended up working for me at a couple of my restaurants, initially as a manager and later, when my own role changed from chef to office boy, as an area manager. He remains a great friend, and as well as being a great mate he is a consummate professional at what he does best: developing restaurant groups.

When Martin moved on, another Martin, Martin Romney, arrived. He was a terrific bloke too, but one who had really been through the mill. He was recently divorced, and had had to sell the hotel he owned. He had put his share of the proceeds into an investment fund, which then ripped off all its clients, rendering their investments worthless. I had lost the same kind of money myself after my divorce, but at least it was through my own mistakes. With Martin it was pure robbery. We all know that shit happens, but there's nothing worse than shit happening outside your control. To earn a few quid he used to do the books for me, for KWT and to start with for the restaurant, too, all by hand, as neither of us was computer literate. His accuracy was amazing, even if the figures he came up with usually showed a loss.

Jessica Road was a lovely house full of memories for me, both good and bad. As well as the dinner parties and drinking sessions, it had seen the demise of my marriage to Mish and my break-ups with Ronda and now Suzie. But after my divorce and the collapse of KWT, and with it my cashflow, it had to go. Unfortunately, my food factory was not the only casualty of the recession. By this time, owing to the property market crash, not only could I not afford the hike in mortgage rates but I couldn't sell the house, either. One morning I woke up, depressed again by all the bills coming out of the woodwork, and thought, fuck it all. I took the keys, wandered into Barclays Bank on Gloucester Road and chucked them on to the manager's desk. 'It's yours,' I said, 'and if you think you're getting any more out of me, you can take a running jump.' And out I walked, a burden lifted from my shoulders.

Once the house was sold there was still a shortfall of approximately £60,000. To be fair to them, Barclays could have made me personally bankrupt, but they didn't. Instead they wrote off the majority of the debt, preferring to gamble on my future. I think they bet the right way, because by sticking with me they've more than made up for what they lost. In return I have remained loyal to them, and in these days of no allegiance to anyone or anything we have built a strong relationship. They have great personal managers and I don't have a bad word to say about them. I hope I will still feel the same in twenty years, but I have my fears that by then my computer will be talking to their computer, and my managers and me will be down the pub.

So now, though I wouldn't exactly describe myself as a phoenix, it was time to focus on rising from the ashes. My comeback was just round the corner, and was launched by three fresh opportunities. First of all, Roy Ackerman, my chairman at 190 Queensgate, put my name forward as a potential creative consultant to a new restaurant due to be opened in Soho by another company with which he was involved, Simpson's of Cornhill plc. Secondly, I was approached by a young lady, Fiona Lindsay, who offered me her services as an agent. Given my record at managing myself, it seemed like a good idea, especially since Fiona was evidently a formidable woman; the sort of person who would chew men up and spit them out before breakfast. But she had a little twinkle in her eye, too. She had previously worked with Anton Mosimann, the famous chef who had featured quite a bit on television in the eighties, and who was well known for his incredible Swiss efficiency. She promised me the world, something that didn't impress me, but at that stage of my career, what did I have to lose? So I signed, and fifteen years on, I'm still with Fiona and her partner, Linda Shanks, and their company, Limelight Management. And against all my expectations, they've managed to produce the goods.

The third factor was the development of my television career. Apart from a couple of guest slots on BBC2's *Food and Drink* with my mate Brian Turner in the mid-1980s, my few appearances on the box had so far been confined to the USA and Australia. One of the *Food and Drink* programmes had involved working with the Navy on a destroyer, HMS *Birmingham*, which we joined off the coast of Gibraltar. Things did not get off to an auspicious start. The director, Wilfred Emanuel Jones, an ex-chef himself, got on the wrong side of me to the extent that I flipped my lid, pinned him to a wall by his throat and shouted: 'Don't you ever fucking talk to me like that again, or you can stuff your programme up your jacksy!' I think he was a little shocked, but it helped clear the air. I don't know whether his brusque attitude was the norm in TV then, but I wasn't prepared to put up with it. It was a shame, really, because outside work he was a really nice guy – bright, witty and quite a gent.

My next appearance on *Food and Drink* was directed by possibly the best food director in the business, David Pritchard, who was instrumental in the success of Keith Floyd and, later, Rick Stein. He was able to get the best out of his presenters by cajoling and encouraging rather than by resorting to intimidation.

When I was offered a stint as a presenter with a BBC programme called *Hot Chefs*, I jumped at the chance of displaying what I could do in this new shop window. The series, filmed in Birmingham, involved about ten chefs, each of whom had a ten-minute slot every weekday morning, airing just after nine o'clock, for two weeks. It was this show that really marked the start of cookery programming as we know it today, replacing the more formal approach we were used to from Anton Mosimann, the Roux brothers and Raymond Blanc, the TV stars of the 1980s.

Gary Rhodes, another of the new faces on *Hot Chefs*, must have thought the same, because we both coincidentally went for a similar style of presenting, introducing a bit of a bossy-chef, abused-commis double act with our assistants. My TV commis was Kate Weatherall, in real life my sassy manageress at 190 Queensgate. We worked well as a team and had a laugh together, which made for a relaxed partnership considering it was the first time either of us had done any proper TV. Kate became a bit of a star in her own right and received quite a lot of fan mail, whereas I got hate mail for my on-screen treatment of her.

Hot Chefs taught me one important thing: not to be afraid of being seen to make mistakes. Everyone does something wrong occasionally, and I think you seem more human to the viewers if you reveal your own fallibility. People appreciate that, and identify with you. On this show, and indeed on many others since, the lid of my liquidizer blew off, covering me on this occasion with tomato soup. The director asked if I wanted to go again, but I reasoned, 'If it's going to happen to me, then it's going to happen to cooks at home. Let's leave it in.' Not everyone was as relaxed: one chef from a top London hotel did exactly the same thing and refused to carry on.

Off-screen, 190 was doing brilliantly, thanks in large part to the Bistrot. Ironically, Bistrot 190's success was based on the dynamics of the very recession that had caused me so much personal damage. I had realized that people still wanted to eat out, but they had to pull in their horns, and, in the case of business customers, they had to be seen to be pulling in their horns, especially if they were the owners or management of large companies. When staff are being made redundant or having their wages slashed, there is nothing worse for industrial relations than for the chief executive to be spotted eating out at a swanky restaurant.

Bistrot 190 was one of the first fashionable restaurants to provide realistic value for money. Not one of our main courses cost over £10, and we served rustic French fare, lots of slow-cooked food. The only problem was that most chefs were still in nouvelle mode, wanting to cook pretty pictures on plates, and it was hard to find a chef who had ever eaten a stew or casserole, let alone cooked one. I would tell them that this was the food of the future but they turned their noses up at it.

But the Bistrot proved my point. Some nights this forty-eight-seater restaurant would do the best part of 200 covers. It was a little miracle, and it rescued 190. Our policy of not taking bookings except from 190 members guaranteed us a full bar as customers waited for tables. It was a restaurant that spawned more of its ilk as the culinary world woke up to the fact that its clientele was trading down. Sadly, this period saw many high-profile chefs losing their jobs and many expensive restaurants folding, but it also saw the birth of London's café society.

As for the customers, they enjoyed the experience. They were able to go out and relax and enjoy good food without seriously damaging their wallets, and they could afford to do so regularly. In many ways, together with the boom in supermarket ready meals and the more interesting takeaway offerings, the emphasis on value-for-money eating out sowed the seeds of the demise of cooking at home. Other notable restaurants of the time that had similar pricing policies were the Red Eagle, Charles Fontaine's Quality Chop House and Kensington Place, which was one of London's first 'cool' restaurants and the forerunner of the bigger 'see-and-be-seen' eateries developed by Sir Terence Conran. But what KP achieved that the other large restaurants didn't was consistency of quality, thanks to its fab chef-cum-partner Rowley Leigh, and a fantastic client list like a walking edition of *Hello!* magazine. In fact it could be argued that it was KP that started Britain's fascination with celebrities, though it's possible that Langan's would dispute that claim. One thing is certain: KP had a much better class of customer.

Thanks to Roy Ackerman, Simpson's of Cornhill offered me the creative consultancy at their new Soho restaurant. With 190 Queensgate and Bistrot 190 doing so well, the board were understandably not overjoyed at the prospect of my attention being distracted by another restaurant, but Roy smoothed things over with them, emphasizing that my role there would be purely a consultancy.

We named the new restaurant Dell'Ugo, after my favourite olive oil at the time. At Dell'Ugo I decided Mediterranean was the route to take. Italian restaurants – San Lorenzo, San Frediano, La Famiglia, Sal e Pepe, La Meridiana and others – had been the cornerstone of trendy sixties, seventies and eighties dining, but after the ten years of nouvelle cuisine, the British appetite for different food had been whetted. By choosing Mediterranean I could encompass both French dishes and exciting new tastes, offering the pleasures of sun-kissed, healthy food from various countries. 'Mediterranean' was perceived as the south of France and Italy, but also I explored Spain, Greece, Turkey and North Africa.

My team at Dell'Ugo came mainly from 190. My housemate Martin Romney became general manager and the wild Troy Clayton came as head chef. Francesca Hazard, Martin's number 2, was an interesting choice. When I had advertised for management staff at 190 she had applied through a mutual friend, despite the fact she worked in financial PR and didn't have any restaurant experience. But I took her on at Dell'Ugo on the basis that she was bright, attractive in a peaches-and-cream English way and there was something trustworthy about her. She turned out to be a little diamond. She picked up the job incredibly quickly, and once she had conquered a slight shyness with people she proved to be a natural. Dell'Ugo was an instant success and, together with Alastair Little at Soho Soho, we helped to put this London village back on its feet. It had become rather run-down as the recession drove many of the media and advertising groups that had been based there out to other areas of London, but within a couple of years the place was buzzing again.

CHAPTER TWENTY-SIX

RESTAURANT REVIEWS ARE RARELY OBJECTIVE. THEY DEPEND VERY much on the mood of the reviewers on the day, on who they're dining with, and on whose bed they slept in the night before. I know one critic who gave brilliant write-ups when he was with his bit on the side and poor to average ones when he was with his wife. So the impression the outside world gets of your restaurant can be at the mercy of factors beyond your control.

Fortunately Dell'Ugo opened to very good reviews, with the exception of the one written by Jonathan Meades in *The Times*. I think he gave us marks of five out of ten: not disastrous, but not brilliant, either, especially if you bear in mind that he gave us eight out of ten at 190 Queensgate.

The night Jonathan came to Dell'Ugo, the receptionist managed to piss him off at the start by reprimanding him for arriving late. And he was forty-five minutes late, so I think he should have accepted this gracefully, although I admit that the receptionist could have handled it more diplomatically. Anyway, he took offence, and from then on it was downhill all the way.

It is discourteous to be late, but the worst crime is not showing up and failing to call to cancel the table. During the restaurant boom of the eighties this problem became almost an epidemic, and I earned myself a certain notoriety when my radical policy for dealing with no-shows was publicized on television. My solution was to phone the offending customers at about 3 am and ask them whether I could let my staff go home now, or whether they would like me to hold their table until they arrived. These inquiries were usually met with voluble abuse, but the next day the errant customer would often get the point or see the funny side and call to apologize properly. It was certainly an effective way of putting the message across. We were seeking no more than a modicum of consideration. The most common offender was the gold-medallion type who habitually made half a dozen reservations at various restaurants months in advance so that, having boasted to his friends about the clout he had, he could casually invite them to choose where they would like to eat on the day and make out that he had got a table at short notice. Very impressive, I'm sure, and there is no law against it – all we ask is that the flash git picks up the phone and cancels the other five bookings. Good manners cost nothing.

On the subject of manners, it is doubtful whether there can be a ruder customer than the film director and so-called restaurant critic Michael Winner, who really gives food reviewers a bad name. To my knowledge he has on only two occasions eaten in any of my restaurants, once at Downstairs at 190, which he didn't write about, and once at Bistrot 190, about which he was quite complimentary. But you need only chat to any restaurateur who has had dealings with him, or indeed just read his columns, to know how rude he is. He gets me so annoyed that at one stage I put up 'Not Wanted' posters in my restaurant bearing his picture and offering a free bottle of champagne to anyone who saw him in the vicinity. The campaign caught on and received full coverage in many national newspapers. In all we sent out over 200 posters to restaurants around the UK and even some in other countries, including his beloved Barbados.

If I were him I would just have ignored it, but the campaign got to him to such a degree that he wrote to me, first to tell me I was preventing him from doing his job, and then intimating that I was no different from the Nazis who persecuted his family during the war. When this didn't produce results he sued me for comments I'd made in *Caterer and Hotelkeeper* magazine (can you believe he actually reads the *Caterer*?) and for using his photograph without permission. The matter was settled before it got to court and I paid a small sum into the charity he supports for the families of murdered police officers.

It was water off a duck's back. I simply commissioned Michael Frith, an artist friend of mine, to paint me a watercolour of Winner to replace the photograph. Then I had 100 seats made for the restaurant lavatories featuring copies of the painting. I actually wanted to put the picture in the bowls of the loos, for obvious reasons, but the cost was prohibitive – my disdain for the man doesn't run that deep.

Mr Winner continues to be banned from my restaurant, although I'm sure the ban is by now unnecessary. Leaving him out of the equation, I think food critics have a valuable job to do and that, for the most part, they do it well. And we chefs and restaurateurs have nothing to gain by letting reviewers get to us, because if we do it is invariably us who end up the losers. Over the years I've met and got to know quite a few restaurant critics, so allow me to introduce you to my personal Top 10. Number 1 in my book is Fay Maschler, who has over thirty years as restaurant critic for the London *Evening Standard* behind her. Even after all that time she still writes with enthusiasm and, of course, with a great depth of knowledge. I have joined her for a few test meals and she usually tastes everyone's food, makes her own judgement and is generally, I think, very fair. She and her husband, Reg Gadney, and her sister, the restaurateur Beth Coventry, have become good friends of mine, but that hasn't stopped her giving me a good kicking when she has thought I've deserved it. Her reviews of Drones and the Atrium, which we'll come to later, were particularly nasty, but unfortunately her comments were justified. Fay's column is the one to read if you really want to know about the actual food.

At number 2 is A.A. Gill, probably the best journalist in his field on the prose front. My wife and I fight over the Style section of the *Sunday Times* on Sunday mornings. You're not necessarily going to learn a lot about the restaurant he is reviewing until you get to the last two paragraphs, but you will get an in-depth look into A.A.'s mind. Having read him since he took over from Craig Brown, I reckon I now know enough about him to become his psychoanalyst. He loves anything to do with sex; he's the world's biggest piss-taker; he regrets not being able to drink; he has a strong feminine side, although publicly likes to be seen as a bit of a chauvinist; he is an arbiter of good taste; he yearns to direct porn films; he hates the countryside and all that it stands for, but is slightly confused about that because he often dresses like a country squire. He hates arse-lickers and loves cars, although is not a great driver. And the food? He doesn't do poncy well, but he adores good food prepared simply and cooked to perfection.

Number 3 is Matthew Fort, the longstanding food editor of the

Guardian. He works for love and not much money (go on, editor, pay him more, you know he's worth it). For years he was the Bertie Wooster of food critics, barely able to say boo to a goose. He writes like the Old Etonian he is, which makes the left-wing *Guardian* seem like an odd choice of vehicle, but he knows his stuff, even if occasionally he can be a little pedantic about such matters as sticking to the letter of a recipe. Life moves on, Matthew, and so does food, so why not base your review on whether you like a dish rather than on whether there's an additional ingredient or an ingredient missing, or on the fact that a chef (all right, me) has combined three different regions of Italy to create a dish? My customers loved it, and I'm sure the Italians would have too, if they'd thought of it before I did.

Jonathan Meades, at number 4, recently retired after a decade and a half with *The Times*. He was another knowledgeable writer and, you often felt, probably a frustrated restaurateur. In my experience, he was one of those critics who was more likely to give you a better review if he was enjoying the company at his table, and by the time he reached the end of his career, you had the feeling he had grown rather bored by it all. He, too, was prone to a bit of pedantry. Take cassoulet, for example. He insisted there shouldn't be tomatoes in the dish, and yet he was taking as his standard the traditional recipe from just one area of France, where they omitted tomatoes. Originally cassoulet was a peasant dish of beans and preserved meats and some cooked it with and some without tomatoes, but that is beside the point. Surely what matters is whether or not he actually liked what he ate. Jonathan had a great reputation among chefs, many of whom were as desperate to earn ten out of ten on the Meades scale as they were to be awarded a Michelin star. Generally you could trust his scoring. My lowest from Jonathan was five for Dell'Ugo, my highest eight.

Craig Brown, A.A. Gill's predecessor at *The Sunday Times*, where his name was on everyone's lips, gets fifth place in my Top 10. He was a brilliant food writer, but rather shot himself in the foot as far as this strand of his work was concerned when he moved to the *Telegraph*. In his day he was exceptionally powerful: his great review of Dell'Ugo put £12,000 on our weekly turnover. His wit, which was in much the same vein as Gill's, was superb, and he used to have me in stitches. He was refreshingly irreverent about food and even more so about chefs, and he wasn't afraid to say what he thought. But you always believed that he was writing from the heart and that he meant every word. I remember him being pretty damning once about Nico Ladenis's restaurant in Victoria. Nico was given the right of reply and retaliated with a how-dare-you sort of piece, and then I chipped in with an article headed 'If you can't take the heat, stay out of the kitchen', in which I defended the food critic's right to voice his own opinion. As long as reviewers do not support their stated views with factual inaccuracies, they must be allowed to offer their personal judgements.

Nico was arguing that a bad review could wipe out the hundreds of thousands invested in a restaurant. So it can, but the same is true of the movie and theatre worlds. Why should the restaurant trade be any exception? We have to remember that the customer is king, which is a maxim Nico had a reputation for forgetting. This was the man who refused to serve gin and tonics and to put salt and pepper on the table. Great chef, but all the time he had a screw loose. Someone seems to have managed to tighten it up for him now, but he stopped speaking to me after I wrote that piece and I doubt cordial relations will ever be restored.

Number 6 is Jay Rayner of the *Observer*. As he is a relative new-comer on the scene, the jury is still out on him to some extent, but he recently won the Glenfiddich Prize, for which I was one of the judges. Jay is the son of Clare Rayner, although he hates people bringing that up. I like him, although he probably thinks I don't after he wrote a long article bashing my political leanings. But I thought it was a fair piece. Jay has brought back to restaurant reviewing some of the elements others seem to have phased out. He writes about the whole experience, food and ambience, in a straightforward way. Since Jay joined the great food writer Nigel Slater at the *Observer*, I've added the paper to my Sunday reading list. Shame it's so left-wing.

At number 7 is Caroline Stacey, who writes mainly for the *Independent*. I'm sorry Caroline is so far down the list. She would be higher if she wrote for one of the bigger guns in restaurant-reviewing terms. She, too, is a Glenfiddich winner, and I think she's fab, a great all-rounder. She makes me laugh, she relishes her life, likes a drink and enjoys her job, and her warmth and personality shine through her columns, as does her wrath, from time to time.

Number 8: Lindsay Bareham. I love her to bits. She used to appear everywhere, including in *Time Out*, but seems to have stepped out of the limelight, which is a great pity because she knows her stuff and puts it down on paper really well. Recently she has concentrated on food writing as opposed to reviewing restaurants. She has a daily recipe column in the *Evening Standard* and has produced a series of great cookbooks that for the most part concentrate on a single ingredient such as potatoes, onions and tomatoes. They are part of my library of over 4,000 cookbooks, and I use them regularly.

Matthew Norman, a sarcastic bastard who writes entertainingly on many subjects and who is another newcomer as a restaurant-reviewer, is my number 9. His pieces in the *Sunday Telegraph* are an easy read and fun with it; a breath of fresh air. Not long ago he came to my current restaurant, Notting Grill, clearly determined to hate the experience. It was certainly quite apparent that he hated me. (What is it about me, I wonder, that seems to drive writers to lash out at me on such a personal level? A pussycat like me? I just can't understand it.) But in spite of having a pop at me, Matthew did at least give my restaurant a glowing recommendation, and although reading it made me squirm a bit at certain points, I did enjoy the review.

At number 10 is Bill Knott. Why Bill is not published more often baffles me. He used to be at the *Telegraph*, did a stint at *Eat Soup* and now writes for the British Airways in-flight magazine, among other glossies. He's a great writer whose work benefits from the fact that he has been involved in the catering trade himself. He has the ability to get under the surface of a restaurant and explain to the reader what it really is all about, for instance, the factors involved in formulating prices, so unlike most critics he is able to present informed arguments for and against a restaurant, and he does so with style.

Well, that's my Top 10. As for numbers 11 to 1,000, I'd need another book to cover them. Suffice it to say that Michael Winner would be in 1,000th position, and Jan Moir of the *Telegraph* would also be there or thereabouts. I love Jan's character assassinations. She is an excellent writer of profile pieces, but as far as her contri-butions to the food pages are concerned, she seems to have been put there for the quality of her writing alone, rather than for any knowledge of food and wine. I suppose this opinion will be per-ceived as sour grapes, as she gave Notting Grill a bit of a pasting, but the fact is, over the last twenty-five years I've been pretty good at taking criticism on the chin. I've only ever written two letters complaining about a critic and one of those was to Jan Moir, whose piece about me was biased and unfair. But some you win and some you lose and, back at Dell'Ugo, trade didn't seem to be unduly affected by Jonathan Meades's lukewarm five out of ten whereas Craig Brown's review, as I mentioned, noticeably increased our business.

I enjoyed Soho and it was a convenient base for my second consultancy. This was for the Zen group, whose chief executive was the lovely Lawrence Leung, a man who never went anywhere without his entourage of four henchmen. The group had a fabulous restaurant in St Christopher's Place in the West End which was way ahead of its time. Too far ahead, in fact, because its prototype 'fusion food' wasn't working. They approached me to run the place: my concept, my team but their wage bill. We opened with a new name, Zoe, and simplified the menu by dividing it into two sections, 'Town' and 'Country'. 'Town' was trendy food, light Cal-Ital style; 'Country' was more rustic – earthy food, big flavours, big portions. It took off like a bomb; it was packed from the day it opened.

I installed my mate Sam Kemp as general manager. Sam was a great character, a great handler of staff and a man born to organize, and with him masterminding operations I knew I had no problem, apart, that is, from his occasional flapping.

Sam had worked for me at 190 Queensgate and was highly competent at his job, but clearly not everyone there liked him as much as I did. While I was away another director took the opportunity to sack him, and I returned to find it was a fait accompli – there was absolutely nothing I could do. After I put Sam at the helm at Zoe he stuck with me for another half a dozen years, showing a loyalty that is rare in the catering industry.

With three restaurants on the go, all of them doing well, it must have seemed to the outside world as if I was really rolling in it, though of course it wasn't quite as simple as that. It is true that I was earning reasonable money, but I needed to. I had nothing in the bank, no property to call my own, a divorce to fund and a large outstanding tax bill to pay off. But the important thing was that I had turned the corner. When your luck's out and nothing seems to go your way, there are times when you think you will never recover. At least I now had a foot back on the ladder.

Even so, there were times when I couldn't even afford to put petrol in my car. I was now driving a lurid green Volkswagen Golf GTi – the Porsche was long gone, as was Ronda's Morgan. Looking back, I think that, after women and pride, cars were probably my

biggest Achilles' heel. It began with a massive Merc 500 coupé. I
should never have chosen one in gold – far too Costa del Crime –
and in keeping with my boy-racer mood at the time I had it fitted
with massive wide wheels with gold and alloy trim. It was fast, it
was flashy and, let's be honest, it was tacky. Two days after taking
possession of this beast I went to drive it to work in the morning
and found it propped up on bricks with all four of its wheels gone.

The Porsche was even more of a disaster. I had hankered after a
Porsche turbo ever since completing a racing driver's course at
Brands Hatch. Two regulars at Ménage à Trois were car-dealers,
and they said they'd keep an eye out for one for me. It wasn't long
before one of them was on the phone. 'We've found you the perfect
car, a turbo in red. Wait until you see the number plate.' I rushed
down to the garage, there she was, a beauty, registration number
MOI 3911. My customary response to any accusation was 'What,
moi?' To have the word on my number plate, followed by the
figures 3911, so appropriate for a Porsche 911, was just too good
to be true. I paid the money and drove it away.

The dealers seemed like nice blokes but they definitely saw me
coming. As I purred away from the showroom it occurred to
me that I ought to have the car checked at the Porsche garage on
the Fulham Road, so I called in there on my way home. They found
so much wrong with it that the list went on for six pages. But the
friendly Porsche mechanic offered to fix it for me on the quiet in his
spare time, no worries, if I paid him cash. It sounded like a good
deal, so I agreed, and the following weekend I took the car to him
for its first round of repairs.

At 2 am on the Sunday I had a phone call from the mechanic's
brother. The mechanic had been out in my Porsche impressing the
girls and had been involved in a serious accident. He was in
hospital and the car was a write-off. The police were involved, of
course, and they told me to get in touch with my insurers. I'd
thought that at least the mechanic would be insured to drive any
vehicle. He was – but only when he was working on authorized cars
at the garage. His extracurricular activities weren't covered.

Things went from bad to worse. The insurers investigated the
Porsche and, surprise, surprise, found that no such registration
number existed in the UK or in Ireland. Further digging revealed
that it had in fact never been a whole car: it had been put together
from various bits of six stolen Porsches. By now the insurers were
washing their hands of the entire business, but unfortunately the

police were not. It took me two years of legal wrangling to get my money back. As for my 'friendly' dealers, they escaped prosecution because the car was deemed to have been bought by them in good faith.

Lucky car number 3 was the bright green VW Golf. About half an hour after I bought that I decided to take it for a spin around Knightsbridge. I was driving up the hill towards the Albert Hall, part of a one-way system, made a left turn and went smack into another car coming out of it in the wrong direction. My Golf was not quite a write-off, but it was out of action for six weeks and – you've guessed it – the other driver was uninsured.

By this time I was living in one bedroom above 190 Queensgate, courtesy of the Gore Hotel, 190's landlords. It wasn't exactly glamorous, but it was somewhere to lay my head. My furniture was all either at Shiplake or in storage, I had no responsibilities and most of my waking hours were spent working, in Soho by day and at 190 Queensgate by night. There were no lasting relationships with women: it was an emotionally arid period of one-night stands, usually with customers of the hotel or the restaurant. I knew by now I was definitely a relationship man. I just had to learn to make them last.

And then Clare Crawshay-Williams reappeared. I had met her at Sebastian Snow's wedding – she was an ex-girlfriend of his, in fact – and she was as plummy as her name suggests. A raunchy girl without being classically beautiful, she was very fit and had the best legs in the business. She told me later that I had been rude to her twice, once at that wedding and on another occasion when she had dined at Bistrot 190. It's amazing how attractive rudeness can be to many women. As I'd never been terrific at making the running with the opposite sex I used it to get a girl to notice me. She would think to herself, I can't believe he just said that, and all of a sudden I became interesting to her because nobody else had ever spoken to her like that. It's a sort of reverse psychology. Obviously it got Clare's attention, anyway, because she remembered both incidents so clearly. It doesn't always work, of course – I've had plenty of slaps and several drinks poured over my head in my time – but it seemed to do the trick when it counted. And it counted with Clare.

Clare called me. I was a little taken aback. She was gorgeous but just not my sort at all. Outwardly she had all the trappings of a classic Sloane, but there was more to her than that. She was a good-time girl in the nicest sense of the word; she liked to enjoy herself.

She kept our relationship a secret from her Sloaney friends for quite a while, but slowly it developed into a bit more than clandestine visits to my hotel bedroom and she wheeled me out to meet them. Her change of heart might have had something to do with finding out that my own background was closer to hers than she had imagined and there was more to me, too, than the simple sweaty chef she had taken me for.

Clare was great company. As well as being fun, she was intelligent and had bags of class and style. She relished the finer things in life, good food and good wine. Her biggest passion of all was tennis. She was a member of Queen's Club and I was deeply impressed by her athleticism and her game. My tennis days had pretty well begun and ended at school, but now she reintroduced me to the sport, and under her tutelage I improved considerably, though I was never good enough to take more than one or two games off her in a set.

One of Clare's tennis partners, and another good player, was Sebastian Snow, who was horrified at our relationship. To Sebastian I was always a bit of rough and he couldn't understand how any woman could go out with me. In fact he once asked my current wife: 'What on earth are you doing going out with that ugly sod?' It is a question I'm sure has been asked of many of the women I've been involved with, and it remains one of life's mysteries.

Sebastian and Melissa had by this time left 190 and opened their own restaurant, Snow's on the Green, near Brook Green in Hammersmith. They went with my blessing: they had both done a fantastic job for me, and it always gives me a buzz when someone I've employed goes off and makes a success of an enterprise of their own. Sebastian is still there today, though unfortunately the pressures of running a restaurant put more strain on his marriage to Melissa than it could withstand, and they eventually parted company.

A career as a restaurateur or a chef is tough on relationships, and casualties are frequent. Your partner has to be exceptionally understanding, monumentally trusting and to have the patience of a saint. The hours are invariably awful, the pay is crap, at least initially, and your other half has to put up with living with someone who always comes home smelling like a bag of chips.

My affair with Clare was probably the strangest I have ever had, in that although we shared a bed for well over a year, we never really shared each other's minds. I did have strong feelings for her, but I never really communicated that to her and so the relationship never properly took root. I always assumed that I was just a bonk to Clare, and vice versa, and yet, in truth, if we had sat down and frankly discussed how we felt, I think we would have realized that we were only a hair's breadth away from getting it together.

In 1993, Simpson's of Cornhill plc gave me another restaurant to oversee. Palio, on Westbourne Grove, was idling on a turnover of about £6,000 a week, although its design and facilities justified a much higher one. I wanted to maximize its appeal as an old-fashioned Italian trattoria, giving good value, great buzz. I saw a happy hour, live jazz two or three times a week and a whole new team running the show, but it would take me a few months to persuade my directors at Simpson's to let me have my way. They had bought out 190 Queensgate and made me a full director of the company. My role was creative director, with a portfolio of 190, Dell'Ugo and Palio, and I was also allowed to keep on my consultancy with Zen, though my brief was to try to use it to get the Zen group to sell Zoe to Simpson's, which eventually they did. These were exciting times, and Simpson's seemed to be a great team to work for.

190 was still my baby, although it was a frustrating business to run. The problem, ironically, was the success of Bistrot 190. I had helped to set up a deal for 190 to take over the catering at the Gore Hotel when it was bought by a couple of well-to-do guys, Peter McKay and Douglas Blaine. The Gore Hotel had been a pretty sleazy joint: unbeknownst to the management, the night porter had been doing a roaring trade arranging hookers for businessmen. It had once had great character but it had been allowed to run down. Peter and Douglas changed all that, completely renovating the rooms with great panache and packing them full of antiques.

Before we took over the catering, all that was on offer were sandwiches, soup and scampi-in-a-basket. My senior directors at 190 wanted to negotiate the deal with the Gore, and they offered them 15 per cent of turnover with no ceiling on the payments. When I urged the board to put a cap of £100,000 on the agreement, they told me I must be mad if I thought the turnover would reach a level where that could become an issue – it was, after all, only a forty-eight-seater restaurant. My pleas were overruled. Maybe it wasn't my place to get involved in the finances, but they should have listened. The new owners of the Gore would have jumped at £100,000. As it was, in my best year at Bistrot 190 we paid the

Gore £220,000, in the process setting the dubious record of shelling out the highest restaurant rent in London on a square-footage basis, a success but a crying shame.

CHAPTER TWENTY-SEVEN

MY LOVE LIFE WAS PRETTY TANGLED BUT MY RELATIONSHIP WITH Simpson's of Cornhill was trucking along nicely. True, they had recently made a disastrous purchase – thirty Muswell's restaurants, most of them on their last legs – but thankfully these weren't part of my portfolio. When my latest love interest failed, I threw myself into my work. Simpson's had also acquired some Whitbread pubs, and I was given one of these to run, in the City of London, a building of great character in a vaulted arch beneath London Bridge Station. We opened it as Café dell'Ugo, and I appointed my chef from Queensgate, an Australian called Chris Millar, who had worked marvels at 190, to oversee its launch.

Chris was, like me, not the most organized guy in the world, but he was one of the finest young chefs I had ever encountered, and by this time I had seen a few. Two of my chefs from Ménage à Trois, for example, Stuart Busby and Chris Suter, had won the Young Chef of the Year award in different years, achievements that made me very proud. And another Aussie, Philip Johnson, who worked for me twice, first at Ménage and later at dell'Ugo, went home and opened a restaurant in Brisbane called Ecco, which was named the best restaurant in Australia. Chris, too, eventually had to return to Oz, his visa having expired, but not before he gave Café dell'Ugo a fantastic kick-start. He later returned to the UK to work on several occasions and has become a very good friend of mine. Whenever I'm in Australia visiting my children, I try to catch up with him. He is now, I am glad to report, making a name for himself out there.

Chris's replacement at Café dell'Ugo was every bit his equal but had even greater potential, not least because of the time she had on her side. This was Kille Enna, who wrote to me from Denmark asking me to interview her. She was eighteen years old. So determined was she to be considered that she flew over from Denmark at her own expense for the interview. In all my years of hiring chefs I have never encountered so much passion for food, especially for fish. She told me that to get a proper feel for fish she had taken up swimming. Extraordinary.

I thought to myself at the time, this girl will turn out to be either a genius or a complete fruitcake. And when it comes to chefs, the dividing line between the two can be extremely fine. You need only look at Marco Pierre White and Gordon Ramsay to see that.

I took Kille on at 190. It was a gamble, but it worked. At least, it worked brilliantly for me, though I can't speak for the rest of my staff. Kille's passion for the job was well beyond the call of duty, and she had a strong self-belief. Her one fault – and in this she was very much a girl after my own heart – was that she told it like it was. Within her first couple of weeks she managed to get up the nose of every chef at 190 by telling them that their cooking was crap. I loved it. It was like looking at myself twenty years earlier. But, again like me, she was also uncontrollable, and if I had let her stay it would have cost me all my other chefs at 190.

I didn't want to lose a talent like Kille's so, against the judgement of everybody else, I took another gamble. I made her head chef at Café dell'Ugo.

A nineteen-year-old head chef was completely unheard of, and I was widely assumed to have taken leave of my senses, but, once I had coached her in the finer arts of personnel management, Kille didn't let me down. She had a very abrupt manner, but once you got to know her she was an angel. She was, I suppose, a bit of a teacher's pet, and I treated her very much as the daughter I had not yet had. At weekends and during her holidays she used to stay at my cottage at Shiplake. In the kitchen she was frustrated by the inadequacy of those around her, but here she was very much at peace with herself. She loved the countryside, she loved gardening, and when she was visiting we'd cook together and talk food for hours. She had a wonderful calming effect on me.

Our affection for each other was misunderstood, and the usual gossip that abounds in kitchens, fuelled by the jealousies of my other head chefs, led to rumours that I was having an affair with

Kille. It wasn't true. Much as I loved her, it was a paternal kind of love. But rumours like that are very destructive, and in the end the attitude of the other chefs drove her away. My loss became Denmark's gain. Kille is now a real star over there. She has already written a couple of cookbooks and has her own television series. I hope she goes from strength to strength.

In the early part of my second stint as a restaurateur I had some seriously good young talent working for me. One guy who went on not only to become a really good chef, especially in pastry work, but also to launch a television career was James Martin, who I discovered at Scarborough Catering College, although I often joke that I discovered him on the streets of Scarborough selling copies of the *Big Issue*.

I was up in Scarborough judging the students' cookery at the end of a course they did with Brian Turner. As we wandered around the kitchens watching the students prepare their dishes, it was obvious James was a star in the making. His dishes were excellent: they seemed to stand head and shoulders above the others. At the end of the day's work, before Brian could get in first, I offered him a job at 190 Queensgate, which he accepted. I have been critical of colleges for some of the badly trained students they turn out, but I have to say that Scarborough was an exception, and I have taken on several of their graduates.

I am often asked by parents how their kids should go about getting started in catering. My advice to youngsters is to find a restaurant or hotel you really like and write to the management asking for a job. And don't give up. If you are rejected, write again, this time saying you'll work for a couple of weeks without pay doing anything, even the washing up. That will show potential employers how keen you are and how much enthusiasm you have for the job. When I hire someone it is enthusiasm that I want to see above all else; a desire to succeed. You do of course need a grounding in the basics, for which I would recommend a day-release course at a catering college, but there is no substitute for working on the shop floor. You develop speed, you build up confidence, you gain a grasp of reality. I see so many college kids who might well know their theory inside out floundering as soon as they are faced with the real world. All too often they just lose the plot and throw in the towel.

In a kitchen you will learn teamwork. You learn to accept criticism without taking it personally, to have a joke, to laugh. It's

A very happy day.

Left, from top: Preparing a canapé party at No. 10 with the focus on food for kids – Cherie obviously just ate the snail; with my middle white pigs. The big one is lunch, the others crackling!; never the shrinking violet – advertising organic milk. **Opposite:** At Notting Grill, our restaurant; she's a nice girl, really – mates Brian Turner and Aldo Zilli with Anthea Turner; Ann Widdecombe and Ainsley on *Ready, Steady, Cook*.

Opposite: Shooting *Food & Drink* in my kitchen; all in a good cause – making an exhibition of myself with the Full Monty on *Children in Need*. Ainsley Harriot, James Martin, Brian Turner and Tony Tobin. **Right, from top:** *I'm a Celebrity* . . . in the jungle with Sian Lloyd; caught like a kipper; doing my bushtucker trial; leading the jungle revolution: 'f**k the calorific value'.

Above left: Jaybe on honeymoon – at the Colombe d'Or in St Paul de Vence. **Below left:** Jaybe's tottering totty – Stringfellow girls. **Below right:** My new family – Frank and Maeve Shiel, Jaybe's parents.

Above: Toby-Jack gets his first food lecture. **Below left:** Our little monkeys – Toby-Jack and Billie-Lara. **Below right:** The old and the new at Notting Grill. Toby-Jack, me, Billie-Lara, Jaybe, Blake and Sam.

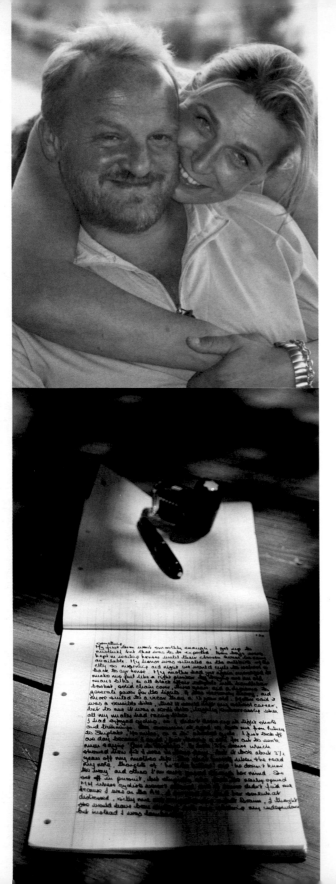

Top: Happiness is a girl called Jaybe. **Bottom:** No ghostwriters for mc. A page from the manuscript for this book – note real pen, real ink. What's a computer?

hard, often punishing, but once the team see that you are not going to let them down and that you put your heart and soul into your work, you'll be welcomed into a great fraternity and doors will open for you.

James Martin did just that. Within a few days of coming down from Yorkshire he had slotted into the team. It was swim or sink for him. On only about his second day, the pastry chef had a hissy fit and walked out, and James had to step into his shoes. He did so well that we never needed to replace the pastry chef. It was a very busy restaurant, but James absorbed the pressure and showed that he had the steel to deal with whatever circumstances threw at him.

Of course, you can't keep keen youngsters for ever. You have to let them fly the nest and develop their careers. Sometimes they return, sometimes they don't, but if you've treated your staff properly there will always be respect for you and they never forget. James has always kept in touch and has never been afraid to pick up the phone to ask for advice, or just to have a chat, and we remain great mates.

When James needed an agent he approached Limelight Management, who look after me, but because he went in cold, without any introduction or recommendation, he got turned down. So I gave them a call and pleaded with Fiona and Linda to take him on. 'He'll be a star,' I told them. 'Trust me.' They did, and he has never let them down. Since then James and I have done several television programmes together, including of course *Ready, Steady, Cook*, and now, when I see him doing well, I get a fleeting glow of paternal pride and think to myself, That's my boy!

I had a lot of good friends among my staff at that time, including Mark Emberton, my new head chef at Dell'Ugo, Francesca Hazard, the assistant manager, Sam Kemp at Zoe and my feisty secretary, Luisa Alves. We all enjoyed each other's company and spent a lot of our spare time together. Luisa, a Zimbabwean, was good, bad and loud, and at first she managed to get up quite a few noses, including that of Martin Romney, my general manager at Dell'Ugo – they were always fighting – but I stuck to my guns and kept her on. There was something about her that warmed the cockles of my heart. She was more of a PA than a secretary; in fact sometimes it was worse than having a nagging wife. For a while she often fulfilled the social duties of a wife, too. When I wanted a partner to accompany me somewhere and left it too late to consult my little black book, she would be there at my side: drinks parties, openings, book launches, even the occasional dinner. But she became overprotective. She would refuse to let callers speak to me and her telephone manner often appalled me. But she was great company and was a terrific listener. She was always telling me it was time to stop screwing around and settle down, to which I would reply: 'There's no rush. If you go looking you'll never find. Take life in your stride and someone will come out of the woodwork.'

And I was slowly rebuilding from the ashes of the divorce, the failed relationships, the repossession of my property and the loss of my business. I wrote a wine and food companion called *Supernosh* with Malcolm Gluck, a spin-off from his very successful *Superplonk* wine guide, which went on to achieve good sales, and secured a column in the *Sunday Times* called '30-Minute Menu', both of which had been instigated by Limelight Management. So the funds were coming in, and even though for the most part they were going out again just as quickly as I desperately tried to pay off my debts, I was getting there. I even had a reasonable car again: a Jaguar XJS. In truth it was a bit of a brute, but it was a vast improvement on the GTi.

It was time to take a step up to the next rung of the ladder and, as had happened when I had first put my foot back on it, three events combined to give me a leg up. The first was that I met the girl I was going to marry, though of course she didn't know it at the time. Secondly, I was promoted to managing director of Simpson's of Cornhill, a promotion that brought with it a hefty pay rise, and third, along came *Ready, Steady, Cook*.

My future wife, Jacinta Shiel, was about to become the oldest commis chef in town by taking a position at 190 Queensgate. I had admired her for some time, although she was unaware of that. She was chief 'tutu' at Stringfellow's nightclub (I should point out this was well before the days of the 'Cabaret of Angels' and the lap-dancers). Peter Stringfellow had been quite a good mate of mine since the time when I used to drop into his club to unwind after finishing for the night at Ménage, and I'd got to know him better when I ran into him on holiday in Greece one year.

I had been invited by Fay Maschler and her husband Reg to stay with them at a villa they were renting there. I was rather surprised by the invitation, but I accepted and had a fabulous time. Reg, Fay and her sister Beth Coventry, who was also there, all loved Greece, and they put me at my ease and helped me relax. My idea of relaxation might sound a bit like a busman's holiday to some people, because I just love cooking when I'm abroad. I mooch around the local shops and markets, buy wonderful fresh produce and take it home to do some spontaneous creating. In Greece we all joined in with the cooking, and in such an unstressed, laid-back way that I didn't feel at all uncomfortable about preparing meals for the doyenne of food critics. One night I even took over the kitchen of a local restaurant and produced dinner for a group of Fay's friends – among them Peter Stringfellow, who happened to be staying in the same village – and we all had a ball.

After that holiday I began popping into Stringy's again, where I would join Peter at his table. He is an incredibly generous man, and was always a brilliant host. In some ways our later lives have followed similar paths. We've both had extreme highs and lows and then new highs, we can both be a little incautious with our money and we both live life to the full, although I probably get to bed a little earlier than Peter does.

The girls who worked at Stringfellow's were all pretty exceptional looking, but Jacinta stood out even in their company. Not surprisingly, I didn't have the bottle to chat her up. And in any case, I was well aware that she must have been propositioned by hundreds of the clients at the club, and no doubt had a wide selection of well-rehearsed put-down lines at the ready. Besides, I learned that she already had a long-term boyfriend, another Tony. So for now it would just have to be admiration from afar. But just as the *Titanic* and the iceberg were destined to meet, so were Jacinta and me, but with much nicer consequences.

One morning, having spent about five years at Stringfellow's and a dozen in clubland in total, Jacinta woke up and suddenly decided, that's it, I've had enough. She felt it was time to revolutionize her life, and that included putting her relationship with her boyfriend on hold. She fancied learning how to cook and signed up for an intensive course at Ballymaloe Cookery School in Shanagarry, near Cork in Ireland. It was a good choice. Ballymaloe, run by a whirling dervish called Darina Allen, is one of the best cookery schools I know. Darina has often pushed her students in my direction and over the years I've had some marvellous Ballymaloe graduates. The fact that not one of them has been a failure is a tribute to her great teaching skills. One of Jacinta's fellow students on the course was the talented Irish youngster Eddie Walsh who, after working with me for a couple of years, went off to join one of my heroines, Alice Waters, in Berkeley, California.

The school is set in magnificent grounds, where Darina grows and rears organic produce. She and her husband Timmy have created a magical business here, the perfect partnership for the world-renowned Ballymaloe House hotel. Every three years or so I take a three-day course at the school as a guest chef and we have a whale of a time. Everyone is so friendly. I stay at Darina's cottage overlooking Ballycotton Harbour, the most perfect setting in the world. It's one of the reasons I fell in love with Ireland.

After completing her cookery course, Jacinta – Jay for short – was taken on at 190 by my young, eccentric head chef, Harry Greenhalgh. She accepted the job in spite of Darina Allen's words of warning: 'You watch out for that Antony Worrall Thompson. He's a bit of a womanizer.' I was away in the States when she joined us, returning to find Harry all of a flutter. 'Let me introduce you to the new commis from Ireland,' he announced. 'She's a bit of all right,' he added, out of earshot.

And there she was. A dream come true. I was so gobsmacked that on being introduced to her I was completely lost for words. Instead of speaking I just looked at her up and down and walked away. Jay was not impressed. She denounced me to Harry in fairly scathing terms, basically expressing the view that I was appallingly rude.

Over the next few months, I rarely went into the kitchen at 190 except when I knew Jay would be working. Even then I didn't go there to cook: I just wandered in to check on things. I always made a point of giving her a hard time about something she was doing wrong and then just striding off. She thought I was ghastly.

On her nights off, Jay worked at a club in Soho. She decided to celebrate her twenty-ninth birthday there in May 1994 with a group of friends and I was very surprised when she invited me to join them. I said I would try to make it, but instead I stayed at home and told her the next day I was sorry, I'd had to wash my hair. I was playing games, I know. But put yourself in my place. This beautiful woman was used to men throwing themselves at her at Stringfellow's, including quite a few famous names, and she had turned them all down. If I made a move for her she'd run a mile. My only hope was to make her come to me. It wasn't going to be easy, but then, that's half the fun.

I remembered my grandad telling me: 'To win the war you've first got to win the battle.' He had written a book called *Letters to my Son*, and in the chapter entitled 'How to Choose the Perfect Woman', he advised waiting until at least the age of thirty before contemplating marriage (I wish I had read it earlier than I did) and then to pick someone who was roughly half your own age plus seven years. It was meant to be: I was forty-four and Jay was twenty-nine.

I continued with the frosty approach, generally acting the boss and keeping any conversation curt in the hope that Jay's curiosity would get the better of her and she would start to wonder why it was I behaved so rudely towards her. Don't ask me why, but I felt confident of success. I was having coffee with my PA, Luisa, in the Bistrot one day when Jay wandered through in a very short turquoise dress, a dress that fitted her like a glove, accentuating her every flawless curve. Noticing my eyes following this vision, Luisa remarked: 'You like her, don't you?'

'Yep. And you know what, Luisa? I'm going to marry that girl.' Luisa was shocked: someone had finally come out of the woodwork.

That very same evening, as I was sitting with a group of girls in the bar at 190, Jay came in with her flatmate, Kate. I learned much later that she said to Kate then: 'Kate, I'm going to have him.'

Uncanny, or what? Though the magic of that meeting of minds was perhaps slightly tainted by Kate's less-than-flattering reply.

'What, that fat git? You've got to be joking.'

Before they went home for the night, the staff usually had a glass of something in the Bistrot to unwind after the last customer had left. As I returned from my restaurant rounds one night, I noticed that they were still there and tried to sneak past without being seen. But Jay spotted me and came after me. 'Don't be an old stick-in-the-mud,' she said. 'Come and buy us a drink.' It was obvious that they had had a couple more than the one drink they were officially allowed. I bought a round anyway and went over to sit with the team. Although there were plenty of other seats available, Jay came and settled herself on my knee. If the rest of the staff seemed a little taken aback, they weren't half as surprised as I was. Still, I kept up my cool façade, though I felt anything but cool. When I had finished my drink and said it was time to turn in, Jay suddenly planted a kiss smack on my lips – and it was no chaste, 1930s film kiss, either.

This was a thrilling development, but now what? I was intrigued when, about a week later, Jay asked if we could have a chat. But my hopes were dashed when I discovered that what she wanted was not so much to have a chat as to give in her notice. She could no longer afford to live on the £9,000 a year I paid her, which was quite understandable given that she had taken a huge drop in income from the big bucks she had been earning at Stringy's. She also pointed out that, since her long-term ambition was to own her own restaurant, her reason for coming to the Bistrot had been to learn from me. Yet so far she had not once seen me cook in the 190 kitchen. She was right. At this stage of my role with Simpson's I had rather lost the plot on the cooking front and was more of an office boy or director than a chef.

I advised her not to be too hasty about leaving altogether and asked her whether she would be interested in an assistant manager's job I had coming up at Palio. Jay saw that the front-of-house experience would be valuable. She accepted. In the meantime, I promised her that before she left 190, I would cook one night in the Bistrot. And although the other staff were highly pissed off at this disruption of their routine, and grumbled that she was rocking the boat, I kept my promise.

It was not until after she had left that I launched my opening gambit. I was organizing a Friday-night birthday dinner party for Fay Maschler at her home in Hampstead, and asked Jay whether she would like to help me with it. I was encouraged by the speed with which she agreed. So far, so good. The assistant arrived at Fay's punctually at 5.30 pm as arranged, but the chef – with all the food – did not make it until 6.45. I was greeted with some annoyance. 'How could you leave me alone for over an hour with people I don't even know?'

'What's the problem?' I chuckled. 'Fay and Reg don't bite.'

But it took Jay some time to calm down.

She had told me that she would need to leave at 9.30 to go to her club job in Soho, but at that stage we hadn't even served the main course. Jay said she would stay on a bit longer. A good sign, I thought to myself. We were getting on really well. Jay admitted to me later that by then she was beginning to see me in a different light. Towards the end of the evening, we were sharing drinks and cigarettes astride Fay's dustbins in the back garden.

Of all the stupid things I have done in my life, taking up smoking at the age of forty and a half must be one of the stupidest. Since my early childhood, when lighting my mother's cigarettes had been one of my filial duties, I had always been firmly anti-smoking. My downfall was that all the girls I fancied when I became single again were smokers. The message of that old advertising campaign was absolutely true: they did taste like old ashtrays, and from that point of view, kissing them was pretty grim. Being a chef, I thought the solution would be to acclimatize my taste buds to theirs, so to do this I used to smoke the ends of their cigarettes. And, as all smokers know to their cost, it doesn't take long to get hooked. Dumb, dumb, dumb.

Back in Hampstead that night, Jay never did make it to work. After all the guests had gone and we'd cleaned up, she and I stayed behind for a drink with the hosts. I was getting knowing looks from Reg conveying approval of my choice of assistant. And it has to be said that by this time she was being very friendly. We must have looked to him as if we were an item.

We finally left at about 2 am and I offered to drive Jay home to the flat she shared with Kate in Highbury. As we pulled up outside she tried to give me a kiss and, sticking resolutely to my game plan, I turned my head away. Short and sweet has nothing on long and sweet, and I didn't want to give her any opportunity to blame anything that might have happened otherwise on drink. I wanted Jay in the right circumstances, and that meant I had to be patient.

So she just got out of the car and went into her flat. I found out later that she was furious with herself. 'I can't believe I tried to kiss him!' she exploded to Kate. 'How embarrassing! And what's even worse, he refused to kiss me. He's so *rude*. He just has to be gay.' I'd have had a good giggle to myself if I'd been a fly on the wall.

Having had the weekend to puzzle over my behaviour, on the Monday evening she popped into Dell'Ugo with Kate – they were 'just passing', said the girl who had never set foot in Dell'Ugo before, even though the club where she worked was just a few doors away. Yeah, right, I thought. We repaired to Stringfellow's, where a good time was had by all and Jay demonstrated her 'dancing' skills. After I walked Jay and Kate back to their car, which was parked in Soho Square, she tried to kiss me again, and again I presented her with my cheek. I'd love to have heard the conversation in the car on the way home.

'He's definitely gay.'

'No, he's not, Jay. I think he really likes you.'

'OK, I'm going to give it one more go, but if he still doesn't show any interest, that's it.'

She was back at Dell'Ugo the following night, where she found me having a meeting with my then managing director, Mr Paul 'I want clubby not pubby' Reece from Nottingham. I motioned to Jay to wait for me. She did, and that evening we gelled at last. We relaxed together and laughed, and I showed my true colours – I knew the moment had come to drop the act, and I couldn't have timed it better if I really had heard that dialogue in the car the night before. Fay Maschler's dinner had been the turning point, but I had needed to go the extra few yards to be absolutely sure of Jay. It had taken a huge amount of willpower – after all, it had been love at first sight for me from the moment I laid eyes on her at Stringfellow's – but it had paid off. From then on I dedicated my life to one person, to Jaybe – my pet name for Jacinta. It took us another four days to cement the foundations of our life together, but what great foundations they were.

CHAPTER TWENTY-EIGHT

IT WAS SHORTLY AFTER JAY AND I GOT TOGETHER THAT I WAS promoted to managing director of Simpson's of Cornhill – a decision that surprised many people, including our chairman, Roy Ackerman. Up to this point my portfolio had consisted solely of restaurants I had opened myself – 190, Dell'Ugo, Palio, Café dell'Ugo – but on my appointment my operations were widened to include some new restaurant purchases: the Atrium, a parliamentary restaurant on Millbank; De Cecco, a very busy Italian joint in Parson's Green; the Lexington in Soho; the City Jamaica Inn; and a real plum: the restaurant after which the group was named, the original Simpson's of Cornhill.

It was the purchase of Muswell's that had proved my predecessor's downfall. Paul Reece was a nice guy and he taught me a lot, but this group had been losing money hand over fist and taking more than a big bite out of the profits my portfolio had been making. Paul had already managed to sell quite a few of the outlets and when he left the company he took most of the rest with him, but on becoming managing director I urged Sandy Singh, the chief executive of Baldwin, our parent company, to sell the few that remained. In the meantime, I gave them an improved, stopgap menu. Even so, as they were scattered all over the south of the country they were very difficult to control.

Roy Ackerman had employed a great executive chef, Mick Geraghty, to oversee the food in Muswell's. Mick was a great operator, and although he was strict, he was a guy who looked after his staff. He worked in the same way as I did, favouring inspiration and incentives over intimidation, and he and I got on like a house on fire. But he was always going to be fighting a losing battle, with little help from the board and even less from his front-of-house executive, an old-school caterer called Jürgen Schmidt, who preferred to rule with a rod of iron. When Mick finally threw in the towel it was a sad day. He had taught me a lot and we had built up a great friendship.

Among Mick's many talents, he was the best man I knew for organizing large functions, so he was the first person I went to when I was asked to put on a banquet for 750 in aid of the Royal Marsden Hospital, which specializes in treating cancer, at the Guildhall in the City of London. The event was to be attended by many dignitaries, with the Princess of Wales, who was president of the Royal Marsden charity appeal, as special guest. We decided to make it an all-star occasion in the kitchen as well. We called it Chefs of the Decade, a title that appealed to the egos of the culinary world, and consequently not one of the chefs we approached refused the invitation. In all I attracted about forty of the best, among them both Roux brothers, Marco Pierre White, Brian Turner, Richard Shepherd, Anton Edelmann and Peter Kromberg. Looking back, I don't quite know how we managed it. And it was a brilliant dinner, with all the attending chefs, who were as always incredibly generous with their time, really pulling their weight. Thanks to them it turned out to be one of the best dinners I have ever helped organize, and it raised £100,000 for the charity.

The function I am most proud of having staged, though, was the British lunch to mark the opening of the Channel Tunnel in Folkestone on 6 May 1996. I remember the date because it was the day of my son Blake's twelfth birthday. There were to be 1,500 guests, including the Queen and President Mitterrand of France, the whole Cabinet and the opposition front benches, plus celebrities from both sides of the Channel, and security was extremely tight.

I had been approached the previous year, along with five other top chefs cooking in the UK, and asked whether I would devise one of the courses. Three of the six of us were French. I told the organizers that I would be honoured to contribute. 'But why have you invited three French chefs to cook the British lunch? Don't tell me the French have invited any Brits to cook in France for their celebrations,' I said, adding that I thought a team of seven British chefs would be more appropriate. I was making what I considered to be a valid point, not trying to be awkward, but when a few months passed and I heard no more about it, I concluded that I must have upset the organizers and they had decided to drop me. But with only seven weeks to go I was contacted again – and suddenly, I was being asked to construct the menu on my own, working with a team of professional caterers.

This was the kind of challenge I love, and I was raring to sock it to the French. May is the perfect time for some terrific British produce – new-season lamb, asparagus, seakale, early summer fruits and some great wild salmon – and we took full advantage of everything available. We even served a couple of very acceptable English wines. I had a team of about twelve chefs, under Mark Emberton's leadership, working with the caterers and making sure everything was done to the letter, with a complete ban on any hint of a packet stock or sauce. It all went like clockwork and, most importantly as far as I was concerned, the production seemed to impress the French guests.

There were only two minor hitches, one of which was the dandelion for my salad mix. The Kent vegetable supplier had assured us he understood what was required, but when it was delivered we had a bit of a surprise. Instead of gathering the wonderful bitter, yellow leaves of the plant, some poor farmer had been out in the fields of Kent picking the heads off 7,500 dandelions. So needless to say, dandelion was off that day.

The other hitch involved the long arm of the law. The hotel where my team and I were staying was about twenty-five miles from Folkestone, all the local places having been booked up by journalists for months in advance. We spent the day before the event working hard at the venue and returned to the hotel at a reasonable hour, ready for a good night's sleep. We had been warned by Kent Police that, because of the tight security, if we did not arrive by 8 am we ran the risk of not being allowed in. But when I awoke the next morning I realized to my horror that it was already 7.15. We had all overslept.

It was just like that opening scene of *Four Weddings and a Funeral*. 'Fuck . . . fuck . . . FUCK!' Into the shower – 'Fuck! Fuck!' – into the car and wham, hit that motorway. I was booting it at about 120 mph when a blue flashing light zoomed up behind me. It was the Chief Constable. I explained the urgency and he was very understanding, but he still got his driver to book me. Then he gave us a police escort to the tunnel.

When I appeared in Folkestone Court I was charged with driving

at only 108 mph. Very generous. Against the advice of my friend
and lawyer Simon Bowen, I didn't appoint a legal representative. 'It
will be an automatic ban if you don't,' Simon warned me, but I had
this sneaking suspicion that given the circumstances I would get
away with it.

'It was like this, sir,' I said to the magistrate, 'I had to make a
choice between letting down Queen and country or accepting that
I may be caught speeding—'

He cut me short. 'Yes, yes, yes, Mr Worrall Thompson, we know
what you were doing, there's no need for any sob story. We've
decided in the circumstances to let you off with a caution.' Simon
couldn't believe it and I was very chuffed: as well as escaping a ban,
I had saved myself £500 in legal expenses.

Even an impending court appearance did nothing to take the
shine off the day. It was great to be part of an historic moment.
I was very proud, too, of my young team that day, and the privilege
was all mine.

Supporting me in everything, by this stage, was Jacinta. It was a
match made in heaven. I felt almost as if she had somehow been
sent specially to me: I had admired her from afar and now we were
together. With her clubland background, it would have been understandable if I had worried that she might turn out to be a bit of a
hard nut; that perhaps her beauty hid a heart of ice, and once she
had cracked my carapace of rudeness she would she just blow me
out in bubbles. But if I had any such concerns – and I honestly don't
recall that I did – they would have been quickly dispelled on our
first 'date'.

I had arranged to pick Jay up at her flat in Highbury. I was not
going to mess this one up: everything had to be right, so flowers
and champagne were the order of the day. When she opened the
door to me she looked amazing: a white Ghost outfit, white
trainers, a gentle tan and just enough make-up. I'm not a great fan
of slap-it-on foundation. I much prefer the natural look. Jay usually
looks as good in the morning as she does last thing at night.

I was playing our date by ear so I hadn't made any reservations.
We ended up in an oriental restaurant, but the venue was irrelevant.
The point was that I was with her; that I had time alone in her
company to get a proper sense of her. I noticed her nose (perfect),
ears (lovely), eyes (gentle). Jaybe was surprised. Other men had
always commented on her body rather than her face. Don't get me
wrong, that was flawless as well, but I have a special appreciation

for noses because my own nose and I have never really seen eye to eye. As a baby I had a great nose, but it didn't last long. Seven broken hooters later you get philosophical, but still, I would have liked a nose like Jay's.

That night, and after the next couple of dinners we shared, she was quick off the mark to pay the bill herself. That's the kind of girl Jay is, generous to a fault, but it was a bit disconcerting. I'm quite an old-fashioned boy – I like to pay, and to open doors for women, all that kind of thing – but her generosity was endearing.

To start with our relationship was very cloak-and-dagger. If it got out that a junior member of the 190 kitchen staff was having an affair with the boss, it was hardly going to make for harmony between her and her workmates. So if I stayed at her place I would drive her to work in the morning and drop her off at the Albert Hall; if she stayed with me, she would sneak in and out via the basement using the lift. By now the owners had built me my very own love shack on the roof of the Gore Hotel. It was literally that, a purpose-built shed with bedroom, bath and small kitchen/sitting room, but pretty well all I needed was a bed, as I was always either working or out playing.

But what I'm sure Jacinta initially believed was going to be a fling was developing very quickly, and before long we were spending every night together. I took her with me to Italy to help me teach a course at a cookery school, and on our return we went public. It was a tough time for Jay. Workmates can be very cruel, and hers accused her of all sorts of things, including being interested in me only for my money. That was some joke, considering that my bank account was still virtually empty, though happily that state of affairs was improved with my enhanced salary as managing director of Simpson's of Cornhill.

Sam Kemp now came into our central office to help Francesca Hazard, promoted to general manager, while Luisa Alves, my PA, went off to be assistant manager at De Cecco. I had promised Jacinta a management role, but this was not going to be easy in our new circumstances. It was a plan that was not welcomed by Francesca, who thought it a bad idea for me to appoint someone so close to me to a management position, but I stuck to my guns. First Jay did a stint under one of my best managers, Art Duquette, an American who had started as my head barman at 190 Queensgate and gone on to pull Palio up by its bootstraps. He was a gregarious man who could lift the atmosphere in a room just by walking in, and he had introduced jazz and a great buzz to this small restaurant on Westbourne Grove. As a result of his hard work and charisma it became one of the stars of my portfolio. American service can be over the top but Art usually got the balance just right.

My next step with Jay was to make her general manager of the Atrium. Well, I was the boss, after all, and Jay deserved just as much of a chance to prove herself as anyone else. As it turned out, my decision was totally vindicated. She was the perfect appointment for a restaurant packed full of politicians and political journalists. She had exactly the right knack of flattering all those egos while remaining completely in control. The rise of New Labour was very much in evidence at the Atrium. During our first Christmas there, both a Tory and a Labour group had their parties at the restaurant on the same night. The Tories had house wine, while in the next-door room the Labour guests were quaffing champagne.

The crowning glory of 1994 was a totally unexpected event, namely Jacinta, in a bit of a flap, announcing to me that she was pregnant. I was thrilled. OK, so it hadn't been planned, and yes, it was all a bit soon, but what was the point in hanging about when everything was so perfect? I felt I had made a pig's ear of my bond with my Aussie kids, as they now were, and I was really excited at the prospect of having another shot at fatherhood. So I was ecstatic, and Jaybe was relieved.

There was one small problem, however: her parents. She had already been to see them at their home in Malahide, Dublin to explain to them face-to-face that she had a new man in her life, which was no easy task when they had been very fond of her long-standing previous boyfriend, Tony. And quite understandably – he was a great guy.

'I've got a new boyfriend,' she began.

'Oh, that's nice for you.' Doubtless they were wondering what had been wrong with the last one.

'He's an older man.' (Thanks, Jay.)

'How much older?'

'Fourteen years.'

Raised eyebrows.

'And there's more. He's been married before and he's got kids.'

Their reply was sympathetic and magnanimous. 'As long as you love him and he loves you, we can't see a problem.'

'Actually, he's been married twice.'

Slightly less sympathetic and magnanimous this time. 'Once is just about understandable,' said Jay's father, Frank. 'Twice is damned careless.'

And now, on top of this bombshell, Jaybe had to inform them she was having my baby. They were due to make their first visit to check out what their daughter had got herself into and were going to stay with us at my cottage in Shiplake. Jay asked me if I would be there to greet them and help her break the news, and I suggested it might be better if they absorbed this piece of information first and then met me. Thankfully, as parents always do, they took this hurricane in their stride, even if inwardly they were shocked at the speed at which everything was happening.

Later that day, after a couple of stiff drinks, they came up to Soho to meet me. I had decided to invite Francesca, Luisa, Sam and a few other close colleagues to join us at the local Pitcher and Piano in the hope that their presence would reduce the likelihood of any awkward silences at this important meeting. Safety in numbers, in other words. Although I was shitting bricks, the encounter went smoothly, Jay's parents were charm personified, warm, endearing, funny and welcoming. Maeve, Jay's mother, was slim and glamorous, with a wicked twinkle in her eye, and, just like her daughter, could win an Olympic gold in talking. Frank, who was much quieter, was, as I was to discover over the years, probably the kindest, most generous man I've ever had the pleasure of knowing.

It was later that evening, over dinner at Zilli's, that I received a grilling from Maeve. It was pretty daunting stuff but I did my best to win her over, warming every moment to this woman who obviously loved her daughter more than life itself. Jaybe kept inter-jecting, 'Oh Mum, I can't believe you said that,' as she slid lower and lower into her chair. But dinner was lovely and I think I passed my exam in loving her daughter, though I definitely failed the one in heading immediately for the altar.

Despite the third degree I was relieved and happy. Jay's parents were like the parents I had always wanted. They were a proper couple, two sides of a coin, with Mum doing the talking and Dad chipping in when the rare opportunity occurred. Although Frank had less to say, even at that first meeting his face expressed a warmth that made me want him as a dad. So from the very beginning, I never perceived the in-laws as outlaws. When I see such a harmonious, 'normal' family, it brings back the unease I have always felt about my own – a hotbed of discontent, not a family at war, exactly, but certainly not a loving family. Of course I loved my mum, but it was love at a distance. I needed some recognition from her, a few kind words to my face. Kind words about you to a third party are never quite the same. Jaybe, luckily for me, had the insight to see through my mother's aggressive façade, and slowly she broke down the barriers, something I had never really been able to do.

And once Mum had accepted that Jacinta was to be a permanent fixture in my life, she warmed up towards me. The three of us would have lunch together from time to time and I actually started to enjoy her company. We were due to meet for lunch one Sunday late in July 1995 when she called to cancel. She had a chest complaint, she said. I told her I hoped she would soon be better and arranged to see her the following Sunday instead.

The next day I flew out to Sardinia to do a programme for *The Travel Show*, which I was looking forward to. It's great sometimes to be invited to participate in programmes that don't involve cooking, and Sardinia, of course, was where I had got involved with my first-ever restaurant, the Rosemary near Porto Cervo, which we revisited during the trip. It had grown somewhat in the intervening years, but the atmosphere was the same. The garden was just as I remembered it and the picture of the cow was still there.

On the Tuesday evening I had a call from my new PA, Marie-Regine, to say that my mother had been taken into the Royal Berkshire Hospital with a chest problem. I rang the hospital to check on her condition, but they refused to give out any information.

'Look,' I said at last. 'I'm in Sardinia. Could you please tell me whether I should be booking an early flight home?'

Finally the penny dropped.

'Oh, I see. Well, I wouldn't worry – she'll be out by the weekend.'

Hallelujah. I rang off and phoned Jay to ask if she could pop down and visit Mum.

Jaybe was fantastic, visiting every day. On the Wednesday my mother was sitting on the side of the bed sharing sandwiches with her, but on the Thursday Jay arrived to find a completely different woman: bedridden, unable to hold a conversation, drugged up to the eyeballs with morphine. Jay was appalled. She asked the doctors what the problem was, and now she found herself up against the wall of silence. They refused to tell her what was going on, even though she was eight and a half months pregnant with my mother's grandchild. She had to find out from my great-aunt Morna, who had visited earlier that day, that the doctors thought Mum had cancer. Jay called me that night to warn me to prepare for the worst. She didn't want to mention the C-word; she simply told me that the doctors were carrying out tests. I couldn't believe it. One minute my mother was in hospital with a cough and dodgy chest, the next she was lying there dying. I flew back from Sardinia early on the Friday morning and went straight to the hospital.

When I saw her I was completely choked up. My mother was a shadow of her former self. She barely recognized me, and she couldn't speak, although I could see that she wanted to. And I really needed to speak to her. I asked her if she wanted to come off the morphine so that she could talk to me, and she nodded.

The next day, Saturday, she was lucid and managed a two-hour conversation with Jacinta and me. We talked about everything: we cleared up the past, and for the first time she told me she was really proud of what I had achieved. I cried. Over the previous year we had become so much closer, thanks largely to Jaybe, who had been the bridge we both needed to cross the divide. Mum was so looking forward to being a grandmother again, but sadly she would not live to see her new grandchild.

We returned to the hospital that evening to find her back on the morphine. I had had my last conversation with her. She managed to squeeze my hand and raise a smile, and a tear tumbled down her sallow cheek. It was the last time I saw her alive. At six o'clock the next morning – the day of the postponed Sunday lunch, put back by just one week – the hospital rang me to tell me to rush over as she was slipping away. She died five minutes before we got there. I cried my eyes out, great, big heaving sobs. Jaybe cried with me. I kissed my mother on the forehead to say goodbye.

I was in a dreadful state, not only because I felt I had been robbed of a mother I was finally getting to know and understand, but also because her new grandchild would never know its grandmother. She missed the birth by only a couple of weeks.

If any funeral can ever be said to be a happy occasion, my mother's was a happy funeral, at least insofar as she had the send-off she wanted. As an actress she would have been delighted that the final curtain came down to a full house. All her friends and what was left of our family turned up, together with many of my friends, some of whom had never actually met my mother. But that is what friends are for, and they were a great support. My team from head office volunteered to help, preparing a great lunch for the guests, and as well as taking charge of the catering they did everything they could to keep up my spirits, which was beyond the call of duty. But of course, it was still a choking occasion, and it took a supreme effort not to break down as I offered up a tribute to my mother at our beautiful little church in Shiplake.

There is a terrible feeling of finality about losing the last member of your immediate family. Even if you haven't been close, you have a sense that there is no one left to turn to. While I may not have asked my mother very often for advice, she had always been there if I needed her, and the knowledge that she was gone affected me much more than I'd ever imagined it would. My strength came from Jaybe. She was a rock during those ten days between my mother's death and the funeral, and the support she gave me was even more remarkable given that she was about to go into labour for the first time at any moment.

Twelve days after we said goodbye to my mother at the hospital, and only four days after her funeral, it was hello to her grandchild, Toby-Jack Duncan Worrall Thompson. Duncan was in honour of my mum, her family name.

Toby was the first of my children to be helped into the world by the NHS. I have no complaints about the Royal Free Hospital, though the bedside manner of the South African nurse who gave Jay her final scan could have done with some brushing up. 'Do you want the good news or the bad news?' is hardly the kind of question you want to hear at that stage of the game.

'The good news,' she went on, 'is that your baby is a perfect-sized boy. The bad news is he has rather a big head. It's nothing to panic about. It's just that your baby's head is at the top end of the head scale.'

'Takes after me, then,' I remarked, trying to make light of news that had clearly alarmed Jay. Big head means pain and, tough cookie that she is, she isn't good with pain.

In spite of a few wobbles at the beginning, up till then Jay had taken pregnancy in her stride. Even when, three days before Toby's birth, I woke Jay with a jolt in the middle of the night by throwing all my weight on top of her, shouting: 'Stop! There's a red light!' and then rolling back to my own side of the bed again, in a deep sleep, she wasn't unduly concerned – except of course about the possibility of me having squashed the baby. Ever since I was five, when I was found sleepwalking on the Brighton seafront, I have walked and talked in my sleep, and by this time she was used to my occasionally strange night-time behaviour.

But she was annoyed, if not surprised, when, two nights later, I leaped on her again. This time I said: 'We've got the green light. It's a go.' Half an hour later her waters broke. Whether I had a premonition, whether I precipitated things by jumping on top of her, or whether it was just pure coincidence, I wouldn't like to say. It was four o'clock on the morning of 11 August 1995, and we were staying at Love Shack 190. After a couple of baths, Jay decided it was time for us to head for the hospital and for me to participate in the birth of our first child (as if I hadn't done enough already). I pointed out that the contractions were still coming only every twelve minutes, reminded her that we were supposed to wait until the gap had narrowed to five, and persuaded her that we should go to Soho for breakfast. I thought it would help if she did something to take her mind off things. And I was starving.

Breakfast at the Old Compton Café that morning was a surreal experience. The only other customers were a bunch of transvestites, all still in their ballroom glad rags from the night before. I was as excited as Jay was nervous, but we managed our breakfast. I wolfed mine down; Jay did the best she could in between contractions. I can't imagine what an American tourist – or anyone else, for that matter – walking into the Old Compton Café would have made of that scene: twelve Lily Savages, one woman in labour and a man who seemed oblivious of it all. Well, I was enjoying my breakfast.

We left the café at 7 am to discover that my car had been decorated with a parking ticket issued at 6.35. Bastards. We drove over to the Royal Free. Jaybe was desperate for gas and air, and I could have done with some myself. She progressed on to pethidine and then the epidural. I think she would gladly have accepted a general anaesthetic if it had been on offer. Then she asked me to shoot back to 190 for some clothes and things, which we'd neglected to bring with us, promising to call me if lift-off approached before I returned.

As I was leaving 190, loaded with armfuls of knickers, I met Rory Bremner coming in. So I put them down and joined him for another breakfast. I had first met Rory with the television presenter Penny Smith, his girlfriend at the time, and the two of them had spent a couple of days with us at Shiplake over Christmas. They made a great couple. Penny, bursting with brainpower, a wicked sense of humour and a lust for life that was exhausting, is absolutely gorgeous. On my list of desirable women she is beaten only by Jodie Foster and, of course, Jaybe. Rory, by contrast, is a shy man. He too has an amazing brain, and great talent, but he is very reserved. Sleeping with him must be like sleeping with a different man every night of the week, though I suppose the excitement of that would pall a bit when he's being John Major or Michael Fish.

Fortified by my second breakfast of the day, I was back at the hospital in plenty of time for the birth. Jaybe, even at the height of the worst contractions, still managed to look beautiful. I really appreciated the care the NHS took of Jay and Toby – no excuses or unnecessary instruments, just a big, kindly, capable, motherly woman who had probably delivered hundreds if not thousands of babies. She was in total control. One of Jay's legs on her hips and the other on mine – it was as simple as that. No doubt Jay didn't see it quite like that, but still. Poor Mum, who is doing all the hard work, misses all the excitement of that first sight of the head appearing – in our case with a little encouragement from me. 'Come on, my son. Jaybe, push harder!'

Not surprisingly, the response from Mum was: 'What the fuck do you think I'm doing!'

And so Toby-Jack arrived, at 6.25 pm, weighing 8lb 1oz, after a fourteen-hour labour, including breakfast – and it was only a few days before he started to look like me, except without the broken nose. As for Jaybe, she was up having a shower within half an hour of the birth, and two days later we all left the hospital together. Remarkably, Jay stepped straight into her jeans, and she looked great. From the hospital we headed directly for Foxtrot Oscar, where I had organized a group of friends to wet the baby's head. At that Sunday lunch two important decisions were made about Toby's future: his religion and his education. However, I can't pretend these were arrived at by reasoned discussion. We spoofed for them. Actually, I let Jay win as far as religion was concerned, although she will deny this. So Toby would be Catholic, which is fair enough – it's not as if I am any great shakes when it comes to matters of the Church. The second game I won fair and square for the right to choose which school he should attend. The perfect compromise.

CHAPTER TWENTY-NINE

BEFORE TOBY-JACK'S ARRIVAL, WE HAD DECIDED THAT ONCE THE BABY was born we would move out to Shiplake, in my view a much better environment for bringing up kids than the city. Grandmother's two cottages had now been passed down to me and it made sense to knock them into one. I am a great subscriber to the theory that if children grow up surrounded by nature and learn to respect animals and plants, they're far more likely to respect human beings.

It was the first big step we made together. Jaybe, very much a townie, was worried about it, and I understood her reservations. For a young, urban woman, the prospect of living down an isolated country lane miles from everyone and everything she knew was pretty daunting. But, as I pointed out, it was only an hour away from London, and her mates would probably enjoy a day out in the country. She was bound to make new friends locally, too. Jay, however, remained unconvinced. In the end we compromised by agreeing to give it six months. Then, if she wasn't happy, we'd move back to London.

The friend who would miss her the most was Kate, her Highbury flatmate. It took Katie quite a long time to warm to me. She had been very much a fan of Jay's ex, Tony, and the three of them had always got together on Friday nights, when it was something of a ritual for Kate – a real raven-haired temptress, dangerous but exciting, like her namesake in *The Taming of the Shrew* – to transform herself into a stunning, come-and-get-me vision of loveliness before they all hit the town. Then I had come along, and not only had I split up London's answer to the Liver Birds, but now I was responsible for one of the party animals going off to have a cub. So there was a bit of friction between Katie and me for a while. I did try to be pleasant to her, but perhaps not hard enough. Whatever the case, Jaybe had made her choice and Kate was going to have to accept it. To her credit, she persevered with me, and I am glad that she did, because we're all great mates now.

To Jay friendship is all important. At home in Ireland, her home had been full of affection and laughter. Her parents had dished out love in equal quantities to their four children and still had plenty left over for others who entered their lives, and their door was always open to friends and neighbours. In our first couple of years together, I was a bit stand-offish when she had her friends round for a meal. Once we'd finished eating I'd be up and out, making my excuses to retreat to the tranquillity of my garden. Underneath it all, I guess I'm actually quite shy. I don't know why, but I find small talk impossible. If I can get my teeth into a good debate, that's another matter. But Jay has me house-trained now, and I have belatedly developed a few social skills.

Jaybe's two closest friends, Kate and Nicky, provide her with great support. Nicky in particular has become almost part of the furniture. It is well known, among women, at any rate, that men are not great on the phone and that women are. By this definition, Nicky must be the greatest woman who ever lived. After some false starts, Jay also made real friends locally. Her pals Nadine and Emma have none of the Henley airs and graces. They take the piss out of me remorselessly, but I am such a sucker for their company that I often gatecrash their girlie lunches. Girlie gatherings fascinate me. For between two and six hours, nobody draws breath: every subject in the world gets covered – and then they are all covered again the next time the girlfriends meet. Nadine and Emma are terrific friends to have for me as well as Jay, not only because they're such stimulating company themselves, but also because they are with two great guys, Terry and Nigel.

So as Jay and I settled into life at Shiplake, all was sweetness and light at home. But on the business side it was another story. It soon became clear that my role as managing director of a public company was not worth the paper it was written on. Sure, I was earning a reasonable salary, but it seemed that I was not shaping up to be the kind of MD Sandy Singh, the chief executive of the parent company, had in mind. My own restaurant division was running smoothly enough, but problems arose when it came to new additions to the fold. As regards these new restaurants, what Sandy appeared to want was a yes man, and whatever else I am, I have never been, nor will I ever be, a yes man.

He had bought a restaurant in Pont Street called Drones, a classic Hooray hang-out favoured by the Nigel Dempsters of this world as the perfect place in which to pick up establishment gossip. In essence it was a great upmarket hamburger joint, it just hadn't kept pace with the times. All it needed to be returned to its former glory was a thorough update.

Sandy had allowed me to successfully put my own stamp on the other restaurants, but Drones was to be his baby, and he wanted to rebuild it completely, money no problem. As far as the food was concerned, Sandy wanted this to be a restaurant where he could entertain and impress his friends and business colleagues, and upmarket grub was the order of the day. Once again I employed the services of Chris Millar, back from Australia, to recreate my ideas. There was no doubting that the food was great, but it wasn't right for Drones. We were panned by Fay Maschler and other critics. It turned out that what Sandy was really after was another Daphne's, an ambition that could be discerned from his design. Unfortunately, Daphne's had the posh celebrity market cornered, and we were never going to compete with it by simply trying to imitate it.

Sandy was a desperate man. One day he was running a profitable restaurant group and the next, it seemed, a single restaurant was suddenly draining the profits to the tune of about £18,000 a month. He had got the concept wrong and I had got the menu wrong. Swift action was needed. But sadly, Sandy's remedy was wrong, too. He decided that the person to solve the crisis was my ex-lover, Annie Foster-Firth.

Annie had been fronting Daphne's, and had been doing an excellent job, too. I'd be the first to give her the credit for being a fabulous front-of-house operator, but after all that had happened between us, there was no way we were going to make a good working partnership again. When Sandy consulted me about this appointment, I told him in no uncertain terms that it was impossible. But it soon became apparent that in seeking my blessing he was just going through the motions. In fact, I suspect he had already done the deal. When he refused to be swayed I even had to resort to sending him a formal letter in my capacity as MD of the company, reiterating that I was 100 per cent against the move. But Annie got the job.

I then wrote officially to the chairman, complaining that the terms of my contract had been breached. It was water off a duck's back. All I received were assurances that Annie's role would be confined to Drones. It wasn't long before the ructions started. Within a matter of days, Sam Kemp, now my general manager at Drones, was being undermined by a girl engaged by Annie, a charming young woman called Antonia who was pleasing on the eye and a lovely person with it, I'm sure, but someone who had little knowledge of running restaurants.

Then things went from bad to worse. Annie wheedled her way into other operations, restaurants that were performing perfectly well as they were. I ran a tight ship: all capital expenditure had to be signed off first by me and then by Sandy Singh, but suddenly Annie was spending in all directions. My position as MD became a nonsense. Under Mr Singh the company appeared to be careering along regardless, and his decision was the only one that mattered. I knew my days there were numbered.

With all this happening behind the scenes, I was grateful that at least my media work was going well. When he had interviewed me before my promotion to managing director, Sandy had made no bones about his intention to use me as a product on which to build his restaurant division. I was to be the front man of the group, and as far as the public and press were concerned, the restaurants were mine. So my contract allowed for unlimited television and other media work. At the time any media exposure for the company was something to be greeted with open arms, but I think Sandy later regretted having agreed to such a free arrangement. He seemed to become increasingly jealous of the amount of publicity I received, and it was this resentment, combined with the tensions created when Annie joined the firm, that caused the first cracks in our relationship.

Just after I met Jacinta, my media profile had been given a further boost when I was offered a key role in a new television series. TV cookery had been revolutionized by chef Keith Floyd, whose successful series shifted the genre further away from its factual and educational base and into the field of entertainment. As a result programme-makers were constantly on the look-out for new concepts for this type of food show. *Ready, Steady, Cook* was the brainchild of Peter Bazalgette of Bazal Productions, now Endemol, who offered me a contract as one of the programme's chefs. Of course I jumped at the chance and signed up immediately.

It wasn't until after the deal was done that Jay and I sat down together to watch the pilot show. It was awful, very American with lots of audience participation. Shit, I thought. What have I done? All I can say now is thank God I didn't see the programme before I signed the contract, because Baz and his executive producer, Linda Clifford, ironed out the glitches and toned down the audience involvement, and from day one the show was a brilliant success. It even gave Channel 4's *Countdown*, which had had the late-afternoon television audience more or less to itself, a run for its money.

The format was simple: two chefs, partnered by two contestants and refereed by presenter Fern Britton, later succeeded by chef Ainsley Harriott, were given a bag of ingredients costing under a fiver and twenty minutes to create a meal from them. The first programme featured Brian Turner and me, great mates and also great rivals. Looking back, it was very tame compared to what we can do nowadays. I think we only produced a couple of dishes each. It wasn't long before my nickname became 'A Dish Too Far': my record for a live show was eleven. But after that I was limited to four by the production team, who find it difficult to fit them all into the overhead camera shot.

The two questions those of us on the programme are most frequently asked are 'Do you know what's in the bag?' and 'Do you really only get twenty minutes?', to which the answers are, hand on heart, no and yes. I often wish we did know what ingredients we were getting because I'm sure if we did we could be far more creative. But then the programme would lose its spontaneity. The only tiny bit of help we get that you don't see on TV, but which anyone who has ever come along as part of the studio audience will know, is a breathing space of six to eight minutes after the bags have been turned out, just to get our brains and equipment together before the clock starts counting down the twenty minutes.

Not only was *Ready, Steady, Cook* an instant hit, but over 1,000 programmes down the line it's still a great show and I won't hear anything said against it. It is a winning combination of three essential components: entertainment, competitiveness and information, enabling the viewer to pick up a few cookery tips for future reference. And the recipes, of course, are available afterwards, too. It has been sold to a number of countries around the world, and wherever I go I meet people who have seen it. I was even accosted once in a remote airport in Zimbabwe by a couple of ladies who were avid fans.

The team of chefs and cooks on the show are a fabulous bunch. If I was pushed to choose the colleague I like working with best it would have to be Brian Turner, as we go back such a long way and the rivalry between us gives our partnership a special piquancy. But each of the team has something different to offer. James Martin, whom I consider to be my prodigy, but who in truth, of course, is very much his own man, is also a great favourite. Lesley Waters, the only woman, is very much one of the boys; Nick Nairn and Paul Rankin are the terrible twins. Patrick Anthony and Richard Cawley might appear to be joined at the hip but at the same time they are complete opposites. Phil Vickery, a lovely guy, won the best prize of all, the cunning devil: he married our first presenter Fern Britton. Kevin Woodford, confused by many with Brian Turner, I know less well as he's always rushing off back to his beloved Isle of Man, but we spent some time together on a recent trip to South Africa to launch the BBC Food channel, and I really warmed to him. I discovered that there is a great guy lurking behind that cheeky smile.

And yet, for all its success, *Ready, Steady, Cook* has its knockers. To its critics I say, for goodness' sake, get a life. This show goes out at 4.30 in the afternoon, when the children are coming home from school and when programme-makers are catering for an audience of all ages. Visiting schools seven or eight years ago, I found children who didn't even know that milk came from cows or ham from pork. Nowadays, not only does every pupil know who I am, but they have no difficulty in telling me all about crème fraiche or chillies, any vegetable you could think of and many cuts of meat and varieties of fish as well. For those who don't learn about food from their parents, *Ready, Steady, Cook* might well be the only cookery education they get. Cooking and eating are fundamental to the fabric of our society and if we allow cookery skills to fall into disuse we are jeopardizing the very heart of the family unit. And while we may have some wonderful British chefs at present, where is the next generation going to come from? I for one want to enjoy food in my old age rather than being reduced to popping a few nutrient pills. The government needs to have an urgent rethink. I am sure the current food technology teaching is useful if all you want to learn is how to stock your fridge, clean your kitchen surfaces or design a sandwich, but from what I hear from most students, it doesn't really deal with real food or real cooking. If we can get food education right, and start it young, think of the savings there will be to the NHS.

One of the aspects of appearing regularly on television was having to get used to the attentions of a whole different batch of critics from those I faced as a chef. One who does have a foot in both camps is A.A. Gill. I enjoy reading his TV review in the *Sunday Times* and, as I have said, I also rate him very highly as a restaurant critic.

Television reviewers in general, like all critics, have their own tastes, and I can understand that it is far easier to dish out brick-bats than it is to lavish praise, but what I can't get my head round is why so many of them seem to find it necessary to launch such personal attacks. By all means lay into the performance, but what is the point in trying to analyse the performer when you don't know him and nobody gives a shit anyway? What the reader wants is your opinion on whether the programme was worth watching, not your uninformed prejudices about who is in it.

Gripes about (some) critics aside, the media element of my work was going great guns and I was learning a lot from it. As well as doing *Ready, Steady, Cook*, I had a couple of cookery books published in successive years. Before my collaboration with Malcolm Gluck on *Supernosh* (which was not really a cookbook, but if you knew a bit about food there were lots of ideas there to recreate), there had been a nine-year gap since the publication of *The Small and Beautiful Cookbook*. In 1994 I made up for this fallow period with *Modern Bistrot Cookery*, which included dishes based on menus at some of my restaurants, among them Zoe and 190 Queensgate, and then, in 1995, with *30-Minute Menus*, a collection of the recipes featured in my *Sunday Times* column. The publishers, Headline, made a beautiful job of *Modern Bistrot Cookery*, which was illustrated by my friend Michael Frith, whose watercolours appeared in the *Sunday Times* colour supplement. It sold well, better than the average cookbook, but it was not something I was going to get rich on. The watercolours were exquisite but unfortunately what the reader wants in a cookery book is photographs. I soon realized that coming up with a product that is tasteful and aesthetically pleasing to your own eye doesn't guarantee success. If that were the case, there would be chainstore designs in Conran shops and supermarkets based on Selfridges Food Hall.

On the question of individual taste, I've often wondered why it is that certain foods become the exclusive preserve of gourmets. Is it really because they are so delicious, or is it simply a matter of their rarity value – in other words, snobbery? Are oysters genuinely out of this world or are they prized only because they are so expensive? After all, what is so appealing about swallowing a puddle of sea-water enclosing something limper and chewier than a raw sweetbread? Personally, I like oysters. But don't tell me the first person to eat Beluga caviar immediately enthused: 'Oh, yum. Now, that is something else. I must tell all my friends.' Can you imagine someone spotting a frog and thinking that those back legs would make a delicious snack? And why not the rest of the poor animal? It must have been a desperately hungry person who noticed the slime trail of a snail and said: 'I'm going to have you for supper! In fact, I'm going to have twelve of you sitting in garlic butter. Delicious!'

What if, on the other hand, the potato were a rarity? Now you're talking. Surely it would be well worth its weight in gold: not only tasty but incredibly versatile. But because it is commonplace and cheap it is taken for granted. What about the wonderful onion, or the fab avocado? Even previously exotic fruit like the pineapple is far less expensive than it was thirty years ago. The wide and year-round availability of perceived delicacies has dealt a cruel blow to some of our more everyday produce, and because we choose to ignore the seasons we suffer from burn-out with certain foods. I don't like strawberries any more, and asparagus has become boring. It's sad when you remember what a treat it was to enjoy their short seasons as a youngster. I have now resolved to eat produce like this only when it is in season in Britain. British can be, and should be, best for the fresh fruit and vegetables that suit our soil and climate, as others are in other countries in which they grow most successfully.

Take the peach. I can barely remember the last time the juice from a peach dribbled down my chin as I bit into it. How long is it since you ate an apricot that didn't have the texture of cotton wool? And when were you last able to hull a strawberry by twisting the green stem? You can't put all the blame on the supermarkets: if the public didn't want the produce, they wouldn't stock it. I understand that we all enjoy the convenience, but who are the losers in the end?

As the stormclouds gathered at Simpson's of Cornhill, having Jay and Toby-Jack to come home to made all the difference. Now that we were settled as a family, the M-word began to come up. Jay had indicated on a couple of occasions that perhaps we should do the right thing. After all, we had a child and she came from a good Catholic background. But I was in no rush. Although it made sense to tie the knot, I had already made two mistakes on the marriage front and this time, when it came to the crunch, everything had to be perfect. I was determined not to make a mess of things again. I worshipped the ground Jay walked on, but how could I be certain that her love for me was real?

Men are notorious for keeping their problems bottled up – many of us would rather self-destruct than relieve the pressure by talking over our difficulties with a friend – but Jaybe and I could talk to each other about anything and everything. So often, as I had found to my cost, relationships start with pyrotechnics and then quickly burn themselves out. But this time I knew Jay and I were running on slow-burning solid fuel and there were glowing embers at the base of our fire. Yes, getting married was the right thing to do.

At Christmas we met up with Jacinta's whole family – her parents, two sisters and brother and their partners – at Frank and Maeve's home in Malahide, and I decided that this would be the time to do things properly and ask Frank for his daughter's hand in marriage. I picked the ideal moment, when Frank had just returned from Mass on Christmas Eve with good thoughts in his head. I had just plucked up the courage to waylay him when suddenly Peter, Jaybe's sister Ciara's boyfriend, intercepted me and asked Frank if he could have a word in his ear. I couldn't believe it: he, too, was going to pop the question.

As soon as Frank and Peter had finished talking, Paul, partner of Jaybe's other sister, Rufina, appeared, sweating like a trooper, and did exactly the same thing. And then John, the brother, announced that he and his girlfriend Christa were going to tie the knot. All three of them in the space of an hour? My head was in turmoil, so God knows what state Frank's must have been in. After all that, I couldn't possibly go through with it. I wasn't going to join a queue, for God's sake. Poor Jacinta. She was overjoyed about her brother's and sisters' news, but gutted to be left out of the roll call herself. She should have been top of the list, especially as she was the one with the first grandchild, but I had just been too slow off the mark. I am just not the kind of person to be badgered into anything. I like doing things in my own time. And besides, as I've said, with Jay everything had to be perfect. I didn't want us to be part of a block booking.

I did eventually broach the subject with Frank before we left Malahide, though I didn't say anything to Jay at the time. I wanted to choose the right moment to propose to her. Frank was as brilliant as ever. Obviously he did have concerns about the fact that I had already been married twice before, but even so he gladly gave us his blessing. He agreed to keep the news to himself until I had asked Jacinta.

In the New Year we were going on holiday to Zimbabwe with Luisa, my ex-PA, heading first for Lake Kariba, where Luisa's parents had a boat, and then on a week's safari. Lake Kariba was a fabulous setting, but the circumstances were wrong for a marriage proposal – too many people. Before leaving on safari we decided to take a trip to the Zambezi to go white-water rafting. Arriving at the Victoria Falls Hotel the afternoon before our expedition, Jay and I decided to have a kip before going to see the falls, accessible via a private path from the hotel. This was my big chance: what better place could there be to ask someone to marry you than in front of one of the most beautiful sights on earth? I established that the entrance to the falls closed at 5 pm so I asked Luisa, who wasn't intending to take a nap, to call us at four. But she fell asleep as well and we didn't wake up until 4.40. I was furious. I knew we wouldn't have another opportunity to go to the falls because the rafting trip started very early the following morning. Jaybe, of course, was completely baffled by my rage. I was so grumpy that she threatened not to come with me at all, but I managed to persuade her, though she still couldn't understand why it was so important – we already had a spectacular view of the bridge and the gorge from the hotel. So much for my perfect plan: the way things were going, there was every chance she would turn me down.

We got to the falls just before the entrance closed. They were magnificent. I asked Jay to step over the protective fence so we were as close as possible to the edge. What I hadn't realized was that the spray from the falls made the ground very boggy and immediately we were almost up to our knees in mud. Very romantic. Anyone watching us must have wondered what these two very short people were up to.

But finally I was able to ask Jay the question I'd been waiting to voice since Christmas Eve. Tears welled in her eyes as she said yes. I was so happy – and relieved, too. I'd achieved my ultimate proposal at last, though it had so nearly gone horribly wrong. Everything fell into place for Jay, and she realized why I had been so desperate to get to the falls. But even at that happiest of moments she found the time to give me a bollocking for my behaviour earlier. I didn't care. By that stage I was feeling no pain.

Back at the hotel that evening there were celebrations all round. We were joined by Rory Bremner, who was on his way back from his own safari and had decided to join us for the white-water rafting. That turned out to be scary stuff. I loved it, but I'm not sure it was my new fiancée's cup of tea. I hadn't been aware that she was no great fan of water at the best of times, let alone the raging rapids of the Zambezi. If you overturn it seems to take an age for you to get back to the surface and you become very disorientated. We were lucky only to capsize once: some of the other boats went over five or six times. When the boat righted itself, there was no Jay. I was in a bit of a panic until I found her, still under the boat. It would have been downright careless to have lost my fiancée quite so quickly. Rory's face was a picture. He looked as if he had just seen his wallet go floating past.

It was a wonderful holiday, and it still feels like a soft-focus dream when I look back on it. But all too soon it was over, and time to return to the real world.

Our news was greeted with surprise at the office. Even after Toby was born, nobody had really thought that Jay and I would last. But my colleagues, who were well aware of my track record, had been basing their predictions on the old me. Now I was a changed man, and loving every minute of it.

CHAPTER THIRTY

THERE WAS NO QUESTION THAT THE EMPLOYMENT OF ANNIE Foster-Firth at Drones was an unmitigated disaster for me. If Sandy Singh had thought everyone would soon adjust to the situation and carry on as if nothing had happened, he was very much mistaken. It was not Annie's fault, but her arrival ultimately destroyed the team.

With hindsight, I realize I should have resigned as soon as it became clear that my position as managing director was being compromised. But it is not always easy to step back and see the whole picture when it is being eroded gradually. I enjoyed being MD, there was work to be done and, until the acquisition of Drones, my young and enthusiastic team had been going places.

So, still convinced that Sandy was wrong to have brought in Annie, I constructed a brick wall around myself in my dealings with her, which made it impossible for us to work together. My staff were not fully aware of our history, and I should not have allowed them to be influenced by my prejudices in the way I did. Francesca, Sam and my PA, Marie-Regine, were all demoralized by the tangible tension.

Sandy Singh was still pleasant enough to my face, but I could no longer trust his judgement. It was clear that he regretted promoting me, but he couldn't challenge me on the performance of my restaurants, except for Drones, and with Annie's arrival that was out of my hands. Instead he was slowly pulling the rug from under my feet. It was time for me to leave a paper trail. As I covered my arse on every executive decision, a mountain of notes and memos built up. I even resorted to secretly using a tape-recorder whenever I had a meeting with him.

All this put me under a great deal of strain and Jay was worried about me. She had never seen me stressed before; usually I weathered any storm in a reasonably calm and happy-go-lucky manner. But my future happiness with her was much more important to me than office politics at Simpson's, and I wasn't going to let anything spoil that. We had scheduled our wedding for September, and plans were well under way. Since the groom was a twice-married non-Catholic, a church wedding was off the agenda, so it would have to be a civil ceremony at the Chelsea Register Office, with lunch afterwards for a select group at my favourite restaurant, Riva in Barnes. The official reception would follow a blessing the next day in our lovely Shiplake church, St Peter and St Paul, which was small enough to be intimate but just about large enough to hold all our guests.

With the numbers amounting to about 250, we decided to put up a marquee for the reception on a smallholding we have opposite the cottages. We were expecting a big Irish contingent – a great crowd of aunts, uncles, cousins and friends as well as the immediate family. In their honour I painted the side of our cottage Irish green. Actually, I got the shade a bit wrong, but the thought was there. Our neighbours at the Mill House next door were horrified, but we've never repainted it and it's still green today.

Chris Millar agreed to prepare the food. The singer Kim Wilde was getting married the week before our wedding, and we were organizing the food for her reception, so Jay and I decided to opt for the same menu to give ourselves a dry run. I had a great rapport with the Wildes, having catered several times for Kim's father, Marty, but I'm sure he didn't realize that his daughter's wedding was also serving as a dress rehearsal for my own.

With the help of my very generous suppliers the menu for both weddings was luxurious but simple. It began with a wonderful platter of shellfish: langoustine, scallops tartare, crab, lobster, baby brown shrimps, cockles, native and rock oysters, clams, mussels – you name it, if it swam and had a shell on it, it found its way on to each table's platter – followed by roast meats, including sirloin of Aberdeen Angus beef, pure bred and selected by Arthur Alsop, an old friend from Scotland who knew everything there was to know about beef. To finish, a range of Irish cheeses and big bowls of strawberries and raspberries were placed at the centre of each table for the guests to enjoy in their own time. It's always a good idea when you are organizing an event for yourself not to go for a menu that requires a complicated service, and in the event this worked flawlessly for us. It is probably the only time I've ever sat down to my own catering without interfering.

Since I'm not really a guy's guy, and a lot of my closest friends are female, deciding on a best man wasn't easy, but I didn't think it would be the done thing to have a best woman. In the end I asked Steve Thomas, an old friend I'd known since my Ménage à Trois days. He turned out to be a great choice. He wasn't too familiar with my past, which was probably no bad thing, and cut an imposing figure. When I first met him he scared me to death: he was a bit of a rocker, sort of Alvin Stardust meets James Dean; tall, slim and trendy and always dressed in his trademark black with brightly coloured socks.

The weather at the beginning of September was lousy but by some miracle the sun shone on two consecutive Saturdays for both Kim's wedding and ours. We'd arranged for a horse-drawn carriage to take Jay to the church and bring both of us back to the reception. She looked stunning in a gorgeous, body-hugging wedding gown in silver on white made by the champion Irish designer Lyn Mar, who has since become a great friend and has supplied some further fabulous outfits for Jay. While Jay went for silver on white, I had opted for a rather dapper number in gold on black. Gold with silver? Yes, I know, but that's what happens when the bridal outfit is so secret that the groom is not even told what colour it is, never mind allowed to see it. But maybe it will catch on.

We'd done an exclusive deal with *OK!* magazine for the rights to cover the wedding. It didn't amount to megabucks but it was just enough to cover the cost of the event and make a contribution towards the honeymoon. However, like other couples before and since, we got our fingers burned. I suppose it was a bit naive of me not to expect trouble when one of the guests was a top freelance paparazzo. I had made it clear to him that he couldn't sell any of his own photographs until *OK!* had published their piece, and re-iterated those instructions in the churchyard minutes before the service. 'Yes, yes, I understand,' he said. I always liked the guy, and I still do – and he does take a great picture – but you can't trust a paparazzo. It is like trusting the devil. If there's a shot to sell, he'll sell it, and hang the consequences.

The first picture appeared in a tabloid soon afterwards, followed by a double-page spread in the *Mail* accusing us of insensitivity in compiling the guest list. They thought it was tactless of us to have invited Penny Smith with her friend, Kevin Ball, when Rory Bremner, from whom she had parted a few months earlier, was also going to be there. They told how Rory had been seen sitting alone in our garden moping because he was so upset. What bullshit some of these journalists dream up. We knew that Rory and Penny were still friends, but in any case we had checked with both parties before sending out the invitations, and everyone was fine about it. Rory was in the garden on his own seeking a bit of peace and quiet to write an ode to Jaybe and me to deliver at the dinner later. And anyone who knows Rory will tell you that when he is preparing to perform, whether it is in front of the television cameras or at a private function, he is the ultimate professional, and he doesn't drink anything or socialize much.

The newspaper coverage was bad enough, but what really peeved *OK!* was the pictures being plastered all over the pages of their biggest rival, *Hello!* They published the official piece anyway but refused to pay us. Simon Bowen took issue with them, arguing that Jay and I had played no part in the spoilers: we hadn't known that the paparazzo was going to sell his photographs ahead of *OK!*'s feature, and in any case we had no control over the actions of our guests. In the end we settled, but we lost a big chunk of the money we'd been promised. Still, looking on the bright side, there haven't been too many weddings covered in both glossies at the same time, and perhaps the famous curse of *Hello!* was counteracted by the *OK!* spread. At any rate, all I can say is that we're still very happily married.

The only effect all this had on our wedding day itself was that the *OK!* photo session, held during drinks in the back garden on our return from the church, took so long that by the time we finally went over to the marquee for dinner many of our guests were already pissed. One of Jay's girlfriends from Stringfellow's was asleep with her head in her plate before the main course arrived. I dubbed Stringy's delegation the Tottering Girls, because they all wore tall stilettos unsuited to both the uneven flooring of the marquee and the very soft lawn of our garden.

The dinner was a triumph. The front of house was fantastically well organized by Richard Whittington, a friend of David Wilby's, and most of the rest of the staff had volunteered their assistance with the preparation on their days off. Their performance could not have been bettered. As they had already staged the same production the week before for Kim's wedding, there were absolutely no hitches, even though we were all an hour late sitting down. You know it has been some bash when no less a personage than Michel Roux phones your office the following week to ask for the name of the caterers, and when he, Andrea Riva and Brian Turner, who scarcely ever miss a Saturday-night service at their own restaurants, have all stayed on for the dinner.

As I surveyed the scene nervously from the top table, I couldn't quite believe it was happening. From time to time I glanced surreptitiously at my new wife – not only the most beautiful woman in the room but also such a terrific person. I almost had to pinch myself to make sure I wasn't dreaming it all. Was I lucky, or what? It had taken me just over two years to get to the altar, an eternity for someone as impulsive as I am. But I wanted to grow old with Jacinta, and I had to be sure that I had grown up; that I was absolutely ready to make a third and final investment in marriage.

The wedding was something of a marathon – it began at 1 pm and finished at about five in the morning, with the Irish invaders easily taking all the prizes for stamina and capacity for drink. The speeches were traditional, except that Steve Thomas's was surprisingly nice for a best man's contribution – I had expected the customary character assassination. Frank, Jay's dad, overcame his nervousness to talk movingly in his captivating Irish lilt about his beautiful daughter. He warned me that in marrying a Gemini I would not be marrying just the two different women but seven. He never spoke a truer word.

But I think the real AWT is an evolving creature, and one of my ambitions is to prove that a leopard can change its spots. When you truly love, and that love is truly reciprocated, it is all-powerful. It washes over you, bringing you an inner peace, a serenity – never to be confused with complacency – and dispelling doubt and insecurity, those demons that stand in the way of you being the real you, the complete you. When I met Jacinta I was not a complete person. To outsiders I may have seemed content, but there was always an emptiness beneath the mask. Now, after two years with Jacinta, I was casting off the past.

Before the wedding someone had told us to be sure we stopped and took a step back from time to time to savour the moment. It was wise advice: so often these landmarks in our lives have flown by before we know it. Rory Bremner's ode to us was a highlight of the evening – he is so talented and quick-witted. Talking of talent, I surprised my new wife with a trio of solo songs, accompanied only by a friend with a tuning fork. But I am pleased to report that my rendering of that old Irish favourite 'Danny Boy' held the audience spellbound. You could have heard a pin drop.

Our guests thoroughly enjoyed themselves. Fay Maschler was rocking her toes off with Michael Proudlock, Ainsley Harriott was singing his heart out with the band, Rex Leyland and his wife Melissa were catching up with my ex-wife Mish and her partner, Charles. Mish had been keen to come and was reunited with many of the friends she had left behind in the UK, including Blake's godmother, Suzie, and her husband Mark Hix, executive chef of the Caprice and the Ivy. I hadn't invited Annie Foster-Firth. In other circumstances I would have done, but with the friction levels at Simpson's of Cornhill sky-high, it would not have been right. Nevertheless, I had asked Sandy Singh, though he had declined, sending us a very nice set of Lalique wine glasses as a wedding present.

By 2 am our departure was long overdue, but it seems a shame to leave your own party in full swing and we were having a ball. I did eventually manage to drag Jacinta away, though not before she and the Tottering Girls had given an outrageous performance of 'Patricia the Stripper'. All I can say is that it epitomized my wife's wonderful zest for life.

For our wedding night I had booked a fabulous room at Robyn and Michel Roux's Waterside Inn, just seven miles away. Antonia, Annie Foster-Firth's lovely Sloaney assistant at Drones, who had helped Richard Whittington out front, volunteered to drive us there. In our room we found a trail of rose petals leading to the bed and a bottle of Cristal champagne on ice. It was the perfect finale to the perfect wedding.

The next day it was off for lunch at our local pub, the White Hart, to pick up where we had left off the day before with the friends and relatives who were still around. God, those Irish have some staying power. Everyone mucked in to help clear up the last remnants of our glorious day. Frank and Maeve were absolute stars throughout. For them it was one daughter down, two to go. I may not have been the quickest off the mark with my proposal, but at least Jaybe managed to be the first sister up the aisle.

On the Monday we flew off to Nice for a two-week honeymoon which passed in a haze of happiness. With the indispensable assistance of my PA, Marie-Regine, I had mapped out a tour taking in France and Italy, starting at the Colombe d'Or, the beautiful hotel in St Paul de Vence packed full of history and art. At my friend Serge Meudjisky's art gallery opposite we let the credit cards take the strain, buying a Picasso, a Dali and a Tobiasse, but hey, you only live once. Some days I agree with Samuel Johnson that it is better to live rich than to die rich; other days I'm more inclined towards Bertolt Brecht's view: life is short and so is money. Our honeymoon was obviously a Johnson interlude. Not only did Serge help us to make up our minds over the paintings, he almost persuaded me to buy a restaurant just outside St Paul. I was very tempted, and had I known what was around the corner at Simpson's of Cornhill I might very well have taken his advice.

Every night we sought out good food, visiting several Michelin-starred restaurants, including Roger Verge's in Mougins. I had been really excited by my own gastronomic tour sixteen years earlier, but not any more. It seemed to me that French food had gone off the boil. Alain Ducasse's Louis XV in Monte Carlo provided spectacular food but at spectacular price. And elsewhere the cost was the only thing that was spectacular.

For the price of a starter at Louis XV we had one of the best meals of our trip up in the hills above Monte Carlo, in the company of the owners of the De Cecco restaurant in Parsons Green in London and a director of Sony. The Monagasque restaurant, apparently a favourite with racing drivers over for the Monaco Grand Prix, offered a fixed menu at £30 a head, including its own selection of wine. Although there was no choice, it was terrific: the food just kept coming until you were screaming for it to stop. It was this experience that inspired me to open Woz the following year. The sickening thing is that I can't for the life of me remember what the restaurant was called, so I'll probably never find it again.

From St Paul we moved on to the sleek, modern Eden Roc over-looking the sea at Cap d'Antibes, a complete contrast to the rustic charms of the Colombe d'Or. The staff were lovely, and couldn't have been more helpful; we had a beautiful room and a memorable balcony. I say memorable because that is where our second child was conceived.

Somewhat strapped for cash (they don't take plastic at Eden Roc), we headed north-east for Lake Garda in Italy, where we stayed at the Villa d'Este, a magnificent hotel set in beautiful grounds by the lake. It was a shame that the food didn't match up to the surroundings. What northern Italy needed was a Riva to shake out the cobwebs – and fortunately for us we found one, in the shape of Andrea Riva's brother, who had just opened a superb restaurant, La Felicia, a few miles away. He served us a veritable feast and refused to take a penny. Andrea had been on the phone asking him to look after us, which was typical of Andrea. He is so generous. I could live in that part of Italy. Mountains, lakes, culture, climate, seasons – it has everything.

Our whole honeymoon couldn't have been more idyllic. I felt as if my life was just beginning. But before that new life could be fully savoured, the situation at Simpson's of Cornhill had to be resolved once and for all. The crunch finally came in January 1997. Worries over my untenable position marred what should have been a very happy time for us – our first Christmas as a married couple, and a New Year that saw both Jacinta's sisters getting married within a month of each other – and to make matters worse, as a result of the stress I was under, I succumbed to a very severe dose of flu. On 6 January I was called to a disciplinary hearing in Sandy's office. A confidentiality clause to the eventual settlement prevents me from sharing the details here, though I would dearly love to. Suffice it to say that I was preparing to attend the meeting when one of my managers at Dell'Ugo called to tell me that the locks to my office had been changed. Not much room for misunderstanding there, then. I rang Simon Bowen, who insisted in no uncertain terms that I should not go to the hearing. Instead he sent a letter of resignation on my behalf, citing constructive dismissal. We had stolen Sandy's thunder, and boy, did the shit hit the fan. I have a lot to thank Simon for over the long time I have known him, but in this case his decisive action was crucial. It was a further two years before the issue was finally settled, during which period Sandy and his big guns continued to try to break me. But I knew it was right to stand my ground. That bulldog thing must be catching.

That day in January was one of the worst of my life. I had been persuaded to walk away not only from a £100,000-a-year job but from a huge chunk of my whole existence: a team I had built myself over many years and a group of restaurants that felt as if they were mine, and were mine in a lot of ways. I was utterly distraught. And yet at the same time it was a massive relief, like emerging from prison after serving a long sentence. The horrible thing was, for all I knew I could have been emerging into a wilderness in career terms. For eight months I stayed within the cocoon of my family,

Jay, now expecting our second child, and Toby-Jack, planning our future. Jay's strength, together with the independence I had carved out of my childhood, made me strong and saw me through.

My bad experience with Simpson's and those months working from home with Jay gave me a sense of proportion and taught me not to let stress get to me. No longer do I allow a traffic jam to raise my blood pressure. A licensing hearing at a magistrates' court has lost its capacity to make me feel like a criminal. A bad restaurant review doesn't get my hackles up. I take note of it, but in a chilled way. So Toby has been naughty at school? I just think, that's my boy. You only have to look at my school career to see that he has a long way to go before I need to worry. Jay says she stresses for me. I wish she wouldn't. There simply isn't any point in letting it affect you.

Jacinta has never seen me really lose my temper. We both raise our voices sometimes, of course, but that's all it is. When I get upset it is usually because she is getting upset about something trivial. I want to live a lot longer, and I want her to go on living with me, not wear herself out with anxiety. Stress kills. It damages our immune systems. We are always so busy worrying about saturated fat, smoking, alcohol, sugar, lack of exercise that we forget about stress. Ideally we shouldn't be worrying at all. Irresponsible advice? I don't think so. Clearly we need to be sensible about all of these dangers, but in my opinion stress is the biggest killer of them all, not to mention the biggest disruption to family life. So keep it all under control. And if you can't control yourself, try taking up yoga.

Jay also taught me the importance of spending time together away from the pressures of work. When we got married we promised each other that we would take one holiday each year on our own together and one with the children. We've been able to fulfil the first part of this promise largely because of the wonderful Lizzie Wilson, a complete genius with children, who has been with us now for nearly six years. In the aftermath of September 11, we were able to leave the children with Lizzie and go to New York to see my friend Drew Nierpoint who runs Montrachet in the Tribeca district. He organized a system whereby local restaurants provided free food to all those who worked so hard to clear up the World Trade Center site. Of course, Jay and I have been able to go on some more traditionally relaxing holidays too, but going away together, wherever the destination, plays a vital part in keeping me sane. Thanks, Lizzie!

I also learned to appreciate the power of a garden; the pleasure and the returns it can give you. It is something I should have recognized much earlier from observing my grandmother. It was in her dungarees working in her garden at Shiplake that she was at her happiest. When she went back to Chelsea for the winter she was always uptight, Mrs Angry, buzzing around like a blue-arsed fly. Perhaps it is no coincidence that my mother, who never took much interest in the garden until her twilight years, was never at one with herself.

I now understand how important it is to stop every so often and smell the roses, and I try to make some time every day to potter in the garden, even if it is only to walk around admiring nature or to sit for a moment with a glass of wine or a cup of tea and absorb it.

That June saw the birth of my fourth child. I was preoccupied by the small matter of watching England playing Brazil at football on television when Jay told me that her waters had broken. She wanted to go to the hospital immediately but the contractions were still a long way apart. I felt I was an old hand at this by now, and tried to get her to relax and wait. 'You know you're not supposed to go until the contractions are coming every five minutes. If you turn up now, they'll only send you home again,' I reasoned. She was due to have the baby at the Royal Berkshire Hospital in Reading, so there was going to be no need for any mercy dashes. But Jay was adamant. She told me that if I didn't take her immediately, she would book herself a taxi and leave me to the football. Sure enough, within an hour we were back. When things accelerated a bit I drove her to Reading again in plenty of time to usher our first daughter, whom we named Billie-Lara, into the world on the morning of 11 June 1997.

I was so convinced the baby would be another boy that when the nurse told me I had a daughter I asked her to check and make certain. I was absolutely over the moon. They say it takes a real man to produce a daughter. Maybe it was the sunset and the lapping waves in Cap d'Antibes that worked the miracle. At any rate I guess that now makes me a real man, thanks to Jaybe.

Back at home with my expanded family, I soon came to realize that losing Simpson's could have been a lot worse.

At least money was not an issue. I was now writing regular columns for the *Sunday Express* and a couple of trade magazines. One of them, *Theme*, gave me a platform for voicing my concerns about the catering industry. Sainsbury's commissioned me to write a couple of recipe books in their 'Quick and Easy' series, one on winter warmers and another on fish. With the help of Limelight Management I was making a fair number of well-paying personal appearances, and my media profile remained high, thanks mainly to *Ready, Steady, Cook*.

Whatever plans we make, life has a way of setting its own agenda, and so it did for me once again in the form of the godfather of all cookery shows, the BBC's *Food and Drink*. It had always been a dream of mine to front the cookery section of the programme, and when presenter Michael Barry suddenly decided to leave, I snapped up the role as soon as Baz offered it to me. The first series was very difficult for me as I wasn't at all used to working directly to camera or to having to conform to a certain way of speaking. On *Ready, Steady, Cook* it was just a question of being filmed interacting normally with Fern Britton and my contestant, and staring into a cold, impersonal lens instead of talking to a human being was alien to me. My performance was not without problems, so I didn't expect to get another series, but the programme-makers persevered with me and next time round things changed considerably for the better. Producer Tim Hinks was promoted to executive producer and the day-to-day production was taken over by a new girl, Elaine Bancroft. I'm not sure how popular she was with the diehards and she lasted only one series, but she was great with me. She had the knack of getting me to relax, and gradually I began to feel good about my work on the show. I owe Elaine a lot.

Elaine's series was the last to be filmed in the studio. After that the cookery slot was relocated to my house in Shiplake and the wine section, presented by Jilly Goolden and Oz Clarke, went out on the road. Sadly, that left no place for the main anchorman, Chris Kelly, a class act. I loved him to bits: he had been really good to me as the new boy. Oz was nice to me, too, but as for Jilly, well, she was one cool customer. It took me almost a whole series to chip away at the ice to find her soft, squidgy centre.

Once I was working in my own home I relaxed even more. I was joined by an assistant, Emma Crowhurst, who took over the job of analysing produce in the supermarkets. She had been a top lecturer at Leith's cookery school and she certainly knew her onions. In the next series Emma was given her own cookery slot and began to come into her own. Jilly decided to give up the show, and Oz joined me to present the wine segment from Shiplake. We were given a new director, Claudia Lewis, a very young, determined woman who built on what Elaine Bancroft had started. She knew what she wanted and got it, and didn't take any nonsense from anybody, but at the same time she was open to ideas and always prepared to listen. She really made the camera talk, and for the most part her direction was stunning, though I wasn't too impressed when it strayed into Jamie Oliver territory, with the shots jumping all over the place and the use of that deliberate side angle on your face when you were talking, which made it seem as if you were looking into the wrong camera.

Claude, as she became known – she also had other nicknames which I can't divulge – was, like many artists, very fiery. I liked her a lot. In fact our relationship was rather like a surreal love affair without the sex. There were days when we wouldn't speak to each other and just stomped about until one or other of us conceded a point. I, of course, was always in the wrong, because I should have been doing what the director dictated, but I'm sorry, there are times when you know that a particular instruction is going to make you look a complete fool, and I am quite capable of achieving that on my own without any direction, thank you. But if that makes it sound as if making the programme was a constant battle, I am creating the wrong impression: most of the time we were like the proverbial big, happy family.

Oz is the ultimate professional. He really knows his wines and has a superb palate, but he avidly rehearsed his part of the programme, whereas I would wing it, relying on my own cooking skills and the sterling work of Anna-Lisa, the home economist. Together with the queen of the back-room cooks, Orla Broderick, Anna-Lisa made sure each dish worked by rigorously testing and retesting it beforehand. Presenters simply couldn't function without the valuable back-room staff. If even the tiniest trifle is overlooked, it can rebound on you big-time.

I hoped there would always be a place for *Food and Drink* on our television screens. It was a timeless, grown-up food programme that was not swayed by the latest fleeting fad. But sadly, in 2003 the BBC decided to axe it after over twenty successful years. It had been very good for me, especially coming as it did in the wake of the Simpson's fiasco, and I will miss it. It did wonders for my confidence, both on and off screen, and it made me appreciate that whatever the current culinary fashion, the general public always value simple food well cooked. But it's strange, as one door closes another one opens. I was soon to be offered *Saturday Kitchen* by the BBC and it was there that I was reunited with my favourite producer, now editor, Elaine Bancroft.

CHAPTER THIRTY-ONE

RUNNING A RESTAURANT IS LIKE A DRUG. THERE ARE SO MANY elements of the experience that give you a high – the pleasure you give your customers, your interaction with them, the insanity of the kitchen, the close-knit relationship with your staff. No two days are ever the same, and it's rare for everything in any one of those days to run smoothly. And when you are working in the independent sector, it's a personality-led business. It is akin to being on the stage: each lunchtime and evening you are performing, you have a new audience to impress, and you have to be ready for the curtain to rise. I am fortunate in that because of the way my career has developed I don't have to appear in every performance. I'm getting old, for Christ's sake; I have a young family that needs me and I want to spend time with them. Nevertheless, once you are hooked, that is it. Try as you might to give up the drug, a sniff of any one of those elements can bring about a relapse at any time.

So it was on the cards that before long I would be looking for a new restaurant. I found it in a small place in Golborne Road, a cool street near Portobello Road, full of antique and junk shops, Portuguese cafés and delis, with a small market and an excellent wet-fish shop. At times it was hard to believe you were in London and not Portugal. At weekends the famous Portobello Road market spilled over on to Golborne Road, enriching its Bohemian atmosphere. By day there was an amazing community spirit to the place; it was the night-time that we failed to take sufficient account of. When the sun set, this buzzy environment turned into a ghost town, where the only life was low life. Drug-dealers hung around in doorways and the healthy hustle and bustle of the daylight hours was replaced by the crime and violence associated with the financing of drug habits. It was, I have to say, a little scary.

I should have been warned on day one of the renovations, when a rather shifty bloke approached me and asked about a job. 'Me wash up, very good,' he assured me.

'No, thanks.'

'No, you no understand. Me wash up, you never have any problems.'

Christ. The guy was offering me protection.

I played dumb. 'Give me your address and phone number, and if something comes up, I'll let you know.'

Needless to say, no contact details were forthcoming.

Once the renovations were under way, we prepared to launch the new restaurant, Woz, with a private party. Why Woz? Well, a few years before, in the same way as the footballer Paul Gascoigne's nickname was Gazza, Fay Maschler had dubbed me Wozza. Finding it considerably less long-winded than my real name – which, fifty years on, even I still find a mouthful – several other journalists picked it up and it stuck. So Woz it became.

Woz the restaurant was, if I say it myself, one of my best. The concept was very simple: Clarke's (Kensington Church Street, West London) meets that restaurant Jay and I had so enjoyed in Monaco. Both of those restaurants serve a no-choice dinner, although Sally Clarke, after training with Alice Waters in California, takes a more American approach, whereas we decided to go more Mediterranean. Woz was like going to a dinner party, very family and very rustic. None of the food was plated. First came five dishes of antipasti, two hot, three cold, with country breads, followed by a dish of fish, pasta, a composed salad or soup, then a whole roast or braised dish, casserole or similar, with one accompaniment. To finish with there was one perfectly ripe cheese and/or pud. The food was placed at the centre of the table for the customers to help themselves. They could even carve their own joint or chicken if they wished, though most preferred us to do it for them.

On the opening night everything went beautifully. The concept was well received by our invited guests and the mood was buoyant. Fay Maschler and her sister, who had been out to dinner nearby, popped in for a drink and to check out Woz with a view to returning to eat another night. We were downstairs chatting when one of my waiters appeared and reported that four guys had walked in off the street wanting a meal. They had been told it was a private party but refused to take no for an answer. Before I could get upstairs to sort things out, I heard the thump of a chair falling over. I rushed up to the restaurant to find that the would-be customers had left – but not before forcibly removing a Rolex watch from the wrist of one of our guests. It had all happened so quickly that no one had had a chance to intervene, which on reflection was probably no bad thing – in my experience, if you know what's good for you, the hero in you should be a bit circumspect about stepping in.

What a great start. We managed to keep the incident quiet for a couple of months, but from that day on we employed a bouncer – and I do mean a bouncer, not a smart doorman. This was a gorilla in a leather jacket. Not surprisingly, some of our customers found this measure a little intimidating. And eventually the opening-night story did make the newspapers because of a spate of other Rolex muggings. They say there's no such thing as bad publicity, but that patently isn't true. Some people might like living on the edge, but apparently not enough of them to fill a restaurant, even a small one.

It was a crying shame, because in other respects Woz was a real hit. I had never opened a restaurant to such universally glowing reviews, about thirty-eight of them were good to great. There were even some reviews in the States. A.A. Gill put a bit of a dampener on matters in his own inimitable way, but I'm a man, I can take that. Fay Maschler, on the other hand, most unusually gave Woz and me a whole double-page spread. That kind of accolade does wonders for morale.

With a reception like that, you'd have thought we were well set up, and at first everything was fine. During the first flush of success I opened a second restaurant, Wiz, a name that sounded just right with Woz. Unfortunately, in my innocence I was unaware of the American usage of 'whiz' – across the pond, I discovered, to take a whiz means to go for a pee – but so what, this was London, and I liked it. I envisaged Wiz and Woz as two cartoon chefs spawning a merchandizing extravaganza: the book, the movie, the T-shirt. Wake up, Walter Mitty.

Wiz, in Clarendon Road, London W11, had previously been a restaurant and before that the Britannia public house, apparently a hang-out for the boys from Wormwood Scrubs. It was a lovely building – high ceilings, bags of character, with a pleasant roof terrace – seating up to a hundred. Wiz was cheap, but overheads were too high for its back-street location, so what we gained on the roundabout we lost on the swings. With some very useful assistance from Fay Maschler, we got the concept right: international tapas, if there can be said to be such a thing. Small bites and street food from around the world; food to share; social dining. Wiz was quick to establish itself. We didn't get many reviews, but word soon spread. Luisa Alves was its first manager, but I came up against the difficulties of trying to handle Luisa as both an employee and a friend. So, in the interests of maintaining our friendship, we agreed to part company and Luisa went off to become PA to the media moguls' restaurateur, Aldo Zilli.

It was goodbye to one old mate and hello to another, David Wilby, with whom I had worked on and off for nearly twenty years, most recently at Simpson's of Cornhill. Since then we had catered some outside events together – among them London Fashion Week and the press day at the Motor Show – now it was time for him to return on a more permanent basis. He agreed to join our company, Chakalaka Ltd, as operations director.

In all the years I have known him, from the days at Ménage à Trois, where he was head chef and saw me through the ups and downs of life with Annie Foster-Firth, to the Simpson's of Cornhill débâcle, David has always been a tower of strength. In my final dark days as managing director of Simpson's, his support was rock solid. In fact he was one of the few, along with Sam Kemp and Marie-Regine, who resisted the heavy pressure to join the conspirators in stabbing me in the back. He is the exception to the rule that friendship is a fatal formula for a business relationship, and I would trust him above anyone else I've ever worked with, apart from my wife, of course. Operating together at the sharp end we gel well, too. If I am having a bad-hair day he is always immediately aware of it and quietly backs off, and if I find that Mr Unflappable has come off the rails then I will give him a quick wind-up, put him back and beat a hasty retreat. It helps that we have different and complementary roles. David, for example, is a terrific organizer and in love with his computer. I, on the other hand, wouldn't know how to switch one on. I guess I will have to learn one day, but in the meantime I thank my lucky stars that I am able to afford a PA to do it for me. I prefer to be the creator; David makes the ideas happen.

Jay and I are very close to David and his wife Margot, a feisty Kiwi. When I have an early appointment in London, I usually stay at David and Margot's the night before, which is marginally better than facing the morning rush hour. I say marginally, because we often end up sitting round the table till 4 am sharing a bottle of wine or three, talking about absolutely nothing. Or at least, not anything we can remember the next day. David and Margot have also helped enlarge our group of friends by introducing us to John and Helen Lederer and Mark and Shel Rawley, two great couples who are similarly fond of getting round the table and enjoying food, drink and conversation. John, as a restaurateur himself, has helped us out with some tricky restaurant situations and indulged us in some great food and wine. The value of good friends is something I desperately underestimated in my early life, and for teaching me how important they are I owe a lot to David as well as to Jaybe.

Meanwhile, at Woz, it seemed that it was the mugging rather than the excellent reviews that remained indelibly imprinted in the memories of prospective punters. Gradually, the weeknight covers dwindled and the place was rarely full except at weekends. And as we all know, customers in London like full restaurants, so the quieter they become, the more people stay away. Woz was drawn into this vicious circle and started to lose money. I should have closed it down a lot sooner than I did, but a combination of pride and loyalty to a great bunch of staff, ably managed by Amy Prior, clouded my judgement.

I decided to rename Woz and change the concept: Bistrorganic was born. I had been a supporter of the organic movement for a couple of years by now, and with all the flak from the BSE crisis flying around, it seemed the way to go. As with any reasonable new restaurant, there was an encouraging honeymoon period, but the business was slow to grow. It was a real hassle finding British organic produce. Imports were no problem, but I felt that it rather defeated the object of the organic ethos to use food that had been flown in from thousands of miles away, contributing to the contamination of the planet in the process.

Perhaps I was just a bit ahead of the game. Organic suppliers were not yet very professional when it came to operating on a commercial scale, and there was still a touch of the hippy attitude to the whole thing. The failure of Bistrorganic to establish itself quickly enough meant that we weren't able to keep it open very long. I am sure it would have worked eventually, but sadly we just didn't have the financial resources to see it through tough times. I had a meeting with Jay, David and our bank manager, Simon

Purdom, on the terrace at Wiz and, being a believer in democracy, reluctantly allowed myself to be persuaded to close it. I did so the very next day. I acted so quickly because I was in a major huff with democracy, but also, I guess, because deep down I knew that I had to put the wounded beast out of its misery swiftly. It had been open only six weeks and closed just two days after a one-star review from Fay Maschler. I was gutted. A great concept down the pan – what a waste. But in the real world you can't always go where your heart leads you.

Although I understood that on a business level, a bit of my heart went with Bistrorganic. I began to lose interest in Wiz. Instead I threw myself into other work. I wrote my best cookbook to date, *The ABC of AWT*, a compendium of my favourite recipes based on an alphabetical list of single ingredients. Again published by Headline, under the guidance of the wonderful Heather Holden-Brown, who had recently joined them from BBC Books, it looked great: lovely design, good content, something for everyone. I had learned from Delia Smith to keep it simple: simple language, simple dishes. I might have had a run-in with Delia later but she is nonetheless a woman to be admired; a woman who has been on our television screens since 1973 and who has sold about 12 million books.

And at this time, as well as writing the book, I pushed myself through a welter of television work. I loved doing *Ready, Steady, Cook* and *Food and Drink* for the BBC, but I also took on what seemed like hundreds of programmes for the Carlton Food Network, or Taste, as it was known for a short time before its demise. The main programme-maker for the Carlton Food Network was a production company called Transmedia, run by a chum of mine, a larger-than-life character called Bruce Burgess. Bruce is a lovable guy but unfortunately he is a bit like me in that he often lets his heart rule his head. He is an inspired man with a wonderfully creative brain chock full of good ideas, but at Transmedia he was turning these into bargain-basement shows put together on tiny budgets. The production values of some of the early programmes were distinctly suspect, the camerawork was poor and the editing even worse, but the quality improved as he developed relationships with more professional directors and crews. At one stage Transmedia was the seventh-largest in-dependent production company in the UK, but as is so often the case with people who have great creative talent, Bruce's administrative skills left something to be desired, and the old Tesco dictum 'pile 'em high, sell 'em cheap' didn't hold true in his business. He lived life to the full, probably to overflowing, and he seemed to lack the strong management he badly needed to keep everything under control. As a result his company finished up in liquidation. He'll be sorely missed by me, though not, I am afraid, by everyone.

Working on TV gives me a great buzz. I know I have been one of the lucky ones in getting the opportunities I've had. To some degree it is a question of being at the right place at the right time, and I am fortunate in that the progression of my career has coincided with the height of the boom in television cookery. So even if it should all dry up tomorrow, I can count my blessings. I particularly enjoy being invited to appear on programmes unrelated to cookery – it makes a nice change and gives me a broader media profile – and I'm delighted to have been asked to contribute to so many different productions, from game and comedy shows to serious current affairs programmes, among them *Call My Bluff*, *Family Fortunes*, *This Morning*, GMTV, *Richard and Judy*, *Ruby Wax*, *Closure*, *Confessions*, *Blankety Blank*, *Dispatch Box*, *The National Lottery Show*, *Ricky Gervais* and *Patrick Kielty*.

I did a couple of editions of *Shooting Stars*, one of which got quite out of hand but was huge fun. Another crazy but equally brilliant experience was doing *The Kumars at No. 42*, the spoof chat show purportedly broadcast from the Wembley home of an Asian family, hosted by Sanjeev Bhaskar, with his 'mother', 'father' and 'granny' all chipping in. Great formula, great cast, great fun. I didn't know whether I was coming or going, but on that programme it doesn't matter – you just have to go with the flow. But it must have been the masochist in me that agreed to appear on *Have I Got News For You*. My appearance came in the wake of accusations by a previous guest, a smart-alec journalist, that the whole thing was orchestrated. Well, he might have had his hand held, but the only steer I got beforehand was a run-through of the format of the show and a big pile of newspapers in my dressing room. Ian Hislop may have a waspish exterior but he was very kind to me. He came to my dressing room before the recording and gave me some advice. 'If you're a wimp, we'll walk all over you,' he explained. 'But if you go for it, you'll be fine.' Well, I am hardly a shrinking violet in front of the camera, so I went for it and indeed I was fine. There is no point in trying to match the wit of Hislop or

Paul Merton, or the dry put-downs of host Angus Deayton to which we were still treated then, before his fall from grace. They are the real stars, which is as it should be.

Although I have regularly appeared on news slots on both television and radio, the prospect of being on the panel of a seriously grown-up programme of the calibre of BBC 1's *Question Time*, chaired by David Dimbleby, was pretty nerve-racking. Because I was a *Question Time* virgin, for nearly a week beforehand a production assistant would ring up every other day pumping me for my views on various topical subjects, not to prime me in any way – nobody has any advance warning of the questions – but merely to test my ability to give an on-the-spot answer to whatever was thrown at me. I am an avid reader of newspapers and generally fall asleep with BBC News 24 or Sky News still giving me the latest developments, and I pride myself on being someone who has an answer to everything, right or wrong. But even so, this was scary Mary, especially as I would be sharing the platform with such seasoned politicians as Shirley Williams. But I've recognized from being a regular viewer of *Question Time* myself that what the studio audience – and no doubt the television audience, too – appreciate are common-sense answers. So often the politicians on the panel toe the party line and skirt round the actual question. I think that if anything the studio audience tends to lean more to the left than to the right, but most of the time all they want is honesty. I was quite nervous at the start, but it's amazing how quickly the confidence comes flowing back once you get a good round of applause for one of your responses. I tried to concentrate on giving those honest answers, and I hope I succeeded.

The programme that most threatened my vow not to let stress get to me was not *Question Time* but *Food Junkies*, a mini-series highlighting the problems in our eating habits. The edition in which I made my main contribution was about sugar, and the fact that owing to our overconsumption of the stuff, about 20 per cent of the adult population of the UK are in a pre-diabetic state known as Syndrome X. I was seen as an ideal candidate for testing for the programme – overweight, underexercised and a smoker – and out of a morbid curiosity to see whether I was among that 20 per cent, I suppose, I agreed to be their guinea pig. The test is not yet available on the NHS, and I hadn't bargained for such a lengthy and extensive procedure. It was carried out at a university hospital in Glasgow, where two whizzkid professors put two drips, containing glucose and insulin respectively, in my left arm while my right arm was put in a sort of makeshift oven, which was very hot and uncomfortable. I had to sit there for two hours, with blood being drawn from the oven arm every ten minutes and centrifugally processed to enable the medics to construct a graph of my insulin resistance.

The upshot was that I did in fact have Syndrome X, which I must admit surprised me. I have always enjoyed great health. I am hardly ever ill, I have loads of energy, I sleep well, I eat healthily, if a tad too enthusiastically, and my heart is strong. I was aware of my black marks, too, of course, the weight, the smoking and the lack of regular exercise, but as they had never caused me any problems the result of this test came as a shock to me and, judging by some of the letters I received from viewers, to many of them, too. It takes a jolt like this to get you to deal with your bad habits. But we can all do something about it. Syndrome X is reversible, though it's not so easy to reverse if you progress to diabetes type 2, a condition that is beginning to reach epidemic proportions in Britain. I have recently become involved in a project called Measure Your Mate, which aims to increase public awareness of the fact that something as simple as keeping tabs on your partner with a tape measure can be the first step to preventing diabetes. The danger lies beyond a 39-inch waist for the guys and 35 inches for the girls. So get measuring.

One characteristic I hope you will have noticed about me by now is that I don't let things get me down for long. At least I have the right shape for bouncing back. I may have done some stupid things in my life but I hope that I have finally grown up enough not to do anything so stupid that it is impossible to recover from. Fame often seems somehow to instil a suicidal streak in people. I am only grateful that I have been content to potter around on the periphery of the whole shooting match and have therefore avoided the pressures heaped upon A, B and even C-list figures.

It doesn't need stating that the press can be incredibly cruel, but sadly, that's just the way things are. They build people up and then they knock them down again. It's the nature of the business we are in, and it is no business for the faint-hearted. When we choose to work in the public eye, we have to accept that. We all know what it entails. You are constantly on show, public property, and when the public has finished with you it will be your time to join the others on the scrapheap. The trick seems to be to have a game plan and to reinvent yourself from time to time. As for my own dealings with the press, being a straight talker, I believe in telling it before it is told about me. Jaybe cringes sometimes when she reads one of my columns or hears me talking on radio or TV, but too bad, that's me.

I have been asked, 'Wouldn't you have loved to have done a Jamie Oliver?' I have to give a politician's answer to that one: yes, no, I don't know. I have a lot of admiration for Jamie: the boy's done good and he's a nice guy with it. But it's the same for him as it is for all of us. He can't know how long he is going to be on his particular pedestal, so he just has to make the most of it while he is up there, and good luck to him. I have no time for petty jealousies. As individuals we have to feel good about ourselves and what we've personally achieved. If you don't, nobody else is going to do it for you. And I do feel good about myself. I know that I am a lucky sod, although to some degree you do have to work at being lucky. But I have plenty to keep my feet on the ground. As well as Jay and the children, I have my memories of not having enough money to put petrol in the car and the salutary lesson of two people who had nobody but themselves to blame for the slide in their careers: my mother and father.

On the subject of letting things slide, as I wrapped myself up in my media work, this was precisely what I was in danger of doing with Wiz. The demise of Woz and Bistrorganic had knocked the stuffing out of me a bit but there was more to it than that, and I just couldn't quite put my finger on what. The obvious problem with Wiz was that the location wasn't right. I'm a good concept man, even if some of my ideas have ultimately proved too complicated for their own good, but latterly I had been lousy at choosing locations.

Woz, I am sure, would still be going if it had been somewhere like Kensington Church Street, where Sally Clarke's and Kensington Place are perennially popular. Wiz, meanwhile, needed high street, passing trade; it needed a high turnover of customers. It needed me to be there, head pulled back out of the sand and radiating confidence.

But after what had happened with Woz and Bistrorganic, that confidence wasn't there. And I was doing so well with all the other irons I had in the fire that I asked myself more than once, do I really need this headache? Do I actually need a restaurant? The answer to that, of course, was no. I didn't need one, but I did want one – that drug again. The trouble was, it wasn't Wiz. The final straw was discovering that the manager was on the take. The other staff were wonderful – old faithfuls, bright stars – but Wiz had to go.

I knew, though, that it was not a good time to be selling, so I had to make contingency plans in case it didn't move quickly enough. I've always liked the way New York restaurateurs cope with a moribund business. They understand that in the Big Apple a restaurant will often have no longer than a two-year shelf life, so when they sense stagnation setting in, instead of selling their premises they reverse the decline by simply changing the concept, reinventing themselves.

I decided that if necessary I would follow their example, and in the event it was a good thing I did. There was a bitter irony in the fact that the city that had inspired my remedy was itself the biggest victim of the atrocity that exacerbated the problem. As the effects of the destruction of New York's famous landscape on 11 September were felt around the world, trade deteriorated, and we calculated that if we did not do something to save the situation, by March 2002 we would be forced to put the company into liquidation.

An idea had been planted in my mind by my friend Tim Etchells, the godfather of the Good Food Show, London Fashion Week and many other high-profile events. He took me to dinner at the Popeseye Steak House in Olympia to road-test a concept he thought might suit me. The Popeseye serves only steak. But this was no Angus Steakhouse-type chain restaurant. This was prime, well-hung beef, with no poncy frills, just good chips, a salad, a small selection of puds. It also served some excellent wines, mainly reds, at very reasonable prices. I was impressed. And the biggest plus for me as a professional restaurateur was that there was only one chef. This, I felt, was a concept well worth nicking.

The various friends I told about it, not to mention Jaybe and David, thought I'd taken leave of my senses. 'It'll never work. What about BSE? What about foot and mouth? The public have no confidence in meat,' they said. Precisely. All the more reason for someone to give them meat they could trust. Jaybe and David were harder to convince, but I pointed out that we had nothing to lose. If carried on with Wiz we'd be closed within three months anyway – I wasn't prepared to plough any more hard-earned money into it. They were also worried about how much converting the restaurant would cost. I had done a few sums and I assured them we could do it for £10,000. They read that as £20,000, but they, and Simon the bank manager, eventually came round to the idea.

I settled on a name, Notting Grill, and a colour scheme, blood or claret red, both of which seemed appropriate. I had given David five weeks to go off and visit his in-laws in New Zealand, and I was determined that Notting Grill would be ready on his return. It was – and we closed the restaurant for only twenty-four hours, for the final cosmetic make-over, during the whole process. In the end we got the job done for £11,000, a feat we managed by getting everyone we could muster to muck in. Sean, a friend of a friend, did most of the exterior paintwork. January is hardly the ideal month for outside painting, but he eventually got it done, as well as some of the interior, although I had to get my mates Charlie and Paul and Jaybe up a ladder as well to finish on time.

When David and Margot left for New Zealand on Christmas day, the embryonic Notting Grill was more or less a clone of Popeseye; by the time they returned five weeks later, it had been transformed into something quite different. Although Tim Etchells and Popeseye had inspired the concept, Notting Grill became its own creature. I hate the idea of ripping off another restaurant – it's happened too often to me. Sure, steak was to be the key, but in addition I had decided that there would also be a 'chop of the day', 'fish of the day', 'shellfish of the day', and 'comfort food of the day'. I also planned to introduce my own Middle White pigs to the menu – no, not as customers, but as suckling pig or chops. I find pork is usually the most disappointing of all meats. Such is the prevailing paranoia about fat that more often than not it does not have enough of the stuff to prevent it from turning out dry and leathery. My Middle Whites, however, have a generous covering of fat, producing the best crackling in the world, succulence, flavour and the tenderness of non-PC veal. It's a superb product, but unfortunately a little too fatty for those who insist on breeding the lean machines we see in supermarkets.

In essence what had attracted me to Popeseye was simplicity, but it was a difficult U-turn to get my head around. After all, my restaurant successes had been based on complication, on using every corner of my chef's imagination and every conceivable ingredient, sometimes all at once. Here my main courses were all grilled, apart from any game and the comfort food dish. A little salt and pepper were their only partners, together with a side dish of béarnaise sauce, hollandaise sauce, green salsa or onion marmalade as appropriate.

But to indulge the chef in me, while David was away I had also decided to include starters on the menu. It makes sense, after all. If the customers are sitting around waiting for their steaks they might as well be enjoying something first, and I might as well be taking their money. I think starters make a meal, and if I wasn't going to be able to muck about with the meat, at least I could channel some of my creativity into the smaller courses.

As far as the main courses were concerned, I redirected the energies I would previously have devoted to researching a variety of produce and dishes into trying to acquire the very best meat and fish possible. If you are going to dress it up, you might be able to get away with the odd deficiency; cooked and served naked, it has to be the best. I discovered salt marsh lamb, Highland lamb, Herdwick lamb. I buy chickens that have had a proper life lasting at least 100 days, so that they reach a weight of 6lb. They cost me £15 each. My accountant, of course, would prefer me to buy factory-farmed £1.99 chickens, but then, what do accountants know about food? My beautiful, diver-caught scallops are £1.75 each in the shell. I could buy five dredged ones for that, but they wouldn't have that meaty quality, that sweet, tender flesh. My sea bass, unlike that served in most restaurants, is wild, not farmed; my prawns, which I serve with garlic and chilli, are the cold-water variety for that unbeatable taste of the sea, not those cheap warm-water prawns from the Far East. Most of the vegetables, salads and herbs are home grown, without the use of chemicals, on my plot near Henley; my chips are hand cut.

But it is the beef that I made into a real mission. I trawled suppliers and farms from all over the country. I tried out Welsh Black beef, Longhorn beef, red Dexter, Aberdeen Angus 50 per cent, Aberdeen Angus 100 per cent, Hereford. I studied books, talked to my old Scottish mate Arthur Alsop, who lived and breathed beef, and prize-winning butchers like David Lidgate. But instead of the holy grail I was seeking, what I found was surprising inconsistency. Irrespective of breed, there was good and bad and often the meat was no more than average. The key thing was how the animal was reared and looked after and, most importantly of all, how it was fed. During the spring and summer months, when the grass was growing, the quality of meat was generally good, and in the winter it fell away. Diet, and in particular a finishing diet of barley, was responsible for that tightly muscled meat with very white fat and a lean, red eye with little or no marbling – by which

I mean those little rivulets of fat in the red muscle. Because this is the look that the supermarkets prefer, and because most cattle now have to be killed before they are thirty months old in accordance with regulations introduced after the outbreak of BSE, farmers have become conditioned to fattening their stock on barley, a cheap and not too labour-intensive feeding method. So now I had to find sources of beef where the animals had a winter diet of grass silage and occasionally linseed cake, which was easier said than done.

The next thing I discovered was that it is rare to find a pure breed of cattle such as Aberdeen Angus or Hereford because so many farmers cross their stock with continental breeds like Charolais, Limousin or Belgian Blue, which are much larger animals than our traditional breeds and not really suited to the EC thirty-month rule. They are much better kept for forty-eight to sixty months. Perhaps it's time more farmers returned to our own traditional breeds and concerned themselves more with quality than with the yield of each animal. The Aberdeen Angus programme is all very well, but legally only 50 per cent of the breeding pair has to be full pedigree for the offspring to be entitled to the name. What's wrong with 100 per cent?

Until we recognize that not everything should be about price, price, price, we'll never get the kind of meat we should all be demanding. Pork, in particular, would benefit from a return to the traditional breeds – Gloucester Old Spot, Saddleback, English Lop, Large White, Middle White, Tamworth. It can't happen overnight, of course, but we could make a start by at least crossing the hybrid commercial pig with one of these traditional breeds. Anything that might improve the quality.

I extended my market research to New York, where the reputations of the steakhouses stand or fall on how good the meat is. US beef is always incredibly tender, thanks in some part to added hormones we're not allowed in Europe (thank God), but what it gains in tenderness it tends to lose in flavour. One leaf we could take out of their book, though, is to try overwintering our cattle on corn which, unlike barley, does produce those wonderful flecks of fat in the red eye of the meat. My quest for the perfect beef continues, but in the meantime I think I've probably got the best steaks in London, aged for at least twenty-eight days in my special ageing rooms, and my customers love them. Food fashion now seems to have come full circle. The nouvelle cuisine craze gave way in turn to cuisine terroir or grandmère, Mediterranean and North

African, until finally everyone said, 'Enough – just give me plain food I can trust.' And that's Notting Grill.

The same may be happening with wine. From French we went Californian, Australian, Chilean, Argentinian, South African and now, it seems, going by my own customers' choices, French is making a comeback.

With Notting Grill up and running, there remained one missing piece: a good front-of-house man. Because of the emphasis for so many years on chefs, the importance of character out front is often neglected by restaurants, but it should be much more of a priority here than in the kitchen. Margot, David's razor-sharp wife, provided our missing link in the shape of George, an ex-area manager from her days with the Café Rouge group.

He was an immediate hit. Not only does he have a wicked sense of humour, but terrific confidence. He has the knack of creating a buzz and of charming the bolshiest of customers, he gets a great work rate out of his staff and, best of all, he is not afraid to take risks when necessary. George has made the customers his own and they love him. Long may he stay with us.

At Notting Grill, I always try to encourage George and his staff to be themselves, real people with real lives, and to treat the customers likewise. The right attitude means confidence without cockiness, no suggestion of inferiority but no arrogance, either. I know a couple of famous, fashionable restaurants where it is so impossible to get a table, unless you are a 'regular', that they might as well be private clubs. If you call to make a reservation they will automatically tell you they are full, but take your details 'in case there's a cancellation'. On the day of your booking, they go through the list they've compiled and decide on the basis of your postcode who to favour. If you live in an expensive area you will be phoned and told that there has been a cancellation. Would you still like a table? Of course, you immediately say yes, because a reservation there is as rare as hen's teeth.

What a performance. I am far happier spending my four nights a week sweating away at Notting Grill, taking great satisfaction in the knowledge that we can hold our heads high in any company. In terms of London's grill restaurants, I would rank us alongside the Popeseye and Smith's of Smithfield for the quality of our product. I know of nowhere else that can touch us. I'm proud of what we've achieved at Notting Grill, and pleased, not to say relieved, that my gut feeling was right: most people secretly love a good piece of meat. Their fondness for beef had merely been driven into the closet by BSE and foot and mouth, and the key to unlocking it was to provide top-of-the-range produce they could enjoy without worrying. And that's what we give them.

CHAPTER THIRTY-TWO

LIFE DOESN'T STOP AT FIFTY. I MAY HAVE FOUND DOMESTIC BLISS AND developed a healthier perspective on life, but I am still brimming with ambition. So what next? The temptation, of course, is to open another restaurant. After all the research and development I have put into Notting Grill, I know where to buy meat, my fish is top-notch and my smallholding at Shiplake can supply vegetables for more than one outlet. In David and George I have the support that would allow me to expand. But, having had my fingers burned in the past, it is perhaps the confidence I am lacking rather than the resources.

If I do decide to go for it, I would open a place in my local area. I am certain that the Notting Grill concept would work there, because while we are blessed with plenty of gourmets' delights within a thirty-mile radius – among them the Waterside Inn and the Fat Duck at Bray, and Le Manoir aux Quat' Saisons near Oxford – as well as a plethora of Italian, Indian, Chinese and Thai restaurants and several gastropubs, there is nowhere offering good, honest, plain cooking using top-quality ingredients. So you never know, I might take the plunge.

I have already dabbled in a couple of business interests in my area, first with a 40 per cent share of the Greyhound pub at Rotherfield Peppard, a beautiful thatched inn with great potential which wasn't, in the end, the success I'd hoped for. My other involvement in the Henley area is a small function venue near Hambledon called Luxter's, a beautiful old barn set in the middle of an English winery and microbrewery. I have always thought that most function food is awful: plastic pre-made stuff positioned on plates with no care, no heart. At Luxter's I'm trying to change all that. It's working out well, and our customers have been ecstatic about the results.

Whatever happens next, I am sure I won't be doing it on my own. My friend Mary-Leese Parker has helped me out one way or another for several years. She reminds me a lot of myself: she is a girl on a mission, though where to I'm not sure she knows herself. On the outside she appears very scatty, a bit Boris Johnson, a bit mad. She's a disorganized cook, so messy you could sometimes be forgiven for thinking she must have fallen into a bowl of fish slops. But on the inside she is very driven, and doesn't suffer fools gladly. She hasn't quite found her niche yet, but I have great faith in her. In fact, I think she could be the Nigella Oliver of television cookery: beauty, brains and balls all in one package. What more could a television company ask for?

But then, you never know quite how the public are going to perceive you. I've had my own problems in that department. I seem to have acquired a bit of a reputation as the guy who gets up everyone's nose. I can't imagine why. I suppose my widely publicized run-ins with Delia Smith and Gordon Ramsay haven't helped, and neither does the fact that the press are always attributing bitchy comments about Jamie Oliver to me. I'd like to put the record straight here. I love everyone. Well, almost everyone.

I certainly don't hate the godmother of television cookery. Delia might not be my personal cup of Tetley's, but her recipes are user-friendly and they work. She is beyond criticism, really – a genuine phenomenon with millions of fans. My spat with her was rooted in a simple misunderstanding. I made the innocent mistake of describing our Delia as the Volvo of TV cooks, and she took that to mean I thought she was boring. She obviously doesn't know her Volvos. Not only are they pretty racy cars nowadays, but their big selling point is that they are almost as safe as houses. And that's all I intended to convey by the comparison: that Delia's is the safest pair of hands on the telly.

My second clanger was another well-intentioned if naive remark, made during a court case in Manchester in which I was called as an expert witness. The local council was bringing an action against a caterer accused of poisoning a large number of people with his chocolate mousse. I didn't know the guy from Adam, but I sympathized with his plight and felt strongly enough about it to support him. At that time salmonella was rife, and councils all over the country were advising chefs to produce hard-boiled eggs, leather omelettes, poached eggs like rocks and scrambled-egg nuggets and to dispense altogether with mousses, mayonnaise and hollandaise sauce, anything which required raw eggs. This chef, like the rest of us, had used raw eggs for years without ever encountering a problem, and always obtained them from the same supplier. But what he hadn't been aware of on this occasion was that the supplier, having run out of his regular eggs, had delivered imported ones instead.

There was no way he could have known the eggs were imported, as this was before British ones had returned to having the lion stamped on their shells. Equally, when you break an egg into a bowl, there is absolutely no way of telling whether it is carrying salmonella, as the bacterium doesn't affect the egg itself. I reminded the court that on the rare occasion a restaurant inadvertently poisons someone with an oyster, we are not prosecuted as long as all the regulations have been followed and the oyster in question is fresh and has been correctly stored. Instead the council goes back to the supplier and checks that his filtration plant is working properly. Why, then, should it be any different with eggs?

In my witness statement, I tried to make the point that a lot of people ate their eggs lightly cooked. I even asked the magistrate whether he liked to dip soldiers into the yolk of a soft-boiled egg. He smiled, but replied, 'I'll ask the questions, thank you, Mr Worrall Thompson.' On our television screens the previous week, Delia had been teaching us all about toast and eggs in her *How to Cook* series. She had prepared some lightly scrambled eggs, very runny and smooth – very unBritish, in fact, more like a French version of the dish – and I suggested to the court that, given her amazing influence over the country's kitchens, after watching this programme a lot more of her 5 million viewers would be adopting her method and leaving themselves open to salmonella poisoning. In describing Delia's scrambled eggs, I said they had the consistency of baby sick. What I hadn't bargained for was some student journalist sitting in the public gallery who thought all his Christmases had come at once. He contacted the national newspapers, and the press had a field day. 'TV CHEF ATTACKS DELIA'S EGGS', 'DELIA'S EGGS ARE LIKE BABY SICK', ran the headlines the next morning. They took the remark completely out of context and, in many cases, bent it to suit their own stories. I am not surprised Delia took umbrage.

I drew some consolation from the fact that we won the court case. In fact, it was something of a landmark victory. It was the first time a council had been defeated on this issue, and it set a precedent for future egg cases.

Although I never intended to insult Delia, she obviously didn't see it that way. We all know that revenge is a dish best eaten cold, so I wasn't surprised that she retaliated, but it was the way she decided to do it that was somewhat unexpected. Her chosen instrument of torture was a full-page interview conducted by my *bête noir* of the critics, Jan Moir, in the *Telegraph*. The published article revealed a Delia we had never seen before, a Delia with the gloves off who proved that she wasn't after all a puppet operated by some BBC producer.

If her comments ('Antony Worrall Thompson is the most repulsive man on television' and '*Food and Drink* is the most disgusting programme' – ouch, ouch!) had been made by someone else, I might have been cut to the quick, but as it was, in a masochistic kind of way, I was rather touched to be the focus of Delia's attention. In spite of the fact that her *How to Cook* programmes had copied the series I had made a year earlier for the now-defunct Carlton Food Network, *Simply Antony*, it seemed that, when the chips were down, this was what she really thought of me. Magic.

Of course the press enjoyed themselves hugely over this. Every newspaper put its own slant on the story, and it even made it to America. It was a hilarious week. I appeared on several radio and TV chat shows whose producers were clearly hoping to be broadcasting the agonized howls of a mortally wounded animal. They had reckoned without the AWT resilience. Sticks and stones and all that. It's not true, of course, that words can never hurt you, but for some reason, coming from Delia, these words didn't hurt. Funnily enough, they seemed to draw me closer to her. Perhaps it was the fact that at last Miss Perfect had reacted in a normal, human, red-blooded manner. By way of a response, I should have bought her a year's subscription to *Autosport*, so she could get to know the real Volvo, and dispatched a note reading: 'Delia, that's the last time I sleep with you.' It was all great fun and I'm sure in the end she saw it for what it was, too, because for my fiftieth birthday she sent me a photograph of herself sporting an 'Antony' T-shirt and holding one of my cookbooks. The note with it said: 'Antony, I love you really.' It was a fitting end to a little cheffie spat.

My other well-documented cheffie spat, with Gordon Ramsay, is still ongoing. In spite of the fact that he has had a telly series or two of his own – though I grant you, they had more in common with horror stories than television cookery – Gordon has a thing about TV chefs, especially me. He's auditioned for other programmes as well. From what I heard, he even wanted to be on *Celebrity Big Brother* until his close family talked him out of it. Is this really a man who doesn't want to be a celebrity? I don't think so.

He kicked off this mini feud by describing me as a squashed Bee Gee. That didn't worry me. I thought it was quite sweet, actually. It's when he gets seriously vindictive that my hackles rise. After the Delia incident he told the London *Evening Standard*: 'Give me Delia's cooking any day. Antony Worrall Thompson can't cook to save his life.' I wouldn't take issue with his preference for Delia – her talent is not in doubt, and he is entitled to his opinion – but the rest of his statement was downright libellous and could even have damaged my career. This time he had gone too far, and I couldn't let it go. I turned over the options in my mind. Should I sue, or should I just send round one of my boys?

In the end it was a man for whom I have a great deal of time, Gordon's mentor Marco Pierre White, who persuaded me not to take legal action. I realized that Gordon's bitterness stemmed from the prospect of living in Marco's shadow for the rest of his life, and that this was probably punishment enough. Gordon is a brilliant chef, arguably verging on the genius, but in my view, he will never be as great as Marco, the acknowledged genius. There are times when I think Gordon has crossed that fine line between genius and insanity.

If you are thinking that I am not immune to bitterness myself when it comes to Gordon Ramsay, you probably have a point. But it's not something that eats me up. I have better things to do with my life. He is no more than an occasional irritation. There's no law that says we have to like everyone we come across and it's sometimes quite satisfying to have an annoying fly to squash. Talking of which, I wonder if Gordon would accept a best-of-five challenge on the programme he calls 'Ready, Steady, Twat'?

I can't think of anyone I hate. Well, certainly no one I hate for no good reason. Yet there are times when I can wander innocently into a pub and look around the bar, only to be met with a greeting such as: 'Who do you think you are looking at, c**t?'

Perhaps it's my face. I check the mirror regularly to see whether I'm going cross-eyed, and I must admit I do have one of those faces that looks as if it used to enjoy a fight. The kindest thing you can say about it is that it's very lived in. I've often wondered whether I should have it changed, but can you imagine the bill? In any case, I'm rather attached to it.

Perhaps it's my personality. It is true that I am fond of a good debate, and some would say I am argumentative. I relish taking on people in positions of authority, especially politicians, and the fact that I have a view on everything can get up a few noses. It certainly annoys the hell out of my wife. But if you believe in something, it is not only your right but also your duty to fight your corner. You just have to realize that you can never please everyone. I reckon that as long as I am pleasing more people than I upset, then I'm getting somewhere.

I've had several run-ins with politicians on television or radio. Invariably, true to their reputation, they won't give a straight answer. They have normally planned what they are going to say before they even know what the question is. We need more presenters like Jeremy Paxman, the proverbial dog with a bone. He just won't let go, and in the end the politicians he is interviewing are usually forced to reply. Half of me would love to have a role like his, maybe on the radio, but the other half has a hankering to be the politician. Jaybe thinks I've taken leave of my senses as far as the latter ambition is concerned.

I'm keen at least to broaden my involvement in food education issues. As well as being in favour of the introduction of compulsory cookery lessons in schools, I believe there are many other steps we can take to ensure that future generations live a healthier lifestyle. We should start by removing some of the temptations placed in their path. In an era of increasing obesity, advertising directed at children, particularly television commercials pushing junk food and sugary drinks screened at times when they are likely to be watching, is potentially even more dangerous than cigarette advertising was. The same goes for the practice of marketing these products by offering free toys for kids to collect. It puts pressure on parents and makes trying to shop in a supermarket with children a nightmare.

We should also remove vending machines dispensing unnecessary fizzy drinks and unhealthy snacks, which dull the appetite for real food, from school corridors. The presence of these products here sends out completely the wrong message. It would make sense to reinstate school meals for all children at the same time. Perhaps the appointment of a Loyd Grossman-type figurehead to create nutritionally balanced but more exciting dishes would revitalize the image of 'school dinners'. If it can work in hospitals, where people are hardly in the mood to eat anything, surely it would succeed with active children whose interest in food has at least been kindled by *Ready, Steady, Cook* or Jamie Oliver.

To nurture that interest, I'd like to see an organic garden in every school. In my experience, children who understand how vegetables grow are far more likely to eat them. In spite of having sold off so many playing fields, most schools will have a spare plot of land somewhere – what better use to put it to than educating their pupils about the power of the soil and the sun, the importance of water, the destructive capabilities of bugs and organic treatments for them?

Another string I have added to my bow recently is product development, and perhaps it is here that my future lies – who knows? I agreed to get involved with Breville, the inventors of the sandwich toaster, when they approached my agent, but only on condition that I was involved in design discussions: style, colours, practicality, necessity, usefulness, everything. I was determined to do it properly. I am especially pleased with our slow-start liquidizer. All liquidizers are very aggressive, and if you've seen me regularly blowing the lid off the one on *Ready, Steady, Cook* when I'm blitzing up hot soups, you'll know where I was coming from there. In fact we now have in excess of fifteen great electrical appliances on the market, all of which I've helped to develop, and I'm chuffed to bits with them all.

From electrical goods, I went on to pots and pans with Ultimate, knives with the Japanese Knife Company, then small kitchen gadgets with Eddington's and food containers with Butterfly Elite. They are all subject to the same stipulations: whatever is out there with my name on it must work efficiently, have style and be the best within its price bracket.

I've now taken my next step in product development with a range of edibles: about to hit a shop near you are biscuits, cakes, organic stock, teas, rustic breads, goats' milk yoghurts, soups, jams, sausages, sandwiches, ice cream, chocolates and mineral water, all made by excellent, mostly small, British companies. This is a difficult line to get right, and for the moment some compromise has been necessary. Originally, I wanted all the food to be home-produced and organic, but this proved to be impossible, mainly because it would have priced it out of the supermarkets, so instead I have laid down four criteria to be followed. The products should beat the competition for taste; they should be made where possible by small manufacturers; these manufacturers should be British companies using British ingredients; whenever price allows, organic produce should be preferred. The formula should always include the first criterion and one or more of the others. Again, I have played an active part in developing the range, and all the recipes have gone back and forth for testing and adjustment until I've been happy with the result. Inevitably, this has meant the occasional item hitting the buffers, but pride and integrity are paramount. I'm in it for the long term, so I have to be patient. In conjunction with my agent, I'm working with Jonathan Townsend of the Partnership to find manufacturers that can come up with the quality foods I want for my range, and I think we have the makings of a great team.

I'm still so competitive that even a recent losing streak on *Ready, Steady, Cook* depressed me. I just hate losing. I'm sure every other *Ready, Steady, Cook* chef would say the same if they were being honest. We're all mates on the show, but I love Brian Turner even more when I beat him. We are similar characters. We're both Taureans, we both love our food, we're both stubborn and, although our catering upbringings were different, in the last few years our careers have followed similar paths. I love him like the dad I never really had. Three years ago we were both approached by our friend Roger Jupe, who was hoping to organize a bunch of TV chefs to run in the London Marathon. I think we both had the same reaction. 'You're having a laugh, aren't you? Look at the state of us!'

I thought no more about it until a couple of other requests made me start to wonder whether somebody was trying to tell me something. The first came from Weight Watchers, who invited me to become a personality slimmer. Then, out of the blue, a case of aspirin arrived in the post. It was sent to mark the hundredth anniversary of our best-known cure-all. The accompanying letter told me I was the perfect person to benefit from taking half a tablet a day for my heart and to help spread the word that aspirin was more than just a headache pill. The message from Roger, Weight Watchers and now the aspirin people was the same. You're a fat bastard and you've got to do something about it.

I was on the phone to Roger the very next day. 'I'll do your bloody marathon,' I heard myself saying. Then I told Weight Watchers to sign me up and began conscientiously taking my half-aspirin daily. What had I let myself in for? I hadn't run in ten years, and my only exercise was walking upstairs to bed each night. I hadn't seen my feet for many a moon, and they hadn't seen the inside of a pair of trainers for just as long.

The easiest bit was Weight Watchers. There was no hassle, no embarrassment, just this lovely lady who came to my house once a week. Rather than chastising me she encouraged me, and it worked. From a 16-stone colossus of rippling fat, I got down into the 13s, a great result. It was the marathon training that was the nightmare.

Jaybe decided to join me, and we were entrusted to the care of a fabulous trainer, Jane Wake, who came up to Henley from London. Sensibly, she started us slowly, but even fast walking gave me gyp. I started to get terrible pains in the soles of my feet and down my shins. You think all the parts work – I get out of bed no problem, I'm able to reach the car and I have been known to walk the dogs, all incredibly efficiently – but the moment you ask even a little extra of your body, it rebels. We decided massage might help, and Jane put me in touch with Randy Baptiste, a mountain of a man more suited, it seemed, to an American basketball team than to administering the gentle pats of a masseur.

I thought massage was supposed to make you feel good, but Randy's didn't. I dreaded every visit. He'd plant me on his special table and then the punishment would begin. It was as if he was jointing a chicken for a Hell's Angels ritual. His fingers dug between the muscles and seemed to pull them apart. There were times I'd want to scream and had to hold back the tears, and every week was worse than the last. He tried to reassure me, explaining that while I had well-developed calf muscles, unfortunately, instead of having the flexibility of rubber, they were brittle like plastic and could snap at any time.

Of the forty weeks' training I had planned, I managed eight. I wouldn't say it was ever exactly enjoyable – the knees would seize up, the back would go, every muscle would be assailed by cramp – but at least, living where I do by the Thames, I was able to suffer in lovely surroundings. With Radio 5 on my Walkman to take my mind off things, and Jaybe by my side, I went through pain barrier after pain barrier, and eventually, against all the odds and with the big race only ten days away, I reached my training target of eighteen miles. The race itself would be twenty-six miles. A book was opened at Foxtrot Oscar on how much of the course Brian and I would complete, whether we would finish, even whether we would actually start the race in the first place. I was heavily backed not to start. But bets like those served only to spur me on. One day my stubbornness will probably kill me.

As well as Randy the torturer I was also regularly consulting my GP, for heart advice, and an osteopath. Three days before the race, they both said, 'Don't do it.' One of them even made me sign a release form relieving him of any responsibility. Jaybe was extremely worried about me going ahead, but I hadn't come this far to give up now.

Because of our television-personality status, Jaybe and I and Brian and Jane, who was going to run with him, were allowed to start in the front row. I found myself next to Frank Bruno, who grabbed my generous breasts with his massive hands and laughed his head off. 'You're having a laugh,' he jested. Another reason for me to get round, I thought to myself. Jane had advised us to start slowly, but after Frank dented my male pride, I shot off on the signal. Only half a mile into the race, I realized I had left Jaybe, Brian and Jane a long way behind and that my shins were already killing me. I started to panic. I needed my mainstay, Jaybe, with me, but where was she? It was like looking for a needle in a haystack.

Eventually I picked her out on the other side of the stampede. How I managed to reach her I don't know. The heart monitor read 165. My doctor had told me it shouldn't go above 155. Oops. I couldn't slow down any more, I was walking as it was. Jaybe could have completed the twenty-six miles in a much quicker time if she'd gone it alone, but thank goodness she decided to stick with me, because I'm sure I would have packed it in without her strength and encouragement.

The crowds of onlookers were fabulous, a magnificent support. They called out to us so often by name that a couple of Kiwi girls, who obviously never watched cookery shows and didn't know who we were, asked if they could run with us. 'You seem to know so many people, it's a great morale-booster.' Sweet. At nineteen miles everything started seizing up and I didn't think I would be able to carry on, but I managed to drag my legs to a St John Ambulance recovery post where a wonderful great big woman pummelled life back into my destroyed limbs.

By the time we got to the Embankment they had closed the underpass so, in excruciating pain, we hauled ourselves up some steps near the Tower of London and down the other side. It was an additional punishment we could have done without. But reaching the Embankment does lift your spirits: you know then there are only four miles to go, though it feels like forty.

Jane, having seen Brian Turner home forty-five minutes ahead of us, a victory that hurt me even more than running the race did, came back to escort Jay and me home, so she ended up running nearly thirty-four miles herself. She must have been mad, but her help was very much appreciated by us. She is a real star.

Birdcage Walk became Birdcage Stumble and seemed to go on for ever, but nothing could stop us now. We had done it. Jaybe burst into tears. I manfully held mine back. In the best, or should I say worst, part of seven hours, I had drunk 13 litres of water, peed about 12, sweated about 6, lost nearly 14lbs in weight, and for all that time my heart rate had not dropped below 150. But I was ecstatic. OK, our time was nothing to write home about, but we had put a cork in all those doubting mouths predicting that never in a month of Sundays would Brian and I complete the course.

We staggered the mile to the Savoy Hotel for a real drink. Brian and Roger Jupe – who, having roped us in, was not in the end able to run himself owing to some physical malfunction or other – had organized a little gathering there and, more importantly, a thorough massage. That extra mile to the Savoy prolonged the torture but it was probably a good way of winding down. The moment either of us was tempted to stop everything started seizing up.

When asked earlier in an interview what he would be looking forward to most after the marathon, Brian had said, 'A chip butty served on a platter.' I went along with that, although it was a bit northern for me: I needed a glass of champagne to go with it. Anton Edelman, executive chef at the Savoy and himself a seasoned marathon runner, had been hugely generous, setting aside a room in the hotel for Jay and me as well as laying on a spread for the runners and organizers. The relief of having got round the whole course was overwhelming; now I just wanted to have a good time. Unfortunately, it wouldn't be for long. Whether it was the superb chip butty, the excellent pint of champagne or the cigarette I don't know, though I have a sneaking suspicion it was the cigarette, but one of the three made sure of that. One minute I was walking across the room and the next I was flat on my face, poleaxed. Jaybe thought I'd had a heart attack but she couldn't do much to help because she couldn't move herself. Her own legs had locked completely.

My heart monitor was still on my wrist, so Brian Turner checked it and announced in his dour Yorkshire way that I was still alive. I had fainted. The cigarette I had smoked had probably used up the small amount of oxygen left in my body. When I came round, I wanted to resume partying, but was persuaded to go to our room. It was a lovely room, I'm sure, but I hardly saw it: I was out cold for the next fifteen hours. Yet when I finally surfaced the next day I had surprisingly little stiffness in my legs.

It would be a lie to claim I'd love to run another marathon, but I never say never. If I were able to give myself a whole year to train, increasing the distance by one mile every two weeks, I might consider it. I just have to listen to my body. If my body says yes, then who knows?

The *Ready, Steady, Cook* group do a fair bit for charity, both individually and occasionally together. We get a lot out of our success so we all feel it is important to put something back. I would like to do even more, but you tend to be overwhelmed by requests – I probably get about six or eight such letters every day – and in the end you have to be strict and limit yourself to helping out half a dozen charities a year. Mine are mainly child-based – the NSPCC, Save the Children, Children in Need, the Child Bereavement Trust. I do work for others but both the cause and the charity itself have to grab me by the heartstrings. The trouble with a lot of organizations now is that the minute you give them an inch they seem to want a mile. Too many of them employ hardened salespeople who don't know how to take no for an answer. I'd rather deal with someone who is charming and patently personally committed to the cause than with some ruthless hard nut who would be equally at home selling double-glazing.

Of course, some charity work can be great fun, especially the BBC's annual telethon in aid of Children in Need. On one of these shows, Gary Rhodes, Brian Turner, Ainsley Harriott and I, all dressed in bright red suits, performed as the Four Chops, with Ainsley as the lead singer and the other three of us as his backing group. Moving and grooving has never been one of my fortes – I seem to have a problem getting the legs and arms synchronized, never mind the bum – and our choreographer, Nicky, clearly had no idea what she was taking on when she agreed to train us. Having said that, in the end Gary wasn't bad and as for Ainsley, he turned out to be a natural. The crowd went wild and, most importantly, we brought in big bucks. The veteran crooner Barry Manilow, who was on after us, said to us sweetly: 'How can I follow that? Do you want to come on tour with me?' I'd rather raise money that way than run a marathon any day. Not that it wasn't scary, but at the same time it was incredibly exhilarating.

On the back of that success, a couple of years later I agreed to participate in an even more demanding act with Ainsley, Brian, James Martin and Tony Tobin. This time the five of us, two fat boys and three fit boys, were asked to perform our own version of the Full Monty. When I found out we were going to have to bare all, I wondered whether this was going too far. Singing and gyrating about a bit is one thing; getting your kit off when you have a body like mine was perhaps pushing it. But in for a penny, in for a pound.

Nicky the choreographer once again managed to turn a couple of sow's ears into silk purses. As was only to be expected in a parody of a striptease, her dance moves for this show were more complicated in that they involved a fair bit of sexual thrusting. Needless to say, my bum always seemed to be going in a different direction from everybody else's. I never seem to have any trouble doing the real thing, but somehow doing it to music without anybody to do it to confuses my already rudimentary coordination. In the end, Nicky devised a rather crude but effective method of keeping me on track. 'Just imagine there is a woman in front of you,' she said. 'On the forward thrust say, "Fuck 'em," and on the reverse thrust say "Leave 'em." Fuck 'em and leave 'em, in time with the beat.' After that I realized where I had been going wrong. I had been leaving them before I had fucked them.

The next problem involved trying to remove my prison warder's jacket, tie, belt, shirt and all the rest of it at the same time as fucking 'em and leaving 'em or doing a twirl. There have been plenty of times when I've had enough bother just getting my kit off at night without falling over, let alone dancing and undressing at the same time. I fervently wished I had Ainsley's natural talent.

But I wouldn't be beaten. Weeks of practising in front of the bathroom mirror got me to an acceptable if not outstanding level. Brian and I had made a pact to go on a diet, but there was one major obstacle: food. Come the final rehearsal I had, if anything, put on weight. Brian hadn't fared much better, but he had at least had sufficient forethought to sneak off to some desert island to bronze his expanse of flesh. I hadn't been nearly so organized.

On the day of the performance, I was doing a personal appearance in Edinburgh. After my plane touched down at Heathrow I made an emergency dash to a tanning studio I knew of in Kensington, where I spent an hour on the most powerful machine. Boy, did I sweat, but I told myself it was all in a good cause. Arriving at the BBC studios in Wood Lane, I went off to get changed and discovered, horror of horrors, that not only was my whole body the colour of cooked lobster, but I had two particularly violent red patches where my backside had been in contact with the hot plastic. The BBC's make-up department, whose ministrations are normally confined to my face, had to come to the rescue rather more comprehensively, to my acute embarrassment.

There was a long time to wait before we were on as our party piece was being broadcast well after the nine o'clock watershed, no doubt to the relief of those watching. Having nothing to do but hang around worrying about it was horrible. We all tried to keep the nerves at bay in different ways. Tony was attempting to read and smoke, James was pacing around, and even having a drink or two, which is very unusual for him. Ainsley was doing sit-ups and Brian and I hit the sauce, chatted to Nicky and tried to practise our routine.

By the time we were given our fifteen-minute call, Terry Wogan and Gaby Roslin had done a sterling job in securing millions of pledges from viewers who for reasons best known to themselves wanted to see our performance. We checked our make-up, mentally ran through the act one more time, straightened our ties and arranged ourselves on the studio floor, where we were hidden from the live audience by a muslin curtain. As the music began, their cheers were deafening. Raucous was not the word – they were rocking in the aisles.

All went according to plan until I took my belt off, at which point I realized immediately that there was something amiss with the Velcro fastener on my trousers and they were starting to fall down on their own. Oh, Jesus, what could I do now? There was only one thing for it: I had to hold up my trousers with one hand while attempting to remove my shirt with the other. At that point I couldn't have cared less whether my moves were in sync with the others. All that mattered was keeping my trousers up until they were supposed to come off. Thankfully, I managed it, and after that

I was so relieved that the rest of the routine seemed like plain sailing, and suddenly, amid rapturous applause and a cacophony of screams, it was over.

Our Full Monty was a triumph, and we were all on a high for several hours afterwards. It was shown a second time later in the programme and repeated in the following year's telethon. Apparently, it ranks as the third most successful act in the history of Children in Need. I am really glad that I overcame my initial reservations to take part, because in the end it was tremendously worthwhile.

Being asked to participate in charity events is a powerful reminder of your own good fortune, and none more so in my case than a ceremony at Buck House to which I was invited to present the Duke of Edinburgh Awards achievers' certificates. Many of the winners were from disadvantaged backgrounds, but were clearly determined not to let that stand in their way. They had all had to fight hard and overcome different kinds of adversity to earn their prizes. Talking to them in the sumptuous splendour of the palace, such a world away from some of their stories, really brought it home to me just how far I had come in my own life.

CHAPTER THIRTY-THREE

JACINTA SAID I MUST BE MAD, MOST OF MY FRIENDS TRIED TO PERSUADE me not to do it, but I had to. Something drew me to the unusual world of *I'm a Celebrity – Get Me Out of Here!*, the reality-TV programme where a bunch of celebrities get to spend up to two weeks in a clearing in the rainforest, far away from their mobile phones and hairdressers but under the constant gaze of cameras. I'd enjoyed watching the first series and I felt honoured when I was invited to take part in the second. So I accepted. It would be a real challenge. I would raise money for charity, and I'd raise my own profile too, reaching an audience in excess of my usual four million. And they were a great bunch of talented people to go with: Toyah Willcox, musician; Sian Lloyd, TV weather forecaster; Phil Tufnell, England cricketer; John Fashanu, former England footballer and now diplomat; Chris Bisson and Danniella Westbrook, actors; Wayne Sleep, ballet dancer; Catalina Guirado, model, and TV presenter Linda Barker.

Me, I've always said it as it is. I call a spade a shovel. What most worried my wife and friends, it turned out, was that I would say something I shouldn't, do something to offend, not be able to hold myself together 24/7. Even my agent tried to persuade me not to do it. I must admit, although I didn't tell my wife at the time, I was a little fearful of my big foot myself. But at the age of fifty-one surely I had grown up enough to control my outbursts.

And what about the jungle itself? What fears for me there? None, actually. No word of a lie. Snakes: no problem. Spiders: well, I'm not sure I'd *enjoy* a funnel-web spider crawling over my face, but when all's said and done, I'm big, they're small, and they squash easily. Rats: no sweat. Leeches: nothing a drop of salt or a fag-end wouldn't fix. The jungle darkness was a big unknown – but there was only one way to find out about that. My real fear was of the other people: nine complete strangers. How would we cope in such proximity to one another with thirty-two cameras breathing down our necks every minute of the day? What would these public figures be like when exposed to such scrutiny? Only one way to find out about that, too.

There was one other thing: I sleep with my mouth open, and I didn't fancy the idea that some small creature might find the warmth of my mouth ultimately more inviting than the chill of a night-time jungle . . .

It was an early start and a forty-minute helicopter ride into the jungle, but before that we were subjected to a fairly rigorous search for illegal items. We were allowed the uniform that was provided plus three pairs of underwear each, but all of us managed to get something extra in. Catalina had eighty cigarettes woven into her hair. Me? I had a spice rack strapped to my stomach like a cocaine smuggler. We arrived at camp, all watches confiscated, and grabbed a bed. For me this was like returning to public school. The beds were primitive constructions of poles and canvas. Mine was at 'mezzanine' level among the terraces cut out of the clearing, in between Catalina, Danniella and Linda. Two beds, Wayne's and Phil's, still had to be built. I organized the fire with Chris Bisson and checked out the kitchen equipment: one decent pan and frying pan, two cheap tin cans for boiling water, two wooden spoons, one chopping board and three knives – nothing else. Not even a colander. Our eating utensils were a plastic mug, an aircraft-friendly knife, spoon and fork and two billy cans.

We were given a map showing the boundaries of the camp, and had to select our first day's team leader: Fash. A natural leader but a bit of a nanny: caring bossiness. Later in the day, we were called individually to the Bush Telegraph, our whingeing place, a timber cabin furnished with a bench, two fixed cameras and two microphones. Over the next two weeks we developed relationships with three different voices: Jo (one of the producers), Voicey and one other. It was clear what their instructions must have been: no emotion, no bonding with the celebs, just cold efficiency, with one phrase to fall back on if stuck – 'I'll get back to you.' They rarely did.

To begin with everyone got on like a hut on fire, something the producers of the show probably didn't want. We voted for Fash to do our first bush-tucker trial; after all, he was our team leader. (The public didn't get to vote until the next day.) His challenge was to wear oversize undies and to tip ten buckets of unmentionables down them, a stiff task. He stopped at rats – fair enough. He achieved seven stars, which meant seven meals between the ten of us. But I think he was more scared of walking the wobbly Bridge of Doom to get to the trial site than anything else.

First impressions were already forming in my head. I was excited but at the same time scared, not looking forward to the first night in the jungle. But I was carefree in the daylight, to the extent of padding around the mud in bare feet, hostile environment and all. I got a ticking off from a security guard for that. I made us a supper of chicken stew with carrots and potatoes (even had a little left to make chicken and rice soup for the next day), with carpaccio of pineapple for pudding. Food never tasted so good. Danniella was showing signs of missing her husband and kids, who'd flown back to England that day. Catalina spotted a huntsman spider over her bed, which I killed but Catalina still screamed, making me jump out of my skin, knocking Chris flying. He nearly took his head off as he fell on a tree stump and needed to see Doctor Bob – it was a lucky escape really. Then I was nearly executed by a large falling plant, loosened from its spot by the heavy rain we had that day. It made a right mess of my bunk. And I got reprimanded over the tannoy for killing the spider because it's a protected species. If it's between me and a spider, the spider goes, in my view. To bed, tired and wet, fire blazing, all of us fully dressed, looking like we were in body bags.

We woke early on the second day, all of us still wet from the day before. The presenters of the live show, Ant and Dec, came bouncing in with the result of the first viewers' poll. The viewers had voted for Catalina to do the second bush-tucker trial. It meant swimming in a pool of crocodiles: one large one chained up (security with guns were at the ready) and three smaller ones released into the pool. She won all ten stars, meaning a meal for every one of us. Very strong woman, not to mention rather cocky. I could have killed for a cup of tea that day, but we had no teabags or milk. Water from the local brook had to be boiled and kept in a suspended canvas water-carrier. No Evian, no off-camera canteen, no hot showers – we washed in the leech-infested brook. We had no dry clothes, so we rigged up a washing line over the fire, but it had to be removed when it got in the way of the cameras. The camera crew follows anyone who leaves the campsite but isn't allowed to speak to us. You are never off camera.

We had daily tasks: boiling water, fetching logs, keeping the fire going. I should have soaked soybeans overnight but forgot. It turned out the two smallest members of the team, Wayne and Toyah, needed the most food; they both started feeling faint. I was trying to budget the rice and beans. We had two cups of rice for ten each day – not enough. No salt or pepper, so I was glad of my contraband spices, but halfway through the second afternoon we were told to hand in smuggled goods. A couple of us carried out the first celebrity-chest task: following clues to find a chest and then bringing it back. We got access to the treats inside only if we answered a question correctly. We got the question wrong and opened the wrong half of the chest, and missed out on coffee, tea, milk and sugar. Our first row was over food, but thankfully supper – kangaroo meat, Brussels sprouts, sweet potato, apples and tomato, plus two ugli, very ugli, fruit – was all right. The kangaroo was filling but tough as old boots. The uglis were delicious, and their peelings made excellent ugli tea. The Terrible Trio, as we were to become known, started to emerge: me, Linda and Phil. Linda had an infectious laugh and Phil cracked us all up.

Boredom is setting in already on day three. More logs, more water, more bloody rice and beans. Ant and Dec tell us that Wayne has been chosen by the public for the day's bush-tucker trial. His task was to crawl through a tunnel-like hutch full of rats with waffles tied to his body. Rats seethed all over him and knocked off his glasses and he found it hard to locate the keys he had to find. He ended up with only two stars. But we had a pact that if someone couldn't face the task or was unlucky however hard they tried, there would be no repercussions. We'd survive on reduced rations. But two meals between ten was going to test my cooking skills. We got the celebrity-chest question wrong again too. Supper was a bloody miracle: stretching two chicken legs into a casserole with rice and beans for ten. I even put in kiwi fruit, I was that desperate. And we had one grapefruit segment each as an appetizer. This turned out to be Fash's favourite meal. Wayne and Toyah got us all to put on a performance of *Cabaret* in exchange for treats. One bottle of white wine for Phil, Linda and me, and cola for the others. The wine put a little extra amusement into after-dinner chat but had us wanting more, so off went the Terrible Trio to plead with the Bush Telegraph for extra alcohol – no joy. We let our guards down for probably the first time and ended up giggling like kids.

The next day, day four, Fash got voted by the public to do the bush-tucker trial. He had to climb a rope bridge that kept collapsing but he got eight stars. It was a good upbeat day – and my birthday too. Linda, who is really clever at making stuff, gave me a pair of star earrings and a rope bracelet, and Phil gave me the title of 'Camp' Chef. Linda and I went off to hunt for the celebrity chest – a easy find – and this time we answered the question correctly, earning ourselves coffee, tea, sugar and milk powder. God, did we need those cuppas. We must have got four cups of tea from each bag. We were learning to stretch everything. I had to make a tough decision in the evening: choosing between a handmade birthday card from Jay and the kids, and extra booze for the Trio with brownies for the non-drinkers – mind games from the production team. I had to go with the needs of my Jungle family and I shed a few tears making the decision at the Telegraph. The team were over the moon, and I just had to hope that Jay and the kids would understand.

Day five saw Danniella's turn for the bush-tucker trial – probably the nastiest trial of the fortnight. In swimwear, she looked drop-dead gorgeous – before she went in, that is – and though she shed a few tears before crossing the bridge she was mentally strong for the challenge. She had eel slime poured over her, followed by loads of different maggots, bugs and stick insects. She completed all the tasks but because everything stuck to her face she couldn't see the stars dropping along with the bugs and she caught only three. We were proud of her anyway. Linda was leader for the day and she turned out to be a right tyrant. We nicknamed her Miss Whiplash. I had to have a word in her ear to tell her to calm down; she thought I was joking, then realized she'd gone a bit too far. She improved later in the day, but we were low-spirited. We were hungry, the weather was wet, and we failed on the celebrity chest. Supper was three quails with a few mangetout, and some cauliflower and broccoli – not enough for three, let alone ten. Food was the main topic of conversation. Fash was going mad on his physical workouts, and Cat was starting to get on our nerves. She is a talented woman but was so aware of the cameras. I wished she could just be herself. The Trio went begging for booze, selling our souls to the devil by answering Telegraph questions, and earned ourselves a sweet rosé.

Fash got chosen again for the bush-tucker trial on day six. Poor guy. We reassured him the public just wanted to see his muscles. He had to deal with snakes in a pit – not his favourite, so only four meals earned. We got some tough old pork, which I beat out and stuffed with apple and cheese. I served it with patty-pan squash, beans and potato. It was amazing how food you wouldn't look at twice in the real world became a treat in a set-up like this. Toyah is a vegetarian who had put up with meat so far, but she got some tofu today. The Bush Telegraph interviewed us some more. Same old questions; same old games. And boring just got more boring. Fash tried in vain to stop me and Phil swearing; he seemed so straight. Got alcohol today but me and Phil decided what we needed was more cigarettes. We were not surviving on ten each day. The Trio went in for more drunken ramblings on the Bush Telegraph, but no cigarettes were forthcoming, so I decided to make a break for freedom in search of fags and was off in the direction of the Bridge of Doom, which lay between us and the outside world. It was pitch black but I had no fear. I must have been mad; it's hard enough crossing the bridge in daylight let alone in the depth of night. I heard security closing in on me so I started to run over the bridge – mad, mad, mad. They caught me 200 yards into the jungle on the other side and told me I was putting lives at risk. All I want is four cigarettes, I said. They called for back-up. They couldn't carry me all the way home, after all. After an hour and a half I returned to camp, no cigarettes but with a promise of deodorant. I felt I had scored a moral victory. Nobody had ever crossed that bridge in the dark before. If nothing else a little excitement broke the monotony.

Fash got voted yet again to do the bush-tucker trial on day seven. It was as if the public were asking just how tough he really was. This one had him plunging his head into buckets of creeping jungle life. He got nine stars – excellent, especially considering all his many phobias. For the first time we could expect a decent supper. The celebrity chest revealed, despite our answering the question correctly, no more than a tiny bag of unpopped popcorn – Catalina decided to cook it as she felt that, living in America, she had the right qualifications for such an onerous cooking task. She burnt it.

Danniella was having a very bad day – no amount of hugs could console her. She packed her bags to leave and went to the Bush Telegraph to utter the magic words: 'I'm a Celebrity – Get Me Out of Here!' The psychiatrist persuaded her to stay until after the first eviction. Supper arrived two hours late: nine sausages, twenty-seven mangetout, twenty-seven macadamia nuts in shells, nine pieces of cauliflower – an insult to Fash's achievements. I persuaded the group that consolidated action was required. We went en masse to the Bush Telegraph. Insults flew, even the girls were swearing, and 'We'll get back to you' was the reply. It was not good enough. We stormed across the stronger bridge: a revolution was under way. One security guard was felled by a door swung into the crotch. There was no messing with us that night! We threatened to walk: change the meal or you've got no programme left. They knew we meant business – we were all starving. New food arrived – steak, potatoes, beans and carrots – and we were happy bunnies. Late to bed, but I vowed I must try to curb my language.

My turn for the bush-tucker trial next day – a water task. I had to fish down in long tubes under the water for 'starfish', dealing with snakes and eels all the while. I ran out of time and only got five stars. I was disappointed but at the same time on an amazing high. Supper was some really fresh barramundi fish on a salad of tomato and cucumber with a citrus dressing. Phil and Linda did the celebrity chest and we got fancy cakes and tea – it was an upbeat day. Danniella was definitely going to leave, though. She was a gem. Nothing like the girl portrayed in the tabloids. We went to bed dreading the news of the first eviction.

Ant and Dec arrived the next morning to reveal that Sian Lloyd was to be the first out. She was fine about it; she'd been missing her man, lots of tears under the bedclothes, she'd hardly slept. And then Danniella left – she needed the support of her husband, Kevin. Their bond was the strength she was missing. Phil did his first trial and earned eight out of nine meals by swinging on a rope and smashing stars. No creepy-crawlies involved – lucky him. Even the celebrity chest gave us a good result: eggs, salt and egg cups. But we were tired, very tired, and bored, very bored. Fash had upped his workout level; he was a man possessed. We had emu for dinner – it made roo look like stewing steak. It rained all day. It rained all night. (I developed 'jock rot' (very painful) – Phil's term.) I evicted two leeches from my shins. The fire barely stayed alight.

No eviction on day ten because of Danniella's self-imposed ousting. Toyah had to undertake a foul-smelling bush-tucker trial. We could hardly bear to let her back in the camp, poor girl. It was amazing she got as many as five out of eight stars from that gut-wrenching sludge she had had to wade through. Catalina was leader for the day and led a sit-down on the bridge in an attempt to get chocolate; instead she was punished by losing us two meals, so we had to make do with three. Awful kangaroo again with sweet-corn, asparagus, tomato, patty-pan squash and rice. Frustration was setting in.

Day eleven saw Chris evicted. He'd been great: helpful and fun. I was feeling bad: my back had gone and the crotch damage was mak-ing me walk like John Wayne. I had to visit Doctor Bob. Everyone was tense. Toyah snapped at me about some rice. She's 4 foot 11 of solid muscles and not to be messed with. I was stripped of my cooking duties and Phil took over; I was his commis and advi-sor. Linda did the bush-tucker trial and won all seven stars: a meal each for the remaining jungle dwellers. But I was really down, des-perate to see Jay. I went to the Bush Telegraph and asked the British public to vote me off (or, rather, not to vote for me to stay). Phil and Toyah's celebrity chest provided a large tub of cookies-and-cream ice cream. We needed that. We dressed for dinner: me in a toga (my feminine side coming out). But the dinner ingredients were a disas-ter – a wild jungle chicken, fully feathered, tough as shoe leather – precipitating maximum drama from the team. Somehow we got over it. Fash gave me a great back massage; Linda pampered me over a few glasses of wine. Phil and I stayed up late talking about our lives. He's a sensitive, kind guy. I walked in my sleep that night. Apparently I sat by the fire for an hour in the early hours.

Ant and Dec bounced in on day twelve to announce Catalina's eviction. Phil got to do the bush-tucker trial. The trial required stamina and in spite of his exhaustion he managed four stars out of six. Toyah and Fash won a great celebrity chest: salt, pepper, some of my confiscated spices and chilli sauce. Linda was in charge of cooking and produced an excellent supper of pork layered with aubergine and tomato, with a starter of spinach, pear and green papaya. I caught a massive crayfish, but we didn't cook it. We named him Sir Colin Crayfish and he entertained us for the after-noon before we returned him to the safety of the jungle. It alleviated the boredom. We had no idea how the show was going down in the UK, no perception of its massive success.

I boiled some water on day thirteen to have a thorough, all-over wash. I expected eviction and was all packed up and ready to go, but it was Toyah's turn to leave the camp. I was a little dis-appointed. Linda did the bush-tucker trial and got all five stars; her star record is 100 per cent. I expected her to have her knickers on outside her trousers next. Superwoman, but nice with it. But the morning was a downer. Wayne took something the wrong way and thought we were being homophobic, and Phil in turn was upset at that. Phil and me did the celebrity chest and I walked right into a prat-fall. I ventured into a small clearing to pick up a clue from the ground and got hauled up ten feet into the air, snared in a net full of leaves and bugs. Fash was chef for the day; with assistance from me. Sea bream with mash of carrots, potatoes and parsnips and some fried patty-pan squash. There was some soul searching going on that night; the mood wasn't upbeat. I wanted time to take in my thirteen-day sentence and decided to go on a final walkabout. I managed to find a quiet spot away from the cameras to relish my memories in the dark, but security found me. There was never any personal time in the jungle. I returned to the campsite, rebuilt the fire and retired for my last night in the jungle.

On day fourteen I was evicted. I had mixed emotions. I would have loved to go the distance, but I was desperate to see Jay too. We'd been apart before, but never out of contact. I had my post-eviction interview with Ant and Dec and it was sweet; they're great guys. Then I got to see Jay again: hot baths, Jacuzzi, big breakfast, champagne ... I got to see again all the others who had been evicted too. It was an emotional rollercoaster. I was at the top and it looked like a long way down. Such a complete shock to the system, such a trauma. Who'd have thought it would all have such a powerful effect? It was also the day that the *Mirror* published an article called 'Wozza, the Love Rat' by my second wife. Whether that affected the vote, I'll never know.

Wayne came out next. We loved him: funny, a consummate actor. I did wish he could chill out a bit more though. Then Linda: ambitious, competitive, also driven, a mad flirt, sexy, strong of mind, strong of body – Phil and I loved her. We three developed a strong bond, a real friendship. Then it was Fash's turn. I didn't like him to begin with, thought he was a real nanny, but he has a heart of gold and I warmed to him a lot. I learnt something too: give people time. Focused, driven, a natural leader – who else would do 1,000 sit-ups on less than 1,000 calories a day? Then Phil, who won the challenge. Either a brilliant actor or a genuine guy: I believe he is genuine. And I had money on him too, so I wasn't disappointed.

It was hell, but it was an experience not to be missed. I wanted to leave the jungle and take something out of it, and I did. I earnt nearly £80,000 for my chosen charity, Save the Children, I got paid myself, I lost a stone in weight, but there was more to it than that. I realized that when you are a success in your chosen career, you build armour around your vulnerability. Part of that armour consists of wealth and possessions, and then there's the love of your wife and kids. You never let yourself get into a position where you are stripped to the bone, where the trappings of success are taken away. In the jungle everything was removed, from the smallest thing taken totally for granted like putting a kettle on and making tea, to the biggest thing: contact with your loved ones. This show is reality; there's no bullshit, no false pampering. You revert to your core being, and you are with nine other people who are also probably experiencing for the first time in a long while the need to rely solely on their true make-up. No flash cars, no mobile phones, no wrist watches, no fashion statements. It was like old-fashioned communism: zero status, just survival. You are as you were created, with nothing to rely on but your own character. And it was a chance to learn about yourself in a unique way.

What did I learn? Success isn't one big winning box. It's lots of small boxes, mini victories that add up to a life worth living. Enjoy what you have. Enjoy your successes. Plant the roses, enjoy their magnificence, but if you don't stop to smell them, to absorb their perfume, it all comes to nothing.

EPILOGUE

THERE CAN BE NO REAL CONCLUSION TO ANY STORY WRITTEN DURING an active lifetime. There will always be new mystery, new challenges around the corner and an ever-present electric charge of anticipation and suspense. Even so, writing this book has given me the chance to take stock of my life so far; to step back and make a reflective and objective assessment of what has been and what is yet to come. I'm amazed at how many mistakes one man can make before he eventually grows up.

Having finally reached a plateau of emotional calm, I can at last look behind me and see my first fifty years – my background, my family – in perspective. I know that deep down I loved my family, but it was as if I was eaten up by some kind of disease that prevented me from recognizing the good in them. Instead I constantly tried to find and then play on their faults. It wasn't really until my mother died that I gained the distance I needed to reach some understanding of them.

My two Aussie boys Blake and Sam didn't have the easiest of starts, but what a pair of stunners they are. Their childhood was one of constant house moves and changes of school, they have had to deal with the arrival and departure of a stepfather who didn't turn out to be the nicest ingredient in the sandwich and, to top it all, they were always broke. So I am over the moon that, in spite of the failure of my second marriage, it produced two such cracking guys. At nineteen and seventeen, Blake and Sam are normal teenagers with the usual penchant for fast cars and even faster women. I am sure they are destined to break a few hearts: I only hope that doesn't include their own. A bonus is that they are both polite and well spoken. Good luck to both of them – they deserve it. I have their mother to thank for the way they have turned out. Being a long-distance dad is incredibly difficult. I am just grateful that I never abandoned the cause, which I might easily have done when they left the UK as small boys.

I know that I am privileged to be in a position where I can take time to plan a future that is more productive than my past has been. I feel there is still a lot left for me to do. I can't believe I have passed the milestone of fifty already. I still like to have fun, and on *Ready, Steady, Cook* I still wear the silly trousers that set a trend for brightly coloured chefs' pants. In fact I am the proud holder of a Savile Row award (albeit one bestowed in a tongue-in-cheek gesture) as Trouser Wearer of the Year. How long I stay in restaurants remains to be seen. I certainly haven't done my time yet, but one day I will get parole. When that will be I probably won't know until the day arrives, but I don't want to die over a hot stove. I love writing, whether it is for newspapers, magazines or books, and I see that taking me well into retirement. Working on the land with organic produce will definitely continue. I hope my involvement in product development will go from strength to strength and I would like to take my passions for politics and food safety and education a step further.

But whatever path or paths I follow in the years to come, they will be based on the needs of my family. Jaybe is the rock on which I have set my foundations, so she must come first in any decisions I make, closely followed by my beautiful babes Toby and Billie, and Blake and Sam, who may well need my help as they enter adulthood. One thing I do know is that I rarely give up on a project once I've got my teeth into it. The experiences of my life so far have brought with them a little wisdom, at least enough to enable me to recognize that success only has a value if you can use it to try to change other people's lives in some way. My modest status as a public figure provides me with a platform from which to encourage others to think about the mainstay of our existence that has been my vocation: food.

I have seen many food fads come and go, often from a vantage point at the cutting edge, and sometimes I have even been instrumental in starting them, yet if I am honest, I do wonder whether the way we eat is any better than it was fifty years ago. Certainly we in the UK have managed to restore the quality of our cooking to the standards of the turn of the last century. We have thrown off the grey mantle of the Edwardian era, we believe in ourselves again and, most importantly, we believe that we can cook without having to rely on imitating our French neighbours. Even if we do not always cook British dishes or with British ingredients, at least we can cook in our own right. But has the growth of 'celebrity cuisine' distorted the real issues? Are we becoming wrapped up in image rather than substance as far as food is concerned, as we are in so many spheres of our lives? Are we becoming victims of our desire for instant gratification? To give credit where it is due, the quality of precooked and ready meals has improved beyond all recognition, but I still think it is sad that more people aren't cooking.

And whose fault is this? As I said earlier, successive governments must bear a good deal of responsibility for squeezing cookery education out of the school curriculum. And Margaret Thatcher must shoulder some of the blame, not only for abolishing school milk, but for making everyone so acquisitive. To be a part of her brave new world – to be able to afford to buy their council house, the second car, the third telly, the matching washing machine and dishwasher – both partners in a household had to go out to work, which doesn't do family life any good. And I am not being sexist here. It doesn't matter which partner stays at home, but for the good of the family, one of them should. The casualties have been home cooking, time spent together around the table, the comfort of the very idea of home. We might as well be living in hotels. Our busy lives take priority over the benefits and pleasures of the family meal.

And what about genetically modified foods? Whether or not they may be harmful to our health is beside the point at this stage. The jury is still out on that and it will probably be a couple of decades before we know for sure. What is clear is that the UK is too small to take the environmental risk. Given the distances seeds can be blown in the wind and pollinating insects can travel, the 200-metre zone between GM testing fields and other crops is a nonsense. It has been proved that plants can cross-pollinate, creating potential superweeds. If we want to be up there with the rest of the world scientifically then we can develop the gene technology, but growing the crops here is plain daft.

Please don't give any credence to all that crap about genetically modified food saving the starving of our planet. Even some Third World countries, such as Zambia, have refused handouts of GM foods. Good for them. There is plenty to feed us all already: the problem is how to get it to those who need it. Politics, wars, drought and land ownership wrangles all conspire to exacerbate the problem, and of course, since there's no such thing as a free lunch, the system must be underpinned by economics. If our great scientists were to develop plants that didn't need water or could be fed with seawater, or even seeds that could be germinated without the support of chemicals, then I'd listen to the GM argument. Until they do, we have enough on our plates trying to get to the bottom of the ways in which the foods we are already eating are putting our health at risk.

I believe the answer is to get more of the public to eat organic primary produce, because it is in primary produce that you are most likely to encounter chemical residues, and eating organic food will help you steer clear of them. And as a chef, I would always discourage the consumption of too many processed and manufactured foods, although as a chef who is also a realist, while I would prefer people to cook from scratch, I appreciate that many of them either don't want to cook or don't know how to. My message is not rocket science. We know that we are what we eat, yet this is a maxim that is currently being totally ignored by scientists, the government and, worst of all, by the public. The result is that we are no more than human guinea pigs who in the course of our lifetimes are unwittingly testing the effects on the body of thousands of different chemicals.

I think going back is the way forward. We must, for example, find a way of restoring the sustainable farming industry we had before the Second World War. We should be aiming to produce more food for ourselves at a price that works for both the farmer and the consumer. We could grow far more under glass if the planning authorities would soften their attitude towards this type of cultivation. Self-sufficiency is an ideal in which the general public has lost interest in the postwar years, and particularly since the advent of year-round imported food. But you can't tell me that we can't be as productive as the Netherlands or New Zealand, two countries of similar geographical size and not dissimilar climates.

I may be no more than an amateur enthusiast, and I certainly don't claim to have any special scientific knowledge, but I care about what we eat and I know I am not alone in my concerns. The revolution is beginning, albeit from a small base as yet. Join me. Every day a decision is made that should be challenged and accounted for. We must not allow ourselves to slide away from democracy and into dictatorship. It's time to fight back.

Very few of us get an easy ride, and life would be very dull if we did. I can't believe how much I missed out on in my first forty years. I love my world now, my new life, and it is time for me to give back some of what I've taken out. So here's to the future. The best is yet to come.

INDEX